MW00608932

# THE BEATS IN MEXICO

# THE BEATS IN MEXICO

DAVID STEPHEN CALONNE

RUTGERS UNIVERSITY PRESS
New Brunswick, Camden, and Newark, New Jersey, and London

Library of Congress Cataloging-in-Publication Data
Names: Calonne, David Stephen, 1953– author.
Title: The Beats in Mexico / David Stephen Calonne.
Description: New Brunswick : Rutgers University Press, [2022] | Includes bibliographical references and index.
Identifiers: LCCN 2021028273 | ISBN 9781978828728 (cloth) | ISBN 9781978828735 (epub) | ISBN 9781978828742 (pdf)
Subjects: LCSH: Beats (Persons) | American literature—20th century—History and criticism. | American literature—Mexican influences. | Mexico—In literature. | LCGFT: Literary criticism.
Classification: LCC PS228.B6 C34 2022 | DDC 810.9/35872082—dc23
LC record available at https://lccn.loc.gov/2021028273

A British Cataloging-in-Publication record for this book is available from the British Library.



⊜ The paper used in this publication meets the requirements of the American National Standard for Information Sciences—Permanence of Paper for Printed Library Materials, ANSI Z39.48-1992.

www.rutgersuniversitypress.org

Manufactured in the United States of America

In gratitude to the people of Mexico

# CONTENTS

# THE BEATS IN MEXICO

Statue of Xochipilli, Creative Commons

# INTRODUCTION

MEXICO HAS INTRIGUED many American authors including Stephen Crane, Jack London, Ambrose Bierce, John Dos Passos, Conrad Aiken, Muriel Rukeyser, Archibald MacLeish, John Steinbeck, Tennessee Williams, Paul Bowles, Hart Crane, Langston Hughes, Katherine Anne Porter, Lucia Berlin, Ray Bradbury, and Kenneth Rexroth. Herman Melville memorialized his March 28–April 16, 1844 visit to Mazatlán in his novel *White-Jacket* (1850). Europeans such as D. H. Lawrence, Malcolm Lowry, Antonin Artaud, and André Breton became important exemplars for Beat writers—Lawrence Ferlinghetti, William S. Burroughs, Philip Lamantia, Margaret Randall, Jack Kerouac, Allen Ginsberg, Bonnie Bremser, Michael McClure, and Joanne Kyger—who also journeyed throughout Mexico over a period of more than half a century. The centrality of Mexico to the evolution of Beat literature and the American counterculture however has been little investigated. Experimentation and research devoted to entheogens and shamanistic practices—shamanism is featured in Rudolfo Anaya's celebrated novel *Bless Me, Ultima* (1972) with its compelling depiction of *brujeria* (magic) and *curandismo* (healing); the popularity of Carlos Castaneda's *Don Juan* series; the study of Mayan and Aztec history, myth, and language; the exploration of

Mexico's archaeological sites; sensitivity to the plight of women and the oppressed; and increasing awareness about preserving ecological balance: all were of central concern to the Beats. Connections with Mexican literary life were fashioned through Margaret Randall's magazine *El Corno Emplumado* (1962–1969), and both Lawrence Ferlinghetti and Philip Lamantia were friends with Mexican poet Homero Aridjis (1940–). As Daniel Belgrad has observed: "For the Beats as a 'cultural formation' (a term that Raymond Williams used to describe a group engaged in a common cultural endeavor and sharing common cultural practices), travel and residence in Mexico was an important rite of passage and was influential in their evolving aesthetic."[1] Going on a pilgrimage to Mexico became de rigueur for the Beats, just as the Grand Tour to France, Switzerland, Italy, and Greece was an important educational journey for poets and intellectuals in Europe during the Romantic Era.

American authors with connections to the Beats such as Charles Olson (1910–1970) and Denise Levertov (1923–1997) were deeply influenced by Mexico. Levertov lived in Mexico from 1956 to 1958 with her husband Mitchell Goodman. During a trip in October and November 1956, Allen Ginsberg and Gregory Corso stopped in Guadalajara to visit them.[2] Corso, according to the autobiographical note he included in Donald Allen's *The New American Poetry*, composed "most of *Gasoline*" (1958) while in Mexico. The volume includes "Mexican Impressions": "Through a moving window/I see a glimpse of burros/a Pepsi Cola stand,/an old Indian sitting/smiling toothless by a hut," featuring America's imperial capitalism and consumer culture set against Mexico's poverty through the imagistic precision the Beats learned from Ezra Pound and William Carlos Williams. This photographic clarity also distinguishes several Levertov poems which pay homage to the delights of life in Mexico such as "Pleasures," celebrating the luscious *mamey* fruit—*Pouteria sapota*—native to Cuba, Central America, and Mexico.[3] Levertov's "Xochipilli"—the Aztec (a more accurate term for the Aztecs is the Mexica, after whom Mexico is named) god of pleasure, poetry, flowers, and spring—invokes Xochipilli's divine powers: "'From thy dung/the red flowers,' says the god/'From thy bones/white flowers,' says the god./'From this music/seeds of the grass/that shall sing when the wind blows.'" In her essay "The Sense of Pilgrimage," Levertov explained: "From looking at a small statue of Xochipilli, the actions of the God appeared in my mind as knowledge, rather than as uninterpreted visual images. The representation of Xochipilli, I mean, informed me of what his actions would be and from this intuitive knowledge came visualizations and their verbal equivalents."[4]

Hart Crane (1899–1932) was an influence on Allen Ginsberg and on African American Beat poet Bob Kaufman—Kaufman is said to have committed Crane's complete oeuvre to memory—who in "The Ancient Rain" declared: "The Ancient Rain fell on Hart Crane. He committed suicide in the Gulf/of Mexico." Hart Crane had contemplated composing an epic poem chronicling the encounter between Cortes and Moctezuma II and alluded to Xochipilli in "The Circumstance": "If you/Could drink the sun as did and does/Xochipilli—as they who've/Gone have done, as they/Who've done . . . a god of flowers in statued/Stone . . . of love—."[5]

Charles Olson, rector of Black Mountain College from 1951 to 1956, is known for his concept of "Projective Verse" which emphasized measuring spacing of verses on the page—as in a musical score—in accordance with the energy of breath rather than conventional metrical form. Olson was appealing to the Beats since both Kerouac and Ginsberg in their elaboration of a Buddhist poetics advocated spontaneity, open revelation of consciousness and the body's rhythmic powers: *prana* in Sanskrit is "breath" or "spirit energy." Olson influenced Diane di Prima, Michael McClure, Ed Dorn, and Joanne Kyger, identifying with the revolutionary ideals of the Beat and hippie movements: he was also a participant in the early investigations of the psychological effects of entheogens on creativity. Olson published a section from his *Maximus Poems* in *The Psychedelic Review: Aldous Huxley Memorial Issue* in 1964. As we shall see in chapter 9, Joanne Kyger's account of a 1985 journey to the Yucatan, *Phenomenological* (1989)—in which she describes reading Olson's *Mayan Letters* during her stay in Mexico—was published as volume 24 in a series of texts by a variety of writers inspired by Olson entitled "A Plan for the Curriculum of the Soul." Ed Dorn was Olson's student at Black Mountain, and Olson provided his pupil with a reading list entitled "A Bibliography on America for Ed Dorn," advising him to consult sources about Mexico including "Indian texts on migrations, such as the Toltecs being pushed out of Tula by Chicmecs, etc.—also codices in which feet (like on floor after bath) are as arrows in Klee." In his poem "Twenty-Four Love Songs," Dorn lamented the destruction of Maya codices by the Christian Spanish invader: "It is deep going from here/from the old world to the new/from Europa home/the brilliant scrolls of the waves/wave/the runic secret of homeward/when Diego de Landa the glyphic books destroyed." Dorn met Margaret Randall in the late fifties when she was living in Santa Fe, and she provided Dorn—who would later publish Randall in his magazine *Wild Dog*—and Gordon Brotherston with texts which they translated and included in *Our Word: Guerilla Poems from Latin America* (1968).

Cover of magazine *Archaeology in Mexico Today*

Dorn also collaborated with Brotherston to prepare translations included in the groundbreaking volume *Image of the New World: The American Continent Portrayed in Native Texts* (1979).

Olson—along with Lawrence Ferlinghetti and William S. Burroughs—was one of the first countercultural travelers to Mexico.[6] In 1937 at the Convention on the Pan-American Highway, Argentina, Bolivia, Chile, Colombia,

Costa Rica, El Salvador, Guatemala, Mexico, Nicaragua, Panama, Peru, Canada, and the United States agreed to construct a highway connecting their countries, and Mexico was the first to complete its section of the road in 1950. Between 1939 and 1951, the total number of Americans making the journey to Mexico more than tripled. Similar in purpose to the American Automobile Association, Petroleos Mexicanos initiated the Pemex Travel Club which, beginning in 1940, published tourist guides titled *Archaeology in Mexico Today*, which Charles Olson perused.[7]

Olson spent six months in Lerma, Campeche in the Yucatan—the Maya referred to the Yucatan peninsula as *Peten*, or "the Land," and *Mayab*, signifying "flat"—and although Olson never again returned to Mexico, his brief sojourn in the country significantly shaped his poetic imagination.[8] He came to the Yucatan at the beginning of 1951, first reaching shore at Progreso. He arrived in Merida—later a destination for Allen Ginsberg as well—and was eager to begin exploring the archaeological sites he had previously known only through books.[9] Cid Corman, the editor of *Origin* magazine and publisher of Olson's work, ransacked used bookstores back in Boston to find texts for Olson and mailed him Alfred M. Tozzer's *A Maya Grammar*.[10]

Like William S. Burroughs—Olson entered graduate school at Harvard the same year Burroughs earned his bachelor's degree there—Olson was fascinated by Mayan history, archaeology, and language. One-fifth the size of America with which it shares a two-thousand-mile border and composed of thirty-one individual states, Mexico represents a tremendous variety of ecosystems, distinct cultures, and languages. Olson was keen to meet local speakers of Maya. There are about thirty Mayan languages which are still alive today in the states of Chiapas and Tabasco, as well as the three states comprising the Yucatan peninsula: Quintana Roo, Yucatan, and Olson's place of residence, Campeche. Throughout the Yucatan, Lacandon, Mopan, Itza, and Yucatec are spoken. The Maya had been writing for a thousand years when English literature made its debut in the seventh century. They invented their own script and inked inscriptions on paper, painted them on pottery, and carved them in stelae. Olson's references to the Maya appear in *Mayan Letters*—which features seventeen letters composed during his stay in Mexico addressed to Robert Creeley—as well as his essay "Human Universe" in which Olson remarked that the Maya "invented a system of written record, now called hieroglyphs, which on its very face, is verse, the signs were so closely and densely chosen that, cut in stone, they retain the power of the objects of which they are the images." Allusions to the Maya appear in Olson's poem "The Kingfishers": "They buried their dead in a sitting posture/serpent cane razor ray of the sun/And she sprinkled water on the head of the child, crying 'Cioa-coatl! Cioa-coatl!'/with her face to the west." Cihuacoatl, "woman snake"—Olson spells her name slightly differently—is an Earth/Mother goddess worshipped in Postclassic central Mexico and is one of the goddesses of midwifery. Olson's interest in the Maya was long-standing. In the early forties (nearly a decade before his journey to the Yucatan), he had read *The Maya and Their Neighbors*—a Festschrift for Alfred M. Tozzer—shortly after it was published in 1940. It is possible William S. Burroughs knew this text as well, for it contains reflections concerning the Maya priests which, as we shall see in chapter 2, recall a central theme in Burroughs's own view of Mexican history: "Priestcraft waxed until it attained to amazing power over the minds of the people and over all that pertained to the forms of worship. Native art and tradition, and also modern scientific studies, agree in informing us that, from the earliest quasi-historical period, at Teotihuacan and elsewhere in Mexico and in Yucatan and Guatemala, down to and even beyond the time of the Spanish conquest, the people were held fast in spiritual and moral slavery to an enormous and baleful priesthood serving a confused throng of fearful gods."[11]

The Beat affinity for Mexico had roots in cultural currents appearing in American and European culture decades previously. As the overgrown ruins of Chichen Itza, Tikal, Dzibilchatun, Uxmal, Tulum, Calakmul, Ek Balam, Palenque, Bonampak, and Yaxchilan were revealed and their archaeological sites excavated during the nineteenth and twentieth centuries, both scientists and artists were spellbound. And during the early twentieth century, excavations began in earnest at the Pyramid of the Sun in Teotihuacan. The American diplomat John Lloyd Stephens (1805–1852) and British artist Frederick Catherwood (1799–1854) published their illustrated *Incidents of Travel in Central America, Chiapas and Yucatan* (1841). As we shall see in chapter 2, Catherwood's work entered the Beat imagination of Mexico through William Burroughs and Malcolm McNeill's collaboration on the graphic narrative *Ah Pook Is Here*. The stately architecture of the grand pyramids and refined, delicately poised figures in newly discovered sculptures illustrated with lifelike verisimilitude the lives of the Maya and Aztecs. The creative genius exhibited in the art of these ancient peoples—whether one considers the choreographic, poetic pose of the celebrated Chac Mool of Chichen Itza, or violent scenes of bloodletting on the elaborately carved stone lintels of Yaxchilan—seemed eerily palpable and relevant to American writers and poets. Public interest in the Maya increased during the 1893 Chicago World's Columbian Exposition where gigantic replicas of the facades of buildings from Labna and other settlements in the Puuc region of the Yucatan were displayed. During the twenties, what has become known in the history of architecture as the "Maya Revival" began. Throughout the United States, from Illinois to California, a vogue commenced for erecting buildings in the Mayan style as demonstrated by Marjorie I. Ingle in *Mayan Revival Style: Art Deco Maya Fantasy.* Frank Lloyd Wright's Hollyhock House (1917–20), which he built in Los Angeles, borrows features from the imposing buildings of Uxmal and Chichen Itza. Fantastic structures created by architect Robert Stacy-Judd with baroque Mayan figurations sprang up in southern California.

The new love for things Mexican would also catch up in its enthusiasm poets such as Hart Crane and William Carlos Williams. The magazine *Broom* published a "Maya theme" issue in which Crane's poem "The Springs of Guilty Song" appeared, while Williams contributed work on the Aztecs, "The Destruction of Tenochtitlan." Williams also composed an essay on Cortes and Montezuma (1923) and proclaimed in *The American Grain,* "The New World is Montezuma." In a 1941 lecture delivered in Puerto Rico, Williams argued that "from the old and alien soul of America itself, may the reliques of its ancient, its pre-Columbian cultures still kindle something in me that will be elevated, profound and common to us all, Americas. There is that path still open to us." Another author significant to the Beats, D. H. Lawrence, explored in his novel *The Plumed Serpent* (1926) the myths of Quetzalcoatl as a part of his quest for the instinctive "blood-knowledge" which Lawrence associated with sexual and spiritual transcendence. Archibald MacLeish composed a long poem entitled *Conquistador* (1932) employing Bernal Diaz del Castillo as narrator and depicting the Spanish domination of Tenochtitlan. And as Carrie Gibson has remarked in *El Norte: The Epic and Forgotten Story of Hispanic North America,* by the thirties, "Hollywood was booming, and it fell in love with all things Mexican, a fashion that reached its peak during the Great Depression. Even the *New York Times* reported in 1933 on the 'enormous vogue of things Mexican.' The daring romantic heroes of the Mexican Revolution, such as Pancho Villa, had captured the public imagination, and Mexico's proximity played a part in the culture's popularization as well." The American composer Aaron Copland met the Mexican composer Carlos Chavez in 1926, spent four months in Mexico in 1932, and returned to the United States to create one of his most popular works, the rhythmically syncopated, riveting, and tuneful *El Salon Mexico* (1936), based on Mexican folk melodies.

In San Francisco, a number of cultural forces were preparing the way for the Beat fascination with Mexico. The French writer Antonin Artaud (1896–1948) participated in peyote rituals of the Tarahumara Indians. Excerpts from

Artaud's writings appeared in the underground publication *Semina* edited by Wallace Berman, which circulated in California's Bay Area, and Michael McClure's second book, *For Artaud,* appeared in 1959. Artaud was prescient in his intellectual itinerary which presaged not only the Beat fascination with Mexico but their spiritual orientation as well. In a letter composed in 1937, Artaud advised a friend to read "the *Bardo Thodol* [*Tibetan Book of the Dead*], *The Egyptian Book of the Dead,* the *Tao-Te-Ching* and the *Vedas* and *drop all the rest!*": each of these classics would also become favorite Beat texts. The "founder" of Surrealism, André Breton, visited Mexico for four months in 1938. Diego Rivera introduced him to Leon Trotsky, and Breton and Trotsky collaborated on their essay against Fascist and Stalinist repression, "Manifesto: Towards a Free Revolutionary Art." Breton was entranced by Mexico, famously remarking: "I don't know why I came here. Mexico is the most surrealist country in the world." Breton inspired the Guatemalan writer and Nobel Prize–winner Miguel Angel Asturias (1899–1974), author of the novel *Hombres de maiz* (1949) based on the Mayan belief that their flesh was made of corn. Asturias translated in 1927, along with Mexican Jose Maria Gonzalez de Mendoza, the French version of the Quiché Maya *Popol Vuh,* and Asturias also incorporated surrealist elements in his writings. Breton lyrically invoked Xochipilli—as did Levertov and Hart Crane—in his essay "Remembrance of Mexico": "Half awakened from its mythological past, Mexico still evolves under the protection of Xochipilli, god of the flowers and of lyrical poetry, and of Coatlicue, goddess of the earth and of violent death, whose effigies, filled with more pathos and intensity than all the others, seem to exchange over the heads of the Indian peasants (the most numerous and meditative visitors of the National Museum's collections) winged words and raucous calls that fly from one end of the building to the other. The power of conciliating life and death is without doubt the main attraction that lures us to Mexico."[12] In addition to Artaud and Breton, one of the earliest publications of a third Frenchman—Georges Bataille's (1897–1962) "L'Amerique disparue"—was included in Jean Babelon's *L'art precolombien* (1930). Although he never made the journey to Mexico, Bataille investigated the Aztecs as an important aspect of his theorizing concerning the sacred, violence, and transgression. Finally, the Surrealist Spanish director Luis Bunuel (1900–1983) arrived in Mexico in 1946, where he resided for the rest of his life and created several of his greatest films. Beat poets such as Philip Lamantia sought inspiration from their Surrealist predecessors, seeking transcendent powers from the unconscious, from dreams, from allowing the mind to roam free from the constrictions of "logical, rational thought," and discovered in the dark gods of

Mexico a way to contact the primal energies which they felt were still alive in pretechnological culture and which preserved what Gary Snyder called the "Old Ways" of relating to nature and the cosmos.

Margaret Astrov's anthology *The Winged Serpent: American Indian Prose and Poetry*, published in 1946—a volume Philip Whalen recommended to Joanne Kyger—contained two sections devoted to texts from pre-Columbian Mexico, including the Aztec "Prayer to the God Titlacaon" and "A Song by Nezahualcoyotl"; "The Eagle and the Moon Goddess" from the Cora people; as well as Mayan works including "Three Fragments from the Book of Chilam Balam Chumayel" and "Prayer before Preparing Milpa." A. Grove Day's *The Sky Clears: Poetry of the American Indians* appeared in 1951, and by the early sixties, Mexican literature and thought had become increasingly visible in American cultural life. As we shall see in chapter 4, underground magazines such as Wallace Berman's *Semina* (1955–1964) and Margaret Randall's *El Corno Emplumado* (1962–1969) were significant in the dissemination of knowledge about Mexico for the counterculture. Both became important venues where both Beats and Surrealists submitted their poems, essays, translations, photographs, and artwork. The *Evergreen Review* published an issue entitled "The Eye of Mexico" in 1959 containing translations by Paul Blackburn, Lysander Kemp, Denise Levertov, and William Carlos Williams, an article on Aztec culture by Manuel Leon-Portilla, and a review of *Mexican Poetry: An Anthology* compiled by Octavio Paz and translated by Samuel Beckett. Wallace Berman published the fifth number of *Semina*, entitled "Mexico Issue," in 1959. The front cover depicted a Mayan stone phallus from the Stella Museum in Campeche while the back featured the famous painting of Sor Juana Inés de la Cruz by Miguel Cabrera.

Also in 1959, Thomas Mabry Cranfill edited *The Muse in Mexico: A Mid-Century Miscellany*, originally a supplement to the *Texas Quarterly*, volume 2, no. 1. Cranfill included in *The Muse in Mexico* William Carlos Williams's versions of Aztec poetry, "Three Nahuatl Poems," which Jerome Rothenberg also featured in his anthology, *Technicians of the Sacred*. By the late fifties, Tuli Kupferberg (1923–2010)—co-founder with Ed Sanders of the band the Fugs—declared in the first eight-page issue of his magazine *Birth* entitled *Beating* (Summer 1959): "The Beats link themselves & are linked to the new rising energies of Africa & Asia, to the primitive current life-loving peoples of Mexico & the Caribbean, to the old wisdom of Asia, to the crazy Bohemian poets of 19th century France breaking their heads against the coming calamities & yet raging after joy, digging life."[13] Upon the arrival of the sixties, the connections between American and Mexican cultural life had palpably strengthened.

Cover of *Semina*, Mexico issue 5, the Estate of Wallace Berman and Kohn Gallery, Los Angeles

Margaret Randall's *El Corno Emplumado*, *Evergreen Review*, published by Barney Rosset of Grove Press—Grove would bring out *Burning Water: Thought and Religion in Ancient Mexico* by Laurette Sejourne in 1960—and Berman's *Semina* were specifically aimed at the burgeoning counterculture. The rich literary tradition of Mexico—beginning with the ruler of the Chichimec kingdom of Texcoco, Nezahualcoyotl (1402–1472), who was also a philosopher, poet, and the subject of a long work by Ernesto Cardenal, to the great religious poet Sor Juana de la Cruz, to contemporary authors such as Octavio Paz—began to reveal itself to readers in the United States.

This increasing appreciation on the part of American writers for the written and oral literatures of Indigenous peoples had one source in Kenneth Rexroth (1905–1982), who served as a mentor for several Beats including Lawrence Ferlinghetti, Michael McClure, Gary Snyder, and Diane di Prima. Rexroth traveled widely and met Edward Sapir (1884–1939), the renowned scholar of Native American languages.[14] During a trip to the Southwest, Rexroth encountered Jaime de Angulo (1887–1950), the charismatic linguist and anthropologist who had lived among Native Americans and influenced several Beat writers including—as we shall see in chapter 9—Joanne Kyger. Rexroth became interested in Native American poetry and song, learning from several scholars including Mary Austin (1868–1934) and Alice Corbin Henderson: "Mary Austin knew more about Indians, and more about Indian song especially, than anybody else in the country, except Frances Densmore and Natalie Curtis Burlin, whom I never met. She understood my interest in the, so to speak, non-Aristotelian syntax of Indian and African languages a generation before Whorf. She played cylinder records of Indian songs for me, and gave me a list of books to read." Austin was also admired by Gary Snyder as "a very insightful nature essayist."[15] In his review of *American Indian Songs: The United States Bureau of Ethnology Collection*, Rexroth praised Densmore, who visited the Plains Indians—specifically the Teton Sioux—and recorded information concerning the celebrated Sun Dance.[16] In his review, Rexroth included samples of Densmore's translations of songs of the Chippewa, Teton Sioux, Northern Ute, Mandan, Hidatsa, Pawnee, Menominee, Papago, Yuman, and Yaqui peoples.

The "ethnopoetics" movement—the study by Rexroth and Snyder of Indigenous cultures and the effort to "translate" oral compositions into "written texts"—was one component of emerging Beat poetics. Poets began to explore Indigenous cultures and anthropology. The works of Claude Levi-Strauss such as *La Pensee Sauvage* (1962) and *Mythologiques* (in four volumes, 1964–1971) were admired by Gary Snyder, Ed Dorn, and Jerome Rothenberg. Snyder thought Levi-Strauss a "genius," while Dorn featured Levi-Strauss—along with Martin Heidegger and the pre-Socratic philosopher Parmenides—in his epic poem *Gunslinger*. Dorn revealed in an interview: "I feel very close to the mind of Levi-Strauss—very respectful of it because I like the kind of mental nets that he sets up." Rothenberg composed a poem named after a famous Levi-Strauss essay, "The Structural Study of Myth." Another important development in the assimilation of Indigenous literatures into American intellectual life was the magazine *Alcheringa*, founded in 1970, edited by Dennis Tedlock and Rothenberg. Snyder wrote essays for *Alcheringa*, while Ed Dorn and Gordon Brotherston contributed their translations of Indigenous oral tales, myths, and poetry. Rothenberg described *Alcheringa* as "a collaborative project that would bring together poets and scholars in the attempt to uncover and to find new ways of presenting the largely oral and traditional poetry in a contemporary context." As we shall see in chapter 9, Joanne Kyger in her poem "Visit to Maya Land" chronicles her visit to Chiapas in the fall of 1976 through her adaptation of an oral anthropogonic myth of the Tzotzil Maya.

The relationship between archaic oral literatures and the yearnings of the counterculture for new sources of inspiration is apparent in the anthology *America: A Prophecy, a New Reading of American Poetry from Pre-Columbian Times to the Present* (1973), in which Rothenberg and George Quasha presented selections from the *Popol Vuh*, the *Chilam Balam*, the Florentine Codex, and Aztec and Toltec texts, as well as reproductions of Mayan glyphs from the Dresden Codex. The collection also features American authors including Walt Whitman, Ezra Pound, Denise Levertov, Charles Bukowski, Philip Lamantia, and Michael McClure, thus emphasizing a subterranean yet continuing historical tradition of the poetry of the Americas. The title *America: A Prophecy* alludes to William Blake's eponymous 1793 poem, thereby connecting the revolutionary Blake—a hero to the Beats and also a much-admired genius during the hippie dawning of the Age of Aquarius—with the voices of Indigenous peoples. Allen Ginsberg (who had chosen Blake as his "guru"), during a reading in Australia, participated in a joint performance with aboriginal poets. Philip Whalen, in a list of recommended books he sent to Joanne Kyger—which included Keats, Coleridge, Byron, Shelley, and Wordsworth—declared in his typically chatty, funny, and obsessively exacting style: "The best of this whole lot is WILLIAM BLAKE (Complete writings which is to say prose, letters & notebooks as well as all poems with variant readings ed by Geoffrey Keynes, Oxford University Press, which is a reprint of the elegant Nonesuch Edn which was too expensive to talk about)."[17] The Beat immersion in the oral and written literature of Mexico and the nascent fascination with ethnopoetics were part of a developing awareness by American writers of the global context of their own philosophical and spiritual trajectory. The realization heralded by Beat transnationalism that the curriculum taught in American schools and universities has been hampered by a U.S. and Eurocentric bias has in the present day begun to be ameliorated.

The connection of the Beats to Mexico pointed in both directions: Mexican as well as Central and South American writers responded to the liberatory, egalitarian, and joyful energies of the American counterculture. The Nicaraguan Ernesto Cardenal edited, with Jose Coronel Urtecho, the *Antologia de la Poesia Norteamericano* (1963) which contains not only the canonized figures of American poetry—Walt Whitman, Robert Frost, Wallace Stevens, T. S. Eliot, and Ezra Pound—but also an impressive list of Beats including Lawrence Ferlinghetti, Allen Ginsberg, Philip Lamantia, Michael McClure, Gary Snyder, and Philip Whalen, figures in the San Francisco Renaissance such as Kenneth Rexroth, and Cardenal's mentor and friend, the Trappist monk Thomas Merton.[18] Cardenal, in his quest for spiritual values and social justice, was in solidarity with the American counterculture, forging friendships with Beat writers who traveled widely in Mexico such as Ferlinghetti and Lamantia; Cardenal's book *Apocalypse and Other Poems* (1971) also contains translations by Rexroth and Merton. Cardenal made common ground with Indigenous peoples, publishing *Homage to the American Indians* (1973), as did Beat writers such as Diane di Prima, who composed a poem entitled "Montezuma," fought against the injustices perpetrated upon the Native peoples of the United States, and worked as a teacher in an Indian reservation school in Wyoming where she first conceived her great epic poem *Loba*.

Because the Beats felt alienated from the ruling religious, cultural, economic, and political institutional Establishment of the United States, they experienced their predicament in ways which recall the experience of the Aztecs who questioned their "Christian" conquerors and overlords. When the Aztec priesthood encountered at Tenochtitlan the "Twelve Apostles" in 1524—a posse of Franciscan friars on a mission representing Pope Hadrian VI as well as the Holy Roman Emperor, Charles V—the Aztecs inquired, "Why should your rituals and your ideas of divine power be better than ours? How can you *know* you represent the true God?" There was additional irony in the fact that Bernal Diaz del Castillo and Fray Toribio de Benavente had both described impressive libraries—in Nahuatl, *amoxcalli,* "houses of books"—in which the knowledge of the supposedly barbaric and "primitive" Aztecs preserved by priests and nobles had been stored which were then burned and obliterated by the "enlightened" Spaniards. These inquiries by the Aztecs match very closely the unanswered questions the Beats and members of the counterculture were posing to their elders regarding not only religious orthodoxy but institutionalized racism, homophobia, unjust wars, the threat of nuclear apocalypse, and the destruction of the environment: they—like the Aztec priests—were not satisfied with the answers they received from those in authority. A similar failure of the Spanish to fathom the complexities of the Indigenous peoples of Mexico occurred when the Spaniards arrived in Yucatan. In 1588, Antonio de Ciudad Real reported: "When the Spaniards discovered this land, their leader asked the Indians how it was called, as they did not understand him, and they said *uic athan*, which means, what do you say or what do you speak, that we do not understand you. And then the Spaniard ordered it set down that it be called *Yucatan*."

So too the Beats were speaking a different language than their elders, and the two generations had difficulty understanding each other. The Beats were in revolt against monotheism and were eager to explore the traditions of other cultures. Carlos Castaneda's *The Teachings of Don Juan: A Yaqui Way of Knowledge* which investigated Indigenous Mexican peyote rituals would carry on the Beat tradition of fascination with Mexico for the new hippie generation: a primal land where materialism and technology had not yet run rampant and where a vital, archaic, ritualistic, and mythic culture still flourished. Young people who came of age after the Beats during the sixties also made common cause with Native Americans. As Sherry L. Smith has documented in *Hippies, Indians, and the Fight for Red Power*, the struggle of Native Americans for justice and an end to oppression intersected with the counterculture's concern with ecology, spirituality, and communal living. The poster for the January 14, 1967 "Be-In" at Golden Gate Park in San Francisco—where Allen Ginsberg, Timothy Leary, Lenore Kandel, Michael McClure, Gary Snyder, and Lawrence Ferlinghetti congregated together with the new sixties generation—featured Native American iconography with an Indian in full regalia on horseback beneath the title "Pow-Wow: A Gathering of the Tribes for a Human Be-In." The counterculture was now conceiving of its members as a kind of separate "tribe" located but in many ways isolated within the larger American society.

Gloria Anzaldua (1942–2004) in her advocacy for the rights of speakers of Spanish, her struggle against homophobia and freedom for LGBTQ people, her celebration of the intuitive and magical, her questioning of identity and selfhood based on linguistic, "ethnic," or "racial" categories (a more inclusive definition of what it means to be an "American"), and her feminist reinterpretation of Aztec mythology was also part of the countercultural critique of patriarchy, racism, repression, and "rationality."[19] Anzaldua was at the vanguard of a larger American liberatory movement during the sixties and seventies when those who had been disenfranchised sought to validate a sense of identity through establishing a connection with the archetypal symbols of their mythic past. Chicano writers such as Rodolfo Gonzales (1928–2005) in his poem *I Am Joaquin* invokes a litany of names including the heroic Cuauhtemoc—the last Aztec *tlatoani,* or ruler (1520–1521)—Pancho Villa, Benito Juarez, Emilio Zapata, and the Virgin of Guadalupe. And Alberto Baltazar Urista Heredia, known as "Urista" (1947–), published *Festival de flor y canto: An Anthology of Chicano Literature* (1976) which features in its title an allusion to *flor y canto,* "flower and song," which is the Nahuatl expression for poetry. The quest for the ancestors is the search for one's authentic beginnings and identity: the journal dedicated to Chicano studies, *Aztlan,* was named after the mythical homeland of the Mexica who traveled from Aztlan—which means "White Place" or "Place of the Cranes"—to Tenochtitlan.

Merely changing location in physical space is not the goal of many travelers. Rather, one may be eager for a new way of seeing things, a renewal of one's pleasure in life and perhaps a transformation of consciousness. Graham Greene in *Another Mexico* points out: "The border means more than a customs house, a passport officer, a man with a gun. Over there everything is going to be different; life is never going to be quite the same again after your passport has been stamped and you find yourself speechless among the moneychangers.... The atmosphere of the border—it is like starting over again." The *border* with Mexico for the Beats signifies not just an imaginary line on a map but rather entry into the Other, the unknown. As we shall see in chapter 8, they wanted—as Jim Morrison sang—to "break on through to the other side," and in the case of Mexico this meant the break into a primal, ancient mode of being, the quest for ecstatic states, the confrontation with death. Indeed, as Alberto Escobar de la Garma has declared: "Mexico, legendarily, has long been Beat terrain."[20] The sheer beauty of the landscape of the country—volcanoes, lovely beaches, the eerie silence of deserted archaeological ruins, broken stones, cenotes, interminable jungle, men on bicycles carrying bundles of wood on the highway, unfinished cement buildings, straggly thin dogs—makes a powerful impression upon the visitor.

However, there was also a dark side to travel in Mexico. Ambrose Bierce (1842–ca. 1914) mysteriously disappeared in Chihuahua while attached as an observer to Pancho Villa's (1878–1923) revolutionary army, setting the precedent for the deaths of poets Hart Crane and John Hoffman as well as Joan

Vollmer, the common-law wife of William S. Burroughs. Mexico is the stage upon which Bonnie Bremser enacts an often life-or-death struggle against her fate as a sex worker. Neal Cassady—"Dean Moriarty" of Kerouac's *On the Road*—perished along the railroad tracks of San Miguel de Allende. Gregory Corso in Kerouac's *Desolation Angels* (where he is named "Raphael Urso") employs the same imagery he featured in his poem "Mexican Impressions," exclaiming: "There's *death* in Mexico—I saw a windmill turning death this way—I don't *like* it here." Margaret Randall waged a powerful fight against political oppression and was forced to leave the country. In addition, writers have fallen ill—sometimes seriously—while in Mexico: D. H. Lawrence contracted malaria and Jack Kerouac became bedridden during his trip with Neal Cassady. During Ed Dorn and family's 1955 trip they were stricken by a variety of maladies while traveling through Matamoros, Ciudad Victoria, Tamazunchale, Mexico City, Guadalajara, Mazatlán, and back through Nuevo Laredo.[21] Philip Lamantia was afflicted by a nearly fatal scorpion sting which he chronicled in his poetry. And while the author of *Under the Volcano* Malcom Lowry did not die in Mexico, the tragic hero of his novel—the consul Geoffrey Firmin—is murdered. Oscar Zeta Acosta (1935–1974), author of *Autobiography of a Brown Buffalo* and *The Revolt of the Cockroach People*, activist in the Chicano movement, and friends with Hunter S. Thompson, was not immune from Mexico's enveloping powers: Acosta disappeared in May 1974 in Mazatlán.

The Beat response to Mexico was by no means monolithic; each of the Beat authors approached chronicling their travels in Mexico from a different angle and employed a variety of literary genres to convey their experiences: poetry, autobiographical memoir, novel, short story, journal. The Beat relationship to Mexico was also often a *shared* relationship: they wrote letters to each other concerning their experiences in the country and communicated antipathies and enthusiasms in their close friendships with one another. They traveled widely throughout Mexico—from Baja to Mexico City to Oaxaca to Chiapas to San Miguel de Allende to the great archaeological sites of the Yucatan—and the country became an inspiration for their literary creativity. The Beats also sympathized with the oppression of the Mexican people and were in opposition to American "manifest destiny." Mexican president Porfirio Diaz (1830–1915) famously quipped: "Poor Mexico, so far from God, so close to the United States." In this regard, the Beats had an illustrious predecessor, Henry David Thoreau (1817–1862), who opposed the Mexican-American War (1846–1848), spending a night in jail for refusing to pay his poll tax which supported both the enslavement of African Americans and the war against Mexico. Half of Mexico's territory was lost when the Treaty of Guadalupe Hidalgo (1848) ceded California as well as large areas of Arizona, New Mexico, Colorado, and Utah to the United States. Out of this experience of principled rebellion against unjust laws grew Thoreau's great essay "Civil Disobedience" (1849), and Thoreau's position opposing American imperialism would inspire the Beats a century later.

In *The Beats in Mexico* my purpose is to explore in depth five interrelated topics: (1) the importance of hitherto understudied women—Margaret Randall, Joanne Kyger, and Bonnie Bremser—in Beat literary history; (2) the significance of Mexico as a place of spiritual exploration and mystical experience for the Beats, especially their interest in shamanism and the use of entheogens; (3) the Beat confrontation with the "Other" in Mexico; (4) the centrality of Mayan and Aztec history, archaeology, and literature in their works; and (5) the ways the Beats adapted and incorporated ancient Mexican myth—such as the myth of Quetzalcoatl—into their poetics while simultaneously commenting on contemporary issues. The organization of *The Beats in Mexico* is chronological: I have arranged the chapters to reflect roughly the order in which the Beats each arrived in Mexico across the decades. Chapter 1 begins with the first Beat to set foot in Mexico, Lawrence Ferlinghetti. Ferlinghetti made several trips to the country and in his Mexican writings, refers continually to other authors and creates an intertextual pastiche through which he weaves his own voice. In chapter 2, I discuss William S. Burroughs's lifelong fascination with the Maya as well as his collaboration with artist Malcom McNeill in the creation of their "graphic novel" *Ah Pook Is Here*. In chapter 3, I explore Philip Lamantia's travels throughout Mexico, his important friendship with poet John Hoffman, and several poems which incorporate Mexican themes. In chapter 4, I study the importance of Margaret Randall's pioneering magazine *El Corno Emplumado* and the ways her feminism and political activism are reflected in her work; I also analyze her poems devoted to archaeological sites. In chapter 5, I review the ways Neal Cassady influenced Jack Kerouac's prose style in his Mexican writings as well as the desire Kerouac expressed to find in Mexico a place of spiritual retreat. Chapter 6 is devoted to Allen Ginsberg, and I analyze several poems including "Siesta in Xbalba" and the ways Ginsberg continues the quest of William Burroughs through his study of hallucinogens and his familiarity with the Madrid Codex. In chapter 7 I continue my survey of Beat women writers with Bonnie Bremser, analyzing the ways Bremser developed Kerouac's spiritual search in Mexico from the female perspective and how her voice provides an important complement to the predominantly male Beat perspective on Mexico.

Michael McClure and Jim Morrison are the subjects of chapter 8. I discuss McClure's friendship with the biologist Sterling Bunnell and their work in collecting psychedelic mushrooms in Mexico as well as several McClure poems including "Song of Quetzalcoatl." I also analyze the ways McClure's friend Jim Morrison explored Mexican themes in his songs and poetry. And last but not least, in chapter 9, I explore an unjustly neglected writer, Joanne Kyger, reviewing the ways her studies in philosophy affected her writings about Mexico. In the epilogue, I draw the various strands of my argument in *The Beats in Mexico* together, emphasizing the ways the Beat vision of Mexico still remains relevant today.

# 1 ⁕ LAWRENCE FERLINGHETTI

## The Mexican Night

LAWRENCE FERLINGHETTI (1919–2021) HOLDS the distinction of being the first Beat author to set foot in Mexico. In the summer following his second year as an undergraduate at the University of North Carolina at Chapel Hill in 1939, Ferlinghetti hitchhiked and took freight trains with two friends, one of whom was the nephew of the ambassador to Mexico, Josephus Daniels.[1] Among the Beats he also achieved the longest record of continuous journeys to Mexico as well as sites of Mayan culture commencing in 1939; he made regular visits during the sixties, and in 2010 he visited Yelapa, Mexico, as well as the archaeological site at Labantuum in Belize. References to Mexico appear in Ferlinghetti's poetry and prose from the beginning of his career to his latest book *little boy*, published just prior to his hundredth birthday in 2019. He traveled throughout the country: Baja, Mexico City, Guadalajara, and his favorite place, Oaxaca. The political struggles of Mexico are reflected in Ferlinghetti's *The Mexican Night* which includes an important letter from Margaret Randall discussing the harassment by the Mexican government of her magazine *El Corno Emplumado*. In the compendious anthology *Writing across the Landscape: Travel Journals 1960–2010*, Ferlinghetti chronicles his many journeys to Mexico. An entry entitled "Mexico, Again" from May 1972 is packed with the visual detail that typifies Beat writings about Mexico: "Mountain towns, north of Tecoman, Tecolotlan, and Ciudad Guzman—upward, toward Guadalajara—all day the dry, brown landscape floating by—a certain sadness in the landscape, on the brown plains, in the adobe and brick houses—lone burros, cows and men, a dead horse just fallen at a crossroads, harness still on. . . . From where, this loneliness on earth. Of course, the floating landscape is symbolic of time itself. It is only as we pass through it, as through a stationary wave, that time seems to flow past. Otherwise, it exists without us, immobile."[2] For Ferlinghetti, Mexican Earth, Mexican Time, Mexican Night emerge as central characters. He emphasizes his habitual need to travel alone, indeed to court "loneliness," a sense of solitude which echoes the title of the classic book on Mexico, *The Labyrinth of Solitude* by Octavio Paz.

As co-founder with Peter Martin of City Lights bookstore in 1953, Ferlinghetti published virtually all the Beats—Burroughs, Corso, Di Prima, Ginsberg, Kaufman, Kerouac, Kyger, Lamantia, McClure—as well as figures in the San Francisco Renaissance such as Kenneth Rexroth and Robert Duncan. Ferlinghetti was thus at the center of the American literary counterculture from the early 1950s to the present. Indeed, City Lights also published a number of South and Central American authors such as Pablo Neruda and Nicanor Parra from Chile; the Nicaraguan Ernesto Cardenal's *From Nicaragua with Love* appeared in the Pocket Poets Series, number 43 (1986); and the anthology *Volcan: Poems from Central America* (1983) features poets from El Salvador, Guatemala, Honduras, and Nicaragua. Other important Mexico titles published by City Lights are *First World, Ha Ha Ha! The Zapatista Challenge*, which explores the Zapatista army and the uprisings in Chiapas; a translation of texts from the sacred book of the Maya—Christopher Sawyer-Laucanno's *Destruction of the Jaguar: From the Books of Chilam Bilam*; and a re-issue of R. Gordon Wasson's *The Wondrous Mushroom: Mycolatry in Mesoamerica*.[3] Ferlinghetti also developed a close friendship with Mexican poet Homero Aridjis—a friend of Philip Lamantia's as well—whose book *Solar Poems* (published by City Lights) Ferlinghetti admired and whose ecological concerns he shared.

Ferlinghetti traveled to Mexico more frequently than to any other country; during the sixties, he rode in his old Volkswagen bus and took along his dog. *The Mexican Night: Travel Journal* (1970) contains writings composed from the fifties to 1969. Ferlinghetti's style is elliptical, telegraphic, compressed, employing dashes between phrases to flash brief images of Mexico—Bob

Lawrence Ferlinghetti and Homero Aridjis, courtesy of Betty Ferber

Dylan under the influence of Beat poetics evolved the concept of "chains of flashing images" in his song lyrics—as well as incisive observations on the social and political conditions in the country. The genre of *The Mexican Night* is ostensibly a travelogue, yet as Larry Smith has observed, the book "combines aspects of the novel, poetry, and poetic prose, frank political statements on the injustices and suppression of the student revolution during the Mexican Olympic Games, and a salute and elegy to rebel leader Che Guevara; all this encompassed within the mythic yet personal journal of the self in a land enveloped in the night's darkness yet bathed in the sun's reality."[4] As with Joanne Kyger's Mexico writings, Ferlinghetti also dates his observations, and *The Mexican Night* opens with an entry from the fifties marked indecisively, "April 22–27, 195?":

> Pardon me if I disappear in Mexico, wearing a mask and strange suspenders. Puncho Villa. Wandering about, speaking my curious 'spagnol. The trees are coming down, we'll to the woods no more, mad mind and black sun, we'd better find an island quick. Though there's no longer any "away." Southbound through the Toltec debris, the dark horse still a free runner. Under what volcano.... My soul in various pieces and I attempting to reassemble it, mistaking bird cries for

> ecstatic song when they are really cries of despair. And poetry a precession of waterbirds in flight mixed with motor accidents. . . . Where am I? Leaving Alamos on a local heap of a bus, full of vaqueros in hard cowboy hats, smoking Sonora Gold on the backseats, stoned blind in the dusk.[5]

This introductory fanfare sounds the recurring themes of *The Mexican Night*. Mexico is a place where Ferlinghetti is able to "disappear" for a time as he seeks his identity, which is in a liminal, fluid state: he is "wearing a mask" occluding his real Self. Pancho Villa (1878–1923), the great Mexican revolutionary, is invoked in the humorous alteration to "Puncho Villa"—Ferlinghetti is "wandering" like a comical rebel as in a Punch and Judy show—in search of a renewed soul. He also desires—like the rebel Pancho Villa—to initiate a revolution to create a just society. Stylistically, Ferlinghetti indulges in his favorite habit of allusion and pastiche. Just as his Surrealist novel *Her* (1960) is suffused with allusions to Djuna Barnes's *Nightwood*, Dante's *Inferno*, T. S. Eliot's *The Waste Land*, and James Joyce's *Ulysses* and *Finnegans Wake*, so too throughout Ferlinghetti's Mexico writings a number of disparate voices weave in and out. "We'll to the woods no more" is a direct quotation from A. E. Housman's (1859–1936) poem which begins: "We'll to the woods no more,/The laurels are all cut,/The bowers are bare of bay/That once the Muses wore."[6] Housman laments the disappearance of poetic inspiration in the loss of "laurels" and "bay"—traditional symbols of poetic genius in ancient Greece—and so too, Ferlinghetti is seeking inspiration, but he finds only a "mad mind and black sun."

The "mad mind and black sun" are likely allusions to Harry Crosby (1898–1929), the infamous founder, with his wife Caresse, of Black Sun Press, which published D. H. Lawrence, Hart Crane, and Charles Olson; Crosby's life ended in madness and suicide. In pre-Columbian Mexico, death and melancholy were symbolized by the black sun, and this depressive theme is further emphasized by the reference—"under what volcano"—to Malcolm Lowry's celebrated *Under the Volcano*, set in Quauhnahuac, Mexico, on November 2, 1938, during the *Dia de los Muertos*. The novel depicts the psychological descent of its protagonist, the alcoholic Consul Geoffrey Firman.[7] Lowry's *Selected Poems* was published in the City Lights Pocket Poets Series, number 17, and Ferlinghetti frequently alludes to him. For example, when Ferlinghetti visited the magnificent archaeological site of Mitla in 1968, six miles southwest of Oaxaca, he spent time in a small church where he noted: "'Jesus mio Misericordia'—one of those Bleeding Christ churches one stumbles into in all the small sad towns of adobe Mexico. . . . Inside, not one but three bloody bleeding Christs—one stretched out under a garden-green trestle like a birdcage . . . only his head with crown of thorns showing—like an invalid in bed asleep, blood on the forehead & the lips dripping with it." Malcolm Lowry's poem "In a Mexican Church" featured similar imagery: "Christ, slashed with an axe, in the humped church—/How shall we pray to you all pied with blood,/Yet deader by far than the hacked wood?"[8] Thus the gruesome iconography of Christ and the crucifixion in Mexico reveals the suffering and poverty of the country's oppressed people, and Ferlinghetti echoes Lowry in his evocation of the heavy weight of sorrow on their souls.

As Ferlinghetti seeks a way out of this psychological labyrinth, he travels south "through the Toltec debris"—a reference to the Toltecs who arose in Tula, Hidalgo, and whom the Aztecs viewed as their cultural predecessors—in an attempt to "reassemble" his fragmented spirit. Waterbirds appear—flying creatures, which one might associate with poetic inspiration and flights of fancy, proliferate in Ferlinghetti's Mexican writings—but here they are singing only "cries of despair." Ferlinghetti openly questions his geographical and spiritual location—"Where am I?"—as he departs Alamos, a town in Sonora in northwestern Mexico on a bus "full of vaqueros in hard cowboy hats, smoking Sonora Gold on the back seats, stoned blind in the dusk." Marijuana and the employment of drug lingo of the counterculture—"stoned"—signals another avenue of "escape" or "entrance" from/into the self. This opening passage of *The Mexican Night: Travel Journal* illustrates Ferlinghetti's approach: a highly condensed, allusive poetic prose—as we shall see, he often creates a pastiche by obsessively referring to or quoting directly from writers he admires who visited Mexico—deployed in the effort to both describe his own existential situation as well as evoke through striking images the indelible experiences of his journeys through the country.

In January 1959, Ferlinghetti attended, with Allen Ginsberg, a conference sponsored by the Communist Party at the University of Concepcion in Chile. On his return, he traveled with his wife Kirby through South and Central America and on to Mexico City, where they enjoyed walking through Chapultepec Park.[9] Two years later, in the second entry of *The Mexican Night* entitled "'Lower' California"—that is, Baja California—dated October 24, 1961, Ferlinghetti informs us: "A visionary journey without visions, in a stone blind land—the new Mexico still the Old Beat Mexico—that huge dark foodshit smell still here (which I first smelled in dank woodwork of a Mexico City pension, 1939). . . . Ensenada, Baja California—bah on this baja—who stole the sun? . . . Only the kids and dogs have anything left in them—and the dogs can't stand it—they lie around stretched out with flies all over them in the gutters, a curious race apart. . . . Perhaps I could learn to love this land if I stayed awhile—tho it's the third or fourth time I've been to Mex already." Jack Kerouac also noticed the omnipresent Mexican canine during a stay in Navojoa in Sonora, one of the "strange towns" in Mexico where he went for a solitary walk "and saw, in the market outdoor affair, a butcher standing in front of a pile of lousy beef for sale, flies swarming all over it while mangy skinny fellaheen dogs scrounged around under the table." Three days later on October 27, Ferlinghetti grew increasingly exasperated with Ensenada—the subject as we shall see in chapter 8 of a poem by Jim Morrison—complaining, "I can't stand it any longer, I'll leave in the morning," and alludes again to Lowry's *Under the Volcano*, for people here "act as if they still had some great slur of hope somewhere. While consuls drink themselves to death."[10] This—as Ferlinghetti guesses—was indeed the "third or fourth" trip he made to Mexico, following his initial 1939 visit as a university student, the uncertainly dated "April 22–27, 195?" journey, and his 1959 voyage back to the States from Chile through Mexico City.

As in the opening paragraph of *The Mexican Night*, Ferlinghetti registers ambivalent reactions: "A visionary journey without visions." He reports the unpleasant odors he experienced back in 1939 are still redolent, as well as the omnipresent poor, straggly, thin, hungry stray dogs which are omnipresent in the literature about Mexico from Lowry to Kerouac. Ferlinghetti's "Dog"—which comically portrays the world from the viewpoint of a loveable and curious canine—is one of his best-known, bravura poems; thus it is expected that he would take note of the omnipresent mutts of Mexico. Ferlinghetti also composed a surrealistic piece of fiction starring man's best friend—"*El Perro Humano*, Human Dog, dog of my days, tail wagger in eternity, barker in the dusk, in the dust, yapper extraordinaire, flea-bitten Mexican wolfhound, mongrel, woofer and pooper, friend of the poorest man, digger and barker, earthly sniffer, alone in the universe"—composed during a trip to Nicaragua and Mexico in July, 1989, entitled "The Dog." However, even with all Mexico's indignities, he muses he "could learn to love this land if I stayed awhile," and in this ambivalent push/pull, attraction/repulsion to Mexico he resembles D. H. Lawrence, who in his letters, essays, and novels also records a constantly shifting sequence of positive/negative emotional reactions to both present-day Mexico and its historical past.

In a revealing entry dated October 28, Ferlinghetti continues his itinerary by bus, from Ensenada to Mexicali through Tijuana. Approaching the town of Tecate, he "passes thru hill country strewn thickly with rocks from road to horizon, nothing but rocks . . . rock mountains, Tibetan peaks (one of those border mountains north of Tecate, on U.S. side, inhabited by American translator of *The Tibetan Book of the Dead*)."[11] This unnamed "translator" is W. Y. Evans-Wentz (1878–1965), the distinguished Tibetan Studies scholar who lived at Mount Cuchama, a few miles away from Tecate near the Mexican border. Cuchama, known to the Diegueno Indians as the "high, exalted place," was employed by them as well as the Luisenos and Chochomis "in secret initiation rites long before the white man arrived."[12] Evans-Wentz would purchase approximately three thousand acres of land north of Tecate where he wrote a monograph on the spiritual history of the area entitled *Cuchama and Sacred Mountains*. This episode is illuminating for it illustrates Ferlinghetti's familiarity with *The Tibetan Book of the Dead*, a popular book for the Beats during the fifties and sixties: Diane di Prima and Andy Warhol participated in a ceremony following the suicide of dancer Fred Herko (1936–1964) which featured readings from *The Tibetan Book of the Dead*. The allusion to this famous text thus reveals the ways Ferlinghetti connects the Mexican landscape with important American countercultural spiritual currents.

As he arrives at the border town of Mexicali, Ferlinghetti observes the signs he sees displayed along the border: "'Narcotics Addicts & Users Are Required by U.S. Law to Register Before Leaving Country.' Also: 'Warning: Cats & Dogs Leaving U.S. May Not Be Allowed to Re-enter.'" He proceeds to parody the signs, and indeed the reader is left to wonder if perhaps these peremptory warnings have been invented by Ferlinghetti: "Do not pee on the wrong side of the fence. Show your dogtags. Borders must be maintained!"[13] Jack Kerouac in chapter 2 of *Lonesome Traveler* entitled "Mexico Fellaheen" registered a similar reaction: "When you go across the border at Nogales Arizona some very severe looking American guards, some of them pasty faced with sinister steel rim spectacles go scrounging through all your beat baggage for signs of the scorpion of scofflaw." Ferlinghetti's solution to the absurd, inhumane, and sometimes deadly situation of the United States-Mexico border differs markedly from the recommendations on offer by conservative politicians in America today who have separated refugee parents from their children and imprisoned them in cages: he suggests that we "declare an immediate moratorium on all liaisons, partnerships and marriages between all people of the same color, everyone immediately to seek union with someone of a different color, all national flags made into snotrags or bandages to be used in maternity hospitals. . . . In the meantime, I wander about the landscape, making like that American Indian whom Henry Miller wished to have at his side when he crossed the continent in this unconditioned Nightmare, the one he wanted to have with him when he viewed the smoking steel mills by roadbeds of Pittsburgh in an *Inferno* Dante never dreamed of."[14] If humans mated only with people who are "ethnically different," gradually racial and national boundaries would disappear: we wouldn't be able to tell "who is who" or by whose "flag" to define one's identity, which would be for the better. Ferlinghetti alludes to Henry Miller's *The Air-Conditioned Nightmare* (1945), which recounts Miller's travels across the United States by automobile with his artist friend Abraham Rattner and chronicles his often disgusted reaction to his native America upon his return from his decade in Paris.

In "The Road to Topolobampo May 1962," the recitation of famous writers' names continues: on one page we find Antonin Artaud and Albert Camus, as well as the author of *Under the Volcano*: "The ghost of Malcolm Lowry skulks from behind a bush carrying his sign: Le Gusta Este Jardin?/Que Es Suyo?/Evite Que Sus Hijos Lo Destruyan!" This is from chapter 5 of *Under the Volcano* and the passage from the novel reads: "The Consul stared back at the black words on the sign without moving. You like this garden? Why is it yours? We evict those who destroy! Simple words, simple and terrible words, words which one took to the very bottom of one's being, words which, perhaps a final judgement on one, were nevertheless unproductive of any emotion whatsoever, unless a kind of colourless cold, a white agony, an agony chill as that iced mescal drunk in the Hotel Canada on the morning of Yvonne's departure." Later in *Under the Volcano,* Lowry corrects the earlier error in the translation of the sign, providing the proper version of the Spanish: "Do you like this garden, the notice said, that is yours? See to it that your children do not destroy it!" Lowry created this cryptic sign as an allusion to the Jewish Kabbalah, intending the message to suggest the allegory of the Garden of Eden where there were "both the tree of life and the tree of forbidden fruit, with the contingent responsibility on man to exercise his choice freely and to act responsibly or else to suffer for his abuse of that freedom." Kabbalah became popular among San Francisco poets such as Diane di Prima, Robert Duncan, and David Meltzer, and Ferlinghetti seeks to convey the hidden spiritual message of the sign in the Garden.[15] Ferlinghetti—like Lowry—has embarked in Mexico on a journey toward authentic selfhood and sometimes appears lost in the labyrinth of existential choices with which life confronts all of us: what action to perform next may have positive or negative consequences and the Garden of Eden—Planet Earth—is ours to fructify or destroy.

This passage is followed in Ferlinghetti's text by: "*Au pays du Tarahumara,* that wild junkie landscape Artaud apprehended. Still I'm not with him, I'm with Camus who also rushed too fast into his unknown, in this *cama alta* . . .

no windows upon the mescal landscape, a bunker in space." Antonin Artaud, as we have seen in the introduction, was a major influence on the Beats and their travels to Mexico. Artaud resided with the Tarahumara Indians of northwestern Mexico and participated in their peyote rituals, while Albert Camus died prematurely—"who rushed too fast into his unknown"—in an automobile crash. Ferlinghetti also evokes the "howling of the robot radio tuned to one of those crazy Mexican stations emitting a hilarious mixture of dramatic advertisements for shoes, American jazz played by violins and cornets, church bells thrown in to punctuate special announcements, sexy male announcers ... all mixed together with mariachis." Anyone visiting Mexico will remark upon the verisimilitude of this description of the sonic kaleidoscope of Mexican radio. Yet he also notes lyrically what he perceives as the tenderness of the Mexican people he encounters: "It is *innocence*, it is their seeming *innocence* which presents itself incessantly, as you see the *camion* passengers so gravely taking in everything the hotrod announcer throws at them. . . . All sit there still groping on into the falling dusk. Innocence persists, insanely intarissable, in spite of all. The road does not end. It is as if the radio were not playing at all. There is a stillness in the air, in the light of the dusk, in the eyes fixed forward, in the still end of life, an intolerable sweetness." This is an "innocence" which Charles Olson also admired in the Mexican people with whom he traveled on a bus trip through the Yucatan, an innocence which Ferlinghetti finds "inexhaustible" as he switches to the French language with *intarissable*.[16]

The narrative of *The Mexican Night* now shifts six years later to 1968 and Ferlinghetti's journey to his favorite Mexican city, Oaxaca, where he enjoys time "under the jacaranda trees and the great Indian laurels, roots still in the Ganges, in the plaza de Oaxaca. . . . And then at night by the circular bandstand listening to the marimba music, everyone out strolling or on the park benches in the semi-dark, the high lamps shining through the trees." The state of Oaxaca, which borders Chiapas to the east, is located in a mountainous landscape—Zempoaltepec, a dormant volcano 11,125 feet above sea level, is one of the several famous volcanos of Mexico—and is positioned where the eastern and southern Sierra Madre mountains converge, occupying approximately 95,000 square kilometers: it is the birthplace of the president of Mexico Benito Juarez (1806–1872) and home of the great Zapotecan archaeological sites of Mitla and Monte Alban. Oaxaca was much beloved by D. H. Lawrence, where he spent the winter of 1924–1925 composing *The Plumed Serpent* and *Mornings in Mexico*.[17] In a letter dated November 14, 1924, Lawrence wrote to William Hawk: "Oaxaca is a little town, about 30,000, alone in the south, with a perfect climate. The market is full of roses and violets, the gardens are all flowers. Every day is perfectly sunny, a bit hot at midday. The natives are mostly Zapotec Indians, small, but very straight and alert and alive: really very nice."[18] *Terry's Guide to Mexico,* published in 1923 and Lawrence's companion during his travels, describes Oaxaca as "one of the most attractive and interesting cities of the Repub., with train-cars, electric lights, telephones, and a progressive administration." It is clear why Ferlinghetti admired Lawrence: his observations about Mexico are incisive, lyrical, vivid, evocative, and life-giving. Ferlinghetti created a nude, 23" x 28" charcoal portrait of Lawrence in 1997 which he included in his album of artwork, *Life Studies/Life Stories.*[19] In 2013, Ferlinghetti also visited Taos, New Mexico, where he participated in a celebration of the legacy of D. H. Lawrence and read his poem "The Man Who Rode Away"—the title recalling Lawrence's novella *The Woman Who Rode Away*—recounting his visit to the shrine containing Lawrence's ashes: "shrine locked—/booby-trapped for burglars—/plumed serpent stoned/into a gargoyle!/ . . . You stand still a moment in the still air./Your eyes have a Mexican look/turned south/over the arroyos/*ahora y siempre*/Winter is coming/ You have your ticket."[20] These verses effectively catch Lawrence as he is about to leave Mabel Dodge Luhan's ranch in Taos, New Mexico, to travel south to what Lawrence sometimes called "Old Mexico."

The archaeological sites the Beats visited in Mexico fall into five distinct geographical locations: (1) Oaxaca's Mitla and Monte Alban; (2) the great pyramids of Teotihuacan near present-day Mexico City; (3) Palenque in Chiapas; (4) Chichen Itza; and (5) the sites accessible on the forty-one-kilometer-long *Ruta Puuc*—*puuc* means "hill" in Maya. This region of the extremely flat terrain of the Yucatan peninsula features rolling hills and the legendary cities of Labna, Kabah, Sayil, and Uxmal. In addition to his observations concerning the landscape, religious life, and political situation in *The Mexican Night,* Ferlinghetti includes descriptions of several archaeological sites including his March 1969 entry, "Uxmal, Or the Flight to the Sun." Uxmal—which in Maya means "thrice built"—was a favorite destination for Margaret Randall, Joanne Kyger, and Allen Ginsberg and is located in a densely wooded valley with low hills to the north and south. The city is one of the most impressive marvels of Mexico: Frank Lloyd Wright considered it a supreme masterpiece of inventive, architectural genius. The massive site contains extended facades, one-story buildings, and pyramids including the Palace of the Governor, Pyramid of the Magician, the Nunnery Quadrangle, and—a typical feature of Maya city planning—a Ball Court.

Ferlinghetti's account of his visit contains surreal passages: he earned his doctorate in literature at the Sorbonne in Paris, and Surrealism surfaces in his early novel *Her* (1960) and throughout his prose and poetry. The Surrealists relied upon their dreams for access to unconscious sources of creativity, and in "Uxmal, Or the Flight to the Sun," Ferlinghetti mixes his actual experience of the ruins with a kind of surreal-fantasy-dream sequence:

> At Uxmal, in the rain forest, I am climbing up a great unfinished pyramid, its base hidden in jungle. Through the mouth of the rain-god Chac I entered the Pyramid of the Magician and now climb up & up, dragging a huge basket of stones for the construction of the pyramid. I am wearing a loincloth and a hat of pineapple leaves. My skin is dark brown with green tints, and it glistens with rivulets of sweat. . . . The sun itself rolls down on top of me, spinning. It is made of peyote and white hot sperm, jism of the universe. I am part of "Space Odyssey 2001" but I am also a bloodshot Indian prince seven feet tall. The white hot sperm falls in showers. The moon rises and drenches us in pulverized peyote. . . . I hear sun adazzle through a silkscreen overlay, a near moon wings by, a Quetzalcoatl phoenix fills the upper air, dripping yellow sperm of light, there is no other paradise . . .[21]

The passage bears resemblance to several of the surreal sections in Henry Miller's—an author Ferlinghetti admired and unsuccessfully sought to publish under the City Lights imprint—*Tropic of Capricorn* as well as Miller's "Rosy Crucifixion" trilogy, *Sexus, Nexus,* and *Plexus*. And Ferlinghetti knew the Beat tradition of the "meditation on ruins" such as Allen Ginsberg's "Siesta in Xbalba": "Late sun opening the book,/blank page like light,/invisible words unscrawled,/impossible syntax/of apocalypse—Uxmal: Noble Ruins/No construction—."[22] Ferlinghetti imagines himself back in time as one of the builders of the great pyramid, and allows himself to spin out spontaneously a kind of improvised riff in which the sun—prime symbol of creative life and power for both the Maya and Aztecs—becomes an amalgam of peyote and sperm, launching him into a cosmic flight which he associates with the film *2001: A Space Odyssey,* directed by Stanley Kubrick and released in 1968. Some moviegoers—hearing about the film's spectacular special effects and original employment of classical music such as Richard Strauss's *Also Sprach Zarathustra*—ingested a variety of entheogens such as LSD before going to the cinema to enhance their psychedelic experience. So too, Ferlinghetti encounters in his own interior cosmic voyage the ecstasy of

San Miguel de Allende, from the collection of David Stephen Calonne

a peyote-fueled trip where the most important god of Mexico, Quetzalcoatl the feathered serpent, appears in all his magnificence "dripping yellow sperm of light, there is no other paradise." Mircea Eliade in his essay "Spirit, Light, Seed" analyzed the relationship between the symbolism of light and sperm, or "seed," and Ferlinghetti intends to suggest a connection between the creation of the cosmos, sexual power, and the atavistic energies he encountered at Uxmal.

Thus far we have seen how Ferlinghetti responded to several significant Mexican locations—from Ensenada and Oaxaca, to Mitla and Uxmal. Yet one of the most central places in Beat literature and mythology is San Miguel de Allende.

Many Beats visited this idyllic town. Pierre Delattre (1930–), founder of the Bread and Wine Mission in San Francisco where Bob Kaufman, Joanne Kyger, Philip Whalen, Robert Duncan, Gary Snyder, and Richard Brautigan congregated, settled in San Miguel where he taught writing at the Instituto Allende. San Miguel is celebrated for its cobblestone streets, stately architecture, and lovely weather. However, it also has a more dramatic significance in Beat literary history, for Neal Cassady died in San Miguel on February 4, 1968. After describing the plaza—"trees of the Jardin full of boat-tailed grackles"; "Conchero dancers with armadillo guitars under the Indian laurels in front of La Parroquia"—as well as a bad marijuana trip which afflicted him at a party, Ferlinghetti declares: "I a strange bird flapping, wearing leather, creaking sandals. I keep creaking forward in them, I not Neal Cassady who died here in the rain at night along the railroad tracks, counting the ties to Celaya, this year, still high on life, he never walked but ran to wherever he was going, and so arrived there first, I not Neal whose lostandfound manuscreeds I'm here deciphering."[23] Cassady had traveled to Mexico in January 1967, staying in Puerto Vallarta, Jalisco, but left in May. In late January 1968, he returned to Mexico, attended a wedding celebration in San Miguel, and passed out on the railroad tracks on his way walking to Celaya, a town about forty-four kilometers from San Miguel: the exact cause of his death remains uncertain but it was likely due to a drug overdose. Pierre Delattre in his memoir *Episodes* (1993), recalled that following Cassady's death: "The police knocked on my door saying they had a corpse in their truck; my address was in his pocket. . . . As I walked along the railroad track where he collapsed for the last time on a mixture of speed and tequila, I remembered his telling me that he was tired of being a cult figure; he just wanted to go back to working on the railroad like his father." Ferlinghetti also refers here to the "manuscreeds"—the manuscripts which Cassady left behind—which City Lights would publish three years later in 1971 as *The First Third*.

Ferlinghetti's travels in Mexico inspired not only prose such as *The Mexican Night* but also poetry. In May of 1972, he journeyed again to Mexico where he composed "Carnaval de Maiz"—dated "11 Mayo 72"—which was published in the collection *Open Eye, Open Heart* (1973).[24] Ferlinghetti returns to the imagery featured in his description of the church in Mitla: "In the churches of Cholula/the bleeding Christs groan/their Indian misericordias/

as Christian saints in cages/wring their wood hands/over bloodblack rosaries/wailing & bewailing/Great God Death/in Churrigueresque chapels/wherein sweet Indian faces/had their burro-vision bent/into 'Heaven-sent'/baroque monstrosities/While Christ Quetzalcoatl was predicted/and did indeed land/and did indeed take that land in pawn/And still riseth up ruined & raunchy/with barbaric yawn/in the dawn of a new debacle/As we walk into it chewing chicle/carrying cameras and Oaxaca blankets."[25] Ferlinghetti makes an oblique allusion to Walt Whitman's famous "barbaric yawp" but altered to "barbaric yawn"—an example of his fondness for comic asides—and notes how the native peoples possessed an earth-centered "burro-vision." Their orientation to the world was rooted in their connection to the cycles of the cosmos and harvesting of corn—the "maiz" of the title "Carnaval de Maiz"—but they were "converted" by the Spanish conquistadors into a belief in a Christian heaven symbolized by the "Churrigueresque chapels," churches built by architects such as Jose Benito de Churriguera (1665–1725), who covered over obsessively every surface of his buildings in a display of baroque stylistic madness. It was believed that Quetzalcoatl would return again, and when Moctezuma II encountered Hernan Cortes, he thought Cortes was indeed the incarnation of Quetzalcoatl—thus Ferlinghetti's "White Christ Quetzalcoatl was predicted/and did indeed land."

However, while the poem describes the cultural depredations wrought by the Christian Spaniards, and the church in Cholula symbolizes what some call "medieval superstition," it holds a message for us, for people in the United States "have indeed abolished Death/and no longer need/such monuments & consolations/We have banned it forever from our lives/and seldom see anyone dying anymore/except on TV in some foreign country."[26] The Aztecs honored the god Mictlantecuhtli—also known as Tzontemoc, usually depicted as a skeleton adorned with bloody spots—who, with his wife Mictecacihuatl, ruled over Mictlan, the land of the dead. In modern Mexico, Aztec conceptions of death are continued in the renowned *Dia de los Muertos*—the Day of the Dead—which is celebrated from October 31 to November 2. Margaret Randall in her recent autobiographical *My Life in 100 Objects* (2020) observes that in their homes, Mexican families construct altars which recently "have also taken on sociopolitical issues such as domestic violence or the immense numbers of citizens murdered by the drug cartels. This is in sharp contrast with our Halloween when children dressed as witches and ghosts go from house to house asking for handouts of candy. Rather than trafficking in fear, ridiculing death, or turning it into a bizarre parody, Mexicans confront it head-on, opening a space in which to feel and talk about the phenomenon."

Ferlinghetti's poem—published a few years after Elisabeth Kubler-Ross's *On Death and Dying* (1969)—recapitulates her argument: in contemporary society, we have attempted to shield ourselves from Death, to pretend it does not exist, and our culture is thereby "sanitized" and impoverished. William S. Burroughs in *Naked Lunch* elaborated on these traditions: "'Death was their Culture Hero,' said my Old Lady looking up from the Mayan codices.... 'They got fire and speech and the corn seed from death.... Death turns into maize seed.'" In the *Popol Vuh,* man is created from corn, while the Hero Twins have maize plants for alter egos. In Maya cosmology, the Young Corn God as the "dead" maize seed is reborn from Xibalba, the Land of the Dead. Thus the modern Mexicans have preserved their Aztec and Maya awareness of the interrelationship between Life and Death as symbolized in their mythology of maize/corn. In "Carnaval de Maiz," Ferlinghetti deftly explores the ways Western and traditional Mexican cultures have interpenetrated and the lessons that we can learn from the people we have supposedly "conquered."

Another important poem received its impetus from a trip to Mexico. Three years later in 1975, during a reading tour, Ferlinghetti began work in Tepotzlan on his "Adieu a Charlot: Second Populist Manifesto" which he completed in 1978 in San Francisco; the poem appeared in *City Lights Journal* number 4 in 1978.[27] "Manifestos" were significant features of the Surrealist movement as well as the Futurist and many other modernist literary and artistic movements. Here as in the past, Ferlinghetti urges poets in his "Populist Manifesto" to abandon the ivory towers of academia and, as Walt Whitman counseled a century previously, to become the democratic bards of the people, to enter the streets, and to employ the language of everyday American life: "Sons of Whitman sons of Poe/sons of Lorca & Rimbaud/or their dark daughters/poets of another breath/poets of another vision/who among you still speaks of revolution/who among you still unscrews/the locks from the doors/in this revisionist decade?"

Ferlinghetti again creates a pastiche by weaving in Whitman's famous exhortation in *Leaves of Grass* to "civilized" people to open the doors of perception and cast off the killing weight of repression and tradition: "Unscrew the locks from the doors!/Unscrew the doors themselves from their jambs!" Ferlinghetti tells us that he has met a young poet in Tepotzlan in Morelos—which borders Mexico City and is known as the birthplace of Quetzalcoatl—a "youngblood wildhaired angel poet/one of a spawn of wild poets/in the image of Allen Ginsberg."[28] When Ferlinghetti intones "Sons of Whitman sons of Poe/sons of Lorca & Rimbaud," at the opening, he is situating his poem and audience within the context of a Hispanic-American-European nexus. He goes on to tell us: "I speak to you/from another country, another kind of blood-letting land/from Tepotzlan the poets'lan'/Land of the Lord of the Dawn/Quetzalcoatl/Land of the Plumed Serpent/I signal to you/as Artaud signaled/through the flames." Because Ferlinghetti is in Quetzalcoatl's place of origin in Tepotzlan, he creates a rhyme with the last syllable of Tepotzlan, "tzlan," which he elides and abbreviates with "poets' land," creating a new word: "poets'lan.'" This wordplay is intended to suggest a community existing between all world poets and the "Land of the Lord of the Dawn/Quetzalcoatl/Land of the Plumed Serpent."

The final section of the poem is devoted to encouraging a new generation of struggling youth to find a path through the confusing labyrinth of modernity. Ferlinghetti counsels them to heed the voices of their inner selves: "Listen says the sea Within you/you with your private visions/of another reality a separate reality/Listen and study the charts of time," an allusion to Carlos Castaneda's *A Separate Reality: Further Conversations with Don Juan* (1971) as well as to the codices preserving the Maya knowledge of astronomy, the relationship of the position of the stars to seasonal change—"study the charts of time." Ferlinghetti draws a parallel between the alienated youth of the sixties and seventies in America and the Lost Generation in Paris as well as expatriates such as Henry Miller who traveled to Greece in search of "the great Greek dream/of The *Colossus of Maroussi*." All of these artists were "living out a myth," attempting to find a new reality: "Lived out the D.H. Lawrence myth/in *The Plumed Serpent*/In Mexico Lake Chapala/And the Malcolm Lowry myth/*Under the Volcano* at Cuernavaca." And from these two British writers, he turns to "the saga of *On the Road*/and the Bob Dylan myth Blowing in the Wind/How many roads must a man walk down/How many Neal Cassadys on lost railroad tracks." The American youth of the sixties were following the path of earlier Beat travelers to Mexico in search of a "myth to live by." Charlie Chaplin (1889–1977)—the "Charlot" of the poem's title—is now dead, but Ferlinghetti celebrates his memory as a symbol of "the Little Man in each of us/waiting with Charlot or Pozzo"; Chaplin's Tramp Charlot and Pozzo (along with Lucky) at the finale of Beckett's *Waiting for Godot* wait for the ever-deferred meaning of life to appear, but it never does. Finally, Ferlinghetti declares that he encounters these forgotten Little Men all around him: "On every corner I see them/hidden inside their tight clean clothes . . . /They turn and hitch their pants/and walk away from us/down the darkening road/in the great American night."[29] Ferlinghetti concludes with Kerouac's "American Night" just as he had earlier explored the solitude and infinite spaces of the Mexican Night, and wonders ambiguously where the "Little Men" will go "down the darkening road" of the modern world.

"Tepoztlan, November 1" features one of Ferlinghetti's finest, bravura passages concerning his Mexican experiences. Here he describes ingesting "about a dozen 'San Pedro' mushrooms—very small, dark ones picked on Popocatepetl—tasted gritty. Very mild and gentle trip, 'blissful.' Friendly presence inside me—very strong little fellow, definitely masculine—'myself inside myself.' . . . The snow top of Popocatepetl seen at sunset clearly without clouds, a heart-shaped snow face on its westward side and on it the sign of Aries in black, the whole under a mantle ten miles high. We rode on small little horses down a valley into the sunset. But the sun never set. We rode on and on into it, never tiring, sun never setting. Endless day, endless night."[30] The mushrooms have a special significance for Ferlinghetti since they derive from the great volcano Popocatepetl, central symbol of Lowry's *Under the Volcano*, and are omnipresent in Beat writings on Mexico. The prose as usual is highly lyrical and again veers into the fantastic, the surreal with "sun-stone going round with lights on it. Aztec Wing creaks open like a door flying."[31] Ferlinghetti alludes here to the celebrated massive Sun—or Calendar—Stone which depicts the five creations of the universe in Aztec myth: each creation composed an age known as a "sun." Richard F. Townsend points out in *The Aztecs* that the Sun Stone, "a grand synthesis of myth, history, and cosmological order, demonstrates the conjunction of a recurring mythic date of renewal-time with the calendar year 1427, sanctifying the beginning of empire and the authority of Aztec rulers." This awesome symbol of the relationship between Aztec civilization, time, and cosmogony evokes in Ferlinghetti an imaginative, psychedelic, timeless voyage, where eternity and infinity open their arms to him.

In his writings on Mexico of the eighties, Ferlinghetti again favors journal form—with dates and toponyms often appended—featuring a blend of personal experiences, surreal passages, and observations concerning the landscape and architecture of Mexico. "Through the Labyrinth into the Sun; August 1982" begins with a zany, surreal riff à la Marx Brothers in Mexico City involving a woman, her pet dog, and a "short bald man." The man approaches the woman who does not wish to be accosted, so "she reaches up and scissors a hole in his crotch. His nuts drop and roll away on the grass like balls in a pinball machine. They careen against a curb and ricochet down the Avenida de la Reforma, bowling over the late morning traffic." The woman then picks up the man's testicles and plants them, from which white trees spring up. The scene takes place in "macho Mexico, and the lady is the eternal *curandera* who will cure modern man with her powerful spells." Ferlinghetti here demonstrates his solidarity with the worldwide feminist movement of the sixties and seventies, which grew in intensity beyond the United States and Europe as women demanded equal rights and challenged the patriarchy. Ferlinghetti also created several drawings in support of oppressed Mexican women. Three artworks created in 2002 chronicle the political struggles in Oaxaca: one is entitled "Policia, Oaxaca," depicting a police wagon rolling over three bodies on the street; the second and third depict naked women crucified on crosses with the words "Por la Liberacion de la Mujer."

In the following entry dated August 15, Ferlinghetti recounts: "At a late afternoon *tertulia,* I meet Octavio Paz. I tell him that in his *laberinto de soledad,* he's not much interested in psilocybin mushrooms as a way I suggest to get out of the labyrinth. . . . He gives me a strange look . . . backing away . . . I'm a real imbecile." Ferlinghetti was invited by Homero Aridjis to participate in the Festival Internacional de Poesia de la Ciudad de Mexico and joined a group of poets on a tour of the ruins of an Aztec temple which had recently been discovered beneath the Zocalo. Ferlinghetti comments upon the "poor *indio* workers" who are doing the digging with their wheelbarrows and spades—a reappearance of the theme we shall encounter in Burroughs and Kerouac of underground labor as symbol of social inequality in Mexico—and are paid three dollars for eight hours of labor. Ferlinghetti also notes the discovery of the temple ruins of a "huge goddess, three yards wide, with head and breasts cut off, buried in the Hill of Serpents. At another place in the ruins, the omnivorous obsidian head of a huge serpent has been uncovered. His mouth is half-open and between the widely spaced blunt teeth a tongue can be seen, about to flick out, petrified in time. His obsidian eyes glare up at the Anglo women tourists."[32]

Ferlinghetti goes on to Oaxaca and names places he has been in Mexico: "many times have I passed alone through Mexico like this. I have passed through San Miguel de Allende, bullfights at Carretera (the most critical aficionados in Mexico), Patzcuaro, Morelia, San Blas, Vaca Cuerna, Mexico City, Oaxaca; stood in endless buslines in broken-down stations waiting for third-class tickets and broken-down buses, drunk mescal in dark dusty cantinas in mountain villages, imagining I was the Consul in Malcolm Lowry's *Under the Volcano,* I have become the Consul, staggering hallucinating down blind alleys . . . as if one had to live out the literary myths, from Hemingway to Kerouac." Lowry returns yet again twenty-two years later in Ferlinghetti's "Oaxaca: February 20, 2004": Went to the café where Malcolm Lowry went—the Café Farola—with Joao Almino."[33] These are intriguing passages which beg the question to which we have alluded previously: To what degree did Ferlinghetti indeed believe that he "had to live out the literary myths, from Hemingway to Kerouac"? And to conduct pilgrimages to locations important to writers he admired in Mexico? Ferlinghetti's texts differ from our other Beat writers on Mexico because his web of intertextual literary allusions is tightly woven. Ferlinghetti identifies to such a degree with other authors that he incorporates fragments, bits and pieces of their texts into his own. This method of pastiche allows him at once to pay tribute and also weave into his own discourse an intertextual pattern of allusions to cultural topoi as well as touchstones which have personal meaning in his own autobiographical quest for selfhood.

Kerouac becomes a central predecessor in Mexico whom Ferlinghetti invokes in relationship to "the Mexican night": "In mescal, the Mexican night comes back. It is all in the worm, the *gusano de maguey* at the bottom of every bottle. It turns in the bottom of the bottle. Colorless, inert, it nevertheless is there, a terrible crawling presence, in the night, primitive, waiting. It is the dark of ancient Aztec Mexico. These kids with their knapsacks on summer holidays from the States eating in the Sol y Luna don't know what it is all about. They have never seen the night-worm turn. They don't know what loneliness is, the worm in the bottle, only one worm, never two, bottled darkness, bottled night, the genie in the bottle a dark insanity. Even Kerouac on a Mexico City rooftop long ago in his *Tristessa* had no inkling of it, except as the Great American night, which is something else."[34] Jack Hirschman, one of the poet laureates of San Francisco, composed a poem sequence based on Mexican themes entitled *The Xibalba Arcane*; the frontispiece depicts a skeleton embracing a bottle of *Gusano Rojo Mezcal*, and Hirschman creates a memorable image: "ribbed like the body of the worm inside a bottle/of mescal which swallows me down to Xibalba."[35] Kerouac often refers to the American Night, for example in *On the Road*: "The whole mad swirl of everything that was to come began then; it would mix up all my friends and all I had left of my family in a big dust cloud over the American Night." And in *Desolation Angels*: "Sometimes, during the night, I'd look at my poor sleeping mother cruelly crucified there in the American night." Kerouac, like Ferlinghetti, wrote of the isolation he experienced in Mexico, composing a poem entitled "Mexican Loneliness."[36] Ferlinghetti's bravura passage ranges from mescal to the superficial young who do not feel the deeply tragic dimensions of the Mexican Night, and we can see the ways Ferlinghetti carries on a dialogue with Kerouac and his experiences in Mexico, continuing his intertextual practice of weaving within his own prose a sequence of writers who share a literary tradition with which he identifies.

During the new millennium, Ferlinghetti traveled to Oaxaca in February 2004 and composed a poem entitled "High Noon, Oaxaca" which describes the political unrest which had begun to gather force in the city: "Converging on the city of Oaxaca from all over the state of Oaxaca/With its sixty percent unemployment/They are the working men and women of the *Unidad Popular*." Two years later in February 2006, he attended a bullfight in Puerto Vallarta, while in January 2008, he sojourned in Yelapa. Finally, in February 2010 he traveled to Belize: "In Belize at Lubaantum, in a Mayan rain forest, a crystal skull dug up by an itinerant woodcutter, a grave robber—long time ago—'Skull of doom,' they call it—causing the death of Atlantis, they say. The cieba tree connected the Mayans to the netherworld, 'the place of fright,' and the whole earth a turtle (here too). And Lubaantun, 'the place of falling stone'—minor Mayan ruin. At Nim Li Punit another minor Mayan ruin—the plumed figure of Quetzal on a stone stele twelve feet high, with a woman carved close upon him—Quetzal's eye stood out very white, as if painted in enamel. I reached up and touched the eye. It was white stone."[37] The reference to Atlantis calls up the esoteric theory connecting the lost continent of Atlantis to the inhabitants of ancient Mexico—a theory promulgated by Edward H. Thompson (1857–1935) in his 1879 essay for *Popular Science Monthly*, "Atlantis Not a Myth"—while "the netherworld, 'the place of fright'" is of course Xibalba, the underworld of the Maya. It is appropriate to end with Quetzalcoatl, the feathered serpent central to the Beats, as Ferlinghetti gazes at "the plumed figure of Quetzal on a stone stele twelve feet high." In reaching up, Ferlinghetti "touched the eye. It was white stone." Ferlinghetti communes with the spirit of Quetzalcoatl, the greatest god of ancient Mexico, who had spread his wings as far south as Belize, as "the noon sun beat down merciless on the jungle." At the age of ninety-one, Ferlinghetti was still discovering new aspects of Mexican history and Maya culture. Mexico was central to Ferlinghetti's life as a poet and political activist and inspired him continuously over a period of seven decades: his work serves as an apt introduction to the central role of Mexico in the works and lives of the Beats.

# 2 * WILLIAM S. BURROUGHS

## Something Falls Off When You Cross the Border into Mexico

WILLIAM S. BURROUGHS ARRIVED in Mexico City in September 1949, escaping New Orleans where he was awaiting trial on weapons and drug charges, and departed Mexico for the final time in January 1953. In Mexico City he became familiar with underworld figures such as drug dealer Dave Tesorero; a shifty, flamboyant lawyer named Bernabe Jurado; and Lola la Chata. La Chata, who appears in *Naked Lunch* as "Lupita," is sketched vividly: "Mexico City where Lupita sits like an Aztec Earth Goddess doling out her little papers of lousy shit"; "A Mexico City pusher name of Lupita—all the big pushers in Mexico are women—Aztec Earth Goddess need plenty blood."[1] Burroughs compares Lupita to the Aztec fertility goddess Coatlicue, "skirt of snakes," mother of war god Huitzilopochtli, depicted in a masterwork sculpture sporting a menacing necklace composed of human hearts, skulls, and hands. Burroughs's fascination with Mexico was perennial: he continued to consult books on Mexico in his personal library in Lawrence, Kansas, such as Linda Schele's *The Blood of Kings: Dynasty and Ritual in Maya Art* to the end of his life.[2] Mexico appears in Burroughs's oeuvre from his first novel *Junky* (1953) to his posthumous volume *Last Words: The Final*

*Journals of William S. Burroughs* (2000). This chapter explores several interrelated themes: the ways Burroughs's pattern of imagery serves to emphasize his ambivalent relationship to Mexico; his lifelong fascination with Maya codices and collaboration with artist Malcolm McNeill; how his concept of "Control" derived from his studies of Maya civilization; and the ways Mexican themes appear in *Naked Lunch, Soft Machine, Electronic Revolution,* and *Ah Pook Is Here,* as well as the trilogy *Cities of the Red Night, The Place of Dead Roads,* and *The Western Lands.*

Burroughs had always demonstrated a keen interest in Indigenous cultures. After completing his degree in American literature at Harvard in 1936, Burroughs entered graduate school at Harvard in 1938 where he enrolled in courses in anthropology and Maya archaeology.[3] The Peabody Museum of Archaeology and Ethnology, founded in 1866 at Harvard, was an important institution pioneering Maya studies. Herbert Joseph Spinden (1879–1967), author of *Maya Art and Civilization* (1913), was curator of the Peabody. Sylvanus Morley (1883–1948), a Harvard-trained archaeologist, made his first trip to the Yucatan in 1907 and became renowned for his excavations at Chichen Itza. These scholarly traditions at their alma mater may have predisposed both Burroughs and Charles Olson toward fascinations with the Maya. Later in 1939, Burroughs would also study anthropology at Columbia University. Jack Kerouac in *On the Road,* part 2, chapter 6, memorably described visiting Burroughs—"Old Bull Lee"—during his trip with Neal Cassady across America and later into Mexico: "In New Orleans he had begun to spend long hours with the Mayan Codices on his lap, and, although he went on talking, the book lay open all the time."[4] As we shall see in chapter 6, in New York City on December 18, 1947, Allen Ginsberg recorded in his journal: "Went down to look at the Mayan codices today—Madrid Codex with Bill, Joan, Huncke at Museum of Natural History."[5] Burroughs was far from being a dilettante in Maya studies, and among the Beats—along with Gary Snyder who researched Native American mythology for his senior thesis on the Haida people while a student at Reed College, and Philip Lamantia who participated in ceremonies with the Washoe in California and Nevada and also studied the culture and language of the Cora people while in Mexico—was well versed in the study of Indigenous cultures. In a sense, the necessity of fleeing America due to his legal troubles was a fortunate eventuality since it permitted Burroughs time to continue his engagement with Mexico through direct experience rather than solely by means of solitary, armchair, scholarly investigations.

Although Burroughs is clearly *escaping* something by leaving America—its rampant homophobia, the legal authorities who are pursuing him on drug charges—he also *seeks* something in Mexico. While living in South Texas, Burroughs had made forays from McAllen, Texas, to Reynosa—a border town in the northern part of Tamaulipas, Mexico—which served as a kind of trial run for his later residence in Mexico City. After arriving in Mexico City, Burroughs first found a house on the western side which he rented, located at Paseo de la Reforma 210, Casa 8, and after his common-law wife Joan and their two children—Billy Burroughs, his son with Joan, and Julie, Joan's daughter with a prior partner—arrived, they moved to 37 Cerrada de Medellin in the Colonia Roma area of the metropolis, conveniently located near Mexico City College where he would matriculate, and a district recently catapulted into notoriety due to director Alfonso Cuaron's successful film *Roma* (2018). Burroughs sent a letter to Allen Ginsberg dated May 1, 1950: "As soon as I sell the Texas property I will buy a house here. A good 2 bedroom brick house in the center of Mexico City costs about $4000 U.S. I am going to Mexico City College on the G.I. Bill. . . . I am learning to speak Mayan, and taking a course in the codices. Mexico is my place. I want to live here and bring up the children here. I would not go back to the U.S. under any circumstances." Burroughs's correspondence with Jack Kerouac concerning life in Mexico City is amusing in its concerted effort to entice his friend to visit by offering as many tantalizing blandishments as possible. As Eric Strand has observed in "The Last Frontier: Burroughs's Early Work and International Tourism": "Burroughs idealized the comparative absence of social control in Mexico." Mexico City at this time was a city of just one million inhabitants—compared to today's population of nearly nine million—and the skies had yet to be tainted by omnipresent air pollution. Burroughs already lamented in a letter from September 18, 1950, to Kerouac that his heroin addiction prevented him from fully enjoying the city's pleasures: "When I am on the junk I don't get around much. I miss experience because I spend too much time in the house. There is more to miss in Mexico than in the States because here no limits are placed on experience."

Burroughs wrote prolifically for over five decades, yet it was not until 2016 that a complete bibliography of his work appeared. His Mexico writings are scattered throughout a number of sources—in letters, stories, novels, interviews, and essays—and as his bibliographer Brian Schottlaender observed, Burroughs "rearranged, recycled, and reiterated obsessively." Burroughs's later publications also often evolved out of earlier manuscripts: thus, unused pages from *Naked Lunch* were later recycled into subsequent novels. Burroughs often returns to specific places in his autobiographical texts through a repeated pattern of imagery. He memorably described Mexico City in the introduction to *Queer* (written 1951–53; published 1985) as having "clear sparkling air and the sky that special shade of blue that goes so well with circling vultures, blood and sand—the raw menacing pitiless Mexican blue." This double imagery painting the Mexican firmament recurs frequently. Early in the novel *Port of Saints* (1973; revised version 1980), we discover: "Blue blaze of Mexican sky, wheeling vultures." And toward the end of the narrative, this stark, eerie music returns: "A room in Mexico, outside blue sky and wheeling vultures over a great empty valley." And in "Hieroglyphic Silence" from *The Third Mind* (1978): "The hawk circles in the shattered blue sky over Mexico." Beat—as Maria Damon has argued—means not only the "beatitude" which defined Jack Kerouac's spiritual quest but also "despair or destitution, being 'beat down to [one's] socks,' in the words of Herbert Huncke, the petty criminal, drug addict, and gifted raconteur who befriended some of the writers." The Beat relationship to Mexico demonstrates this doubleness—both exalted and sometimes terrible. Burroughs associated the azure above Mexico City with both heavenly ("blue," "clear," "sparkling") and ominous ("vultures," "hawk," "shattered," "blood," "menacing," "pitiless") symbolism, which was borne out by the central tragic episode of his life which happened in Mexico City. Burroughs's relationship with his common-law wife Joan Vollmer had been understandably strained given his drug addiction and pursuit of liaisons with men and boys. Joan had even traveled to Cuernavaca at one point to file for separation from Burroughs, but the couple reconciled. On September 6, 1951, while at a party in the apartment above The Bounty bar during an inebriated game of William Tell, Joan placed a glass upon her head: Burroughs aimed, fired, and struck Joan in the temple. Joan died from a single gunshot wound to the head. Joan was buried in the Panteon Americano cemetery in north Mexico City, near the Tacuba Metro Station. This disaster would become one of the legendary events which marked Mexico for subsequent Beat travelers as not only a sunny paradise but also a somber place of spiritual testing, physical illness, and madness.

In *Naked Lunch,* the first allusion to Mexico City and Dolores Street occurs immediately in the first section entitled "and start west," while in section 3, "the rube," Burroughs describes entering Mexico:

> Something falls off when you cross the border into Mexico, and suddenly the landscape hits you straight with nothing between you and it, desert and moun-

tains and vultures; little wheeling specks and others so close you can hear wings cut the air (a dry husking sound), and when they spot something they pour out of the blue sky, that shattering bloody blue sky of Mexico, down in a black funnel. . . . Drove all night, came at dawn to a warm misty place, barking dogs and the sound of running water.

"Thomas and Charlie," I said.

"What?"

"That's the name of this town. Sea level. We climb straight up from here ten thousand feet." I took a fix and went to sleep in the back seat. She was a good driver. You can tell as soon as someone touches the wheel.

At the close of this passage, the enigmatic "Thomas and Charlie" is an in-joke. Burroughs is referring to the city of Tamazunchale north of Mexico City—which when pronounced aloud sounds like the English names "Thomas 'n' Charlie"—and in addition, Thomas and Charley are slang terms for narcotics. Jack Kerouac on his way into Mexico noted in *Visions of Cody* (written 1951–52; published 1972) that Tamazunchale was a "brown and fetid foothill town," while Ed Dorn during his journey through Mexico spent an enjoyable time at the Saturday morning market. Burroughs employs the double vision we encountered above, his imagery alternating between "shattering bloody" and "blue." Burroughs had read Oswald Spengler's *Der Untergang des Abendlandes* (1918–1922)—*The Decline of the West*—sharing the book with Kerouac and Allen Ginsberg when they became friends in New York in the mid-forties. Spengler introduced the term *fellaheen*—a central concept in Kerouac's writings about Mexico—which Spengler defined as "the peasantry, 'everlasting' and history-less . . . a people before the dawn of the Culture, and in very fundamental characters it continued to be the primitive people, surviving when the form of the nature passed away again." Thus what "falls off" as the traveler goes across the border is also the veneer of "civilization" as one enters an archaic realm of primal, violent human origins, "that shattering bloody blue sky of Mexico, down in a black funnel."

Mexico was significant in Burroughs's literary career for it was the place he found time to dedicate himself fully to his writing and where he created *Junky*, *Queer*, and *The Yage Letters*. In spring 1950 he commenced work on the manuscript of a novel—initially titled *Junk*—which was then published under the pseudonym "William Lee" as *Junkie: Confessions of an Unredeemed Drug Addict* (1953) and ultimately as *Junky* (1977). Encouraged through his epistolary exchanges with Allen Ginsberg, Burroughs mailed him chapters of the manuscript. The autobiographical itinerary follows Burroughs's trajectory from New York, to New Orleans, to Texas, and finally, where the fourth section of *Junky* is set, to Mexico. The narrator informs us: "As soon as I hit Mexico City, I started looking for junk." The narrative follows his homosexual encounters, interactions with drug dealers, as well as specific places in the city: he drinks "in a cheap cantina off Dolores Street," and at the Opera Bar. *Junky* concludes with the narrator contemplating leaving Mexico to search for the drug *yage*—*ayahuasca*—in Colombia.

In the spring of 1951, Burroughs began composing *Queer*—the first half of the novel overlaps chronologically with the Mexico City narrative in *Junky*—and tells us in the introduction that he "liked Mexico City from the first day of my first visit there. . . . A single man could live well there for two dollars a day." *Queer* is notable for its adumbration of concepts Burroughs explores in more depth in his later Mexico-themed works. In chapter 4, the protagonist Lee tells us: "I know telepathy to be a fact, since I have experienced it myself. . . . I have a theory the Mayan priests developed a form of one-way telepathy to con the peasants into doing all the work. The deal is certain to backfire eventually, because telepathy is not of its nature a one-way setup, nor a setup of sender and receiver at all." In *Naked Lunch, The Soft Machine,* and *Ah Pook Is Here,* the power of the Mayan priests and telepathy become for Burroughs one of his various idées fixes. From childhood, Burroughs had undergone a variety of psychic and paranormal experiences which would power his lifelong fascination with the occult. Burroughs devotes a significant passage of *The Cat Inside* to an analysis of a central revelation of his childhood: "When I was four years old I saw a vision in Forest Park, St. Louis. My brother was ahead of me with an air rifle. I was lagging behind and I saw a little green reindeer about the size of a cat. Clear and precise in the late afternoon sunlight as if seen through a telescope. Later, when I studied anthropology at Harvard, I learned that this was a totem animal vision and knew that I could never kill a deer."[6] Burroughs associates this epiphany with the moment in Indigenous cultures when shamans encounter their tutelary/totemic animal, which then marks their vocation as the healer/poet of the tribe. When Lee says in *Queer,* "I know telepathy to be a fact," he speaks for his author since Burroughs frequently emphasized his belief in paranormal, shamanistic, and magical practices. Indeed, André Breton had named Mexico an essentially "surrealist" country; Jack Kerouac called Mexico "the magic land at the end of the road"; Philip Lamantia experienced supernatural visions atop the pyramids of Teotihuacan; the "magic mushrooms" of Maria Sabina of Huautla de Jimenez were ingested by Bonnie Bremser and researched by R. Gordon Wasson. The mystical themes which run through many of Burroughs's Mexican works reflect both the country in which he composed them and his own—as well as the Beats' in general—affinity for the magical, the transcendental, and the esoteric.

In addition to his newfound productivity, Burroughs also now had the opportunity to continue an intense study of the codices at Mexico City College, where he met up again with his friend Hal Chase who had studied anthropology at Columbia University and received a grant to study the Zapotecan language. The Mexico City College Anthropology Department had several distinguished scholars on its faculty including Pedro Armillas and Wigberto Jimenez Moreno. Burroughs pursued his interest in the codices with the head of the department, Robert Barlow (1918–1951), a close friend of the genius of weird tales, H. P. Lovecraft (1890–1937). Burroughs joined the Sahagun Anthropology Club, and in July 1950, embarked on a field trip led by Barlow and Armillas to the Temple of Quetzalcoatl at Teotihuacan. In *Junky*, however, he describes this period of his life in rather casual terms: "For something to do, I enrolled in Mexico City College. The students impressed me as a sorry-looking lot, but then, I wasn't looking at them very hard." The students spent time in a bar—"The Bounty"—and Burroughs reported that he always carried some type of gun while living in Mexico, noting that he shot a mouse in The Bounty with his .22 pistol. Although a "foreigner" himself in the country and representative of an imperial power, Burroughs was cognizant of the depredations of colonialism inflicted by the Spaniards who ruled Mexico from 1524 to 1810. Burroughs lamented the destruction of the Maya codices perpetrated by Bishop Diego de Landa (1524–1579), noting that only the Dresden, Paris, and Madrid codices survived the conflagration: "So there's no way of knowing what the others consisted of. I mean a whole civilization there went up in flames. It's as if you piled all our physics books, Shakespeare, and everything else into a pile and burnt the whole lot, and there was nothing left."[7]

Burroughs's indignation regarding the desecration of the cultural patrimony of Mexico is justified: Bishop Landa burned in an auto-da-fé five thousand "idols" as well as twenty-seven codices in the town of Mani, about one hundred and sixty kilometers from Merida in the Yucatan on July 12, 1562. There is a depiction of the book burning in the Tlaxcala Codex, and according to Landa's *Relacion de las Cosas de Yucatan*: "We found a large number of books in these characters and, as they contained nothing in which there were not to be seen superstition and lies of the devil, we burned them all, which they regretted to an amazing degree, and which caused them much affliction." Burroughs sought to recover and reinterpret the treasures of the Maya's lost civilization. In *Ah Pook Is Here*, Burroughs offers one possible motive for Landa's destruction of the codices: "A glyph depicts the Moon Goddess copulating with a death figure, and we may assume that the books destroyed by Bishop Landa contained many such scenes." It was not only cultural destruction which the Spaniards wrought; Claude Levi-Strauss has asserted that "in the century or century and a half that followed the discovery of America, the populations of Mexico and Peru fell from a hundred million to four or five million, assailed less by the blows of the conquistadores than by imported diseases, made more virulent by the new forms of life the colonizers imposed. These diseases included smallpox, measles, scarlet fever, tuberculosis, malaria, influenza, mumps, yellow fever, cholera, plague, diphtheria, and many others."

Burroughs expressed a distaste for institutionalized Christianity which may in part have been exacerbated by the destruction of the codices by Bishop Landa. Burroughs objected to Christianity due to "the total lack of any spiritual content, or any spiritual discipline leading to tangible gains, comparable to Zen Buddhism: Tibetan practitioners who, through rigorous and prolonged training, can spend a night in sub-zero cold with only a loincloth. The Shaman's Way to achieve the palpable status of the Impeccable Warrior. I fault Christianity for its lack . . . a lack that does not even have the vitality to ache." Burroughs alludes here to *The Teachings of Don Juan* by the UCLA anthropologist Carlos Castaneda (1925–1998) and his concept of the spiritual Warrior. Castaneda's books regarding the visionary practices of the Yaqui shaman Don Juan Matus from Sonora, Mexico, were popular among countercultural youth during the sixties and seventies. Burroughs was particularly interested in Castaneda's concept of *nagual*, declaring that "'genius' is the *nagual*: the uncontrollable—unknown and so unpredictable—spontaneous and alive." Robert A. Sobieszek in *Ports of Entry: William S. Burroughs and the Arts* argues that Don Juan's conceptions "illustrate the process of microperception associated with drug-induced cosmologies, as well as the significance of an out-of-body or 'body without organs' state experienced by spiritual mystics and those in trances." The Maya referred to the shaman as *h-men*—"he who makes"—and the *h-men* was the link between the invisible realm of ancestors, spirits, gods, and the living. Sometimes with the aid of hallucinogens, the *h-men* sought to cure illnesses. John Tytell in his essay "The Beat Legacy" discusses the connection between shamanism and modern literature: "In non-western cultures, the shaman healer often tries to absorb the patient's illness through touching. To the extent that we can be 'touched' by their words, writers like Conrad or Kafka or Pound seem so related by this sort of shamanism that it indeed seems a defining characteristic of the modern literary sensibility. This shamanistic capacity of the artist is also evident with Burroughs." Burroughs himself late in life underwent a ritual supervised by a Native American shaman to exorcise his "Ugly Spirit." Bishop Landa had thus tried to extirpate both the literary and spiritual treasures enshrined in the codices as well as Mexico's native shamanistic practices—Mircea Eliade memorably called them "archaic techniques of ecstasy"—which were considered to be forms of "witchcraft" or the "devil's work" by the European invaders but were welcomed by Beat students of alternative spiritualities.

In Burroughs's literary imagination, Maya culture was central for two significant reasons. Firstly, he continued to be intrigued—as he had been during his studies at Harvard in the thirties—by the quest to decipher the glyphs of the Mayan language. He had demonstrated a similar interest in Egyptian hieroglyphics, devoting himself to researching Egyptology at the University of Chicago, and while living in London during the seventies, he took photographs of the Egyptian, Aztec, and Maya artifacts in the British Museum. Novels such as *Naked Lunch* and *The Soft Machine* feature book covers with drawings suggesting inscrutable letters from mysterious alphabets. Indeed, Burroughs often alludes to Mayan and Egyptian cultures in tandem. In *Nova Express* (1964), the narrator declares: "The screen opened out—I could see Mayan codices and Egyptian hieroglyphs." And in an experimental film Burroughs created with director Anthony Balch—*Towers Open Fire* (1963)—Burroughs depicts himself delivering a lecture on Egyptian and Maya writing. The subject of Maya glyphs is an intriguing intellectual puzzle in itself and during the past decades immense strides have been made in deciphering their meaning. John T. Irwin in *American Hieroglyphics: The Symbol of the Egyptian Hieroglyphics in the American Renaissance* documented the ways Emerson, Thoreau, Poe, Hawthorne, Melville, and Whitman were all deeply influenced in their writings by Jean-Francois Champollion's decipherment of Egyptian hieroglyphics on the Rosetta Stone in the 1820s following Napoleon's invasion of Egypt in 1798. So too, for the Beats, the Maya glyphs become symbolic repositories of multiple meanings. Burroughs in *Junky* intones ominously: "A series of faces, hieroglyphics, distorted and leading to the final place where the human road ends where the human form can no longer contain the crustacean horror that has grown inside it." And as we shall see, Allen Ginsberg in "Siesta in Xbalba" goes questing "in the bleak flat night of Yucatan/where I come with my own mad mind to study alien hieroglyphs of Eternity."

•

Secondly, Burroughs's fascination with writing systems correlated with his desire to understand society's mechanisms of indoctrination and to discover ways to undermine them. Burroughs was particularly obsessed by the question of "control" and its relationship to time and death: How did the Maya use language to achieve power over the oppressed majority of their society? This concept appears in several works with Mexican themes. In the "atrophied preface" section at the end of *Naked Lunch* (1959), a bit of tantalizing dialogue emerges: "'Death was their Culture Hero,' said my Old Lady looking up from the Mayan codices. . . . 'They got fire and speech and the corn seed from death. . . . Death turns into maize seed.'" According to the Quiché Maya epic *Popol Vuh*, or *Book of Counsel* (1554–1558), humans are made in the fifth generation of the cycle of creation, and the Young Corn God as the "dead" maize seed is reborn from Xibalba, the Land of the Dead where the warrior boys Hunahpu and Xbalanque vanquish the Lords of Death. Primal origins are a theme to which modern writers obsessively return, as if to assert alternative creation myths to replace those afforded by Judeo-Christian tradition. Jorge Luis Borges in his story "The Writing of the God" alludes to the *Popol Vuh*—translated as "Book of Counsel" or "Book of the People"—when the narrator declares: "I saw the origins told by the Book of the People. I saw the mountains that rose from the water, saw the first men of wood, saw the water jars that turned against the men, saw the dogs that tore at their faces. I saw the faceless god who is behind the gods." Linda Schele in *The Blood of Kings: Dynasty and Ritual in Maya Art* asserts that the rate of infant mortality among the ancient Maya was higher and life expectancy shorter than today. In addition, sacrificial rituals and warfare were part of daily life. Schele argues that the omnipresence of death "led the Maya to dedicate much of their ritual and art to the defeat of death's final grip on their lives. Depictions on objects of all types treat the whole process of death, from the soul's entrance into the Maya Hell, called Xibalba, to a final apotheosis or rebirth. . . . Death's special imagery is found on coffins, wall paintings, pottery, jades and other objects that accompanied the dead into their graves and guided them through their confrontation with the Lords of Death."[8] Burroughs understood that the iconography of death pervades Maya culture because they conceived death and the regenerative cycles of nature as deeply connected.

In another section of *Naked Lunch*—"islam incorporated and the parties of interzone"—the codices reappear: "Ever dig the Mayan codices? I figure it like this: the priests—about one percent of the population—made with one-way telepathic broadcasts instructing the workers what to feel and when. . . . A telepathic sender has to send all the time. . . . The Mayans were limited by isolation. . . . Now one Sender could control the planet. . . . *You see control can never be a means to any practical end. . . . It can never be a means to anything but more control. . . . Like junk.*"[9] Language is one method of control and social conditioning, and "junk"—or drugs—became in Burroughs's work a metaphor for all forms of social or psychological manipulation. Imperial and theocratic authorities in ancient China, Sumeria, and Egypt, as well as Mesoamerica, possessed control over written documents and signs. Writing was associated with magical powers. "Upward mobility" was granted to those who had access through literacy to knowledge.[10] Writing—and reading—conferred equal powers of control: a repository of knowledge could then be built up over time and kept secret by those who were literate from those who were not.

The topic of "control" appears again in the seventh section of *The Soft Machine* (1961) which Burroughs titles "The Mayan Caper." Jennie Skerl argues that "The Mayan Caper" is the most important section of the novel due to "its central placement in the text, because it is the longest sustained narrative, and because it gives the most straightforward exposition of how a control system works and how it can be dismantled." The opening pages inform us: "The Mayan calendar starts from a mythical date 5 Ahua 8 Cumhu and rolls on to the end of the world, also a definite date depicted in the codices as a God pouring water on the earth—The Mayans had a solar, a lunar, and a ceremonial calendar rolling along like interlocking wheels from 5 Ahua 8 Cumhu to the end—The absolute power of the priests, who formed about 2 percent of the population, depended on their control of this calendar." Burroughs errs slightly here: the actual start of the Maya Era is 4 Ahau 8 Cumku, approximately August 10, 3113 B.C.E. Elizabeth Hill Boone in *Cycles of Time and Meaning in the Mexican Books of Fate* observes: "In Mesoamerica everything that happened and everything that mattered was bound together and controlled by time. Time, as it was organized and codified in the pan-Mesoamerican calendrical system, characterized and qualified all actions and happenings, just as it ordered and linked the present to the past and future. Supernatural, natural, mythical, and historical events—whether important or trivial—were all shaped by this calendar. Supernatural beings came under its influence; the lives of humans were governed by it too." As we shall see, the Dresden Codex particularly fascinated Burroughs, for it "is entirely ritual-astronomical, and tied to the workings of the complex Maya calendrical system." Burroughs adapts his experiences in Mexico to the creation of a science fiction cosmos where "time travel" is possible and introduces his knowledge gained from the Dresden Codex of the astronomical calculations of the Maya. Priests rule people through their control of writing and the passage of time through the calendar: they also manipulate the behavior of the "workers" through telepathic mind control. Although a little-known fact, Burroughs derived his notions concerning the "telepathic" abilities of the Maya priests from Joan Vollmer—they had discussed the codices together—which as we see above is apparent in the exchanges referring to his "Old Lady," another example of Beat women being excluded from the historical-literary record.[11]

Burroughs's conceptualizing about the Maya shares several features in common with the theories of Maya scholar J. Eric S. Thompson, as Byron Ellsworth Hamann argued in his essay "How Maya Hieroglyphs Got Their Name: Egypt, Mexico, and China in Western Grammatology since the Fifteenth Century." Thompson declared: "I conceive the endless progress of time the supreme mystery of Maya religion, a subject which pervaded Maya thought to an extent without parallel in the history of Mankind." Thompson also saw the glyphs in the Maya writing system as holding as yet undecipherable secrets: "The glyphs are anagogical, and we have only a scant idea of the mysteries. . . . If we lift our eyes thence to the heights we may perceive dimly the sublime poetry of time into which the tools of the graver and the legends and myths of the storyteller have transmuted its periods." Hamann argues that—like Burroughs—Thompson thought "the collapse of Maya society was brought about by class revolution, in which peasant-laborers rose up against their astronomer-rulers."[12] The Maya continued to preoccupy Burroughs during the early sixties as well. Heathcote Williams records an amusing anecdote that while Burroughs was living in London in 1963, he "kindly lent me a book on Mayan Civilisation—a subject that was of particular interest to him as he explained that the Mayans had a calendar which prescribed what everyone should feel on certain days. 'Makes things much simpler. If you know that somebody coming towards you has been ordered to be in a good mood that day by the Mayan priests' calendar, well, then they're less likely to kill you.'"

Sections of an unpublished work composed at the height of the revolutionary sixties appeared as *Electronic Revolution*—the cover features Maya glyphs connected in the manner of electronic circuits—in 1970. The entire text has only recently been published as *The Revised Boy Scout Manual* (2018), and the first of five steps Burroughs proposes to achieve deliverance from domination by the Establishment is: "Proclaim a new era and set up a new calendar." The Beats and later hippies were devoted to overturning conventional Western systems of marking temporality and sought a return to the cyclical, cosmos-centered ways of observing the movement of time which characterized archaic cultures. Diane di Prima composed several poems containing references to the equinox and solstice as we see in her "Notes on the Solstice": "The Mexican Indians really did it/kindled new fire FROM THE RAYS OF THE SUN/ focused light/new fire which went on all year/till the next summer solstice." And Bonnie Bremser in a prose text of dated journal entries entitled "Dreams" published in *Coldspring Journal* (1974), demonstrated her familiarity with Mayan time systems: "Feb 12 1971 (1st day of Pop Kan Indian year)." In *Ah Pook Is Here,* Burroughs reflects again on the calendar: "The priests made calculations on their calendar dating back 400,000,000 years. Why?" In *The Revised Boy Scout Manual,* Burroughs again states: "The priest gods in the temple. They move very slowly, faces ravaged with age and disease. Parasitic worms infest their dead fibrous flesh. They are making calculations from the sacred books. '400,000,000 years ago on this day a grievous thing happened . . .' Limestone skulls rain in through the porticos. The Young Maize God leads the workers as they storm the temple and drag the priests out." Matthew Levi Stevens has pointed out that Burroughs refers to "the elaborate system used by the Maya: the interlocking 365-day Solar Calendar called the *Haab,* and the 260-day sacred calendar called the *Tzolkin*—as well as further Lunar cycles, a 584-day Venus cycle, and something known as The Long Count, that dated events in mythological time from the Creation." Burroughs argues in his book of interviews *The Job* that there are distinct parallels between the Maya world and our own: "Now translate the Mayan control calendar into modern terms. The mass media of newspaper, radio, television, magazines form a ceremonial calendar to which all citizens are subjected. The 'priests' wisely conceal themselves behind masses of contradictory data and vociferously deny that they exist. Like the Mayan priests they can reconstruct the past and predict the future on a statistical basis through manipulation of media."[13] Rather like the Wizard of Oz, our modern "priests" hide behind the curtain of Madison Avenue and manipulate, behind the scenes, magic reality shows to control the masses for their own benefit. Burroughs's residence in Mexico furnished him with a set of tropes concerning the relationship of the Maya to time, "control," literacy, psychological conditioning, and political power which would appear repeatedly throughout his writings in his theorizing concerning our own postmodern world.

A brief, eight-and-a-half-page text—"The Bay of Pigs" (1972)—is one of Burroughs's most successful adumbrations of this topic because he weds his intellectual premises to well-crafted, suspenseful storytelling. The protagonist John finds himself in a Mexico City bar where he is irresistibly attracted to "a girl with bright green eyes and the immobility of a lizard. He thought of a beautiful green reptile from remote crossroads of time." He learns from her that the CIA is in Mexico to search for the Mayan books which contain secrets for creating a totalitarian society. She takes him through a "neighborhood of *pulquerias* sandwich booths and market stalls. Men in white cotton pants, in from the country. The sour smell of *pulque* and sweet urine was heavy in the air." The lady—we are given further hints in addition to her green eyes and immobility concerning her hidden identity for she is "wearing flexible low-heeled shoes of green lizard skin"—gives John a potion comprised of herbs and dried "sacred mushrooms." These are the "magic mushrooms" of the *curandera* Maria Sabina of Huautla de Jimenez—which are of course another sine qua non for the Beats in Mexico. John then engages in passionate sexual intercourse with the unnamed woman. She is actually an Iguana goddess in human form: she has a twin brother to whom John is equally attracted and with whom he also makes love. Twins are frequent in Maya myth: Hunahpu and Xbalanque are the Hero Twins of the *Popol Vuh,* while Quetzalcoatl—the name Quetzalcoatl is a pun in Nahuatl and can signify either "Plumed Serpent" or "Precious Twin"—and his twin Tezcatlipoca journey together through the Underworld. In Burroughs's narrative, this twin boy knows about John's past and reveals to him that the Russians, Chinese, and even the Swiss are descending upon Mexico accompanied by Maya scholars in order to find the lost codices and then keep their methods of manipulation and mind control secret. The boy tells John that he and his sister represent the rebellious "Academy" and upon saying this, the boy transforms into a middle-aged man. The Academy seeks to recruit and train the youth of the world "to prepare for all-out resistance" to the hegemony of those who seek to impose totalitarianism upon the world. The Academy seeks to destroy the concept of the nation and to do away with the nuclear family because parents have in the past been "allowed to bring up helpless children in any form of nonsense they have themselves been infected with." John is told as the tale concludes: "The secret of flesh is in the lost Mayan books. All the forces of suppression have now converged on Mexico to find these books and keep this secret from being used to create a new race of beings on this planet." Burroughs's Manichean view of the universe—of "war all the time" in which Creation battles Destruction—is here on full display. "The Bay of Pigs" is masterful. By employing the techniques of mythological narrative—shape shifting, twins, human-animal transformation, magic, hidden identities—Burroughs creates a swiftly paced, modern science fiction/fantasy myth.

Maya themes continued to dominate Burroughs's literary imagination during the next phase of his career. While Burroughs was living in London in

1970, he became acquainted with the young artist Malcolm McNeill. They collaborated—"collaborated" is perhaps too strong a term, for Burroughs at this early stage merely supplied McNeill with text and left him to create the images—on a graphic narrative entitled "The Unspeakable Mr. Hart" which appeared as a series of four installments in the British underground magazine *Cyclops* in 1970: part 1 was published in July, part 2 in August, part 3 in September, and part 4 in October.[14] In part 4, McNeill illustrates in the second panel Burroughs's text: "It must have been a strange world when the Gods literally rose from their sacred books. But Mr. Hart couldn't see the young maize God peering through the corn shoots." John Stanley Hart—a billionaire newspaper tycoon—is a merciless, capitalist thug who is unable to understand the hidden knowledge of the codices, but rather wants to pry from their secrets a formula which he can use to create a "Media Control Machine," employing images of Fear and Death rather like the "yellow journalism" of William Randolph Hearst. Hart recapitulates the depredations of Bishop de Landa, but instead of burning the Maya codices, he seeks to exploit them for his own dastardly purposes. The first panel of the second tier depicts the infamous execution during the Vietnam War of Nguyen Van Lem—a member of the Viet Cong—by a gunshot to the head on February 1, 1968, in Saigon. By including this image, Burroughs and McNeill emphasize the way the contemporary media feeds on images of death and violence—the photograph of Lem's obscene murder was widely disseminated at the time—in order to supply the population with a steady diet of "exciting entertainment," *panem et circenses*.[15]

The *Cyclops* collaboration between Burroughs and McNeill would prove to be both trial run and catalyst for a much more ambitious project because they now began work on producing a "picture book" modeled on Maya texts—*Ah Pook Is Here* (a transliteration of the Mayan god of death, *Ah Puch*)—which continues the narrative of the depredations of the Maya by the corrupt John Stanley Hart adumbrated in their *Cyclops* series. McNeill was inspired by Frederick Catherwood's celebrated renderings of Maya cities as well as the proto-Surrealist Hieronymus Bosch (ca. 1450–1516): ancient Mexico and the apocalyptic modern world come alive through Burroughs's text and McNeill's art. Burroughs explained at the time: "Malcolm McNeil is doing the art work. It is most closely similar to the actual format of the Mayan Codices, which was an early comic book. There'll be pictures in the Codices, and sometimes there'll be three pages of text in writing that we can't read. We can read some of it, and we can read the dates. . . . The story concerns someone who has discovered the control secrets of the Mayan books.[16] Burroughs

*Ah Pook Is Here*, courtesy of Malcolm McNeill

collaborated for more than seven years with McNeill on *Ah Pook Is Here*; however, the funding for the book fell through due to the excessive expense involved in producing an elaborate "graphic novel," although eleven pages—of the more than one hundred original illustrations—were published in *Rush* magazine in December 1976. *The Lost Art of Ah Pook Is Here* was finally published in 2012. The original cover for the book—which did not appear on the Calder edition—depicts the skeletal death god Ah Pook sitting in the lap of a woman and shooting a "gringo" astronaut. As in the depiction of the killing of Nguyen Van Lem in South Vietnam, Burroughs and McNeill again emphasize the collision between past and present by counterpointing the ancient Maya with modern American imperial ambitions—this time in outer space.

The Maya comic book style cartooning with glyphs and narrative seems eerily contemporary: conjoining word and image is precisely the form that modern graphic storytelling—colorful, energetic, and compelling—takes. Burroughs and McNeill had inspected together in the British Museum the magnificent seventy-eight-page Dresden Codex which features the finest draftsmanship of the surviving Maya books. It is also the oldest, dating from the eleventh or twelfth centuries, and came to light in European collections in 1739. McNeill, inspired by the Dresden Codex, was able to translate Burroughs's images from *Ah Pook Is Here* into stunning tableaux. As David Carrasco points out in *Religions of Mesoamerica: Cosmovision and Ceremonial Centers*: "Unlike most other indigenous peoples of the Americas, the Maya developed an elaborate writing system capable of recording the range and meanings of their spoken language. . . . The typical presentation of this writing system combines written texts, carved into the stone, with pictorial programs depicting ritual and political action. . . . Some Maya scholars have called these scenes with their inscriptions Maya 'cartoons,' because they contain frozen framed images with accompanying narrations." McNeill and Burroughs desired—as McNeill explained—"to design a book not as a series of pages but as a continuous panorama or word/image painting." Indeed, a recent picture book for children—*Tales of the Feathered Serpent* (2020)—recounts the myth of the construction of Uxmal by magic through a text accompanied by illustrations. The author, David Bowles, argues that "when I consider the highly visual way Mesoamericans recorded their stories, the closest modern equivalent that comes to mind is the graphic novel. Blending words and images, comics and other sorts of graphica allow our brains to process stories more like our ancestors did, using multiple parts of our brains to understand more fully."

The lively codices—they were painted, it is generally believed, in the Late Postclassic period (c. 1250–1520)—portray the Maya as a palpable presence and give us the sensation that they have not passed away into lost time but are in fact our contemporaries. The Maya fashioned the paper for their codices by making a solution of lime in which they soaked bark fibers which were then pounded into thin sheets. "Codex" is actually a technical term which "normally refers to a book whose pages are bound along one edge, but scholars who specialize in pre-Columbian literature of Mexico and Central America have come to use this term for books whose pages are folded back and forth in the manner of a screen. The advantage of such a format is that the reader can open more than two successive pages at a time, or make direct comparisons of pages that are distant from one another."[17] The detailed drawings of pyramids as well as carefully wrought glyphs McNeill created for both *Cyclops* and *Ah Pook Is Here* accurately depict the Maya attired in their native garb and headdress: McNeill consulted texts, including *The Ancient Sun Kingdoms of the Americas: Aztec, Maya, Inca* (1961) by Victor von Hagen, for models. *The Lost Art of Ah Pook Is Here* is a successful example of the attempt to imagine a species of modern codex inspired by the creative genius of the Maya.

After leaving Mexico in 1953, Burroughs traveled in South America, then lived in Tangier, Morocco, Paris, and London before returning to the United States in 1974. However, Mexico continued to appear in his writings and emerged as an important area of intellectual exploration for the counterculture. R. Gordon Wasson had been the subject of a cover story in *Life* magazine on May 13, 1957, regarding his research into the hallucinogenic mushrooms which were employed in sacramental ceremonies by the Mazatec *curandera* Maria Sabina (1894–1985) in Oaxaca, who became—as we shall see in later chapters—a significant figure for Beat travelers to Mexico. In addition, Timothy Leary met Burroughs and created in the summer of 1962 the Zihuatanejo Project in the then peaceful fishing village of Zihuatanejo in Guerrero, Mexico. Here Leary continued the study of the effects of LSD which he had begun during his tenure at Harvard University, and Burroughs consulted with Leary concerning his research. Leary claimed concerning ingesting mushrooms during his stay in Mexico: "In four hours by the swimming pool in Cuernavaca I learned more about the mind, the brain, and its structures than I did in the preceding fifteen as a diligent psychologist."[18] If Mexico was the place Burroughs sought in order to explore the use of drugs without legal interference, it would also later become the center for academic inquiries into entheogens. Several Beats who followed Burroughs in their travels south of the border pursued the expansion of consciousness through substances found in Mexico including peyote, marijuana, and mescaline.

In Burroughs's later novels, Mexico continues to be an abiding theme. In the trilogy *Cities of the Red Night* (1981), *The Place of Dead Roads* (1983), and *The Western Lands* (1987), Mexico reappears in a number of different contexts. The "Invocation" to *Cities of the Red Night* opens with the dedication: "to Itzamna, Spirit of Early Mists and Showers, to Ix Chel, the Spider-Web-that-Catches-the-Dew-of Morning, to Zuhuy Kak, Virgin Fire, to Ah Dziz, the Master of Cold, to Kak U Pacat, who works in fire, to Ix Tab, Goddess of Ropes and Snares, patroness of those who hang themselves, to Schmuun, the Silent One, twin brother of Ix Tab, to Xolotl the Unformed, Lord of Rebirth, to Aguchi, Master of Ejaculations, . . . To Ak Pook, the Destroyer. . . . To all scribes and artists and practitioners of magic through whom these spirits have been manifested. . . . NOTHING IS TRUE. EVERYTHING IS PERMITTED."[19] One observes in this extended catalogue Burroughs's familiarity with the entire pantheon of Maya gods, and a similar incantation occurs in *Ah Pook Is Here*, illustrating again that Burroughs's texts are often a cross-quilt of thematic kernels or fragments which reappear in a variety of guises in different works. According to Maya mythology, Itzamna is the upper god and creator deity thought to reside in the sky. Although little is known about him, scattered references are present in early colonial reports of the Spanish *Relaciones*; in the Postclassic Yucatan codices, he is also known as the inventor of writing. Claude Levi-Strauss in *The Origin of Table Manners: Introduction to a Science Mythology* notes figures found in a grave in Tikal of a Mayan dignitary or priest which depict Itzamna as "a toothless old man, the master of day and night, and closely associated with the moon and the sun between whom he appears in the high-relief sculpted figures at Yaxchilan." Dennis Tedlock in *2000 Years of Mayan Literature* names him *Itzamnaaj*, meaning "Far Seer" or "True Magician."[20] It is not unusual that magic and the invention of writing are connected within the mythic imagination—for example with the Egyptian god Thoth—since writing possesses to the uninitiated the mysterious power of being able to preserve and pass on knowledge. Burroughs ends his catalogue with a salutation to Ah Pook and connects the themes of magic and literacy in his finale: "To all scribes and artists and practitioners of magic," concluding with an allusion to the most famous saying of Burroughs's hero, the Ismaili assassin and "magician" Hassan-i Sabbah (ca. 1050–1124 C.E.): "NOTHING IS TRUE. EVERYTHING IS PERMITTED."

The second volume of the trilogy, *The Place of Dead Roads*, also has a Mexican genesis, for the title itself derives from a dream Burroughs experienced in which a Mexican attempted to explain to a gringo: "These aren't unused roads, they are dead roads." The novel narrates the story of gay gunfighter Kim Carsons in the American West, and late in the book there is a passage describing Mexico City: "Evening falls on Mexico, D.F. The plumed serpent is suffocating the cities in coils of foul saffron smoke that rasp the lungs like sandpaper. . . . Two men reel out of a cantina and pull their nasty little 25 automatics from inside belt holsters and empty them into each other at a distance

Maquahuitl, Florentine Codex

of four feet." The mood here is typical of many such evocations of the violence and sense of impending doom which characterize Burroughs's memories of Mexico City. The phrase "rasp the lungs like sandpaper" recalls the phrase we examined at the beginning of this chapter from *Naked Lunch*—"a dry husking sound"—regarding the vultures' wings slicing through the sky. An allusion to D. H. Lawrence's great Mexican novel *The Plumed Serpent* (1926)—originally titled by Lawrence *Quetzalcoatl*—appears with the evocative, "The plumed serpent is suffocating the city in coils of foul saffron smoke."

In the final volume of the trilogy—*The Western Lands*—Kim Carsons returns, obtaining a job in a weapons store in Mexico City where he "devises variations on the Maquahuitl. This is the only effective Aztec weapon, consisting of obsidian chips set in wood, the usual shape being rather like a cricket bat. The sharp edges of broken glass with the weight of the hardwood handle, and an advanced warrior, a Blood Glutton or an Armed Scorpion, could cut both free from under his opponent with a single swipe of his Maq." Burroughs again demonstrates his extensive knowledge of Mexican history and culture and showcases his skill at precisely describing weaponry. Vividly depicted in book 2 of the Florentine Codex, the *Maquahuitl* was a wooden club approximately one yard long, four inches wide, and equipped with keen obsidian blades employed in close combat by the Aztec.

Burroughs was known to carry not only guns and derringers but a variety of knives, machetes, swords, cans of mace, and other weapons. He was also quite knowledgeable concerning the proper use of these instruments of self-defense—the primary purpose for which Burroughs obtained them; thus the care with which he describes Kim Carson and his *Maquahuitl* is entirely in keeping with Burroughs's own personal predilections. It is likely that Burroughs derived the names "Blood Glutton" and "Armed Scorpion" from characters in *Aztec* (1980), a popular historical novel by Gary Jennings (1928–1999), followed by a number of sequels including *Aztec Blood* (2002) and *Aztec Rage* (2006).

In *The Cat Inside* (first edition, illustrated by Brion Gysin, 1986; later edition 1992)—Burroughs's homage to his large fleet of felines—recalls his intense relationships with cats in his later years. Mexico is invoked in several brief vignettes. In one, Burroughs combines his interest in the Egyptians and Maya: "Evidence indicates that cats were first tamed in Egypt. The Egyptians stored grain, which attracted rodents, which attracted cats. (No evidence that such a thing happened with the Mayans, though a number of wild cats are native to the area)." Later, Burroughs recalls an incident involving a "white cat in Mexico City. I slapped it across the face with a book. I can see the cat running across the room to hide under a lumpy junked armchair. I can hear the cat's ears ringing from the blow. I was literally hurting myself and I didn't know it." And Burroughs also compares his relationship with cats to past human lovers. His cat Ruski reminds him of Kiki whom he had loved in Tangier, and also "Angelo in Mexico City . . . and someone else I cannot identify because he is so close to me." *The Cat Inside* brings together present experiences with Burroughs's memories of the past in Mexico.

Finally, in the posthumously published *Last Words: The Final Journals of William S. Burroughs* (2000) he recalls in an entry for July 23, 1997, when a man from the agency where he rented his typewriter in Mexico City came to reclaim it: "'When you pay good, okay. When you pay *malo*, is no good.' He repossessed the typewriter and departed forever from my sight. He was middle-aged, gray hair, no hostility in him. Old dust of dead people and places." These brief shards of memory, wispy vignettes, serve to catch vividly lost moments of Mexican time during which Burroughs was so impoverished that he was compelled to relinquish his precious typewriter due to lack of funds. In an entry four days later on July 27, 1997 he remembers "the guard at Lecumberri Federal Prison in Mexico D.F.": this was the prison where he spent time following the shooting of Joan.[21] Burroughs died just a week after making this entry, on August 2, 1997.

As we have seen, Mexico was a central place in the life and career of Burroughs. His original reasons for coming to the country were in many ways practical: he was fleeing the legal authorities; he wanted free access to drugs without the threat of imprisonment; life was considerably less expensive in Mexico; and as a homosexual man, there were fewer restrictions on living a more openly gay lifestyle. Yet there were several other important consequences of his residence in Mexico. First, his writing career began in earnest due in part to the encouragement he received from Jack Kerouac and Allen Ginsberg. Secondly, his fascination with the history, language, and culture of the Maya and Aztecs informed several of his major works and offers a key to some of his central themes regarding "control" and the totalitarian tendencies of modern political structures. And thirdly, the central event of his life—the killing of his common-law wife Joan Vollmer—occurred in Mexico City. Burroughs would later famously claim that this tragedy also compelled him into his career as writer: "I am forced to the appalling conclusion that I would never have become a writer but for Joan's death, and to a realization of the extent to which this event has motivated and formulated my writing. I live with the constant threat of possession, and a constant need to escape from possession, from Control. So the death of Joan brought me in contact with the invader, the Ugly Spirit, and maneuvered me into a lifelong struggle, in which I have had no choice except to write my way out."

It was Jack Kerouac who created one of the most striking portraits of Burroughs in Mexico: Kerouac had come to Mexico City just before Burroughs would leave the country for the last time after three years in residence. Kerouac writes that his friend had "lost everything, his wife, his children, his patrimony—I saw him pack in his moldy room where he'd shot M all the time—Sad moldy cases—old holsters, old daggers—a snapshot of Huncke—a Derringer pistol, which he gave to old dying Garver—medicine, drugs—the last of Joan's spices, marjoram, new mold since she died & stopped cooking—little Willie's shoe—& Julie's moldy school case—all lost, dust, & thin tragic Bill hurries off into the night solitaire—ah Soul—throwing in his bag, at last, picture of Lucien & Allen—Smiled, & left."[22] Kerouac's melancholy evocation of his close friend *in extremis* recalls Emily Dickinson's telegraphic, fond-of-dashes style.[23] Mexico was a place of both death and creation for Burroughs: the wrenching death of his wife, and the birth of his vocation as writer. The mark of his years in the country would be discernible in virtually all of the work he created over his entire literary career. And he also—as we shall see in later chapters—provided both inspiration and a cautionary tale for the later Beat travelers who would follow in his footsteps to Mexico.

# 3 ⁕ PHILIP LAMANTIA

## A Surrealist in Mexico

PHILIP LAMANTIA, BORN in San Francisco in 1927, was—along with Lawrence Ferlinghetti and William S. Burroughs—among the first Beats to travel to Mexico and incorporate themes from its landscape, history, and culture as central aspects of his imaginative vision. Lamantia returned several times to Mexico throughout the fifties and early sixties. He met Margaret Randall in New York, and when she came to Mexico City, Randall participated in the literary salon which gathered in his apartment. Lamantia also forged friendships with Mexican writers such as Homero Aridjis—born of a Greek father and a Mexican mother in Contepec, Michoacan, and a founder with his wife Betty Ferber in 1985 of "Grupo de los Cien," the "Group of 100," devoted to preserving Mexico's biodiversity including the sea turtles and Monarch butterfly—and the Nicaraguan Ernesto Cardenal. Raised in the Catholic traditions of his Sicilian forebears, Lamantia was a prodigy, immersing himself in early adolescence in Edgar Allan Poe and H. P. Lovecraft's Gnostic, eerie, hypnotic, and engrossing tales, as well as David Gascoyne's *Short Survey of Surrealism.* He attended an exhibition of Salvador Dali and Joan Miro at the San Francisco Museum of Modern Art which further catalyzed his curiosity about Surrealism. Following the publication of four of his poems in Charles Henri Ford's avant-garde magazine *View* in June 1943, Lamantia attracted the attention of the maestro of Surrealism André Breton, who praised him as "a voice that rises once in a hundred years." In February 1944 several Lamantia poems also appeared in *VVV*, the Surrealist journal published in New York.[1]

Lamantia's inventive, virtuosic, and wildly creative imagination deserves to be better appreciated than it is at present, for as Kenneth Rexroth argued: "There is nothing induced about his visionary poetry. The language of vision is his most natural speech. A great deal of what has happened since in poetry was anticipated in the poetry Lamantia wrote before he was twenty-one. Of all the people in the San Francisco group his is the work which should have the widest appeal to the counter culture, the youth revolt that took form in the Sixties." Indeed, Lamantia was "psychedelic" before the word had been invented in 1956 by British psychiatrist Humphrey Osmond—*psyche* (mind, spirit) + *delos* (to make visible, manifest)—in his desire to expand visionary religious experience to its furthest limits. Although many of Lamantia's writings are accessible, they also often pose a challenge to readers, for they are replete with allusions to his extremely wide knowledge of a number of anthropological, theosophical, alchemical, and occult sources. In this chapter I discuss the importance of peyote in Lamantia's visionary poetry; the ways Mexican geographical locations such as the town of Jesus-Maria in Nayarit appear as essential locales in Lamantia's spiritual explorations with the Cora Indians; Lamantia's friendship with the poet John Hoffman whose travels in Mexico influenced his use of imagery; and finally I provide a close reading of Lamantia's experiences in Teotihuacan, which he narrates in his poem "Ceylonese Tea Candor (Pyramid Scene)."

As we have seen in the introduction, several Beats were inspired in their attraction to Mexico by the writings of Antonin Artaud. A brief excerpt from Artaud's "La Mexique et la Civilisation" appeared in Wallace Berman's *Semina* 5 in 1959—the "Mexico Issue"—and Lamantia's translation of a poem by the Mexican writer and religious figure Sor Juana de la Cruz was published in the same issue. Robert Duncan observed that "Artaud's *To Have Done with the Judgment of God* (1947) by the early 1950s in a translation by Guy Wernham and preached by Philip Lamantia had become an underground text for us in San Francisco, and, earlier, in 1948, *Transition* 48, issued from Paris in English, had presented Artaud's *Journey to the Land of the Tarahumaras*, opening the prospect of a Nature revealed anew by Cabala and by the drug peyotl."[2] Peyote and its use among the Indigenous peoples of Mexico was an important influence on the Beats. Helen Weaver—scholar of French literature, astrologer, and lover of Jack Kerouac who appears in his *Desolation Angels* as "Ruth Heaper"—translated Artaud's *The Peyote Dance*.[3] Georges Bataille became fascinated by Mexico, and the Aztecs appear in several of his works, including the essays "The Sacred," "The Accursed Share," and in *The Tears of Eros*. For Lamantia perhaps the most significant connection to Mexico was due to the fact that yet another famous Frenchman—his mentor André Breton—arrived in Mexico in 1938, believing it to be "the most Surrealist country in the world." Breton met Leon Trotsky and the muralist Diego Rivera, seeking to establish Surrealism in the Latin American countries.[4] Lamantia himself from his youth identified with the politically radical, anarchistic, antiracist—he became close friends with the African American poets Ted Joans (1928–2003) and Bob Kaufman (1925–1986)—international, egalitarian ethos of the Surrealist movement which would be emphasized in writings by the Chicago Surrealist Group founded by Penelope and Franklin Rosemont in 1965. Like Lamantia, Ted Joans corresponded with André Breton and became friends with Octavio Paz.[5]

The anthropologist Jaime de Angulo (1887–1950) lived in the Bay Area and influenced Joanne Kyger, Gary Snyder, and Michael McClure as well as Lamantia. Henry Miller painted a vivid portrait of de Angulo in *Big Sur and the Oranges of Hieronymus Bosch*: "As usual, Jaime wore a bright headband around his forehead—his dirty snotrag, probably. Brown as a walnut, gaunt, slightly bow-legged, he was still handsome, still very much the Spaniard—and still utterly unpredictable. . . . He was definitely the outlaw."[6] De Angulo studied the work of C. G. Jung, met D. H. Lawrence, and researched the Pomo Indians of California, who fascinated Lamantia as well. For example, in his poem "Mount Diablo," Lamantia alludes to the mountain which according to Pomo myth is the site where the world was created.[7] Lamantia went to Big Sur in 1947 to meet de Angulo who, according to one source, informed him about peyote. Lamantia shared peyote which he had obtained from San Luis Potosi in Mexico with Neal Cassady and Jack Kerouac—in one account, Kerouac fell asleep during this session; however, Kerouac composed a powerful description of peyote's effects in *Visions of Cody*—when they visited Lamantia in Berkeley in 1952.[8] In a recently published manuscript entitled "Vision and Instigation of Mescaline 1961: To Ernesto Cardenal," Lamantia demonstrates that he was ahead of his time, for he perceived the usefulness of peyote not only as a vehicle toward the "beatific vision" but also—as contemporary research is discovering—a possible therapy for psychiatric illnesses: "USA is starved for chemical/vegetable visionary experience—deadly alcohol preferred to beginning wide/awake visionary transcendental bliss producing mystically impulse drugs—Mescaline can help cure alcoholism heroin addiction—natural means to see God! MESCALINE NOW LONGEST LASTING MOST INTENSE READILY AVAILABLE NON-ADDICTIVE VESSEL OF TRANSCENDENT VISION! MESCALINE IS VISION PRODUCING ALKALOIDS OUT OF PEYOTE ANCIENT INDIAN SACRAMENTAL PLANT NATIVE TO RIO GRANDE OF USA AND MEXICO! A REAL HOLY AMERICAN DRUG!" Lamantia also read with great excitement *Unknown Mexico* (1902; published in two volumes)—an important introductory text to Mexico for the Nobel Prize–winner J.M.G. Le Clézio—in which the Norwegian explorer Carl Lumholtz (1851–1922) recounts his travels to the Cora and Tarahumara and their employment of peyote in sacred ceremonies.

In chapter 17 of *Unknown Mexico,* Lumholtz describes the shamans he encountered, observing: "Without his shaman the Tarahumare would feel lost, both in this life and after death. The shaman is his priest and physician. He performs all the ceremonies and conducts all the dances and feasts by which the gods are propitiated and evil is averted, doing all the singing, praying, and sacrificing."[9] And in chapter 11, Lumholtz provides detailed observations of the various plants which, when eaten, create "a state of ecstasy. They are therefore considered demi-gods, who have to be treated with great reverence, and to whom sacrifices have to be offered. The principal kinds thus distinguished are known to science as *Lophophora Williamsii* and *Lophophora Williamsii*, var. *Lewinii*. In the United States they are called mescal buttons, and in Mexico peyote."[10] Lumholtz in his travels to Mexico, during his time with the Tarahumara and Huichols, sampled peyote and reported: "The plant, when taken, exhilarates the human system, and allays all feeling of hunger and thirst. It also produces color-visions." The Norwegian explorer had thus as early as 1902 opened the way for the Beat pilgrims to Mexico during the fifties and sixties such as Lamantia, who viewed their quest for enlightenment through the use of entheogens as replicating the sacred rituals and ceremonies practiced by Mexico's Indigenous peoples. As Thomas Albright has remarked: "Mexican culture had an especially deep attraction for the Beat artists of the 1950s, as it had for Artaud, Luis Bunuel and Malcolm Lowry, with its tenuous balance of violent extremes and complex texture in which the everyday shades into the surreal, the natural landscape into the occult. And of course, peyote, with its insight that all existence is sacred but not solemn."[11]

Lamantia was thus well prepared with knowledge regarding Mexico when he undertook his first trip there in 1950 with Christopher Maclaine (1923–1975), a filmmaker and editor of the magazine *Contour*.[12] Not much is known about this journey; however, Lamantia's return with his wife Gogo Nesbit to Mexico in 1954 is more fully documented. He acknowledged that "Mexico, a Catholic country, was for me, as for Kerouac, a multilayered inspiration. Some of the most beautiful parts of *On the Road* are about his Mexican experiences."[13] Bonnie Bremser was also inspired by Kerouac's vision of Mexico in *On the Road* during the composition of her *Troia; Mexican Memoirs,* and both Joanne Kyger and Margaret Randall fell under its spell. Lamantia traveled to the Cora tribe in the Nayarit mountains of western Mexico—chronicled in several of his poems—trekking up winding trails through the canyons of the rugged Sierra Madre mountain range to the Nayeri people and the village of Jesus-Maria.[14] In his unpublished journal "Notes from my visit with the Cora: April-May 1955," Lamantia exults: "This whole region is the most beautiful area I have ever seen, except for the scene at North Africa: however, perhaps greater, since there are no Coras 'there.'" Lamantia also took great pains to learn the native language of the Cora: he devoted twenty-six out of the seventy-seven pages of his journal to a "phonetic lexicon" and Spanish-Cora vocabulary.

These experiences are documented in a late poem, "Triple V: The Day Non-surrealism Became Surrealist"—the first section of which is titled after Carl Lumholtz, "Unknown Mexico"—in which Lamantia recalled the *Rey Mula* ("King Mule") "who carried me eight hours to the Nayeri people/who in the sacred (oral) text the *Majakuagy-Moukeia* were never conquered by Aztecs; nor later by seventeenth-century Spaniards." It is likely Lamantia learned about the *Majakuagy-Moukeia* of the Cora through an edition published by *El Corno Emplumado* in 1964 by Ana Mairena, translated into English by Elinor Randall, the mother of Margaret Randall.[15] Lamantia's desire to participate directly in the ceremonies of the Cora was perhaps partially inspired by the example of Antonin Artaud, who in *To Have Done with the Judgment of God* includes his poem "Tutuguri: The Rite of the Black Sun" recounting his ecstatic experience partaking in the Tutuguri—which means "song of the owl"—a sacred ritual of the Tarahumara. During Lamantia's two-month stay in Nayarit in early 1955, he was one of the first outsiders allowed to take part in the ceremony involving *yahnah,* a "black, juicy tobacco," which commenced at ten in the evening in a Jesuit mission church: music played throughout the night as a procession of men bearing torches led the celebrants to a temple on the lintel of which a giant iguana was carved. Iguanas and jaguars—central symbols of primal, archaic Mexico—recur in several Lamantia poems.

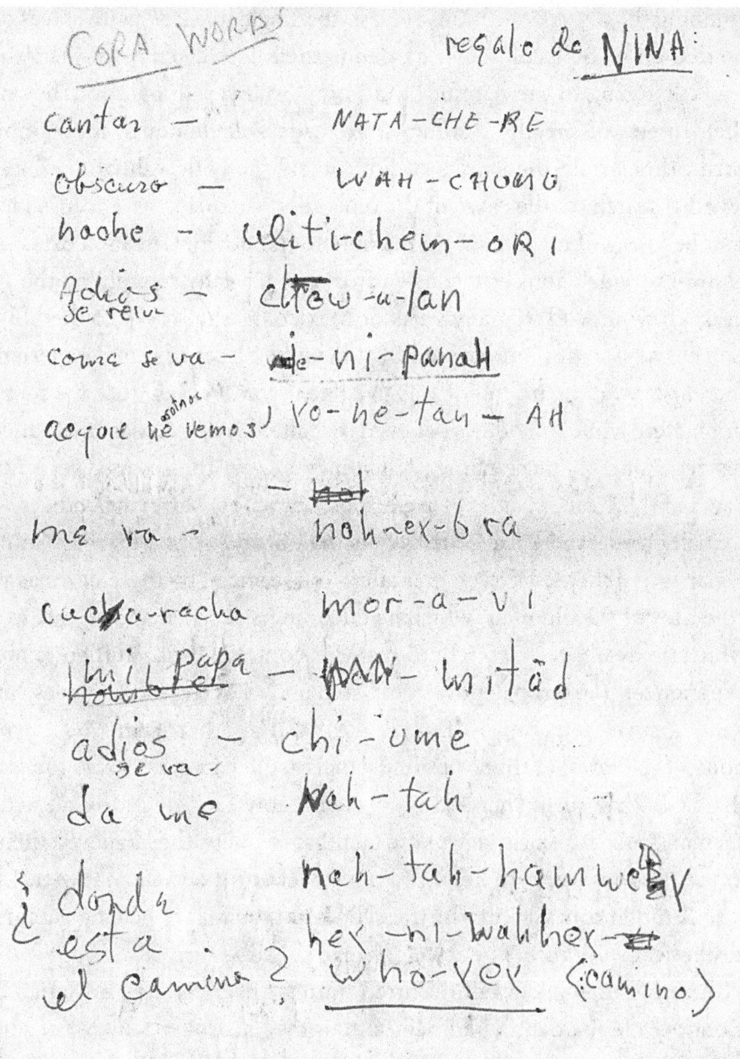
CORA WORDS regalo de NINA
cantar — NATA-CHE-RE
obscuro — WAH-CHOMG
noche — uliti-chem-ORI
Adios — chow-u-lan
Como se va — ni-panah
aquí nos vemos — yo-he-tan-AH
me va — nohnex-bra
cucaracha mor-a-vi
mi papa — witäd
adios se va — chi-ume
da me wah-tah
¿donde esta el camino? nah-tah-hamwey
hex-ni-wahhex
who-yex (camino)

Lamantia notebook, courtesy of Nancy Peters, Philip Lamantia Estate

Another iteration of this experience among the Cora appears in section 36 of *Destroyed Works* entitled "Cora": "Through a village suspended like a star of blood/going into the rites of the old men/silence invaded me, eating the pitayah/Where they took me, the little Indians and where I ended up is a hidden explosion/in history/not, certainly, an ecstasy in the void!/They chanted me out of the night up to their temple of the Two Iguanas/(a real iguana climbing the tower of my house) First, the single line trek/with staves of fire/ up to their high places/music carried in their flesh eaten by the earth and its fruits/listening to the barefoot thud on a hollow slab of wood/hewn from their forests of breathing stone/They made a circle out of me/grinning to each other inside the smoke of hot, putrid, narcotic yahnah. . . . I began a feverish search for the caves of the old gods/—to bring back a cured feather, a stone/a bag of medicines." In his note to the poem, Lamantia explains that *pitayah* is "a delicious crimson red fruit, superficially resembling the prickly pear, growing wild in many parts of Mexico."[16] The "caves of the old gods" Lamantia "searches" are revered worldwide as places of sacred experience. In the *Popol Vuh,* we are told it was in seven "womb-caves" that the first Maya originated, while the Aztecs believed that after leaving Aztlan, their ancestors resided in a holy place named Chicomoztoc, or "the seven caves." And ten pages of the Grolier Codex—the earliest of the four surviving codices—were partially preserved because the codex had been left in a dry cave in central Chiapas as a sacred offering. Lamantia is entranced by these caves as well as "the rites of the old men" which he encounters in "silence"—a state of being which he associates throughout his Mexico poems with authentic mystical experience. The primal powers of archaic Mexico—sacred caves, *pitayah* fruit, iguanas both on the Temple itself and another iguana occupying his house, the "barefoot thud" of ritual dancing, the narcotic *yahnah* tobacco, the shaman's "bag of medicines"—are memorably recorded. The attraction of shamanism for the Beats lay in the fact that as poets, they believed their roles in the modern world to be analogous to that of the shaman/mystic/doctor who through contact with the transcendent transmitted healing energies and aesthetically beautiful poetic language to the tribe.

Another dramatic event occurred during this trip to Jesus-Maria and the Cora people. Lamantia had been bitten by a scorpion which put him in a state of paralysis for at least twelve hours. Vomiting and constantly passing out, he cried, "Ah, Madonna! Madonna, save me!" and was startled at his own exclamation since he "hated the Church" and had abandoned it to become an atheist Surrealist. Lamantia survived the crisis, and his recovery from this near-death experience led him to consider a conversion back to Catholicism.[17] The fact that this transformation occurred is noteworthy, for as we have seen, Lamantia saw Mexico as "a Catholic country . . . a multilayered inspiration." In Mexico, the Virgin Mary metamorphosed into Guadalupe; churches were constructed on the ruins of Maya and Aztec temples. Indeed, Lamantia struggled throughout his career regarding his loyalties to Christianity, Surrealism, and the more esoteric spiritual traditions to which he was equally drawn.

In "The night is a space of white marble," composed while in Mexico City, Lamantia alludes to the *Mystical Theology* of Pseudo-Dionysius the Areopagite: "The night is a space of white marble/This is Mexico/I'm sitting here, slanted light fixture, pot, altitudinous silence/your voice, Dionysius, telling of darkness, superessential light/In the silence of holy darkness I'm eating a tomato/I'm weak from the altitude/something made my clogged head move! Rutman a week at beach at Acapulco." Lamantia supplies his physical location, seated beneath a "light fixture"—an appropriate place for an enlightening experience—with the double meaning of "pot," slang for marijuana and a container for plants. He is also physically high up in space, "altitudinous," referring to the height of Mexico City—7,350 feet—but also to the "high" supplied by the entheogen he has ingested, and to the peaks of religious ecstasy. "Altitudinous" also recalls Sir Thomas Browne's *Religio Medici* (1643): "I love to lose my self in a mystery, to pursue my Reason to an *O altitudo!*" Mexico City for Lamantia, as for William S. Burroughs, was a place for intense experimentation with drugs: both the height of the city and his transcendent state have rendered him "weak." The poem moves from lofty diction to quotidian reality: "I'm eating a tomato," "something made my clogged head move!," and to a friend who is at another place in Mexico known as a vacation paradise—Acapulco.[18] The sudden, surprising, comical reference to eating a tomato is an example of the way Lamantia employs the technique of Surrealist juxtaposition of dissimilar elements to evoke mystery, the supreme oddness of reality, and often humor.

Lamantia then moves in the final two verses to: "Saint Dionysius reminds us of flight to unknowable/Knowledge/the doctrine of initiates completes the meditation!" "Saint Dionysius" is Pseudo-Dionysius the Areopagite (ca. 500–600 C.E.) whose "negative theology"—with which as we shall see in chapter 6 Allen Ginsberg was also familiar—expounds the concept that the Divine cannot be named and must be approached in silence. Lamantia is literally listening to the voice of Dionysius as he speaks to him, and "unknowable knowledge" is the paradoxical truth of apophatic theology. The poem concludes with "the doctrine of initiates completes the meditation!," alluding to the fact that Dionysius—whose works transmitted the Neoplatonic tradition—employed in his writings the language of spiritual initiation which is central to the ancient Mystery religions. In the second and third sections of *The Mystical Theology*, Dionysius speaks of the process of "initiation into the divine" through breaking free "from what sees and is seen." The initiate "plunges into the truly mysterious darkness of unknowing. Here, renouncing all that the mind may conceive, wrapped entirely in the intangible and the invisible, he belongs completely to him who is beyond everything. Here, being neither oneself nor someone else, one is supremely united to the completely unknown by an inactivity of all knowledge, and knows beyond the mind by knowing nothing."[19] The oppositions of darkness and light, silence and sound, unknown and known convey a mystic sense of unity which Lamantia sought through entheogens, the rituals of Indigenous peoples, and Surrealism—all of which were central to his attraction to Mexico.

Following his dramatic conversion experience in early 1955 in Mexico, Lamantia returned to San Francisco. According to John Suiter in *Poets on the Peaks: Gary Snyder, Philip Whalen and Jack Kerouac in the North Cascades*: "In the summer of '55 Lamantia went to a Trappist monastery in Oregon (dedicated to Our Lady of Guadalupe) in his effort to understand his seemingly autonomous reversion to his childhood Catholicism, but by October he was still grappling to make sense of what had happened to him."[20] Lamantia retreated to a monastery created under the aegis of Guadalupe, the central figure in syncretic Mexican Catholicism. In later years when Lamantia recalled this period, he put the experience with the Cora in the context of his approximately eight years living in Mexico: "Mexico City was wonderfully habitable in the 1950s . . . I met Leonora Carrington there . . . I traveled and perched for long stretches in various regions—Oaxaca, Chiapas, and even remote places in the Sierra Madre mountain range in western central Mexico. . . . With the Coras, though their name for themselves is Nayeri . . . it's as close as you can get to pre-European contact. It was there that I began to return to the Church, to my own roots, inspired by their vision and ritual." Lamantia participated in the famous 6 Gallery reading on October 7, 1955, when Ginsberg premiered "Howl." However, Lamantia did not read his own poetry, choosing instead to recite poems by his friend John Hoffman (1928–1952), who had died in Mexico. Due to his recent seemingly redemptive experience in Mexico, Lamantia rejected his earlier Surrealist-inspired work and began to regard his earlier poems as "blasphemous," thus initiating the cycle which would continue throughout his career of entering-into and exiting-out-of the Surrealist fold.

Lamantia's friendship with Hoffman was a significant aspect of his connection to Mexico. Indeed, by reading Hoffman's poems at the 6 Gallery during the premiere of "Howl," Mexico became a palpable symbolic presence at the very beginning of the public initiation of the Beat movement. The Beats were already aware of William S. Burroughs's shooting of Joan Vollmer in Mexico City in 1951, and the death of Hoffman added to the idea of Mexico as a mysterious, beckoning, but also potentially threatening power. In his essay

"The Legend in Praise of John Hoffman," Lamantia recalled: "After his death a manuscript was collected from among his 'effects.' His being stricken down by paralysis, in Puerto Vallarta, Mexico, 1952, and subsequent death in a hospital in Guadalajara are all I know together with the fact that a certificate, in Spanish, mentions cremation." In "Untitled Introduction to *Journey to the End*"—composed in Mexico in October 1954—Lamantia observed that Hoffman "had the wanderlust, and after peregrinating to the central parts of Mexico (he died in Guadalajara in January 1952) he wrote me of a desire to go further south, 'build a raft and make it to Ecuador'; he was fated to make it to the Sun." Gerd Stern recalls encountering Hoffman at the San Remo bar in New York City—he had met both Hoffman and Lamantia earlier in San Francisco—and shipping out with him to South America. On the trip they read *Chants de Maldoror,* the proto-Surrealist poem by Comte de Lautreamont (1846–1870), who was born in Montevideo, Uruguay. Stern claims however that Hoffman's body was found washed ashore on a beach in Zihuatanejo.[21]

Mexico recurs in several Hoffman poems including "Because of the Stripe He Was Forced": "He knew that to the south the skulls of/Mexico whiten in the sun, smiling. He was living thru the end/of history. He welcomed the coming of Time. In the ritual of/Peyotl (which is a place as geographical as any) pots of fire burn/in the bellies of the old gods symbol of time's pure beginning/becoming being. The intricate pattern of the bricks and the/most highly developed calendar in the world. On his back on/the couch the mind carves arabesques on the ceiling." One notes Hoffman's hymning lyricism as well as allusions to the Aztec calendar and ceremonies with which both he and Lamantia were familiar. Hoffman sees the Western world as experiencing "the end/of history" and peyote rituals as creating what Mircea Eliade has called *in illo tempore*: in the activity of ritual, myth re-enacts the events of the beginning of time. The "old gods" of Mexico represent "time's pure beginning/becoming being."

Lamantia's portrayals of Mexico in his poems memorializing the Cora people may be viewed in relation to Hoffman's philosophical quest. Hoffman's "the end/of history"; "pots of fire burn"; and "the bellies of the old gods" recall Lamantia's "a hidden explosion/in history"; "staves of fire"; "the caves of the old gods." Both Lamantia and Hoffman shared a similar vision of Mexico as a symbolic landscape of timelessness in opposition to America's slavery to "clocktime" and the ruthless efficiencies of industrial production. For Hoffman, the Aztecs and Maya had created "the/ most highly developed calendar in the world." And in "Canticle" Hoffman intones: "The coiled sun swings /Like a slow snake/Across/The sky calendar." The verses in their sinuous *s* sounds imitate the snakelike movements of the "coiled sun"—Hoffman likely had the snake-bird Quetzalcoatl in mind—through the sky.[22] Visitors to Chichen Itza in the Yucatan may view how at dusk the sun creates shadow snakes down the steps of the great pyramid El Castillo, the Temple of Kukulcan. When Europeans arrived in America—before the 1582 enactment of the Gregorian Reform—they had not yet created calendars as advanced as those they discovered in Mexico. Gordon Brotherston has observed: "Calendrical science is in fact inseparable from the major intellectual achievements of the New World. Historical and astronomical time were systematically correlated there long before they were in the Old World." Several Beats including William S. Burroughs, Gary Snyder, and Diane di Prima explored alternative ways to record the passage of time: Snyder often dated his works according to vast geological swaths of time such as Jurassic, Mesozoic, Paleozoic, or Cretaceous, while di Prima invoked the changing of the seasons—the equinox and solstice—in her poetry. Thus John Hoffman was a card-carrying Beat in his admiration for the "sky calendar" of the Aztecs and Maya. Allen Ginsberg in "Howl" memorializes him in the verses, "who disappeared into the volcanoes of Mexico leaving/behind nothing but the shadow of dungarees and the/lava and ash of poetry scattered in fireplace Chicago." While Beat poet ruth weiss in *Compass* begins: "JOHN HOFFMAN died in MEXICO . . . JOHN HOFFMAN your poetry lives with PHILIP LAMANTIA . . . this night/in a room/of reflections/the patterns of self on the wall/at the shore of the sea/sparks from the red tide/a movement of self/fire-works on the water/the eye a reflection of stars/what put us here."[23] Hoffman, like Neal Cassady who later died near the railroad tracks of San Miguel de Allende, would become a kind of martyr figure in the evolving chronicle and mythology of Beat journeys to Mexico.

Following his reading of Hoffman's poetry at the 6 Gallery in October 1955, Lamantia contributed to *Semina* 5—the special "Mexico Issue"—edited by Wallace Berman and published in 1959. His friendship with Berman was significant, as Lamantia recalled: "The connection between Wally Berman and Surrealism was definite, as far as I'm concerned. . . . He had all the same books on alchemy and magic that I have, and was interested in the same subjects I've been interested in since I was fifteen. We had many long, up-until-dawn discussions about poetry and the relationship between the oracles, the esoteric—all those matters." *Semina* 5 contained a brief excerpt from Antonin Artaud's "Le Mexique et la Civilisation," as well as showcasing Mexico-themed work: Kirby Doyle, "Mexico after Artaud"; John Hoffman, "Floridas";

John Wieners, "Peyote Poem"; Michael McClure, an untitled poem dated "8/2/58" containing the verses, "A pink and yellow world. Personal, you said with a soft voice./Like sometimes I'm in Mexico. And I saw Mexico,/I missed it when I was there. Full of pastel/adobe houses. Pink, Salmon, and Blue/pinatas and crinoline hens"; Bob Kaufman, an untitled poem, "O mexico your sadness is nut brown . . ."; and ruth weiss, a selection from *Compass*: "mexico the two-sided coin . . ."

Lamantia submitted two works, a translation from the Spanish of a poem by Sor Juana Inés de la Cruz and "Memoria." Sor Juana—born Juana Inés de Asbaje y Ramirez de Santillana (1648–1695) in a village in Puebla and known as the "Tenth Muse" of Mexico—was a precocious child who learned both Latin and Greek from texts in her grandfather's library, entering the Hieronymite convent of San Geronimo in 1669. The subject of a portrait by the Oaxacan Miguel Cabrera (1695–1768), Sor Juana is depicted in his famous painting seated regally at her desk with one hand upon a large open book, at ease among the many impressive tomes on her bookshelves. She may be seen as a protofeminist of the Renaissance who sought equal rights for women, struggling against the hegemony of male power in the Church of Mexico: she had major conflicts with ecclesiastical authorities Manuel Fernandez de Santa Cruz, the bishop of Puebla, and Francisco de Aguiar y Seijas, archbishop of Mexico. American recognition of Sor Juana's achievement began as early as 1823 when a biographical sketch about her appeared in the *New York Mirror*, while the *North American Review* in 1849 provided a more fulsome account of her work. In "Respuesta a Sor Filoleta de la Cruz" (1691), Sor Juana memorably describes how in her intense passion for studying Latin, she would cut off pieces of her hair if she failed to learn a specific lesson, "for there seemed to me no cause for a head to be adorned with hair and naked of learning—which was the more desired embellishment." She composed poems in Spanish and incorporated elements from the Nahuatl language in her carols, *villancicos* and *tocotins*. Lamantia translated section 92 from Sor Juana's *Las Redondillas*, which appears on the obverse of Mexico's two hundred peso currency with Juana's portrait on the front: "Hombres necios que acusais/a la mujer sin razon/sin ver que sois la occasion/de lo mismo que culpais." Lamantia identifies her as "Sister Juana Inez of the Cross" and translates: "Who's the greater culprit/in height of passionate mistake/she who falls by cajoling/or he who cajoles her into falling?/Oh, whose fault the most/although both of them, wrong:/she who sins for pay/or he who pays to sin?"[24] From the outset of his career, Lamantia would be at the vanguard of liberatory politics—he was involved with the anarchist movement in San

Francisco—and so too we may witness here his early celebration of the creative strength of women.

Sor Juana also appears in the introduction to Lamantia's "Babbel." Lamantia defines *Babbel* as "a language extending the sonic level of the poem—in pure song flight—to maximum points," adding that "Sande Rutman and I originated and named Babbel in December, 1960 in Mexico City." Lamantia cites Antonin Artaud, James Joyce, and Hugo Ball as conducting similar experiments with language as well as "certain poems in a Spanish/latin meld by Sor Juana Inés de la Cruz." It is significant that Lamantia admired Sor Juana not only for her brave egalitarian ethos but credits her experiments with innovative poetics as well. Octavio Paz shared this opinion, perceiving "in Sor Juana a poetic program that goes beyond the baroque to anticipate modernism." She also appears in Lamantia's "America in the Age of Gold": "From this north my head is full of you, Sur America/Sor Juana sailing the cloud her back to us from Mexico *real*."[25] Lamantia contrasts North and South America and christens Mexico as "Mexico *real*"—"royal Mexico"—where Sor Juana surfs like an Olympian through the sky. Sor Juana was of keen interest to Margaret Randall as the prototype of a modern, feminist, literary woman proud to stand up for her rights, and as we shall see in chapter 9, Sor Juana also figures in the work of Joanne Kyger.

Lamantia's second piece in *Semina* 5—"Memoria"—is an excerpt from the longer poem which appears in his *Collected Poems*: "Marijuana in black light, marijuana en las puertas del diablo/All night long, the chant charted/and fell/All night long the aztec messengers arrived/and fell stars!/All night long, and of time/jaguar in her eye/Typewriters hung in Ant Eater's Garden/Macchu Picchu loomed—crust of Sky/it fell/Marijuana seeress spoke sibyl sentences silver and cut/the throats of time!"[26] In the longer version of the poem, Lamantia alludes to "Morphia," "kif," "Hashish," before invoking the "marijuana" of the section above. He refers to "Mohammed of the Sacred Plant," "kif of Anghor Vat," thus creating a kind of global geographical list of entheogens and places with which they were associated. Marijuana is—and the poem here shifts to Spanish—*en las puertas del diablo*, "in the doors of the devil." In the verse "aztec messengers arrived/and fell stars!" Lamantia alludes to the etymology of the word *angel*, which in ancient Greek means "messenger," since he associates these aztec—he does not capitalize "aztec"—messengers with falling stars, with heavenly angelic events. The jaguar—the largest cat of the Americas—is one of the archetypal creatures of Mexico, appearing throughout its mythology. The name of the magnificent city of *Ek-Balam* derives from *Ek*—meaning "black" or "star"—and *balam*, "jaguar";

thus, Black Jaguar or Star Jaguar. So too the celebrated Mayan texts named *Chilam Balam, Chilam* being a priest. Chilam Balam was the priest and prophet of northern Yucatan who predicted that Kukulcan—the Mayan name for Quetzalcoatl—would return from his self-exile in the form of emissaries: the Spanish men with beards.

Following his first trips to Mexico in the fifties and during the progressive impact of the Beats on American culture—Ginsberg's "Howl," Kerouac's *On the Road,* and Burroughs's *Naked Lunch* were published in 1956, 1957, and 1959, respectively—Lamantia continued his reflections upon Mexican literature and culture. He returned to Mexico several times in the early sixties and was expelled twice on narcotics charges. His dependency on a variety of drugs including heroin attracted the attention of the legal authorities. Lamantia was depicted in a photograph by "Pantale Xantos"—the pseudonym of Wallace Berman—in *Semina* 5 dated "9.8.59" injecting heroin into his arm with a hypodermic needle. The cover of *Narcotica* (1959), published by Auerhahn Press, was designed by Berman and features a crucifix in the center surrounded by four photographs of Lamantia: one side view with a photograph of Pope John XXIII; one showing him displaying his two open arms with hands facing palm up; and two showing him injecting heroin—one image is the same one Berman included in *Semina* 5. Despite his drug dependency, he continued to evolve as a writer, and the sixties were significant in both his career and in his relationship to Mexican literary life. Lamantia composed several poems with Mexican themes including "Ceylonese Tea Candor (Pyramid Scene)." In addition to his fascination with the pyramids of the Aztecs, Lamantia developed during the sixties a serious interest in Egyptology—like Gregory Corso and William S. Burroughs, both of whom were passionate about Egyptian hieroglyphics—and studied the theories of Schwaller de Lubicz concerning the sacred architecture of the Temple of Man in Luxor, Egypt. Earlier explorers of Mexico and the Yucatan such as Frederick Frost and Channing Arnold—two British travelers—noted similarities between Egypt and Mexico in *The American Egypt: A Record of Travel in the Yucatan* published in 1909.[27]

Lamantia's fascination with pyramids is revealed in a recurring pattern of imagery throughout his Mexico poems. The word pyramid derives from ancient Greek *pyramis,* which refers to a small piece of bread with triangular sides joined at the top. The great pyramids of the Aztecs were intended to replicate the power of the sacred mountain, and for Lamantia they are sources of spiritual energy. Pyramids are symbols of mountains as sacred spaces; from Moses receiving the Ten Commandments, to Friedrich Nietzsche's visionary

Pyramid of the Sun, Creative Commons

insights among the peaks of Sils Maria, Switzerland, which gave birth to *Also Sprach Zarathustra,* to the Tibetan sages in the Himalayas, high mountain peaks have been the locations for epiphanies. In the Aztec world, because mountains are in close proximity to the elemental forces of the cosmos—sky, rain, and sun—they are also near to the divine, and the sacred mountain is believed to be located at the center of the universe. By the same token, the pyramid partakes of this same symbolic power. It was on Easter Sunday in 1961 that Lamantia set out with several friends to visit the Pyramid of the Sun at Teotihuacan, and he dedicated "Ceylonese Tea Candor (Pyramid Scene)" to his fellow explorers: "J.R., le comte A.R. de Sales, and Helene."[28]

These three dramatis personae are Richard J. "Josh" Reynolds III, Aymon de Roussy de Sales, and Helen DuFresne: we possess an account of this episode authored by de Sales entitled "The Fifth Sun" published in *Borderlands* in 1994. This lively narrative gives us a vivid portrait of Lamantia in Mexico by a close friend. Aymon de Sales describes the shift in awareness which evolved as young people in America welcomed the oncoming "Age of Aquarius": "The years passed quickly, the psychedelic revolution, the need to push the world into a new consciousness. It was down there in Mexico—the Indian continent that lay dark, submerged, and away from white man's power. Maybe I'd been reading too much Kerouac, his Dharma Bums about drifting between Los Angeles, Mexico, and New York, a sacred triangle, poets seeking a Bodhisattva vision." De Sales perceived his attraction to Mexico in relation to the descriptions in Jack Kerouac's *On the Road* of his Mexico travels, which as we shall see in chapter 5 depict Kerouac's urge to escape New York and urban America to struggle toward the Buddhist peace of mind he fought to achieve and chronicled in *The Dharma Bums* (1958), his book-length poem *Mexico City Blues* (1959), and the posthumously published *Some of the Dharma* (1997). De Sales also heard enticing tales about Maria Sabina, the *curandera* in Huautla de Jimenez: "There in Oaxaca an old witch lived alone in the mountains, a soothsayer, an oracle for the vanished Indian nation. She spoke of pathways of the mind, a way to see things which we hadn't dreamed about, and with this knowledge you could experience mysteries."

De Sales recalls specific details of his first meeting with Lamantia: "The knowledge of the Sun came to me those thirty-three years ago when I found myself in Mexico City. I was introduced to a poet called Philip Lamantia. He had these enormous dark liquid eyes like a deer, and they burned with an intense fire. He was a mystic, and upon meeting him I became involved with increasing rapidity in a strange set of circumstances." Lamantia wore "a silver crucifix, white shirt and jeans, his crewcut head making him look like a Zen monk." He was "talking a mile a minute. The energy that guy had was amazing, supernatural. He told us about mandalas, crystal skulls in tombs which no instrument could make." Lamantia sought to visit at sunset Quetzalcoatl's temple at the pyramids of Teotihuacan, believing the time was propitious since it was the equinox—Easter Sunday or "MARCH! O IDES!" as he tells us in the poem—proclaiming: "This is the City of the Gods! . . . Here their voices will be heard, their ghosts still walk! This was the greatest of all religious centers in America. Its power extends to the poles!" Lamantia goes on to declare: "The Plumed Serpent is the symbol of rebirth. It must begin again. I know it! You felt that, didn't you?" Thus the fragmented modern world can rise again, as with D. H. Lawrence's own symbols of Quetzalcoatl the Plumed Serpent and the Phoenix rising from the ashes into new life.

The influence of Lawrence's novel *The Plumed Serpent* (1926) may be seen in Lamantia's poetry. Lawrence included in his novel several "hymns" in verse form to convey his ideas concerning the revivification of the ancient worship of Queztalcoatl for modern Mexico. In chapter 11, "Lords of the Day and Night," Lawrence describes a man singing accompanied by a soft drumbeat: "The Lord of the Morning Star/Stood between the day and the night/As a bird that lifts its wings, and stands/With the bright wing on the right/And the wing of the dark on the left,/The Dawn Star stood into sight." Lamantia's "Morning Light Song" begins: "RED DAWN clouds coming up! the heavens proclaim you. Absolute God/I claim the glory, in you, of singing to you this morning/For I am coming out of myself and Go to you, Lord of the Morning Light/For what's a singer worth if he can't talk to you, My God of Light?"[29] In one version of the myth, upon his death Quetzalcoatl is transformed into Venus, the Morning Star, known in the ancient Mayan books as *Chak Ek'*—"Great Star." Lamantia—like Lawrence—endeavors to "speak in the voice" of an Indigenous celebrant, praising the light of the stars as the source of all life and inspiration.

De Sales then informs us that Lamantia warned his fellow pilgrims of the darker side of ancient Mexico: "But beware! Five hundred years ago that Pyramid ran with blood, hearts tossed on sorcerers' altars. The black magicians descending from the north, the spiderwoman's men turning this crystal view upside down. This place has layers of karma—beware of being caught in this cat's cradle!"[30] Lamantia and friends discover a fissure in the pyramid from which they see "a whitish wisp like a vapor escape. In the twinkling of an eye it lost itself in the coming darkness, but its shape, what I glimpsed of it, was like a gnarled hand. The Pyramid had opened! The second thing was a scream. The scream was Philip's (though he claimed later he never knew he made it), but Josh and Helen saw 'something' like smoke come out of his mouth and disappear into the gloom of the Mexican evening."[31] Lamantia declares: "There's things in this Pyramid no one has seen for a thousand years. These magicians were into galactic intercourse. Who knows what went into the world." De Sales corresponds closely to Lamantia's "Ceylonese Tea Candor (Pyramid Scene)": "we raced down/and the Black Shapes hundreds of them cut around us and/wailed a weird banshee sound of hell I couldn't quite believe it/but it WAS TRUE!!! We were being pushed off the/Pyramid of the Sun that IS the mountain of Hell itself."[32]

Lamantia, while preparing to visit the pyramids at Teotihuacan, had told de Sales: "The outcome has been predicted in the form of Huitzilopochtli, the Fifth Sun. It is known that this appears after four others have come and gone, and that this is itself destined to be superseded by another. It was all written down in their sacred manuscripts, the painted texts, that is why the Catholic priests burned them. They told of things that made the Christians fainthearted. There are various indications that the Fifth Sun is the creator of a great and indestructible work, and this work is the freeing of the human brain from duality."[33] Mary Miller and Karl Taube in *The Gods and Symbols of Ancient Mexico and the Maya* point out that the Aztecs believed both the Sun and the earth's population had been created five times: humanity and the current sun were generated during the last, final creation at Teotihuacan, which "was also the birthplace of the gods themselves. According to the Florentine Codex, during the long peregrination from Aztlan that eventually led to Tenochtitlan, the Aztecs went from Tamoanchan to Teotihuacan, where they made offerings and built pyramids over the burials of rulers, thus giving them life everlasting."[34] Michel de Montaigne (1553–1592) in his essay "On Coaches" observed: "The Peoples of the Kingdom of Mexico were somewhat more urban and more cultured than the other peoples over there. In addition, like us, they judged that the world was nearing its end, taking as a portent of this the desolation that we visited upon them. They believed that the world's existence was divided into five periods, each as long as the life of five successive suns." The notion that there is a succession of World Ages is familiar to us from Hesiod's *Works and Days*—Golden, Silver, Bronze, Heroic, Iron—and Ovid's *Metamorphoses*: Golden, Silver, Bronze, Iron.

Lamantia urges his friends to "count the steps, we must count the steps, they contain a clue," suggesting the pyramids occlude mysteries which can be revealed through close study and exegesis. This notion of deciphering ancient Mexico for "clues" to cosmic mysteries returns in Lamantia's poem "Opus Magnum": "I am with banquet of lovers at ruins of Tenochtitlan/swam the Hellespont of ancient mystery/landed on shores of Mu Atlantis Babylon." We may observe in Lamantia a continuation of the tradition of interpreting both Aztec and Maya history in terms of "secret knowledge." D. H. Lawrence in *Studies in Classic American Literature* set the stage for such conceptions when he declared: "The occultists say that once there was a universal mystic language, known to the initiated, or to the adept, or to the priesthood of the whole world, whether Chinese or Atlantean or Maya or Druid—a language that was universal over the globe at some period, perhaps before the Flood." Lawrence's suggestion that there is an esoteric element in archaic cultures would be continued in the notions of "New Age" predictions of the apocalyptic Maya prophecies. As E. J. Michael Witzel has argued in *The Origins of the World's Mythologies*, while the ancient Mesopotamians had a "pessimistic" worldview, "the Mesoamericans certainly were even more obsessed with death, as the imagery of Mexican festivals still shows, and they were equally preoccupied with the renewal of divine, solar power through blood offerings and human sacrifice. Worse, the end of certain of their calendar cycles was an ever-looming threat, as clearly felt at the time of Cortez's invasion of Mexico. The end of the current Fifth World is predicted of an exact date (2012)." One recalls similar anxieties in our own times regarding a correlation between disastrous predictions and the calendar when, during the turn into the new millennium in 2000, a variety of apocalyptic events was predicted. Authors such as Jose Arguelles (1939–2011)—who earned a doctorate from the University of Chicago in the history of art and was affiliated with Allen Ginsberg's Naropa University in Boulder, Colorado—studied the pyramids and calendar in relation to esoteric philosophy; while Raphael Girard in *Esotericism of the Popol Vuh: The Sacred History of the Quiché-Maya* also interprets this classic work within the framework of a tradition of "secret wisdom."[35]

The next section of "Ceylonese Tea Candor (Pyramid Scene)" is itself composed in the pattern of a pyramid. Lamantia experimented with constructing his poems in the form of crucifixes and other symbolic shapes in the tradition of the great religious poet George Herbert: "north of/Mexico City/ once called Ten/och tit lan built one/thousand AD by the Toltecs/after destruction of Teotihuacan/city of the gods. And conquered by/witch/ driven Aztecs, bloody blackmagic/nazi/moloch worshipping sun devils of old/mexico who took the remains of Toltec High/Religion and turned it into degenerate center of Hell's/cult of blood hearts torn open for the pleasure of all the/demons of the seven circles of the seven thousand webs of the/ seven million fallen angels of God's solar paradise."[36] The Aztecs believed the Toltecs had once ruled at Tollan—also known as Tula—and *Tollan* may also refer to any great urban center. Tenochtitlan—a magnificent "lake-borne" city once home to at least 200,000 inhabitants connected by three huge causeways to the land—was considered a *Tollan,* as was Teotihuacan. The Aztecs imagined Toltecs inhabited a wondrous world where Quetzalcoatl reigned. It is to this tradition that Lamantia refers when he accuses the Aztecs of being "witch driven" in their perversion of the "High Religion" of the Toltecs into a "cult of blood." To be called a "Toltec" was a term of high approbation. As Gordon Brotherston observes, "the term 'Toltec' came throughout Mesoamerica to designate craftsman, artist, intellectual. According to native texts, Toltec accomplishment was encyclopedic. These people excelled as architects and masons, scribes and painters, carpenters and sculptors, lapidaries and experts in jade and turquoise, miners and workers of gold, silver, copper, tin, and other metals, makers of mosaics and feather tapestries, potters, spinners and weavers, musicians and composers, medical doctors, experts in astronomy, chronology, and calendrics, and true readers of dreams. Of someone adroit and learned it was said 'He is a true Toltec.'" Denise Levertov in "The Artist," which is her version from a Spanish translation of the Toltec Codice de la Real Academia—Levertov received help from Elvira Abascal with the original Toltec text—confirms this vision of the Toltec genius: "The true artist: draws out all from his heart,/works with delight, makes things with calm, with sagacity./works like a true Toltec, composes his objects, works dexterously, invents;/arranges materials, adorns them, makes them adjust." And Robert Lowell, who spent time in Mexico in 1968, composed an impressive poem entitled "Mexico" comprised of twelve sonnets which appeared in his volume *History* (1970) evoking a similar scenario, depicting a "Toltec Eden" employing his typically lush, dense, churning, violently lovely imagery: "Hope not in God here, nor the Aztec gods;/we sun-people know the sun, the source of life,/will die, unless we feed it human blood—/ . . . We sit on the cliff like curs, chins pressed to thumbs,/the Toltec temples changing to dust in the dusk—/hair of the vultures, white brow of the moon: this too dust . . . /dust out of time, two clocks set back to the Toltec Eden,/as if we still wished to pull teeth with firetongs—/when they took a city, they too murdered everything:/man, woman and child, down to the pigs and dogs."[37] Lowell also portrays the horrors of human sacrifice and the Aztec notion that unless fed by blood "the source of life/will die."

In the above passage, Lamantia employs the word "moloch," borrowed from the second section of Allen Ginsberg's "Howl" where Moloch symbolizes the greed, rapacity, and violence of the modern American technocratic state to which sacrifices must be made, as the ancient Canaanites made child sacrifices. Lamantia posits a version of Mexican history in which the Aztecs perverted what was previously a noble civilization, suggesting a similar trajectory in America where white invaders imposed slavery on Africans and wrested the land from the Native Americans. The violence and terror of American history is mirrored in the Aztecs, whose brutality was indeed horrific. Enemy warriors captured in battle composed the preponderance of victims. Male or female slaves were sacrificed and children were favorite targets of the rain gods. Although extracting the heart was most commonly practiced, death was also accomplished through killing on the scaffold or gladiatorial contests. Corpses were then beheaded, flayed, or dismembered. The *tzompantli*, or "skull rack," was a wooden scaffold placed near temples and which displayed severed heads. Manuel Leon-Portilla in *Aztec Thought and Culture: A Study of the Ancient Nahuatl Mind* argues that the Aztecs represent "a situation similar to that of Nazi Germany in our time, where a mystic-militaristic world view and a genuinely humanistic philosophy and literature coexisted. Indeed, such a mixture of humanism and barbarism seems to be an inherent quality of the so-called rational animal." One recalls the scene in Steven Spielberg's *Schindler's List* (1993) in which the Nazi liquidation of the Krakow ghetto is counterpointed with a German soldier playing the prelude from J. S. Bach's English Suite no. 2 in A minor, thus juxtaposing Nazi diabolic destruction against German creative genius.

In a text dated August 30, 1961, "The Beat Generation," Lamantia states: "A few poets of my generation tried to live in voluntary poverty—tantamount to Sin in the U.S. of the post/atomic period—outside, that is, the

SYNTHETIC/MECHANO/ORGANIZATION of biochemic life, in desperate WILL TO BELIEVE in themselves as much more than ciphers in the proverbial metallic filing cabinets of the jerry/bult/junk/sustained MATERIALIST VOID. We took to the streets and inner temples of Being . . . We go to the end of the apocalypse. It is COME—: AnaAlbion. AmerEnglish poetry awaits the time of Bards, Seers, Oracles, Singers, *the old made new*, the return of Quetzalcoatl, the realization of Artaud's spectacle." We can see a clear echo of this language in the conclusion of "Ceylonese Tea Candor (Pyramid Scene)" where Lamantia again exhorts in capital letters: "if you do not take up your swords of the mind against the/mechanical materialist VOID/if you do not pray for DIVINE ENLIGHTENMENT/if you do not experience god OH POORE MANKINDE!!!/ON THIS PLANET YOUR TIME WILL BE UP!!!/AND THERE SHALL BE HELL TO PAY!!!"[38] The "mechanical materialist VOID" here is reminiscent of Moloch, for America has become a self-consuming machine—Allen Ginsberg was inspired by Fritz Lang's film *Metropolis* which depicts a soulless technologized society—and Lamantia addresses the reader directly, urging us to avoid the fate of the Aztecs who perverted a noble civilization. Lamantia's "take up your swords of the mind" recalls William Blake's poem "Jerusalem," which contains the stirring quatrain: "I will not cease from Mental Fight,/Nor shall my sword sleep in my hand:/Till we have built Jerusalem,/In England's green and pleasant land." Blake became a favorite poet of the counterculture—Ginsberg considered him his "guru"—and Lamantia urges at the close of "Ceylonese Tea Candor (Pyramid Scene)" a worldwide political and social revolution to overturn the old order and to bring the Surrealist dream of "the marvelous" into everyday life.

Lamantia's friend Ted Joans connected Aztec hegemony to the oppression of American Blacks in his poem "Another Dream Deferred? A Take-Off on Langston's Famous Poem." Langston Hughes visited and wrote about Mexico, where his father Charles Langston had become a successful businessman. Joans composed "Another Dream Deferred? A take-off on Langston's famous poem" in Mexico City in January 1988, and he closely follows Hughes's celebrated poem "Harlem": "What happens to a dream deferred?/Does it dry up/like a raisin in the sun?/Or fester like a sore—/And then run?/Does it stink like rotten meat?/Or crust and sugar over—/like a syrupy sweet?/Maybe it just sags/like a heavy load./*Or does it explode?*"[39] Joans compares the plight of African Americans with the sacrifices of the "Aztec executioner." Verses one and three are direct quotes from Hughes. Joans then shifts to "The warm sun the warm winter Mexican sun/Where Aztec executioner priests used to/

Make sacrificial blood run." Joans returns to Hughes in verse eleven—"To stink like rotten meat"—and in the final verse which imitates the close of "Harlem": "Maybe it just sags/like a heavy load./*Or does it explode?*" Just as Lamantia sees in the Aztecs a predecessor of the Fascist state, Joans connects African Americans' struggle for freedom with his condemnation of the violence and exploitation the Aztecs inflicted on their victims.

In poetry Lamantia composed over the next decades, Mexican themes return and a pattern of volcanic imagery emerges in several works. The dramatic symbolism of volcanos in Mexican history is memorialized in book 12 of the *Florentine Codex* in which Cortes and his fellow conquistadors are depicted on their horses traveling in a stately march between the twin volcanos Popocatepetl and Iztaccihautl. Volcanos are a frequent subject in Mexican literature: Mateo Rosas de Oquendo (b. 1559?) composed "Indiano volcan famoso" describing Popocatepetl. Volcanos are primal, sublime, archaic, reaching to the molten core of the Earth's center, periodically hurling fiery lava violently upward and in their convulsions symbolizing the simultaneously creative and destructive energies of the universe. Indeed, the vast crater caused by the impact of an asteroid the size of a city at Chicxulub in the Yucatan peninsula near Progreso—theorized to be the cause of the extinction of the dinosaurs sixty-five million years ago—was originally thought to have been a gigantic volcanic caldera. The asteroid created a hole twelve miles deep and one hundred miles wide, causing huge lava waves to flow outward which solidified into a ring of huge peaks. This recent scientific discovery confirms Mexico as the locus of titanic, elemental, apocalyptic cosmic events.

The Surrealist artist Wolfgang Paalen—who lived in Mexico and edited the important magazine *DYN The Review of Modern Art* (1942–44, five issues) which featured pre-Columbian art as well as texts by authors including Henry Miller, Anais Nin, Miguel Covarrubias, Robert Motherwell, and Pablo Picasso—composed an essay in April 1943 regarding the cinder cone volcano Paricutin, located two hundred miles west of Mexico City near Uruapan, which began erupting lava on February 20, 1943: "The resemblance of the silhouette of the young volcano to that of a pyramid has struck many observers. Moreover Mexico abounds in mountains and hills of volcanic origin which suggest the form of a pyramid. Without doubt the ancestors of the Mexicans of today witnessed the birth of volcanoes, spectacles quite sufficient to generate a myth." The Beats would seize upon volcanos as a central symbol of untamed Mexico and in "Advent," Lamantia recalls the times he spent with Jack Kerouac within the context of volcanic imagery: "Jaguar in a Picasso eye—Stravinsky fires!/Picasso walks hamadryad five hydrant minds/Who make death belch down death/Europe in rains of decapitated titans CUT OFF—/NOW/Over our general motors neon sign I'm walking/With Jack Kerouac/The Juicy endless head of American Prose/We pray loudly in a lotus bowl—the Gentle present Jesus/In blue torrents of our rain/That washed us down mexican volcanos while we climbed/THOSE mountains of/ incense Myrrh Frankincense Aloes/The Cherubic Wanderer Angelus Silesius/Out of the seventeenth century/TIME IS AS ETERNITY IS." The poem commences dramatically with the quintessential Mexican mythological symbol: the jaguar. Lamantia alludes to creative geniuses such as Pablo Picasso and Igor Stravinsky—the driving, barbaric, syncopated, ecstatic rhythms of Stravinsky's *Le Sacre du printemps* were employed in Walt Disney's *Fantasia* (1940) in the extended scene depicting the explosive outpouring of lava from scores of volcanos—who attained heights of creative achievement analogous to mountain peaks, but also to a litany of spiritual figures: during their friendship, Lamantia and Kerouac discussed mystical literature. Lamantia refers to the German Catholic mystic Angelus Silesius (ca. 1624–1677), admired by figures as diverse as Jorge Luis Borges and Martin Heidegger, alluding to his *Der Cherbinische Wandersmann* (1674, *The Cherubic Wanderer*) in which Silesius states: "Time's like eternity, eternity like time,/Unless you do yourself between them draw a line," thus expressing the omnipresent desire among the Beats to escape from clock-time into the eternity of each moment, an experience which they sought in Mexico.

The final section of "Advent" opens: "We come to the great mandala of New York/In church of Saint Francis off Herald Square/Where the blue slippered Virgin Mary guadalupizes the evil serpent." Lamantia creates a compact, dense series of references to Buddhist and Hindu thought with the *mandala*—which in Sanskrit means "circle"—symbolizing the cosmos as well as a camouflaged allusion to Lamantia's experience with the scorpion bite in Jesus-Maria, for here we again have the "Virgin Mary" which we recall he cried out in his moment of crisis, but she "guadalupizes the evil serpent."[40] In the narrative concerning Our Lady of Guadalupe—*Nuestra Senora de Guadalupe*—the Virgin Mary appeared four times before a Mexican peasant named Juan Diego Cuauhtlatoatzin beginning on December 9, 1531, on the Hill of Tepeyac near Mexico City and spoke to him in Nahuatl, his native language. The syncretism of Aztec and Christian spiritual cultures is enshrined in Guadalupe, and Lamantia invents a cool verb—"guadalupizes"—to describe the vanquishing of both the serpent in the Garden of Eden and also, most likely, the scorpion which almost killed him but from whose toxic bite

Lamantia believed he had been saved through the intercession of the Virgin Mary/Guadalupe.

Finally, another late poem which features volcanos—"Mexico City Central Moon"—chants a whole catalogue of memories. The poem opens: "The humid chemic from lobotomized trees/drinking coffee dust off the Alameda . . . labyrinth's eyes a *Pulque* dive at dawn Osirian as Quetzalcoatl . . . 1950 *Calle de Garcia Lorca*."[41] Composed in the early 1980s, the reader realizes that Lamantia has lost none of his Surrealist energy and inventiveness: "lobotomized trees" alone surpasses in imaginative weirdness anything created by Salvador Dali. The Alameda is the great park of central Mexico City, and Lamantia supplies a date as well as the street *Calle de Garcia Lorca,* suggesting that during his first trip to Mexico in 1950 he spent time there. Pulque, an alcoholic, milk-colored drink which tastes like sour yeast, is sold today when distilled as tequila: the state of Jalisco is renowned for its blue Weber agave—*agave tequiliana.* Created from the fermented sap of the agave or maguey plant, pulque is said to have been invented by the Aztec goddess Mayahuel, whose four hundred breasts nourished the gods of drunkenness, the Centzontotochtin. Mayahuel is depicted in the Codex Laud in the Bodleian Library, "decked out in all her finery, with hair ornaments, ear pendants, nose ring, armlets, and fine collar with little golden bells." Bernardino de Sahagun (ca. 1499–1590) in his *Historia general de las cosas de Nueva Espana* warned: "What I principally command is that you shun drunkenness, that you do not drink *pulque,* because it is like henbane which removes man from his reason. . . . This *pulque* and drunkenness is the cause of all discord and dissension."[42] Pulque became part of the Mexican experience of other Beat authors. Jack Kerouac in a letter to Allen Ginsberg of May 10, 1952, recalled his time in Culiacan: "I ate tortillas and carne in African stick huts in the jungle with pigs rubbing against my legs; I drank pure pulque from a pail, fresh from the field, from the plant, unfermented, pure milk of pulque makes you get the giggles, is the greatest drink in the world."[43]

Volcanos return in the final section of the poem: "the Empedoclean suicide in a volcano a green sigil There were the/fountains of hate in the womb of obsidian clothing/the iridescent descent to Toluca exploding the Presidential Plazas/dimly Pancho Villa in Sonoran desert the very thought of mirage/alligator, iguana, armadillo/here too it's prohibited to dream." Empedocles was the pre-Socratic Greek philosopher said to have committed suicide by leaping into the volcano at Etna—and subject of a play by Matthew Arnold, *Empedocles at Etna*—whom Lamantia invokes among his memories of

Mexican volcanos, as well as the black obsidian glass which volcanos create; the great Valley of Toluca was conquered by the Spanish in 1521 and is today the state capital of the State of Mexico; the Sonoran Desert is located in northwest Mexico; while Pancho Villa (1878–1923) is the great Mexican revolutionary, invoked as we have seen in chapter 1 by Lawrence Ferlinghetti. Ted Joans in his poem "Calexico & Mexicali"—dedicated to Lewis Carroll—declares: "Tweedledee rode rough with/Pancho Villa from Calexico/Onto coldheart hawk Chicago/Where Pancho still prevails." Pancho Villa was also one of the heroes of the Surrealists: Villa appears on one of the cards in the Surrealist tarot deck *Le Jeu de Marseilles* along with—among others—Hegel, de Sade, Lautreamont, and Paracelsus.[44] Lamantia's poem concludes in a virtuosic hymn to Mexico: "Monks, lamps, vampiric final rasp Cactus leather stretched to sky/ease to earth;/a sugary throat sends up the steely sand, moon/dust, the twinkle at the zelicon's run/to your hoary rim, Mexico/They call you 'the sixth world.'" Here, "Cactus leather" leads up into the sky like the axis mundi, connecting earth to the heavens, and the "moon" of the poem's title returns. "Zelicon" is the *Papilio zelicaon*—the anise swallowtail butterfly which inhabits the Baja Peninsula and other areas of Mexico—while the "hoary rim" may be the rim of an archaic volcano where cosmic energies gather: "sand" and "moon dust" hover in the atmosphere. Because of Lamantia's ambiguous word placement, "twinkle" may be the sparkle of heavenly bodies including the moon or the "twinkle" caused by the zelicon butterfly's flight through the sky as it arrives at its destination. Lamantia concludes cryptically with "They call you 'the sixth world.'" The American writer on Native American culture Frank Waters argues in *Mexico Mystique: The Coming Sixth World of Consciousness* (1975) that a "sixth world of consciousness" will begin to make its appearance around 2012 according to the Maya calculations, a central concept in "New Age" interpretations of Maya history.[45] Thus "Mexico City Central Moon" encodes Lamantia's personal experiences in Mexico in the early fifties through a joyous blend of pure surrealist style—there is great pleasure to be had in reading Lamantia by simply allowing his words to work their magic without straining too assiduously after "meaning"—with a synoptic history of several archetypical Mexican tropes and a bow at the close to esoteric traditions which had always nourished his imagination.

In this chapter we have seen some of the myriad ways Lamantia incorporated his profound affection for the land and people of Mexico in his works. Lamantia established himself in Mexico City as a literary figure who drew together important writers including Margaret Randall, whose *El Corno Emplumado* became a central source for Beat writers in their relationship to

Mexico, and forged literary bridges to Mexico and Latin America through his friendships with Homero Aridjis and Ernesto Cardenal. He read widely in books about Mexico and the Indigenous people such as the Tarahumara and Cora, synthesizing this knowledge with his own interpretation of Mexican history and places in his poetry. While in Mexico, Lamantia pursued his studies in mystical literature, including the works of Pseudo-Dionysius the Areopagite, texts which would exert a profound influence on several Beat authors. And in his later poetry, Lamantia continued to return to his memories of a country whose people, culture, and ancient traditions he had always loved.

# 4 ✻ MARGARET RANDALL

## Poet, Feminist, Revolutionary, and *El Corno Emplumado*

Born in New York City in 1936, Margaret Randall, nee Reinthal, moved with her parents at age ten to Albuquerque, New Mexico. Coming from a Jewish family and growing up in Albuquerque against what she described as a "backdrop of Indian and Hispanic oppression" would sensitize Randall to the plight of marginalized peoples throughout the world. At age twenty in 1956, she heard "Howl" read at a party and "was mesmerized. For the first time, a poet grabbed me, changed me. I wanted to know Ginsberg, wrote to him care of his publisher, said I would meet him in San Francisco on such and such a night, made the road trip but of course he didn't show. This marked the moment I knew I wanted to write poetry myself."[1] In 1956–1957, Randall learned Spanish while living in Spain—the beginnings of her long career as a distinguished translator—with her first husband, and upon returning to the United States encountered Elaine de Kooning when she was a visiting professor at the University of New Mexico. In her memoir entitled "Elaine," Randall recalled driving to Ciudad Juarez on the Mexican border where she and Elaine often spent the weekends and attended the bullfights on Sunday at the Plaza Monumental: "We always stayed at the same hotel, drank tequila at the same bar, and gloried in the Sunday afternoon display with its bravado and theater. Young and unperturbed by such cruelty to animals, I still subscribed to the excitement of the dubious drama with its predetermined outcome." Elaine de Kooning would provide the cover illustration and drawings for Randall's first book of poetry, *Ecstasy Is a Number* (1961).[2] Relocating to New York City in 1957—the same year that Joanne Kyger moved to San Francisco and encountered the Beats—Randall met painters Willem de Kooning, Fritz Kline, Mark Rothko, and Helen Frankenthaler as well as poets including Frank O'Hara, Jerome Rothenberg, LeRoi Jones (Amiri Baraka), Denise Levertov, Robert Creeley, Hettie Jones, Allen Ginsberg, and Diane di Prima. Like di Prima, Randall desired to conceive a child outside conventional marriage and became pregnant by poet Joel Oppenheimer: "I gave birth to my son Gregory in 1960, when single-motherhood was burdened by social stigma. . . . This didn't concern me. From the moment I was a mother I felt complete."

During the summer of 1961, Randall journeyed with Gregory to Mexico City for a short visit: she was, in her words, "testing the waters" to determine whether or not to relocate more permanently to Mexico. She found that "Mexico's colonial churches were filled with treasures and pungent with the scent of copal. A nation of corn, the air smelled of *nixtamal*, and roasted chile-sprinkled *mazorcas* could be eaten at stalls along city streets." Copal is incense made from resin; nixtamal is the process by which corn is cooked in an alkaline solution to produce delicious tortillas; mazorca is roasted corn on the cob. Randall responded to Mexico's "snow-capped volcanoes—Popocatepetl and Ixtaccihuatl" as well as to "multicolor houses lining cobble streets. Purple, red, and white bougainvillea vines, tall as trees, cascaded over volcanic garden walls and the violet lace of the jacaranda canopy spread its ample branches." This intensely descriptive and poetic incantation is characteristic of Randall's style. She was enticed by the cultural richness of Mexico City: "It had more green than any metropolis I've lived in before or since, a rich Indigenous culture, and you could still feel the spirits of Frida Kahlo, Diego Rivera, Leon Trotsky, and Tina Modotti. Leon Felipe roamed Colonia Cuauhtemoc with his black beret and memories of Spain, writing poetry that brought the war for his country's soul into painful focus. Mexico welcomed refugees from everywhere."[3] Randall determined to move to Mexico City, and a few months after her initial visit, departed with Gregory in late summer 1961 from New York on a Greyhound bus. An outsider to conventional American society, Randall found a welcoming home for a "refugee" such as herself in Mexico. In this chapter I shall review her creation of the seminal literary magazine *El*

*Corno Emplumado*, her dedication to the feminist movement, and the ways Mexico—for example the "meditation on ruins" which became a pervasive Beat trope—appears in her prose and poetry.

While the male Beats are well represented in a variety of anthologies, histories of Beat literature, and university course offerings on the American counterculture, female members of the movement have been marginalized. Over the past two decades however, this lacuna has begun to be ameliorated with the publication of several books, including Brenda Knight's *Women of the Beat Generation* (2000); Nancy M. Grace and Ronna C. Johnson's *Breaking the Rule of Cool: Interviewing and Reading Women Beat Writers* (2004); and Anne Waldman and Laura Wright's *Beats at Naropa: An Anthology* (2009). Recently, Spanish-language monographs have also appeared, such as *Female Beatness: Mujeres, genero y poesia en la generacion Beat* by Isabela Castelao-Gomez and Natalia Carbajosa Palmero (2019). As Eleanor Elson Heginbotham observes in "Witnesses, Wanderers, and Writers: Women on the 'Beat' Road," Beat women "were powerful and self-constructing women who would carve out their own careers in writing, art, drama, and, in almost all cases, in political activism as well." There has also been renewed attention to figures such as Anne McKeever (1928–2002), an artist, model, photographer, and Beat poet who lived near Lake Chapala in Ajijic. However, although Margaret Randall is depicted in three photographs in Fred W. McDarrah's *Kerouac and Friends: A Beat Generation Album* (1985) and a selection of her poems appeared in Richard Peabody's anthology *A Different Beat: Writings by Women of the Beat Generation* (1997), her life and work—although still unknown to many readers—are central to the Beat relationship to Mexico. Randall has continued her early 1956 Beat connection to the present day. In "Notes from Mexico" which Randall contributed to Ed Dorn's magazine *Wild Dog*, she recalls that in 1965, on his way to Cuba, Allen Ginsberg arrived "one night to spend three days, great talk, reading, recording of new work and the beautiful tantric chants learned last year in India, his gentleness permeating the house, reaching the kids, his electric tooth brush tried out all around." Ginsberg had hoped to visit the places in Mexico City where he had spent time with Jack Kerouac, William S. Burroughs, Lucien Carr, Bill Garver, and Joan Vollmer, writing that the city still possessed the redolent aroma of "Mex Tabac and detritus and tropic earth perfume"—but he was unable to tour the city due to an illness.

Thomas Merton (1915–1968)—the Trappist monk who had several ties to the counterculture chronicled in Angus Stuart's essay "Merton and the Beats"—thought highly of Randall's poems. In a letter composed on January 28, 1966, Merton discusses Randall (whom he refers to as "Meg") as well as the Chilean "anti-poet" Nicanor Parra (1914–2018): "Parra seems to me to be a lot lighter on his feet than the gummy and heavy type of thing (at least so it seems to me) we are getting around here. That's why I like Meg's poems, they are less 'heavy.' Ginsberg is articulate but somehow he seems to me to be emotionally or spiritually or something gooey, viscous. I do not deny that he is a very fine poet." In December 1967, Randall read her poetry with Lenore Kandel and Lew Welch at a "Poetry Fiesta" held in Glide Memorial Church, San Francisco. She edited *Poesia Beat* (1977), which included selections by Allen Ginsberg, Jack Kerouac, Lawrence Ferlinghetti, Gregory Corso, and Leroi Jones translated into Spanish, and in an appendix titled "*Nueve poemas mas, de otros tantos poetas beat*," she included Peter Orlovsky, Philip Whalen, John Wieners, Barbara Moraff, Diane di Prima, Jack Spicer, Michael McClure, and Gary Snyder. In her introduction to the volume written in April 1969 in Mexico City, Randall asserted: "The Beat generation constituted one kind of rejection—among many others—of the American Way of Life: it was a group of 'prophets,' a school—or path—of poetry. As literature, it breaks with the English Victorian tradition in a much more public way than the experiments, forty years earlier, of William Carlos Williams, Ezra Pound and others." More recently, Randall edited *Los Beat: Poesia de la Rebellion* (2019). Both anthologies of Beat poetry feature Randall's thoughtful introductions, thus delineating the connection of her own life and career with Beat literary traditions and values. Randall also composed a poem, "I Am Waiting," for Lawrence Ferlinghetti on his ninety-sixth birthday in the style of Ferlinghetti's celebrated eponymous poem, and in 2016, Randall attended the Beat & Beyond Conference in New York City; Ferlinghetti and Diane di Prima were unable to participate, but Randall was joined at the symposium by Michael McClure and Hettie Jones. Randall has also taught at Naropa University—the Jack Kerouac School of Disembodied Poetics—in Boulder, Colorado. It is also evident that Randall identified with the transnational orientation of the Beats: she celebrated the unity of world cultures in her many travels to places including Cuba, Nicaragua, Greece, Jordan, Peru, Honduras, and Mexico.

A prolific author, feminist, and political activist with more than one hundred and fifty books to her credit, Randall has composed poetry, stories, essays, memoirs, worked as a translator, and created several collections of photographs. Her groundbreaking magazine *El Corno Emplumado* (January 1962–July 1969) was vital in the dissemination of knowledge about Mexico for the counterculture and became a vital source where Beats and

Surrealists—as well as the then unknown Los Angeles writer Charles Bukowski—submitted poems, essays, translations, letters, photographs, and artwork. Harris Feinsod in *The Poetry of the Americas: From Good Neighbors to Countercultures* observed that Ernesto Cardenal regarded *El Corno Emplumado* as representing "'la verdadera Union Panamericana' (the true Pan-American Union)" and that Randall had thereby created an important bridge between the literatures of the Americas.[4] Thomas Merton was invited by Randall to contribute to *El Corno Emplumado*, and he replied in a letter dated January 15, 1963, that "Ernesto [Cardenal] sent me some of the earlier issues and I find it lively and full of good ideas. To begin with a bilingual Latin-American literary magazine like this is most necessary, and can fulfill a great function. . . . I am personally convinced that the best American poetry is written in Latin America." Citing Octavio Paz and Cesar Vallejo, Merton went on to tell Randall: "One feels that in Latin America the voice of the poet has significance because it has something to do with life." Allen Ginsberg's "Howl" and "Kaddish" appeared in Spanish translations in *El Corno Emplumado*. Octavio Paz contributed poetry, and drawings of the British Surrealist Leonora Carrington also appeared in its pages. Hermann Hesse sent an unpublished poem, while Henry Miller contributed a section from his unfinished *Nexus II* to the ninth issue, which appeared in January 1964. Julio Cortazar was a supporter, as were Samuel Beckett and Norman Mailer. During *El Corno*'s nearly eight years in existence, thirty-one 100- to 250-page issues—one issue was produced every three months—were printed with an average run of two thousand copies.

Philip Lamantia had helped artist Bruce Conner—Conner would provide the cover art for Lamantia's *Destroyed Works* (1962)—and his wife Jean in October 1961 to come to Mexico City, where they settled in the Juarez neighborhood. Lamantia also became a significant figure in Randall's literary life in Mexico during this period. Randall had given a reading in New York City at a coffeehouse in the Village in a series sponsored by the poet Paul Blackburn where she met Lamantia for the first time: she described him as a "visionary Catholic poet." Lamantia told her to contact him when she came to Mexico in fall 1961, and she and the Mexican poet Sergio Mondragon met at Lamantia's residence in the Zona Rosa in the Colonia Cuauhtemoc: Randall and Mondragon would later marry and settle in Prado Churubusco, on the south side of Mexico City. The Lamantia apartment—presided over by the poet and his wife Lucille—became an international literary salon. Randall recalled that "Mexico's Juan Martinez and Carlos Cofeen Serpas were often there. Ernesto Cardenal arrived from Nicaragua: this was long before he took his priest's vows. Raquel Jodorowsky visited from Peru. Among the U.S. Americans I remember Harvey Wolin and Howard Frankl. Through seemingly endless nights we read to one another, often barely understanding the other's language and almost always missing hidden historical and cultural references. It soon became clear that we needed a forum where we could read new work in the original and in translation, a form free of the strictures so often imposed by the academies or schools then in vogue."[5] Mexican poet Homero Aridjis, Leonora Carrington, Bonnie and Ray Bremser, ruth weiss, and photographer Anne McKeever spent time in the Colonia Cuauhtemoc.

Randall noted that a question which confronted her at this point was: "What did we, from the North, know of Vallejo, of Neruda, much less the expression of our more contemporary Latin American brothers and sisters? What did these poets and writers, whose medium was Spanish, know of our Williams, Pound, Creeley, Blackburn?"[6] Randall clarified the origin of the name of her journal: "I know we talked about creating a title that would reflect the best of the creative contributions made north and south of the border. In the US, we felt that jazz was a major contribution, thus the jazz horn or *corno*. In the south, cultural history was still very much influenced by the pre-Columbian gods and myths, thus the plumes of Quetzalcoatl."[7] Thus jazz music—a central focus of the Beats—and the feathers of ancient Mexico's greatest god Quetzalcoatl were united in a single symbol to represent a bridge between the nascent American counterculture and the history of Mexico. The title of Randall's journal is also significant because it signals the omnipresence of Quetzalcoatl in Beat literature: as we shall see in the following chapters, several Beats including Michael McClure—McClure devoted an entire poem to recounting the Quetzalcoatl narrative—invoke the legendary Feathered Serpent in their writings. Jerome Rothenberg's *The Flight of Quetzalcoatl* (1967) is Rothenberg's translation from the original Aztec via Bernardino de Sahagun's initial translation and Angel Maria Garibay's later Spanish prose version. The surrealist Benjamin Péret, who spent nearly eight years in Mexico, wrote *L'Air Mexican* (1952), translated the Maya collection of calendrical, historical, mythic, and prophetic texts known as *Chilam Balam*—*Le livre du Chilam Balam* (1955)—and compiled *Anthologie des mythes, legends et contes populaires d'Amerique* (1960), pondered the meaning of Quetzalcoatl: "One may also concede that Quetzalcoatl has preserved across the centuries his form as a plumed serpent because his creation expresses a point of equilibrium, precarious without a doubt, between opposing tendencies and contradictory human activities. Under this aspect, he symbolizes in effect the end of the struggle between the eagle and the serpent." Indeed, the present-day Mexican flag depicts an eagle vanquishing a snake, thus presenting a variation on the plumed serpent iconography.[8]

Randall in "Quetzalcoatl: 1961"—dedicated to her husband Sergio Mondragon—which appeared in the first January 1962 issue of *El Corno Emplumado*, invoked the mighty god in a strikingly contemporary fashion:

will we ever
know you
Quetzalcoatl, hanging
in the air / weight

on the faces
of those remaining
Plumed Serpent
whose heart

dismembered itself
to light the sky,
even now / your Mexico
has become

the last bomb shelter
those who followed
stepped on
your MYTH and

looked the other way.
they want to
light the sky too
Quetzalcoatl

your light
is not enough
for them, they
want
to make
a big light
O God:
such a big light

O Serpent:
AND TURN IT OFF!

Randall warns of the threat of nuclear annihilation and the ways humanity has abandoned Quetzalcoatl—"stepped on/your MYTH"—and gone down the path of self-destruction. In the myth, Quetzalcoatl sets himself afire, and as his ashes fly up toward the heavens, his heart, also rising up into the sky, is transformed into the second planet from the sun, Venus, the morning star. Randall retells this section of the narrative as the "Plumed Serpent/whose heart/dismembered itself/to light the sky." However, modern Mexico—indeed the entire world—has lost its connections with the creative powers of poetic transformation and has turned into "the last bomb shelter," as Randall suggests the possibility of nuclear apocalypse. The poem was composed at the height of the Cold War in 1961: the Cuban Missile Crisis, during which America and the U.S.S.R. came within a hair's breadth of mutual annihilation, occurred the following year, on October 16–28, 1962. Contemporary humanity also seeks to "light the sky," not through the altruistic act of self-sacrifice which Quetzalcoatl performed but rather through the chaos and fire of atomic and hydrogen bombs. An early poem, it is not as technically adept as Randall's later work, yet it successfully conveys through the juxtaposition of contemporary chaos with ancient Mexican myth the sense of alienation which defined the Beat generation and gave birth to works such as Gregory Corso's celebrated 1958 antiwar poem, "Bomb."

Randall's absorption in the mythology and poetry of Mexico was typical of the Beats, and *El Corno Emplumado* was significant for its early promulgation of the "ethnopoetics" movement which emphasized translations and adaptations from world Indigenous cultures. The April 1964 issue featured poems from the Comanche, Paiute, Arapahoe, Ojibway, Sioux, Tlingit, as well as the Maya and Otomi. *El Corno Emplumado* was also noteworthy for showcasing work by women. The first issue of January 1962 included "El culto magico de una virgin" by Randall's close friend, the anthropologist Laurette Sejourne—author of *Burning Water: Thought and Religion in Ancient Mexico* (1960)—who explored the "mysteries" of the great archaeological site Monte Alban, in Santa Cruz Xoxocotlan, Oaxaca. In the January 1963 issue, "In Search of the Lost Culture" by Sejourne appeared accompanied by illustrations from the Borgia, Nuttall, Dresden, Fejervarvy, and Borbonicus Codices. Sejourne's lyrical and philosophical style in this essay—which Randall herself translated into English—is apparent when she declares: "It is obvious that the prodigious vitality of prehispanic thought does not lie in anything less than the fact that it went to the deepest roots of human reality. And it is without a doubt this depth, which elevates to the realm of the universal the language with which they transmitted their great vision of the world." Sejourne became a significant figure in Randall's life in Mexico City. Randall recalls their friendship in her book of essays *More Than Things* (2013) as well as in her recent *My Life in 100 Objects* (2020). Here Randall recalls in the chapter "Small Clay Head from Teotihuacan, Mexico" receiving from Sejourne from one of her archaeological explorations what may have been the head of a child's doll: "It measures two inches by an inch and a half. She said it was a minor artifact that would be disposed of or returned to the earth if no one wanted it. It is not minor to me, but symbolic of a people and their culture. I have kept it close ever since." Randall also honors Sejourne in "Laurette at Teotihuacan" which chronicles a day when Randall, her son Gregory, and Sejourne spent time at Teotihuacan: "You try to explain this Palace of the Butterflies,/how ordinary houses spill their secrets,/completing a city/ crowned by pyramids. Sun, Moon./A world you see but struggle to explain/ against official rhetoric." Randall laments the ways scholarship by women has been devalued by the male establishment: "Teotihuacan, where you offer imagination/and I begin to learn what it means/to understand too much/in a world that values tradition/and the ideas of men/over female wisdom, female risk." Sejourne's career exemplifies the ways women scholars have been sidelined by men and their accomplishments often left unacknowledged.

As a feminist and revolutionary, Randall's political beliefs were destined to bring her to the attention of the authorities: the success of *El Corno Emplumado* was to come to an abrupt halt. In October 1968, Randall and Mondragon participated in the student movement in Mexico City, and the government funding of *El Corno Emplumado* was suspended. The XIX Olympiad was set to begin on October 18. On the night of September 7, 1968, Lawrence Ferlinghetti observed a rally of student revolutionaries taking place at the University of Oaxaca. Three days later on September 10, Ferlinghetti was in Mexico City when he went to the University of Mexico campus with editors and poets from *El Corno Emplumado*. The area was now occupied. They walked, Ferlinghetti recalled, "through the barricades into the buildings held by the students like Cuba 1960 with young cats in fatigues & chicks with rifles."[9] On October 2, student protestors gathered on the Plaza de Tlatelolco to voice their grievances to the government. The response was chilling: hundreds were murdered by police and troops.[10] 1968 was the year of worldwide youth rebellion, the dawning of the "Age of Aquarius," and in his novel *Love in the Days of Rage* (1988), Ferlinghetti observed: "Down in the streets a little revolution was giving birth to much hope and euphoria, not just in France but around the world, in the U.S., in Germany and Italy and Mexico City, in Prague, in Portugal, everywhere there was a stirring, more than a stirring, a new spirit, a seething spirit."[11] Ferlinghetti includes in his travelogue *The Mexican Night* a letter "Concerning the Suppression of *El Corno Emplumado*" by Margaret Randall and Robert Cohen, who pointed out that by 1968, their publication received approximately a third of its funding from various subsidies from the Mexican government, and following the killings in Plaza de Tlatelolco: "All magazines in Mexico that dared to cry out against these events immediately suffered withdrawal of subsidy. . . . The repression we have suffered is nothing next to what has been happening to other brothers and sisters in Mexico." After *El Corno Emplumado* was shut down, Randall left Mexico City for Cuba, then lived in Nicaragua, and finally returned to the United States on a tourist visa. She then applied for resident status in order to reclaim her American citizenship. Randall was denied by the Immigration and Naturalization Service, which invoked the 1952 McCarran-Walter Act and ordered her deported in 1985. Randall was accused of expressing in her work opinions "against the good order and happiness of the United States." Randall won her case in 1989.[12]

Randall composed a poem in four sections entitled "Feet Still Run: Tlatelolco, October 2, 1968," and part 1 depicts the carnage perpetrated upon the protestors:

> *Se les paso la mano* I heard someone say,
> *they went too far*: irony as release
> as if anyone believed
> they'd fired to disperse the crowd.
>
> It was early. We didn't know
> the number of victims,
> didn't know we would never know
> who died that day.
>
> White arm bands moving through the crowd,
> bullets shattering air
> over Aztec stone, between colonial walls
> and modern apartment blocks.

Feet still run in every direction
leaving shoes, a beret, a handbag
trampled in the *Plaza de las tres culturas*
as the trapped still fight their way

Into buildings, pound on doors, plead
with terrified neighbors
locked down against sudden war,
cutting lights, swallowing fear,

retreating to silence, pretending
the stairwells aren't sticky with blood
bodies aren't piled on bodies
two stories high.

Randall's disbelief that the troops had "fired to disperse the crowd" was repeated less than two years later in the United States when the Ohio National Guard on May 4, 1970, killed four and wounded nine unarmed student protestors at Kent State University. At the close of the poem, the lesson Randall takes from the slaughter of the Mexican students is: "What power is capable of/when threatened." The special forces of the government attacked using high-caliber weapons and tanks: the official death toll was twenty-six, but according to other sources it was as high as one thousand. She speaks with a "Tarahumara man/who ran a thousand kilometers south/to lend his community's support:/'We've always known what they've done to us/but when they murder/their own sons and daughters/we know they are evil.'" The symbolism of a man from the Tarahumara—the people with whom Antonin Artaud had spent several ecstatic months and renowned for their amazing stamina as long-distance runners——racing 620 miles to support the uprising against the oppressive power of the Mexican government is a moving reminder of the power of political solidarity. Randall acknowledges that every year on October 2, she re-experiences the trauma of that day in Mexico City, waking in the morning and "remembering/what I cannot forget/have never forgotten." "Feet Still Run: Tlatelolco, October 2, 1968" is an elegy memorializing not only those mercilessly murdered but also a threnody recording the sense of loss during an idealistic time in world history when there was still hope for a revolution in human consciousness and an affirmation of the powers of love and community.

That the trauma of this event made an indelible impact on Randall is evident for she returns to the theme several times in her work. In "A Day Like This" from *She Becomes Time* (2016), Randall remembers: "On a day like this we gathered peacefully/At Mexico City's Plaza of Three Cultures,/Circle of concrete apartment blocks/And righteous colonial church/Built over ruins of Aztec glory./Loudspeakers carried the rousing static/Of speeches until gunfire tossed bodies/In piles of before and after,/Turned history on itself."[13] In 1968, Randall published a book entitled *Los "Hippies": Expresion de una crisis*, and this tragedy of 1968 in Mexico City seemed indeed to mark a crisis point, to be the final blow to the idealistic dreams of the Beats and the American counterculture of social justice for African Americans, women, and gays and an end to the war in Vietnam in a year that had already seen the assassination of Martin Luther King Jr. in April; the murder of Robert F. Kennedy in June; and the rioting and violence of the Chicago police at the Democratic National Convention in August. And now in October—every two months with numbing regularity it seems in retrospect—there was another setback to dreams of social justice and freedom, this time in Mexico. Now the violence of gunfire had "turned history on itself" just as gains had begun to be made for oppressed minorities and women in America.

During her time in Mexico, the plight of women had been at the heart of Randall's revolutionary trajectory, and the Beats have rightly been accused of excluding women from their "club" and of misogyny. Randall often singles out Mexican women such as Sor Juana Inés de la Cruz, Frida Kahlo, and photographer Tina Modotti (1896–1942) as inspiring exemplars of independent, vital, and creative women. In "Through Broken Shards of Earth" from *She Becomes Time*, Randall reflects: "Centuries beyond her life, Sor Juana stares at me/Or Frida laughs and swings her missing leg,/Their eyes interrogate my time as I do theirs." In her recently published autobiography, *I Never Left Home: Poet, Feminist, Revolutionary* (2020), Randall recalls: "Living in a tremendously sexist society, toward the end of my time in Mexico I experienced a shift in gender consciousness that changed me profoundly. It was 1968–1969, and the early texts of Second Wave feminism were beginning to trickle down from the north. I read those texts, and something clicked." Randall was living in Mexico City as the feminist revolution in America began to gain full force and was at the vanguard of the movement in Mexico with the publication of her book *Las mujeres* (1970) along with artists such as Leonora Carrington. Carrington painted a poster in 1972 for the women's liberation movement entitled *Mujeres Conciencia* (*Women's Awareness*) which depicts

Eve and Quetzalcoatl in the act of a mutual sharing of sacred knowledge, thus overturning the patriarchal Christian view of Eve/Woman as a destructive, sinister force and creating a new, affirmative symbolism based on Aztec myth. On the back of the painting, Carrington inscribed: "Winged Cihuacoatl (snake woman)/Quetzalcoatl sacred serpent hermaphrodite/rises again in the tree of life where/Eve gives Eve back the fruit/of Wisdom/Women take back the original wisdom."

Randall's commitment to the oppressed and forgotten of Mexico is a central focus of her prose and poetry. "Angelita, little angel" recounts the dark fate of a child prostitute in Mexico City who carries her younger brother "curled in the frayed cloth/of her *rebozo*, smelling of fresh cornmeal/and dried urine, moving in unison/with her sister who walks her territory/on this Mexico City street: broad sidewalk/not quite to the corner where her fiefdom ends/and another child's begins. Back and forth,/slowly, squatting from time to time/against the great wall of Aztec stone,/ancestral temple now Ministry of Public Works/in a country where little angels are/as common as the scent of fresh *tortillas*." Randall creates in the reader a profound sympathy for this exploited child, mirroring the daily treadmill of her existence through the effective employment of enjambed verses carrying us along with her as she treads the streets, "back and forth."[14] The Aztec history of Mexico City is counterpointed with modernity as an ancient temple has been converted into a government building and we witness "modern tourist buses lumbering/through ancient streets." This juxtaposition of ancient and modern is a common technique in the work of Beat writers on Mexico, for even though a modern metropolis like Mexico City appears to be overrun by steel and glass skyscrapers, those imposing buildings are often erected upon the remains of the great Aztec civilization. So here too, Angelita, the descendant of a once proud people, has been deracinated and plies her sad trade—her life and the lives of her sister *angelitas* have been commodified and made as expendable and easily available as "fresh *tortillas*"—along streets filled with blithe tourists on holiday.

Randall's experiences in Mexico during the sixties are also reflected in "The Boy with the Mayan Face," a four-and-a-half-page tale collected in *Part of the Solution: Portrait of a Revolutionary* (1973). Here as in "Angelita, little angel," Randall turns her attention to the youth of Mexico, for the story narrates an encounter with a twelve-year-old boy afflicted with epilepsy. In "The Boy with the Mayan Face," Randall demonstrates a command of swift and economical storytelling, illustrating she is capable of composing prose as fine as her poetry.

*Brothers, Chiapas, 2007,* courtesy of Margaret Randall

The narrative begins: "If you think of it, you seek them out, you find them, you see them—many such faces—it's the remnants of a race powerful enough to have lived in Palenque, complete enough to have invented Zero. . . . It was up a small embankment along the highway to Acapulco, exactly eight kilometers south of Chilpancingo, dusty dry afternoon, six o'clock when the car started going bad. . . . This place was called Petaquillas, Guerrero." Randall prepares the reader for the meeting to come by creating suspense: whoever she meets will be the descendant of historical greatness, relative of a group of gifted people who created Palenque and intellectually brilliant in their invention of new concepts in mathematics and astronomy. As in "Angelita, little angel," Randall contrasts past with present, ancient historical greatness with contemporary loss and grief, Aztec and Maya with modern Mexico. She supplies precise details concerning the location and time of her dramatic experience to assure the reader of its verisimilitude, to dispel any doubt that what she is about to reveal actually happened: "exactly eight kilometers south of Petaquillas, Guerrero"; "six o'clock." Petaquillas was known in pre-Hispanic times as Ayacapitzatlan or Yacapitzatlan—in Nahuatl, "place of the thin nose"—thus setting the scene for the atavistic encounter which follows.

The narrator stops in Petaquillas to repair her car and again describes her geographical location: "The road curved back towards Chilpancingo behind us, Iguala behind us, the Canyon del Zopolote—canyon of vultures—behind us and the mountains hiding Ameyaltepec, Mexica, Mazcala. . . . Before us the road stretched up across the last mountains before the sea—darkness settled and we could see the first faint lights of other cars moving up along the road that humped into the sky, disappearing on the other side of those dark brown mounds to complete the hundred and twenty kilometers to Acapulco, city of bought luxury."[15] This hymning of place names in Mexico recurs, as we shall see in chapter 7, in Bonnie Bremser's *Troia: Mexican Memoirs,* for Bremser also exhibits immense pleasure in the music of these exotic—to a foreigner—often ancient place names with their flow of unusual *z, x,* and plosive *p* sounds. The narrator travels through Mexico by automobile, she is "on the road," and several details in Randall's prose—*the road stretched, mountains, sea, sky, darkness, settled*—recall the close of Jack Kerouac's *On the Road* where Kerouac sings "all that road going": "So in America when the sun goes down and I sit on the old broken-down river pier watching the long, long skies over New Jersey and sense all that raw land that rolls in one unbelievable huge bulge over to the West Coast, and all that road going." Thus Randall, like Kerouac, creates a hushed mood of expectation, an expectant sense of a possible revelation to come hidden in the beckoning Mexican landscape.

As a mechanic works on her broken automobile, the narrator notices a "Boy." "Boy" is capitalized throughout to lend his presence an allegorical power; he is at once nameless and universal. He comes quite close to the window where she is sitting on the driver's side of the car: "He was terribly thin and small and his dark brown head, the exact Mayan features, the very oval black and white eyes, could have been a living mask in the Museum of Anthropology. At once, he was a descendant." She is obviously struck by the archaic, primal power of his presence, recalling the images of the ancient Maya preserved in stone and iconography throughout Mexico. Visitors to Mexico are sometimes amazed when they behold with their own eyes the historical continuity between the supposed vanished Maya and Aztecs, the magnificent works of art which recorded their daily lives, and the people who actually still live in Mexico today—the living descendants. They have not vanished or become extinct, they have not disappeared, they have not been conquered by the Spaniards: they are carrying on their ancestral traditions and still speak their ancient languages. The hushed tone continues as the traveler describes his "very fragile" arms which hang inert along his "thin sides but when he slowly moved them, brought them up slowly in some slow-motion gesture, they contained the limits of everything."[16] This last phrase—"the limits of everything"—now ascribes to the Boy a hint of supernatural powers, a sense that he hides a secret which has not yet been fully revealed.

The Boy then says "*Estoy de pedido*"—"I am asking"—and informs her he is an epileptic. They begin to converse: "As he readied his answers to my questions his face moved up and around, his eyes traveled out in lengths we only sometimes touch." Again Randall emphasizes the intuition which allows the Boy access to "the limits of everything," now sensed as a kind of magical visual perception and insight unavailable to the rest of humanity. "Limits of everything" and "traveled out in lengths" both suggest expanses of space and time open to those gifted with imaginative powers. The fact that he is an epileptic is significant, for among the ancient Greeks, epilepsy was known as "the sacred disease," a sign that the sufferer had been gifted supernatural powers symbolized by bodily spasms which the epileptic "fit" reveals. The visitor feels "assaulted by the impact of a certain kind of knowledge. The creature was telling me something and I was trying to listen. I wanted to listen as hard as I could." The Boy informs her he is one of four brothers and the narrator experiences a moment of illumination:

> The gray-brown earth became part of the sky, part of the earth, the sky came down to the earth and became part of it, there was no noticeable becoming, in fact, it was suddenly all one and the only lights were the awkward mechanic's lamp shining at intervals through the space between the engine and the raised hood, the occasional tiny moving lights which were cars crossing the wide hills above and before us to Acapulco, and the great full round yellow moon directly above us.
>
> At that moment I gave the Boy one orange. I took the orange from a bag of twenty or thirty oranges we had in the car and I put the orange in his hand and the Boy drew in his breath, I could hear the effort in that act, and all of a piece without stopping without stuttering or beginning again he said "Dios te bendiga"—God bless you. And he was gone. Suddenly he wasn't there anymore. After the Boy left there were other adventures not part of this story.[17]

In cosmogonic myth, creation occurs through the meeting of heavens and earth, as we note here: "The gray-brown earth became part of the sky." Something is in the act of creation, of "becoming," and this instant of self-knowledge is accompanied by a proliferation of light imagery: "lights," "mechanic's lamp," "tiny moving lights," "the great full round yellow moon." The tale is dreamlike, the narrative thus allowing us to experience a kind of "once upon a time"—what Mircea Eliade named the *in illo tempore* of myth, "in that time"—a universal, archetypal story localized in Mexico. The events are told realistically, yet Randall creates a sense of magical occurrences, the world as a place of revelation. One may interpret the car breaking down as symbolizing the rush of modern "civilization" coming to a momentary halt to open up for the narrator a moment of communion with this mysterious Christ- or Buddha-like Boy—his fragility and sense of holiness suggest an image of "Beat" in the sense of "Beatitude," an encounter with the angelic and transcendent: Allen Ginsberg, we remember, called his friends "angel-headed hipsters," and in "Sakyamuni Coming Out from the Mountain" Ginsberg imagines the Buddha "in ragged soft robes/wearing a fine beard,/unhappy hands/clasped to his naked breasts—/humility is beatness/humility is beatness."

In "The Boy with the Mayan Face," Randall exemplifies the Beat struggle during their Mexican journeys against "appropriation"—the desire to master or "interpret" the "Other"—and thus reduce the stranger to an amalgam of one's own prejudices and stereotypes. At one end of the spectrum is idealization, in which one attributes to the "Other" qualities perceived as lacking in one's self, thus the "Noble Savage" who is pristine and incarnates all the best human qualities. At the other end is prejudice and racism, in which one does not "see "the "Other" at all, but rather only a reflection of one's own preconceptions. At its worst, this impulse becomes the desire ultimately to reduce, dominate, or destroy the "Other." Georg Wilhelm Friedrich Hegel's celebrated "Master and Slave" narrative (sections 178–196) in *Phäenomenologie des Geistes* (1807)—*The Phenomenology of Mind*—posits that the Master needs the Slave to achieve a sense of identity, a self; he or she appears to be an autonomous, powerful entity, but the Master in fact is dependent on the Other to achieve selfhood. This may lead to a struggle to the death for recognition, for each member of the "relationship" is locked into an inescapable vulnerability. We see the results of seeing the Other as an Object to be reduced to the hegemony of the Subject in Jean-Paul Sartre's famous pronouncement "hell is other people." Hegel's insight became central to later theorizing concerning the "Other" by philosopher Emmanuel Levinas (1906–1995). Yet Levinas turns Hegel upside down and asserts that we must serve the Other, we must be responsible to the Other, we must be attentive to and respectful of the Other, we must honor reciprocity. Prior to other abstract philosophical problems should be our ethical duty to our fellow human beings. Levinas writes in *Totality and Infinity* of the face:

> The face resists possession, resists my powers. In its epiphany, in expression, the sensible, still graspable, turns into total resistance to the grasp. This mutation can occur only by the opening of a new dimension. For the resistance to the grasp is not produced as an insurmountable resistance, like the hardness of the rock

> against which the effort of the hand comes to naught, like the remoteness of the star in the immensity of space. The expression the face introduces into the world does not defy the feebleness of my powers, but my ability for power. The face, still a thing among things, breaks through the form that nevertheless delimits it. This means concretely: the face speaks to me and thereby invites me to a relation incommensurate with a power exercised, be it power or knowledge.[18]

It is precisely the "Face" in "The Boy with the Mayan Face" to which the narrator responds so intensely. She does not ask what she may *take* from him but what she may *give* to him; not what she can *possess* but how she can *respond*; she seeks not *power* but *love*. At the close, the Boy blesses her—*Dios te bendiga, God bless you*—creating a perfect circle of reciprocity. The narrator wants to *listen*, she is "assaulted by the impact of a certain kind of knowledge. The creature was telling me something and I was trying to listen. I wanted to listen as hard as I could." The *Chandogya Upanishad* speaks of *Tat Tvam Asi*, "Thou are That," as does Martin Buber regarding the "I-Thou" relationship in which the Other is not an exterior object but rather the Self in another form. There is also the suggestion of a Gnostic, mystical moment—Gnosticism was a central fascination for the Beats—in the phrase "a certain kind of knowledge." "Gnostic" derives from ancient Greek *gnosis*, "knowledge": not "rational" or "intellectual" knowledge but rather the flash of intuition which opens up to us our true selves. This attitude also marks Randall's relationship to the archaeological marvels of Mexico where she also seeks to "listen" for what "knowledge" they may reveal to her rather than to impose on them preconceived notions about their meaning and significance.

After the Spanish conquered and colonized Mexico, there emerged a vast class and racial divide. Following Mexican independence, as Joanna O'Connell has documented, "the efforts of Mexican intellectuals and politicians to fashion a story of unity from the complex history of colonial dominance and enforced difference grew from a colonial Creole intellectual tradition in which the Indigenous was always thought of as Other even as that same tradition worked to appropriate a pre-Columbian past as its own." This effort to reconstruct the narrative of the "Indian" in Mexico to accord with a new notion of Mexican national identity created by the colonialists—known as *Indigenismo*—of course failed. Jose Vasconcelos Calderon in *La raza cosmica* (1925) expounded the idea of a "fifth race" of the future in which "racial division" would be transcended. In a sense, Randall's relationship with the Mayan Boy dramatizes her attempt to disentangle herself from this history—as a visitor from another imperial power, the United States—of colonial "othering" of the Indigenous peoples of Mexico. As O'Connell correctly perceives, this tension between separating oneself from the "Indigenous" while simultaneously striving to "appropriate" is typical of the ways "identity" and "difference" are negotiated, and cultural imperialism is an issue with which Beat visitors to Mexico also struggled.

This sensation of "Otherness" may move in the opposite direction as well. For example, Randall recalled concerning her arrival with infant son Gregory in Mexico: "There, my son and I were other in ways as confusing as they were challenging. I was the gringa woman, desirable as well as disreputable, even dangerous. A single mother in a place where the condition was certainly less acceptable than it had been in New York, I possessed that aura of white exoticism even as I was a constant reminder of supposed superiority and conquest. My son was the beautiful little blonde boy exclaimed over by everyone who saw him." This, as we shall see in chapter 7, would be precisely the reception accorded Bonnie Bremser's daughter Rachel in Mexico where Rachel often became "an object of worship, our white baby." In Randall's work we can appreciate the ways "Otherness" can be experienced by both the visitor and the resident of a foreign land as well as how we must be alert to the ways we categorize people from different cultures. Randall collaborated with feminist biologist Ruth Hubbard on a book entitled *The Shape of Red: Insider/Outsider Reflections* (1988), in which she pondered the complexities of Self/Other and the ways "many of us move between feelings of belonging and wishing to remain outside a cultural milieu that may feel safe but also stultifying." This is a push-pull dynamic which held true for virtually all Beat travelers to Mexico—and for all humans everywhere—in which one experiences a self in flux, in which one's own sense of identity is challenged through the encounter with that which is "different" and the ways one's presence may also challenge others.

In both the poetry and prose we have examined thus far, Randall is superb at evoking the lives of Mexico's Indigenous peoples. She also draws comparisons between the Zapatista revolution and her own history as the grandchild of Jews who suffered during the Holocaust as we see in the poem "The Difference": "these still earth gods/chamulas huixtecos zinacatecos/rub their bare legs/with the oil of the jungle nuts, walk/the chiapaneco mountains/those legs glistening, shining/in strong sun, cutting black/through fifty kinds of green/those great wide faces close to me in the market of/san cristobal de las casas, eye to eye." The verses are striking for their effective alliteration of "c," "s," and "t" sounds in evoking "these still earth gods." Randall watches the natives of Chiapas looking at her and then reports: "i return the same cold unmoving eyes/caught for one weight of time, one/question, the old jews/still moving in my past, move/today, have never stopped." The repetition of "eye" and the fact that Randall does not capitalize "i" suggest a kind of pun on the way her own sense of selfhood—her "I"—has been reduced to a lowercase letter as she feels a sense of guilt in witnessing the anguish of the people of Chiapas and receiving their gaze "eye to eye." The oppression of Chiapas, which gave birth on New Year's Day 1994 to Subcomandante Marcos and the Zapatista liberation movement, is the background of this poem. In his essay "Time Bombs," Noam Chomsky pointed out that these uprisings on New Year's Day "coincided with the enactment of the North American Free Trade Agreement (NAFTA). The Zapatista army called NAFTA a 'death sentence' for Indians, a gift to the rich that will deepen the divide between narrowly concentrated wealth and mass misery, destroying what remains of their indigenous society." Randall viscerally experiences the suffering of the people of Chiapas, which recalls to her the trauma of her own Jewish ancestors during the Holocaust. At the close, she notices one man who "looks down his mayan nose/at me and i move out/in all ways, on all waves,/asking." The poem concludes inconclusively with Randall questioning her own place as an American among "these still earth gods," the people of Chiapas, who are under siege.[19] Other Beat authors such as Lawrence Ferlinghetti also declared solidarity with the Zapatista revolt, and City Lights published a valuable anthology *First World, Ha Ha Ha! The Zapatista Challenge* (1995) exploring the Zapatista Army and the revolt in Chiapas.

The physical landscape of Mexico and its archaeological sites demand the same kind of sensitivity and care that the visitor must cultivate in relation to Mexico's people. In *She Becomes Time* (2016) Randall included a sequence of seven poems devoted to sites along the *Ruta Puuc* as well as evocations of Chichen Itza and Dzibilchaltun. As an epigraph to this section, Randall includes a verse by Nezahualcoyotl in her own translation: "There where death does not exist,/there where it has been vanquished./there is where I will go." "*Alla adonde no hay muerte,/alla donde alle es conquistada,/que alla vaya yo.*" Nezahualcoyotl (1402–1472) was an Aztec philosopher, poet, and the subject of a long poem by Ernesto Cardenal. In her notes, Randall tells us that Nezahualcoyatl "had an experience of meeting an 'Unknown, Unknowable Lord of Everywhere' to whom he built an entirely empty temple in which no blood sacrifices of any kind were allowed—not even those of animals." Indeed, the "Unknown, Unknowable" are states of being which Randall herself seeks to reveal in her expeditions throughout Mexico. The ruins of Mexico became a common trope throughout Beat literature, recalling the greatness of civilizations past, "the ruins of time." The early Beats, Burroughs, Kerouac, and Ginsberg, all read Oswald Spengler's *Der Untergang des Abendlandes—The Decline of the West*—and the sense of impending doom for modern humanity was widespread since World War I and T. S. Eliot's *The Waste Land.* Following World War II, Hiroshima and Nagasaki—Lawrence Ferlinghetti, who served with the U.S. Navy, was horrified during his visit to Nagasaki six weeks after the atomic bomb was dropped—the Cold War, and the Cuban Missile Crisis, the threat of nuclear war haunted the Beats. Gregory Corso's poem "Bomb" was as we observed above a predecessor to Margaret Randall's "Quetzalcoatl: 1961," and "Bomb" influenced the satirical black humor masterpiece, Stanley Kubrick's film *Dr. Strangelove or: How I Learned to Stop Worrying and Love the Bomb* (1964). The Beats were intensely aware of the precarious nature of American life in a country which sought to pretend everything was "normal" and "happy," and the most important activities among white middle-class suburbanites were making money and purchasing material things. Warnings of apocalypse were everywhere, and during the fifties and early sixties, some Americans went so far as to build bomb shelters in their backyards in case of a nuclear attack. The archaeological remains of the Aztecs and Maya thus become a central focus for the Beat "meditation on ruins," both for what these magnificent structures can tell us of these vanished people and as warnings of our own possible fate.

Diane di Prima—although she only made one brief visit to Mexico, a vacation journey to Puerto Vallarta—shared Randall's respectful concern for the original inhabitants of Mexico and lamented the depredations of Mexico's conquerors. In her poem "Montezuma," she reflects on Moctezuma II (ca. 1466–June 29, 1520) and the meaning of the loss of a city: "to give it away, give it up, before they take it from us./not to go down fighting./the hard part comes later/to see the women taken, the young men maimed/the city/no city is built twice/the long wall down at Athens, the olive trees/five hundred years of tillage/burning, 'not these but men'/i.e., mourn/not these/and yet no city is ever built again." Di Prima was perhaps inspired in her threnody for the destruction of Teotihuacan by Charles Olson's notion of the *polis,* the "city," in "Maximus to Gloucester, Letter 27 [withheld]" in which Olson declares: "I have this sense,/that I am one/with my skin . . . /Polis/is this." Di Prima compares the depredations of the conquistadors in Mexico to the destruction of the Long Walls of Athens—which protected the city and connected the ports of Piraeus and Phaleron to Athens—by the Spartans in 403 B.C.E. following Sparta's defeat of Athens during the Peloponnesian War. So too, Mexico was conquered by Cortes, and as di Prima declares, "no city is ever built again." Di Prima also quotes four words—"not these but men"—from Pericles's speech in 432 B.C.E. before the outbreak of the war as chronicled by Thucydides in *The Peloponnesian War*: "And we must not lament for the loss of houses and land, but for men, for these things do not procure for us men, but men these."[20] Di Prima recalls the horror of "the women taken, the young men maimed" and compares the long historical record of war and destruction from ancient Athens to the fall of Moctezuma II at Teotihuacan.

Randall carries on this Beat quest for what the past may tell us about ourselves, devoting several volumes to her expeditions. *Stones Witness* (2007) demonstrates her talents as a photographer with images of Chichen Itza, Palenque, Paquime (Casa Grandes), and the Mogollon site in Chihuahua and Cacaxtla, near the southern border of Tlaxcala. Randall also chronicles her explorations of Kiet Seel—which means "broken pottery" in Navajo—a site of the ancestral Puebloan people in northern Arizona. In the chapter entitled "Like Me," Randall reveals that she has been propelled in her travels by several questions concerning the residents of this spectacular location: "What did they think? How did an average day unfold? How did they love? How did they relate to one another, and what was their relationship with those beyond their canyon, their center of the world?" She goes on to speak of her treks throughout Mexico: "It is not as if I haven't been to other ruins. I have visited many, from the great Mayan citadels of Tikal and Palenque to the seaside retreat of Tulum and Chichen Itza's astonishing ball court . . . the labyrinthine adobe of Paquime on Mexico's northern desert . . . I have stood in the cave at Xochicalco and placed my hand in the ray of pure light descending from the opening high above: midday in June. The bones of my hand came clear as an x-ray negative; my blood surrounding them a rich coral-red." However, not all of Randall's experiences at Mexico's ruins were sublime. She reports a mysterious terror which replicates that of Philip Lamantia when he visited Teotihuacan: "Outside Mexico City, at imposing Teotihuacan, I have experienced the sudden jolting pull of another dimension and had to flee the site, my stomach and bowels threatening to explode with a violence I could only partially decipher."

Furthermore, for the Beats, the increasing commercializing of these sites in Mexico became symbols of how colonialism and the depredations of capitalism continued to wreak havoc on the country. In "Chichen Itza" from *She Becomes Time*, Randall indicts—as does Joanne Kyger—its commercialization: "Today vendors screech like the howlers/Once leaping through these courtyards/Fake a raucous jaguar growl/On whistles made in Taiwan/Shout *comprame comprame*/As they push a gaudy mask at the tourist/Who pleads

Uxmal, Pyramid of the Magician, collection of David Stephen Calonne

*no money* and walks on." Randall laments that Chichen Itza's glorious dynasties have now become "a Disneyland that draws 1.2 million/To stones that will not reveal their secrets/Through the insulting din."[21] Over the past decades, Chichen Itza has become progressively vulgarized. Randall refers to the Indigenous men—the irony is not lost that it is the descendants of the Maya who are reduced to such a humiliating position to earn a leaving [living]—who hawk whistles which they constantly blow on fiercely to imitate the sound of a growling jaguar in hopes of enticing a strolling tourist to make a purchase. Chichen Itza has now been transformed into the equivalent of a Mexican "Disneyland," a "theme park" intended for purposes of entertainment, complete with tickets, places to eat, merchandise on display for sale, and pullulating crowds. Many of the "tourists" who visit the site have little interest in listening to see if the ancient stones will "reveal their secrets."

In "Uxmal"—another visit to a *Ruta Puuc* site chronicled in *She Becomes Time*—Randall continues to question the ways Western explorers and scholars have related to Mexican culture. As an epigraph, she quotes John Lloyd Stephens: "We came at once upon a large open field strewed with mounds of ruins, and vast buildings on terraces, and pyramidal structures, grand and in good preservation, richly ornamented without a bush to obstruct the view, and in picturesque effect almost equal to the ruins of Thebes." Randall's first stanza serves as a sarcastic commentary on Stephens's prejudices: "Even the visitor who loved it most/evoked Old World splendor./impossible to believe/those graceful facades/were conceived by the ancestors/of those who led him to this place."[22] Although Stephens was the first to celebrate the glories of these "newly discovered" marvels of architectural planning, he was beset however by the typical Western prejudice which declares they were "almost equal to the ruins of Thebes." It is inconceivable to Stephens that the Maya possessed creativity and genius equal to the builders of ancient Greece or Egypt, while it is obvious to any dispassionate observer that their architectural skills were often equal if not superior to the artisans of Europe and Egypt.

Randall goes on in her poem divided into nine stanzas to recount the history of Uxmal, revealing that she knew the intriguing myth popularized by John Lloyd Stephens—related to him in 1840 by a Maya native of the region—in *Incidents of Travel in Central America, Chiapas, and Yucatan* (1841). According to Stephens's version, an old woman—a *bruja* or shaman—employed magic to hatch from an egg a creature who grew into a Dwarf. She then instructed her Dwarf son when he came of age to challenge the *gobernador* of Uxmal to a trial of strength. The set of challenges—all of which the Dwarf wins—culminates in the governor telling the Dwarf that he must now construct a building higher than any other in the city, otherwise the Dwarf shall be killed. Overnight, the Dwarf builds the Pyramid of the Dwarf, the great building which has come to be called the Adivino, Pyramid of the Magician or Pyramid of the Dwarf.[23] This structure is unusual among Maya sites for the ground plan is elliptical—perhaps the origin of the myth of the Dwarf being born from an elliptical egg?—instead of rectilinear and its facing is steep and smooth.[24] For Randall, the site is indeed magical, featuring a tantalizing feast for the ear as well as senses of smell and sight, for if visitors listen carefully they will hear the music "of wooden trumpets, conch shells, drum and rattle" while the stones of Uxmal are wreathed with "clouds of copal incense," and the visitor with keen eyes will see "the blue-green and gold/sheen of Quetzal plumes." Randall in the third stanza retells the myth of Uxmal's origin succinctly and eloquently: "Ask a Dwarf, a boy not born of woman,/to build a pyramid in a single night/and don't be surprised/when that being/hatched from an iguana egg/achieves the impossible." Randall ends the poem with a summary of the meaning of Uxmal: "Believe in the Dwarf, magician/whose rounded shoulders/anchor your line of sight./Believe in Uxmal leading the *Ruta Puuc*/as it retraces its steps/Through a jungle of brilliant green."[25] In returning to the word "believe" at the close, Randall repeats the third verse from the first stanza concerning Stephens, who found it "impossible to believe/those graceful facades/were conceived by the ancestors/who led him to this place." Randall's poem thus serves as an answer to Stephens's ethnocentric interpretation of Uxmal and celebrates its power, counseling the traveler to perceive it not with the rational, reductive intellect but with soul and heart: one must "believe in the Dwarf" in order for the magic of Uxmal to reveal itself. As Randall confesses in *My Life in 100 Objects*: "Of the dozens of Mayan ruins that we've visited, Uxmal is one of those where I've felt most at home. Uxmal and Palenque. Both sites seem to guard mysteries not yet explained in archaeological texts."

If Uxmal represents magic, a key element of the attraction of Mexico's ruins is the way they set the visitor to pondering the concept of time. As we shall see in chapter 6, Allen Ginsberg focuses on the passage of time as a central feature of his poem "Siesta in Xbalba," and Randall in one of her most recent books, *Against Atrocity: New Poems* (2019), includes a poem, "Breakfast with Max," describing a visit to the National Institute of Standards and Technology—NIST—located in the mountains near Boulder, Colorado. She contrasts the Western obsession with making sure that "each minute/succeeds in orderly fashion the one before" with the ways the Maya conceived of time. Randall focuses on the word "*succeeds*," which she interprets not only as one moment *following* another but rather in its other meaning: "Here *succeeds*/also means to succeed as in success:/working in a way that satisfies/those demigods of war and commerce." The "civilized" Western societies see time as requiring "synchronized clocks to run on time,/carrying us punctually from one place/to another, one war to the next." War and Money are our gods, and indeed Frederick Winslow Taylor (1856–1915) espoused a theory—which became known as "Taylorism"—advocating the most "efficient" ways to control employees in modern industry "punching into the time-clock." Larger profits could be made by factories through monitoring labor from the perspective of the most "effective" and therefore brutal management of time.

Randall contrasts this way of seeing time to the "dual calendars" of the Maya: "My heartbeat alternates between their time/And ours, embraces the Long Count/While trying to avoid fascism's blows/To each new generation./In the solitude of the writing space/Or before the next outpost,/I decide each day/To honor Mayan imagination and my own."[26] The Maya devised two systems of measuring time: the *Tzolkin* calendar, which is a repeating cycle of 260 days employed in temple rituals and supplications to the gods, and the *Haab*, the 365-day year, governing the art of divination. These calendars, as we have seen in chapter 2, became a preoccupation of William S. Burroughs in his own thinking about Maya Time.[27] Randall moves back and forth "between their time/And ours," between the archaic sense of unity with the cosmos symbolized by the great mathematical, astronomical, and calendrical achievements of the Maya and our own obsession with "time as money, time as success."

Finally, in addition to her editing of *El Corno Emplumado* and her poetry and prose devoted to the literature and culture of Mexico, Randall is also a talented photographer and has published several books including *Stones Witness* as well as her recent autobiography *I Never Left Home: Poet, Feminist, Revolutionary* (2020), which features a generous selection of her photography. *Women Brave in the Face of Danger: Photographs of and Writings by Latin and North American Women* (1985) is devoted to Randall's pictures of the women and archaeological monuments of Mexico. Randall began taking photographs in Cuba, apprenticing herself to Ramon Martinez Grandal, "and learned the elemental aspects of the art. Later I would continue to improve my photographic skills, and working with images became almost as important to me as working with words."[28] In *Women Brave in the Face of Danger*, Randall "went back over photographs I had taken of women during my last years in Mexico, Cuba, Nicaragua. . . . Bringing a vision of Latin American women, filtered through the prism of my *gringa* eye." The book contains poems by Diane di Prima, Denise Levertov, Rosemary Catacalos, Joy Harjo, Adrienne Rich, and Audre Lorde: their texts accompany each photograph. One page features a statue in Mexico City's Alameda Park entitled *Malgre Tout*—"in spite of everything"—by Jesus Fructuoso Contreras (1866–1902). It depicts a nude woman facedown with her arms tied behind her back. Randall's caption points out that the statue is "surrounded by busts of presidents and Aztec warriors." Accompanied by a poem by Linda Gregg, it is a memorable statement on the oppressive lives of Mexican women.[29]

Thus, we have seen how Margaret Randall's *El Corno Emplumado* developed into a central "underground" magazine which published Beat authors and served as an important bridge between American and world literature. In the Mexico City apartment of Philip Lamantia, a circle of Beat authors and artists from around the world began to form a nucleus of literary life in which Randall played a major role. Randall in her short stories such as "The Boy with the Mayan Face" expounded a philosophy of sensitivity to the "Other" and chronicled the subjugation of the Mexican people in both her poetry and prose. Her poems on the impressive archaeological sites such as Uxmal and Chichen Itza continue the Beat preoccupation with the symbolic meaning of ruins and their significance for modern humanity. Randall, perhaps most intensely of all the Beats or Beat-affiliated writers, knew Mexican culture from the inside because she not only knew Spanish fluently and became an expert translator but lived in the country continuously for many years. Finally—and perhaps most importantly—Randall has been a pioneering revolutionary feminist who sought social justice, and the struggle for equality for women and for the Indigenous peoples of Mexico resonates throughout her prolific writings.

# 5 ⁕ JACK KEROUAC

## The Magic Land at the End of the Road

JACK KEROUAC (1922–1969), BORN in Lowell, Massachusetts, of French Canadian ancestry, spoke the dialect *joual* as a child. Lowell was home to a variety of immigrants, including Russians, Italians, and Poles. Kerouac's friend Sebastian Sampas was of Greek heritage and Kerouac admired the Armenian American author William Saroyan (1908–1981) for his "neat, funny Armenian poetic" and moving portraits of Armenians exiled in America in flight from the genocide inflicted by Turkey in 1915. Kerouac was influenced by Saroyan's lyrical, nonstop, energetic, hip prose style, and allusions to Saroyan may be found in several of his works. It is therefore understandable—given his Greek, Armenian, and French Canadian affinities—that Kerouac would identify with the Mexican people and feel a sense of kinship with those who were considered alien or "inferior" to the White Anglo Saxon Protestant establishment of the United States. As Kerouac explained in an October 12, 1952, letter to John Clellon Holmes: "I'm not American, nor West European, somehow I feel like an Indian, a North American Exile in North America . . . maybe because I have an Indian great-great-grandmother—or have strong Quebec Plain Peasant feeling and general weird Catholic mysticism." Kerouac's grandmother was said to be half Iroquois. This merging of a feeling of kinship with "Indians" and Kerouac's deep interiority also recalls Philip Lamantia, who as we have seen in chapter 2 merged in his poetics a spirituality grounded in the Italian Catholicism of his youth and a radical openness to Indigenous religious practices.

When in 1949 Kerouac caught his first glimpse of Mexico across the United States border while traveling through El Paso, Texas, he was ready to discover a Promised Land and dutifully recorded the moment in his *Journals*. He notes "a reddish wall, a monastery wall too, behind which the sun seemed to be setting, sadly, to the accompaniment of some brooding Mexican guitars we heard on the car radio. I am sure there were no better way for me to see Mexico for the first time. And to think of night settling down behind those mountains—! in secret, soft Mexico, a purple shawl over their vineyards and dobe-towns, with stars coming on so red, so dark; and perhaps that Moorish moon."[1] This sensual description dense with specific details painting the natural landscape distinguishes many of Kerouac's passages concerning Mexico. His praise of the setting sun, stars, night, and mountains recalls the final paragraph of *On the Road* as Sal Paradise hymns: "So in America when the sun goes down . . . the evening star must be drooping and shedding her sparkler dims on the prairie, which is just before the coming of complete night that blesses the earth, darkens all rivers, cups the peaks and folds the final shore in." Even before stepping foot in Mexico, Kerouac had formed a particular picture of the country in his literary imagination. In noticing a seemingly insignificant detail across the border—"a reddish wall, a monastery wall too"—Kerouac prefigures his later view of Mexico as a place of spiritual retreat and exploration.

It was in 1949 that Kerouac received Burroughs's invitation in a September 26 letter: "Mexico is very cheap. A single man could live good for $2 per day in Mexico City liquor included. $1 per day anywhere else in Mexico. Fabulous whorehouses and restaurants. A large foreign colony. Cock fights, bullfights, every conceivable diversion. I strongly urge you to visit. I have a large apt. could accommodate you." Burroughs wrote to Allen Ginsberg three months later on December 24, 1949: "Everything I hear about the U.S. makes me glad I am not there. . . . It is really possible to relax here where nobody tries to mind your business for you, and a man can walk the streets without being molested by some insolent cop swollen with the unwarranted authority bestowed upon him by our stupid and hysterical law-making bodies."[2] Kerouac must have kept these attractions in his memory, for in chapter 3 from part 1, "Passing through Mexico," of *Desolation Angels* he closely echoes the sentiments in Burroughs's letters to both himself and Ginsberg. Kerouac repeats—he was known for his astonishing memory—virtually verbatim Burroughs's comments regarding Mexico City being "cheap" and is amazed by the fact that in Mexico the policemen are accustomed to "minding their own business."[3] Kerouac ultimately made several trips to Mexico beginning in December 1950 and ending in June 1961, during which these early responses would be tested, reformulated, and sometimes modified. The time Kerouac spent in Mexico was fruitful for his writing. During his stay with Burroughs in Mexico City in 1952, Kerouac completed in just five days, from December 16 to 21, a work composed entirely in French: the recently published text entitled *Sur le Chemin*. In this chapter I consider the ways Kerouac would incorporate his experiences in Mexico in *On the Road, Some of the Dharma, Mexico City Blues, Tristessa, Desolation Angels,* and *Dr. Sax*.

Kerouac traveled widely in Mexico, creating memorable descriptions in his novels and letters as well as the poetry collection *Mexico City Blues*. As we can see from his vision of Mexico across the border, for Kerouac Mexico was an "anti-America" where personal freedom appeared to be limitless and the Mexican people also projected an "innocence" which Kerouac associated with pre–World War II United States: life was slower, less hectic, and there existed a sense of community and shared values which became pulverized under the baleful, apocalyptic influence of the Atomic Age and America's rise to Supreme World Power. In John Huston's 1964 film version of Tennessee Williams's play *The Night of the Iguana* (1961), the ex-Episcopal priest Dr. T. Lawrence Shannon played by Richard Burton stops the tourist bus he is taking to Puerto Vallarta on a bridge over a river. Turning to observe the Mexican children happily bathing and women washing laundry below, Shannon declares: "A moment of beauty . . . a fleeting glimpse into the lost world of innocence."

Kerouac's evolving friendship with Neal Cassady also influenced the ways he portrayed Mexico, and with the posthumous publication of Cassady's autobiographical *The First Third*, it is clear how Cassady shaped Kerouac's literary style and approach to depicting Mexicans and Mexican Americans in *On the Road*. Kerouac recalled concerning his literary evolution: "At the age of 24 I was groomed for the Western idealistic concept of letters from reading Goethe's *Dichtung und Wahrheit*. The discovery of a style of my own based on spontaneous get-with-it, came after reading the marvelous free narrative letters of Neal Cassady, a great writer who happens also to be the Dean Moriarty of *On the Road*." In a letter to Kerouac from February 1951 concerning Taos, New Mexico, Cassady tells his friend: "Adobe buildings lined the way: every tenth structure housed a bar. From out their open doors came loud

Mexican music and the aroma of spiced food. Drunken Indians, their long black hair braided under strange hats used the center of the hiway as a path upon which to stagger. Some were singsonging to themselves, none talked, and most passed me in dark silence with cold eyes." Cassady then hitches a ride to Santa Fe, where he walks "by crowded tourist cafes serving well-to-do travelers Mexican and American dishes, catering to their every wish . . . Mexicans chattering and otherwise, whites drunk and otherwise, Indian girls encased in moccasins, Indian squaws encased in fat, Mexican chicks in tight skirts and provocative stride, old Mexican women in more fat and burdened with unwashed infants, white women of all kinds, waitresses, heiresses, etc. and kids, kids every place imaginable, leaping and yelling."[4] Kerouac would learn from Cassady this direct apprehension of tactile reality expressed in long, unfolding, energetic, nonstop sentences which replicate the rhythms of spoken American English as well as the emphasis on visual details of southwestern Mexican American culture and speedy registering of sharp perceptions: Bob Dylan's "chains of flashing images."

As Sal Paradise and Dean Moriarty in *On the Road* first enter Mexico, Sal describes their euphoria during the trip they made in summer 1950 upon first walking the streets of Nuevo Laredo which "looked like Holy Lhasa to us," thus comparing the small Mexican border town to the seat of Tibetan Buddhism and home of the Dalai Lama. The two travelers continue on their way, entering a "smoky lunchroom" where they listen to guitars playing on an American jukebox: "Shirt-sleeved Mexican cab-drivers and straw-hatted Mexican hipsters sat at stools, devouring shapeless messes of tortillas, beans, tacos, whatnot. We bought three bottles of cold beer—*cerveza* was the name of beer—for about thirty Mexican cents or ten American cents each. . . . Behind us lay the whole of America and everything Dean and I had previously known about life, and life on the road. We had finally found the magic land at the end of the road and we never dreamed the extent of the magic."[5] As in the passage from Cassady's letter, Kerouac focuses on the music, food, drinking—in this case *cerveza*—and specific details describing the Mexicans he encounters (cab drivers are "shirt-sleeved"; hipsters are "straw-hatted") in a cinematic style which follows people and objects as they successively enter and recede from his field of vision. Indeed, imagery of looking, sight, and eyes recurs throughout *On the Road*. Dean observes in two passages a few pages later: "There's no s*uspicion* here, nothing like that. Everybody's cool, everybody looks at you with such straight brown eyes and they don't say anything, just look, and in that look all of the human qualities are soft and subdued and still there. . . . I want you par-ti-cu-lar-ly to see the eyes of this little Mexican boy who is the son of our wonderful friend Victor, and notice how he will come to manhood with his own particular soul bespeaking itself through the windows which are his eyes, and such lovely eyes surely do prophesy and indicate the loveliest of souls."[6] As we saw in chapter 4 regarding Margaret Randall's tender experience, the eyes and face of a Mexican boy call out to Cassady as they did to Randall as he encounters "his own particular soul bespeaking itself through the windows which are his eyes."

Cassady echoes here Matthew 6: 22–24: "The eye is the lamp of the body," thereby calling to attention the tenderness which Charles Olson also encountered in Mexico. While traveling on a bus through the Yucatan, Olson observed: "When I am rocked by the roads against any of them—kids, women, men—their flesh is most gentle, is granted, touch is in no sense anything but the natural law of flesh, there is none of that pull-away which, in the States, causes a man for all the years of his life the deepest sort of questioning of the rights of himself to the wild reachings of his own organism. The admission these people give me and one another is direct, and the individual who peers out from that flesh is precisely himself, is a curious wandering animal like me—it is so very beautiful how animal human eyes are when the flesh is not worn so close it chokes, how human and individuated the look comes out of a human eye when the house of it is not exaggerated." Here as with Margaret Randall, Kerouac, and Cassady, we note Olson's sensitivity to the limpid, accepting, open eyes he meets. Yet Kerouac also moves beyond Cassady, for he does not merely observe and notate what he sees; rather, he typically expands into deeper philosophical territory by asking larger questions of purpose and meaning: "We had finally found the magic land at the end of the road." The sense of finality is emphasized by the anapestic rhythm of "at the end/of the road": the sense of swift movement ending in the final heavy arrival of a full stop in "road." The highway is the road of life down which the pilgrims Ray and Dean travel and the "magic land" of Mexico becomes for Kerouac a kind of spiritual Promised Land.

Ray himself then takes over driving duties from Dean, musing, "I was alone in my eternity at the wheel, and the road ran straight as an arrow," driving through Linares and "hot, flat swamp country," across the Rio Soto la Marina to Gregoria, "into the places where we would finally learn ourselves among the Fellahin Indians of the world, the essential strain of the basic primitive, wailing humanity that stretches in a belt around the equatorial belly of the world."[7] Mexico is the place where the Beats will "learn ourselves"—an echo of the Socratic injunction "to Know Thyself"—as well as the Gnostic exhortation to find the inner Self. These are central passages, for Kerouac is abandoning American clock-time—rather like Billy and Wyatt in *Easy Rider* when Peter Fonda casts his watch to the ground, signaling they are now entering the archetypal time of the mythic journey of the hero as they speed across America on their motorcycles—to discover Mexican Time. Erik R. Mortenson in his essay "Beating Time: Configurations of Temporality in Jack Kerouac's *On the Road*" argues that the novel critiques American notions concerning time by contrasting our attitude with the eternal, open Mexican conception. Kerouac describes Mexico City "as a place without physical or temporal end. Sal writes: 'We wandered in a frenzy and a dream. We ate beautiful steaks for forty-eight cents in strange titled Mexican cafeterias with generations of marimba musicians standing at one immense marimba.... Nothing stopped, the streets were alive all night... nothing ever ended.' Here temporality is limitless.... Mexico is repeatedly portrayed in obverse relations to an oppressive America... time sheds its constraining feel." As in *Easy Rider*, the change in temporal order between America and Mexico is symbolized when Dean exchanges a wristwatch for a piece of crystal sold on the side of the highway by a group of Indigenous girls. Kerouac believes the "Indians" have existed from the beginning of time: "Those people were unmistakably Indians and were not at all like the Pedros and Panchos of silly civilized American lore—they had high cheekbones, and slanted eyes, and soft ways, they were not fools, they were not clowns, they were great, grave Indians and they were the source of mankind and the fathers of it.... And they knew this as we passed, ostensibly self-important moneybag Americans on a lark in their land; they knew who was the father and who was the son of antique life on earth, and made no comment."[8]

Entering a realm of timelessness and making common cause with the "Indians" are connected within Kerouac's literary imagination. Yet these passages also contain the "romanticizing" of Mexicans which has been critiqued by Manuel Luis Martinez in *Countering the Counterculture: Rereading Postwar American Dissent from Jack Kerouac to Tomas Rivera*. Martinez finds Kerouac, and the Beats in general, to be guilty of the tendency to "essentialize" "minority groups"—Blacks, Mexicans, Indigenous peoples—and projecting upon them perceived qualities which they believe themselves to be lacking. As we have seen earlier with Margaret Randall, the twin dangers accompanying any meeting with the "Other" are: on one hand, arriving at the encounter with the baggage of preconceived prejudices or overt racism; and on the other, falling into the trap of idealizing and projecting onto the "Other" qualities believed to be lacking in oneself. Cecil Robinson in *With the Ears of Strangers:*

*The Mexican in American Literature* (1963) comments acerbically on the passage I have quoted above: "Mexico, especially in its Indian component, has been viewed as being, despite its primitiveness, seeped in an ancient wisdom which could serve to upbraid the upstart, saucy, essentially shallow technologized societies of the north. Jack Kerouac in *On the Road* makes some observations along these lines, the sensitivity of which suggests that should he outgrow the writing of twinge-of-the-moment diaries, he may some day produce a literary work."[9]

The notion of the "fellaheen"—Kerouac varies his spelling as well as employment of lower- and uppercase as "Fellahin" or "fellaheen"—recurs throughout his oeuvre: for example in "Mexico Fellaheen" from *Lonesome Traveler* he describes Mexicans as having "a fellaheen feeling about life, that timeless gayety of people not involved in great cultural and civilization issues."[10] The ascription of more "authenticity," "mystery," or "spirituality" to "primal" peoples of course is a tendency which has its origins in the Romantic notion of the "Noble Savage." Kerouac acquired his notion of the "fellaheen" from Oswald Spengler's *Der Untergang des Abendlandes—The Decline of the West*—which William Burroughs had shared with him and Allen Ginsberg. Spengler argued that the fellaheen were "the peasantry, 'everlasting' and historyless . . . a people before the dawn of the Culture, and in very fundamental characters it continued to be the primitive people, surviving when the form of the nation passed away again."[11] Kerouac is rightly faulted for the sort of "reverse racism"—which also mars Norman Mailer's provocative essay "The White Negro"—such Spenglerian methods of categorizing humans and interpreting history may imply.

There is however another possibility, suggested by the Martinican author Edouard Glissant (1928–2011) in his book *Poetics of Relation* (1997). Glissant argues:

> If we examine the process of "understanding" people and ideas from the perspective of Western thought, we discover that its basis is this requirement for transparency. In order to understand and thus accept you, I have to measure your solidity with the ideal scale providing me with grounds to make comparisons and, perhaps, judgments. I have to reduce.
>
> Accepting differences does, of course, upset the hierarchy of this scale. I understand your difference, or in other words, without creating a hierarchy, I relate it to my norm. I admit you to existence, within my system. I create you afresh.—But perhaps we need to bring an end to the very notion of a scale. Displace all reduction.

> Agree not merely to the right to difference but, carrying this further, agree also to the right to opacity that is not enclosure within an impenetrable autarch but subsistence within an irreducible singularity.

For Glissant, the way out of the impasse the Beats reach in Mexico between themselves as Americans representing a colonial power and their meeting with the "Other" is to simply acknowledge the *opacity* of the Other, to accept the "irreducible singularity" of the Other. As we have seen earlier with Randall's encounter with the Maya boy, this requires one to "let the Other be" rather than seeking to reduce the "Other" to one's own categories. It is however also the case that what the counterculture desired was that which was *authentic,* and they sought confirmation that something beautiful might be found in the souls and faces of the "Other," perhaps symbolizing or incarnating that which had been lost by contemporary humanity. The young Benjamin Braddock in Mike Nichols's film *The Graduate* (1967) is told by an elder that pursuing a career in "plastics" may be a wise move. But for the youth of the fifties and sixties, if contemporary America was increasingly made out of "plastic" and had become unbearably unreal, the search for the "real" and "true self" in a decaying and empty culture must become an inward, mystical journey. Indeed, during an interview with Mike Wallace in 1958, Wallace asked Kerouac whether the Beats were "mystics" and Kerouac replied: "Yeah. It's a revival prophesied by Spengler. He said that in the late moments of Western civilization there would be a great revival of religious mysticism. It's happening." Wallace then asked: "What sort of mysticism is it? What do Beat mystics believe in?" and Kerouac replied: "Oh, they believe in love. They love children . . . and I don't know, it's so strange to talk about all this . . . they love children, they love women, they love animals, they love everything."[12] The "revival of religious mysticism" which Kerouac notes Spengler predicted is precisely what Kerouac and the Beats sought in their journeys to Mexico.

The counterculture turned to the past and the "primitive" to find a way forward. Indeed, as the editors of *Alcheringa* put it, they sought in their magazine devoted to ethnopoetics to address "the problem of the sacred/powerful dimension of language and its possible restoration in English: just as we have desecrated the landscape, so we have carelessly depleted the potent resources of language. In tribal ontologies, cosmologies, and the poetries that present them may be found the answers, or the beginnings of the answers, to both these problems." According to William Ellery Channing, Henry David Thoreau's—our first great ecologist—last word on his deathbed was "Indians": in many ways, Thoreau felt closer to the original inhabitants of America who lived in harmony with the land than he did to his contemporaries. In addition, Kerouac as a French Canadian was in the tradition of several French predecessors in their spiritual quest: Honoré de Balzac in his "theosophical" novels *Seraphita* and *Louis Lambert*; Arthur Rimbaud in his studies of alchemy and magic and his desire for the *dérèglement de tous les sens* in the effort to—in Jim Morrison's memorable phrase—"break on through to the other side"; as well as figures such as Antonin Artaud and Georges Bataille. As Jane Goodall has argued in *Artaud and the Gnostic Drama*, both Artaud and Bataille were "motivated by an obsession with recovering the sacred and with rupturing the boundaries of the known world and the known self." For Kerouac, this "rupturing" was also a "finding" which he found to be a living tradition in Mexico incarnated in its people.

In his biography of Neal Cassady, *The Holy Goof*, William Plummer observes that this voyage to Mexico "is special because it is the longest, because it is the most ecstatic and raw, because it is Kerouac and Cassady's last road adventure."[13] Sal Paradise later falls dangerously ill in Mexico City and Dean deserts him, leaving Mexico for the United States. This departure may be seen as the beginning of the parting of the ways between them, for while Cassady became interested in the work of Edgar Cayce—the infamous American "clairvoyant"—Jack began to study Buddhism seriously, which would ultimately result in his *Some of the Dharma*, published posthumously in 1997. While in Mexico, Kerouac began having "Buddhist visions" as we see in this excerpt from his notebooks: "REPOSE BEYOND FATE—REST BEYOND HEAVEN! Buddha goes beyond Christ—for I have had a vision of the anxieties of Heaven (Mexico City Benzedrine Vision Dec 1952)." Kerouac began compiling reading notes from his studies of Buddhist texts in December 1953 and completed the manuscript of *Some of the Dharma* on March 15, 1956.[14] In one passage in *Some of the Dharma*, Kerouac considers Mexico as a place to pursue a contemplative life: "I want to practice solitude in the middle of the forest. Where is the forest? Far North in the Gaspe, far South in Mexican lands, both Indian grounds . . . Mexico is best. Mexico is like old India. The jungle in the winter, the desert plateau in the summer. The Tao Morning Ground, the ecstasy of the jewel lotus." Allen Ginsberg during his visit with Margaret Randall in Mexico City on his way to Cuba in 1965, expressed similar sentiments with an added bit of comedy: "Life is too short—I want to go back to Mexico and live in Oaxaca like a peaceful bearded sage and eat tortillas for a year."[15] As we observed earlier with regard to Nuevo Laredo, which appeared to Kerouac as a version of "Holy Lhasa," so here Mexico is a place of revelations: "The Tao Morning Ground, the ecstasy of the jewel lotus." Chapter 8 of the *Tao Te Ching* counsels us: "In dwelling, live close to the ground. In thinking, keep to the simple." And in the most famous Buddhist mantra *Om Mani Padme Hum, mani* means "jewel," while *padme* is "lotus flower." We note in these excerpts from *Some of the Dharma* how Mexico began to enter Kerouac's literary imagination in tandem with Taoist and Buddhist thought as well as the advice of his fellow Massachusetts native Henry David Thoreau to "simplify, simplify" your life.

A year and a half later, this dream of a retreat in Mexico is confirmed in a letter of February 7, 1956, to his friend, poet Philip Whalen (1923–2002), in which Kerouac envisions ways he might be able to earn enough money working in the United States to allow him to live in Mexico for at least a portion of the year: "It would be just the thing for North American bhikku-ing for me, Summer in the mountains earning livelihood, Falls in Mexico (going thru Bay Area en route), holidays and Winter with family in Florida (where they're going to live now), and Springs back in Mex. I'd like to found a kind of monastery in the plateau country outside Mexico City, if I had the money—but I'll start this next Fall with the first of the buildings, my own dobe hut, windowless, with open outdoor fireplace, a rain shelter and nothing much else, you block up the windows, 20 miles outside Mexico City—it seems like a good location."[16] Beat poet Lew Welch (1926–1971?)—"Dave Wain" in Kerouac's *Big Sur* (1962)—in his poem "In Answer to a Question from P.W." recorded similar plans: "In Mexico I'll finish the novel I'll write, rough, while/fire-watching in Oregon./The problem is, what kind of typewriter to pack in?/I ought to be able to live 6 months in Mexico on what I/earn on the Mountain in 4." Thus Kerouac's dream of a "monastery" reappears: as we have seen earlier, Kerouac immediately began to imagine Mexico as a place of spiritual retreat when he first glimpsed the country across the border from the United States. Like the ancient Desert Fathers, Kerouac considered the solitude of deserts, of "the open spaces of American Southwest and Nevada" as places of inner testing and purification, as with Jesus Christ as well as the tradition of early Christian monasticism in the Egyptian desert which began in the third century C.E. But he preferred Mexico since it allowed him to reside in the jungle during the winter and in summer move to a desert location to pursue his contemplative quest. One may observe the ways Kerouac began to associate specific places in Mexico with spiritual yearning in the poem "Heaven" from *Heaven and Other Poems*: "Like going to Xochimilco and seeing/everything with clear loving eyes,/it will be, to go to Heaven/a wise angel of the dead." Founded in the twelfth century and known today as the home of the "floating gardens," Xochimilco—in Nahuatl, "place of flower growing"—is located southeast of Mexico City. Under the ruler Axayacatl, it became a state required to pay tribute to Tenochtitlan. For Kerouac, it is analogous to "Heaven" because he will be flooded with light, with love and able to see into the true nature of reality. Like William Blake who sought "To see a World in a Grain of Sand/And Heaven in a Wild Flower," so too for Kerouac, Xochimilco—"the place of flower growing"—like Heaven will open his inner eye into the true, eternal nature of reality.

This impulse towards Mexico as a place of spiritual pilgrimage may be seen in the life and work of Ernesto Cardenal (1925–2020) who translated into English the Mexican poems of Beat poets such as Philip Lamantia whom he met in Mexico in 1959. Lamantia had himself retreated to a monastery in Oregon following several mystical experiences in Mexico. Cardenal traveled to the Trappist monastery in Gethsemani, Kentucky, to become a novice, spending two years under the tutelage of his mentor Thomas Merton.

Both Cardenal and Merton were students at Columbia University—as had been Kerouac, Ginsberg, and Ferlinghetti—and Merton had considered establishing a spiritual center in Mexico. After completing his studies with Merton, Cardenal traveled to Cuernavaca where he spent two years to become a priest, planning that Merton would one day follow him: they hoped to create together a new monastery devoted to social justice for Central Americans. Merton however was denied by his superiors the freedom to leave the Trappist monastery.[17] Merton had several connections with the Beats. We have seen in chapter 4 that he admired the writings of Margaret Randall and her magazine *El Corno Emplumado*. He also sent stamps from his monastery—he lacked money to contribute—to Diane di Prima to help support her literary magazine *The Floating Bear*. Merton exchanged letters with Lawrence Ferlinghetti, visiting him in San Francisco, while Kerouac dedicated two poems to Merton, published in the magazine *Monks' Pond* (Summer 1968). Merton also contributed an introduction to Cardenal's poetry book *Gethsemani, Ky.* (1965).[18] Cardenal in his memoir recalling his friendship with Merton remarks that he believed "contemplatives today could do as the Desert Fathers did years ago. They were people who didn't only resist the decadent lifestyle in Rome or in the other cities of the Roman Empire, but went instead to the desert and lived separately in solitude. And they hadn't had any religious instruction; they led normal lives in nature, alone with God, for nature is man's natural element, like the fish in water."[19] For Kerouac, the spiritual quests of the Buddhist and the Desert Fathers shared in common the desire for solitude, unity with nature, and retreat from the chaos of the contemporary world. His notion that Mexico might provide a place to

Thomas Merton, photograph by John Lyons. Used with permission of the Merton Legacy Trust and the Thomas Merton Center at Bellarmine University.

establish such a refuge and community—D. H. Lawrence had also dreamed of creating his utopian colony named *Rananim* in Mexico—was one shared by several of his fellow writers.

While Kerouac was indeed seeking a place of contemplation in his journeys to Mexico, he also spent time familiarizing himself with Aztec culture—unlike several other Beats he did not see the Maya ruins in the Yucatan—visiting several archaeological sites, including Teotihuacan. The myth of Quetzalcoatl plays a role in Kerouac's long poem sequence entitled *Mexico City Blues* composed from 1954 to 1957 and published in 1959, comprising 242 "choruses"—which became an important text for Bob Dylan—as well as in his novel *Dr. Sax,* which was written in 1952 and also appeared in 1959. In his introduction to Kerouac's *Pomes All Sizes,* Ginsberg described a conversation he had with Bob Dylan: "'How do you know Kerouac's poetry?' I asked Mr. Dylan after we improvised songs and read some *Mexico City Blues* choruses over Kerouac's gravestone 1976 Lowell's Edson Cemetery, cameras on us walking side by side under high trees and shifting clouds as we disappeared down distant aisles of gravestones. Dylan's answer: *Someone handed me Mexico City Blues in St. Paul in 1959 and it blew my mind.* He said it was the first poetry that spoke his own language." Dylan's own lyrics have been inflected with Mexican themes, such as "Romance in Durango" which features a fiesta as well as a portrait of Quetzalcoatl with his obsidian eyes. Dylan also originally planned to call the Rolling Thunder Revue's 1975 tour, "The Montezuma Revue."[20] Ted Joans (1928–2003)—who traveled in Mexico and celebrated Frida Kahlo, Diego Rivera, and the country's *muralistas*—also paid tribute to Kerouac's *Mexico City Blues* in his elegy "The Wild Spirit of Kicks: In Memory of Jack Kerouac," composed shortly after Kerouac's death in October 1969: "Jack in floppy shirt and jacket loaded with jokes/Ole Angel Midnight singing Mexico City Blues." Finally, Kerouac's *Desolation Angels* also influenced Dylan. According to Sean Wilentz: "In early August, Dylan recorded 'Desolation Row' for his sixth album, *Highway 61 Revisited,* and the correspondences with Kerouac, beginning with the title, were too exact to be coincidental. Various readers have plucked out lines in the novel—Kerouac's description of the poet David D'Angeli (Philip Lamantia) as 'the perfect image of a priest' or of all the authorities who condemn hot-blooded embracers of life as sinners, when, in fact, 'they sin by lifelessness!'—that turn up verbatim or nearly so in Dylan's song. The ambience of 'Desolation Row' is reminiscent of Kerouac's Mexico, a mixture of cheap food and fun (and ladies for hire), but with 'a certain drear, even sad darkness.'"

It is significant that it was Mexico City which would be the place of genesis for *Mexico City Blues,* which is a culmination of Kerouac's studies in Buddhism and provides a chronicle of his spiritual struggles during this phase of his career. Several choruses feature Mexican themes. Kerouac indulges in Joycean wordplay à la *Finnegans Wake* as he does in *Old Angel Midnight* (1956–59; published 1973), which records—in Kerouac's description of his aims in the book—the "babbling world tongues coming in thru my window at midnight no matter where I live or what I'm doing, in Mexico, Morocco, New York, India or Pakistan, in Spanish, French, Aztec . . . the sounds of people yakking and of myself yakking." One of the "Aztec poems" in the sequence of *Mexico City Blues* is the "207th Chorus" which opens with "Aztec Blues," the same two words which begin the 137th Chorus: "Aztec Blues—Imitation of Pound/A God called 'Drink the Flood/Water'—HUETEOTL—/Is a very old God./What older God could you get/GLED-ZAL-WAD-LE,/The Sound of the Feathered Serpent,/cause of the flood./He came from: 'Destroyed-Over-Flooded-Land-/Exiled-Him-Water-Pour,'/Which means: He is Water./He is the Flood/He is the Ocean that Floods/Serpent as the Sign of Flood, Ah/Sax—/Bird-feather is a sign of escape,/flight, exile—/The Feathered Serpent/Snakes that Fly/Nail Eternity/To bye/TONA TI UH:—'Of the Sunken Your Ear.'"[21]

Even by the standards of the at times opaque poems in *Mexico City Blues*—the book was savagely reviewed by Kenneth Rexroth in the *New York Times*—"207th Chorus" is unusually dense. Kerouac here is "riffing"—as in the spontaneous musical composition of jazz—on three gods, Huehueteotl, Quetzalcoatl, and Tonatiuh, within a pattern of imagery involving air, water, fire, and earth. The sudden appearance of "Ah Sax—" provides a clue, suggesting Kerouac is referring to the plot and characters in his eponymous novel *Dr. Sax,* composed during Kerouac's 1952 visit to William Burroughs in Mexico City concerning the flooding of Lowell, Massachusetts, when Kerouac was fourteen years old. Dr. Sax attempts to employ a magic potion to destroy the Great World Snake who is intent upon devouring humanity. This narrative also appears in *On the Road*: "I told her about the big snake of the world that was coiled in the earth like a worm in an apple . . . I told her this snake was Satan. . . . A saint called Doctor Sax will destroy it with secret herbs which he is at this very moment cooking up in his underground shack somewhere in America. It may also be disclosed that the snake is just a husk of doves, when the snake dies great clouds of seminal-gray doves will flutter out and bring tidings of peace around the world." However, in *Doctor Sax,* the potion has no effect, and as the Snake proceeds to attempt his destruction, a great bird suddenly arises, taking the Snake in its beak and disappearing into the sky. In the 207th Chorus, the puzzling imagery of the Feathered Serpent who is the "cause of the flood" is thus a veiled allusion to the historical flooding of Kerouac's hometown during his adolescence.

This counterpointing by Kerouac of his experiences in Mexico with childhood memories in Lowell is not atypical, for in one of the entries from his *Book of Sketches* (written 1957; published 2006)—in which the lines are broken up down the page in verse form—he again recalls the past in relation to the present: "Saturday in Mex City & the streets/lead to all kinds of fascinating/lighted vistas, movies, stores, pepsi/colas, whorehouses, nightclubs,/ children playing in brownstreet/lamps & the sleep of the/Fellaheen dog in some old grand doorway/YES, the end to a perfect meal/is always the grand cup of/black coffee, here or in/Sweets Seafood Restaurant, NY/or in Paree, anywhere, the/warm rich comforter (which/prepares the appetite for chocolates/on the homeward walk, preferably/milk chocolate & nuts)—/It's the exciting hour in MCity/or anycity, 8 on Sat nite, when/the 5 & 10's closing & the show/crowds rush & newsboys shout,/trolley bells clang, like soft/like Lowell long ago when/I had that swarming vision." So too in *Mexico City Blues*, Kerouac emphasizes that "Indian songs in Mexico . . . /are like the little French Canuckian /songs my mother sings." Mexico City recalls Lowell as the madeleine cookie in Proust's—an author Kerouac admired—*À la Recherche du Temps Perdu* recalls Marcel's childhood.

As for "Hueteotl," here Kerouac slightly errs, for the proper name should be Huehueteotl, who was indeed an Aztec "Old God" worshipped from ancient times and uncharacteristically depicted in sculpture as possessing a wrinkled face: it was uncommon in Aztec sculpture to show aged humans or gods. Huehueteotl was conflated by the Aztecs with Tlaloc, the rain god. Kerouac ends with "TONA TI UH," a sun god who usually sports a headdress of eagle feathers, red body paint, and a huge solar disk. In invoking these gods, Kerouac includes all four elements: Quetzalcoatl, Snake and Bird = Earth and Sky; Huehueteotl = Water; and finally, Tonatiuh, who is the sun god = Fire. The puzzling ending, "TONA TI UH:—'Of the Sunken Your Ear,'" may refer to the fact that Tonatiuh is presented in iconography wearing dangling circular earrings.[22] In Aztec thought, as we have seen with Lamantia, during the Fifth Sun which is governed by Tonatiuh, the world will come to an end. We have an adumbration of this same Quetzalcoatlan theme in both *Dr. Sax* and *Mexico City Blues*: Kerouac is presenting Aztec history within the context of his own autobiographical experience, his personal mythology.[23]

In other poems in the sequence, such as the 13th Chorus, Kerouac turns from Quetzalcoatl to Aztec human sacrifice which he also introduces in *Desolation Angels*: "I caught a cold/From the sun/When they tore my heart out/At the top of the pyramid/O the ruttle tooty blooty/windowpoopies/of Fellah Ack Ack/Town that russet noon/when priests dared/to lick their lips/over my thumping meat/heart—/the Sacrilegious beasts/Ate me 10,000/Times & I came back/Spitting Pulque/in Borracho/Ork/Saloons/of old sour Azteca/Askin for more/I popped outa Popocatapetl's/Hungry mouth."[24] The poem contains wordplay, sonic improvisatory jazz riffs, absurd humor, infantile ("ruttle tooty blooty/windowpoopies") burbling—we remember the "babbling world tongues" Kerouac employed in *Old Angel Midnight* as well as Surrealist Ted Joans's perception of Kerouac's "floppy shirt and jacket loaded with jokes"—and stretches of sheer impenetrability. Dennis Tedlock has pointed out, "concerning nonsense syllables or sound poetry that doesn't use words as we normally understand those—there was one mention of Comanche music and that's what I am picking up on—but all over North America there are many songs in which the lines with words and lines with vocables (that's what musicologists call them), the so-called nonsense syllables, something like scat singing in jazz, you always find these things closer to the familiar than you expected to when you think about it." Kerouac composed both *Mexico City Blues* and *Doctor Sax* while ingesting marijuana, which may account for the delirium of some of the poems in the sequence, although as in jazz and improvisation, Kerouac sometimes *did not seek to* "make sense" but rather *non-sense* and to take pleasure—as Tedlock observes—in a kind of "scat singing" in what, after all, are jazz poems titled "Blues." Allen Ginsberg reported that Kerouac wrote *Mexico City Blues* "by drinking coffee, smoking a joint, and writing down whatever came into his head, blending Buddhist apprehensions of *sunyatta* (open, spontaneous, luminous emptiness) with jazz improvisation and Proustian memory flashes."

Kerouacian joy continues with the black humor of catching a cold when your heart is hacked out of your body. Kerouac also jousts with "Fellaheen"—"Fellah Ack Ack." James T. Jones in *A Map of Mexico City Blues* suggests that the repeated "Ack Ack" or "AZTEC BLUES/'A kek Horrac'" in the 137th Chorus are not just nonsense syllables but rather variations on the author's own name: "Jack Kerouac." We also find in the 24th Chorus "Kerouaco's"; in the 110th Chorus, "Kallaquack"; in the 138th Chorus, "Jaqui Keracky."[25] Composers such as J. S. Bach and Dmitri Shostakovich secretly inscribed their identities within the texture of their musical compositions through the translation of the letters of their names into musical tones, so Kerouac's practice is not unusual, especially since he claims to be writing musical "blues" with his 242 "choruses." Kerouac also invokes pulque and getting *borracho*—or "drunk"—in Mexican bars, ending with a childlike tongue twister à la "Peter Piper Picked a Peck of Pickled Peppers" with "I popped outa Popocatapetl's/Hungry mouth." These final verses suggest that he has survived—like a cartoon character—the seemingly inexorable death visited upon him by the priests who had "dared to lick their lips" over cutting out his heart by escaping yet another threat posed by the "Hungry mouth" of Mexico's greatest volcano ultimately unscathed. Antonin Artaud composed a similarly tongue-twisting poem, "Histoire du Popocatepetl"—one of his most scatological—which begins: "Quand je pense homme, je pense/patate, popo, caca, tete, papa." In the following 14th Chorus, Kerouac carries forward the thematic thread of the 13th Chorus, again as in a musical composition: "They'll eat your heart alive/Every time/But there's more blood/I shed/Outa my pumpin heart/At Teotihuacan/And everywhere else."[26] Kerouac has incorporated within the structure of *Mexico City Blues* a recurring pattern of ideas and images rooted in his personal interpretations of Mexican culture.

Kerouac articulates a vision of Aztec history in his visit to the pyramids at Teotihuacan, twenty-five miles northeast of Mexico City, with Allen Ginsberg, Gregory Corso, Peter Orlovsky, and Orlovsky's brother Lafcadio in *Desolation Angels*, book 2, part 1, "Passing through Mexico," chapter 14: "We hop a bus and go rattling to the Pyramids, about 30, 20 miles, the fields of pulque flash by. . . . We start climbing the stone steps of the Pyramid of the Sun." The ever-super-observant Kerouac then notices among the ancient stones a plethora of anthills: "While the Teo [tihuacan] priests goofed up there these ants were just beginning to dig a real underground super market." The trope of the power differential between the ruling classes, oppressed majority, and the resulting revolutionary impulse is a recurring theme for the Beats in Mexico. Jimmy Fazzino in *World Beats: Beat Generation Writing and the Worlding of U.S. Literature* observes: "The power dynamic between the 'Teo priests' on high and the ants down below resonates with Burroughs's own fascination with the priestly caste (of the Maya, in Burroughs's case) as insidious control agents. Neither Burroughs nor Kerouac presents pre-Columbian Mesoamerican society as idyllic or romanticized; they are both attuned to power differentials—made visible by their soaring temples but also suggesting their hidden obverse: the underground pathways of the ants—that shaped those cultures and still provide insight into the workings of control and authority in the present day."[27] Burroughs had most likely discussed his theories concerning the Maya and the priestly system of social control, which we discussed in chapter 2, with Kerouac as their friendship progressed, as well as during the time Kerouac spent with him in Mexico City: Beat literature about Mexico is notable for the ways the themes and obsessions of each author evolve through their discussions with one another and resurface in individual works in differing contexts.

The relationship between upper and lower "classes" also appears in a hitherto unpublished tale included in a recent Kerouac volume in the *Library of America* edition (2016). "Execrable Spanish America'" is a brief, two-and-a-half-page text featuring a character named José who lives in a "well to do middleclass house on the outskirts of a Mexican jungle town." "José" is "an excited Spaniard part Indian businessman with little mustache, large worldwide ego" who "rushes on eager white shoes in the oppressive broiling humid heat of a jungle village, over stinking sidewalks to the heart the Europeanized heart of town." Kerouac portrays him as a deluded soul who tries desperately to inhabit the false facade of a bourgeois existence with all the benefits of "civilization" at the edge of the jungle, rather like the mad attempt to impose European "culture" on the Congo narrated in Joseph Conrad's *Heart of Darkness.* José spends the afternoon "dozing in his father's redbrick and glassbrick house at the outskirts of town among the few well to do Spanish families (their contempt of the sad stinky tortilla Indian, the long dust of filth afternoons, the coyote dogs snapping at flies in rotten meat noon drowse at the Mercado, José's whole being is pointed to disentangling himself from every possible contact with the Indian life which was the basis of his life white Spanish blood or no, Spanish blood or no, glassbrick house or not, 52 Chevy or not." What emerges in Kerouac's character portrait is a man who is ashamed of his mestizo status and strives to eradicate all traces of any connection with his Indigenous "blood" by owning a new American automobile and aping American ways. From the narrator's point of view, José is a lost man, for "there is no hope at the end of the hot dry street & no hope beyond & no hope here & no hope anywhere! And especially no hope in those homes on the edge of town where hope is supposed to be, hope & middleclass solidity, quality, & kind—Bleak as an eye in heaven, as a formal mind struggling to free itself from these bonds of language to a pure sea of images—."[28] "Execrable Spanish America" may have been a trial run for a longer fictional work Kerouac planned to develop, treating more fully a Mexican theme he had not yet explored in depth: the limbo in which those who do not fully belong to any "culture"—in this case "Spanish," "Indian," "Mestizo," "Mexican," or "American"—may find themselves when they seek to define their "identity" in relation to a particular category of being. And José errs in believing that if

Jack Kerouac, Allen Ginsberg, Peter Orlovsky, Gregory Corso, and Lafcadio Orlovsky in Mexico City, 1956, courtesy of the Allen Ginsberg Estate

he can cleave to the "values" of "bourgeois America" that he will have found the Promised Land.

In *Tristessa* (1960)—*tristeza* is "sadness" in Spanish—the only Beat novel entirely about Mexico, Kerouac returns to the theme of his own "French-Canadian-Indian" ancestry in this narrative concerning his love affair with a Mexican-Azteca prostitute, Esperanza Tercerero. Kerouac composed *Tristessa* in Mexico City during the summers of 1955 and 1956, and by November 1956, Kerouac was reunited with his friends: Allen Ginsberg, Peter and Lafcadio Orlovsky, and Gregory Corso all arrived in Mexico City, as chronicled in a famous photograph of the quintet posed before the Fuente de Neptuno in the Alameda Park.

The subject matter of this tale was introduced earlier in the section of *On the Road* chronicling Sal's romance with "Terry," a Mexican American farmworker he meets in Bakersfield in the Central Valley of California, published separately as a short story under the title "A Mexican Girl" in *The Paris Review*. Their affair lasts two weeks, and as Sal works with her among Mexican migrant farm workers in the cottonfields, he believes he has now become "a man of the earth, precisely as I had dreamed I would be, in Paterson." However, this notion that he can live such an agrarian lifestyle quickly fades and he feels he must go back "on the road." This push-pull dynamic is also at work in *Tristessa* as Kerouac begins his affair with Esperanza full of hope—her real name means "hope" in Spanish—for a new life, and the novella excitedly begins in medias res in a headlong rush: "I'm riding along with Tristessa in the cab, drunk, with big bottle of Juarez Bourbon whisky in the till-bag railroad lootbag they'd accused me of holding in railroad 1952—here I am in Mexico City, rainy Saturday night, mysteries, old dream sidestreets with no names reeling in." Kerouac mixes his memories of life on the railroad with his present experiences in Mexico City, the prose giving the reader a sense of unstoppable energy and movement as each image flashes by—life as experienced from a moving car, a moving train, a moving, constantly recording camera eye. However, this thrilling self-delusion cannot last, and is hinted at through Kerouac's balancing in this passage of positive adjectives such as "mysterious," "dream," and "beautiful" with more melancholy ones such as "tragic," "gloomy," "lugubrious," and—one of the favorite Kerouacian adjectives—"sad." Exactly as we have seen William S. Burroughs pair and contrast the opposites of "blue sky" and "wheeling vultures" in the Mexican heavens in works such as *Queer, Port of Saints, The Third Mind, The Wild Boys,* and *Naked Lunch,* so too Kerouac's novella oscillates between *esperanza* and *tristeza.*

In his passion for Tristessa, Kerouac seeks to escape the restrictive rules governing relationships between the "races" in America and to find a kind of redemption through the symbolic erasure of difference and prejudice through his love for her. However, as Nancy McCampbell Grace has argued in her essay "A White Man in Love: A Study of Race, Gender, Class, and Ethnicity in Jack Kerouac's *Maggie Cassady, The Subterraneans* and *Tristessa,*" this struggle to achieve union with

> the fellaheen woman is doomed long before he ever meets her. Metaphorically, the text suggests that democracy and self-improvement cannot be achieved in a

> place apart. The farther one goes from the social body of one's origin, the farther one gets from meaningful progress, certainly from the symbolic fecundity of love. Tristessa's sordid history, especially the abuse of her body, signifies that she is incapable of loving anyone. Jack has no control over her addiction which destroys her mind to the point where he likens her to an Aztec witch threatening to kill him. His deification of her and his belief that he loves her are worthless anodynes and as she becomes more maniacal, her body begins to implode. In Part 1, she has convulsions, and in Part 2, her entire body, particularly the lower stratum, becomes ghastly; her arms covered with cysts and one leg completely paralyzed.

Thus, Kerouac's efforts to "romanticize" the "Other" end in failure. He projects onto Tristessa the desire to transcend "racial," "class," and "national" boundaries. Indeed, seeking salvation in human "love" for Kerouac was a path which ended finally in disappointment, one reason for his obsessive turn toward Buddhism and a life of renunciation.

Finally, if Kerouac interrogated the question of class and ethnicity, he also explored religion in Mexico. Because Kerouac was a devout Catholic in his childhood and revered his brother Gerard, who died when Kerouac was just four years old and was subsequently "sainted" by his family, he responded intensely to the churches of Mexico. In "Mexico Fellaheen" from *Lonesome Traveler*, Kerouac recalls that during his last day in Mexico City, he visited a small church near Redondas and beheld a tremendous statue depicting a "tormented" crucified Christ: "It shows the blood running from His hands to His armpits and down His sides. . . . It shows His body falling from the Cross on His hand of nails, the perfect slump built in by the artist, the devout sculptor . . . a sweet perhaps Indian Spanish Catholic of the 15th century, among ruins of adobe and mud. . . . They understand death, they stand there in the church under the skies that have a beginningless past and go into the never-ending future."[29]

There is a connection between Christianity and the ideology of the Aztecs, both invoking death and sacrifice as salvific. In the case of Christianity, we are redeemed through the death of Jesus Christ on the cross, while the Aztecs save themselves through sacrificing victims to the sun in order to keep the universe itself alive. The Spanish invaders noted that their mythology—like that of the Aztecs—posited a great flood; a lost paradise; rituals that bore similarities to communion, confession, and baptism; and celibate priests. Priests were called *papahuaque* ("those with long, curly, tangled hair" in Nahuatl) by the Aztecs, which is similar in sound to the word "pope" in Spanish, *papa*. Georges

Bataille in his early 1929 essay "L'Amerique Disparue"—"Extinct America"—also noted the ways Aztec rituals resembled those of the Catholic church as well as similarities in iconography: "The sculptured demons of European churches are to some degree comparable (surely they are involved in the same basic obsession), but they lack the power, the grandeur, of the Aztec ghosts, the bloodiest ever to people the clouds of our earth. And they were, as we know, literally bloody. Not a single one among them but was not periodically spattered with blood for his own festival."[30]

Kerouac here touches on a theme familiar to the Beats in Mexico. As we shall see in chapter 9, Joanne Kyger in *Phenomenological,* the account of her journey in February 1985 to the Yucatan, noted that in Sor Juana Inés de la Cruz's play *El Divino Narciso* (1689)—*Loa to Divine Narcissus*—Juana "argues that the sacrifice of the Mexican corn god, and the ritual in which his image shaped in corn dough is eaten, anticipates the Christian symbolism of the death and resurrection of Christ and the Sacrament of Communion. This idea which favors the native Indians was a big no-no to the Catholic Church."[31] And Diane di Prima in her "Notes on the Solstice" (1975) also includes a section in prose concerning Aztec sacred practices regarding Huitzilopochtli: "At the festival of the winter solstice the Aztecs killed their god Huitzilopochtli in effigy first and ate him afterwards. An image of the deity in the likeness of a man was fashioned out of seeds of various sorts, which were kneaded into a dough with the blood of children. The bones of the god were represented by pieces of acacia wood. This image was placed on the chief altar of the temple, and on the day of the festival the king offered incense to it."[32] All of these conceptions—from Europeans such as Bataille to Beats Kerouac, Kyger, and di Prima—are historical iterations of the same theme: obvious similarities exist between Aztec and Christian rituals. The Beats were particularly interested in tracing these connections in order to counter the hegemonic pretensions of Western "Christian" societies to "civilization" and to cultural supremacy. Kerouac in his depiction of the church near Redondas also emphasizes the blood flowing from Christ's hands "to His armpits and down His sides," speculating that the statue of Christ may have been executed by an "Indian Catholic" of four centuries ago. The "understanding" Kerouac claims the Mexicans have of death has its roots in centuries of Aztec religious culture. During his travels in Mexico, Kerouac was deeply affected by the churches he visited, as well as the ways the religion of the "bloodheart sacrifice Aztecs" fused with aspects of his own childhood Catholic faith.

As we have seen, Kerouac explored several differing aspects of Mexico. Influenced by his friend Neal Cassady, he sought to describe its landscape and people in an immediate, highly visual, hip prose. In *Mexico City Blues,* he incorporated his knowledge of Aztec mythological traditions within the context of his jazz, bebop poetic style. He also visited archaeological sites such as Teotihuacan, where—as in other Mexico-inspired works such as "Execrable Spanish America"—he explored themes of class differences and "racial identity." Like the other Beats, he also sought Mexico as a place of spiritual retreat where he could begin to put into action his Buddhist studies, and similar to Philip Lamantia, his Catholic background allowed him to see in Mexico a powerful coalescence of Christian and Indigenous traditions which he recorded in his constant, daily notebooks. Because he spent such extended periods and composed so many important works while living in Mexico, it is clear that in many ways Mexico symbolized for Jack Kerouac "the magic land at the end of the road."

# 6 * ALLEN GINSBERG

## I Would Rather Go Mad, Gone Down the Dark Road to Mexico

THE RELATIONSHIP OF William Burroughs to both Jack Kerouac and Allen Ginsberg (1926–1997) was mutually enriching. Burroughs played the mentor to both younger men, sharing with them texts by the Gnostics, Oswald Spengler's *The Decline of the West*—which as we have seen influenced Kerouac's concept of the "fellaheen" in Mexico—Alfred Korzybski's *Science and Sanity*, Hart Crane, and Arthur Rimbaud. Ginsberg helped Burroughs arrange his manuscripts and find publishers—Kerouac also encouraged Burroughs's literary efforts—and Ginsberg's travels to Mexico were inspired by Burroughs's own expeditions: Ginsberg's reflections upon Mexico appear in his poetry, essays, and letters as well as his voluminous *Journals* which are still in the process of being edited and made available to the public. In the early fifties Burroughs enticed both Kerouac and Ginsberg to Mexico with tales of happy times. Indeed, Ginsberg had already been entranced by the idea of voyaging, by the Romantic lure of enlightenment through world discovery. In *The Book of Martyrdom and Artifice*, several early Ginsberg poems document his preoccupation with the idea of travel, such as "The Last Voyage" composed in 1945: "Others have voyaged far, have sailed/On waves that wash beyond the world/I loved the ancient men who veiled/The image of themselves where swirled/The maelstrom of the holy stream,/And I glided through the smoking air/With sails uplifted by a dream." An apprentice poem, Ginsberg was still struggling to find his own style, and these verses are saturated with Samuel Taylor Coleridge, Rimbaud's "Le Bateau Ivre," and the notion of travel as sacred pilgrimage—Kubla Khan's "sacred river" is Ginsberg's "holy stream."[1] In quest of escape and self-discovery, Ginsberg joined the Merchant Marines, writing to Lionel Trilling on January 7, 1946, aboard the S.S. Groveton: "Right now I'm in the middle of the Gulf of Mexico, in Hart Crane seas, amid 'adagios of islands' and proverbial sunblue seas. Really, I do enjoy sailing in these tropical waters, in watching the stars, in inventing fabulous romances on the prow of the ship as she bounces forward." Ginsberg is quoting—"adagios of islands"—from Hart Crane's "Voyages," section 2: "And onward, as bells off San Salvador/Salute the crocus lustres of the stars,/In these poinsettia meadows of her tides,—/Adagios of islands, O my Prodigal,/Complete the dark confessions her veins spell."[2] Ginsberg demonstrates his awareness of Crane's biography and connection to Mexico—Crane committed suicide by leaping from his boat into the Gulf of Mexico—when he refers to the gulf as "Hart Crane seas."

Ginsberg's yearning for faraway places—he ultimately traveled the world to, among many other destinations, India, China, Russia, Czechoslovakia, South America, and Australia—would lead him inexorably to Mexico. Due to Burroughs's influence, during the mid-forties, Ginsberg was introduced to the cultural patrimony of Mexico. On December 18, 1946, he described in his journal visiting with Burroughs, Joan Vollmer, and Herbert Huncke the Museum of Natural History in New York to view the Madrid Codex—the longest, best preserved, and probably the latest of the four surviving Codices.[3]

Discovered in Spain in the nineteenth century, it is unclear how it reached Europe. Known also as the Tro-Cortesianus, or Troano Codex, the Madrid Codex was constructed from bark paper—*amate* in Nahuatl—and painted on fifty-six sheets on both sides, then folded accordion-style ("screenfold") for a total of one hundred and twelve pages. It contains almanacs, astronomical tables, a description of the New Year ceremony, depictions of deer trapping and hunting, scenes of human sacrifice, and Maya gods familiar to us from Burroughs's work: both Itzamna the god of writing and the Young Maize God whom Burroughs invokes in *Naked Lunch* are depicted. It also famously shows the rain god Chac and moon goddess Ixchel exchanging cacao: it is said that Quetzalcoatl gifted the seeds of the cacao tree to mankind and the wonderful boon of *chocolatl*—chocolate.

Madrid Codex

The influence of the Madrid Codex can be seen in Ginsberg's early poem "Denver Doldrums." Ginsberg wrote Lionel Trilling about the poem in an August 1947 letter and also explained in his journal entry of August 11, 1947, the imagery of the Madrid Codex which had both menaced and intrigued him:

> So the parasitic tics and chiggers and so, the scorpion, a traditional castration symbol, are associated with the demon of Mr. Mayer that follows. The image is from one of the Mayan Codices—the Madrid Codex—which contains a series of drawings of a venomous growth on the loins of a squatting man. The beast grows larger and bolder in each picture and finally dominates the man astride his neck. The evil of the visage of the monster intensifies and grows more complex with each picture, while the Mayan's face is drained of all emotion. Nobody seems to know exactly what the Mayans meant, or knew, by this and a hoard of equally terrifying representations of psychic mortification. I understand that there were priests who had control of these Codices which seem to have prescribed both social routine and psychic ritual. Regularity of thought, stylization of the soul in the culture, and manipulation of these abstractions by the priestly aristocracy (and here I mean to suggest Korzybski's semantic theory) are all elements of my personal myth of the Mayans. I am on a "kick" with the Mayans. As far as that is concerned, I imagine actual seasons of the soul, and an atomic magic (psychology, which was the basis of their society as the machine is of ours) developed by the priests and gone out of control after ages of bureaucratic centralization. So follows an exploration of certain Mayan cities depopulated but intact, like ghost ships.[4]

The passage is noteworthy for its perspicacious analysis of the Madrid Codex, illustrating that Ginsberg paid close attention during his visit with Burroughs to the Museum of Natural History. The Madrid Codex presents a succession of difficult-to-decipher images for the untutored eye. It seems likely Ginsberg is describing what are known as the "serpent pages" which depict a variety of gods making sacrifices to propitiate the arrival of rain. There is a sinuous snake making its way from one panel to the next, and indeed a "squatting figure" as well as a god of death who takes a torch to a deer about to be sacrificed. These frightening monsters invade the final section of "Denver Doldrums," which features the following dark verses: "Substance changes meanings in my sleep/Symbols clang disruptive in the deep,/Mad am I, I mock my own mad error!/Slow round in my chamber I turn in my terror!/ . . . More vivid monsters in my dream attain/More intellectual dignity, more pain,/Like these, vague monsters haunt the sunny air,/Invisible as boredom, everywhere. . . . While all the wide world turns upon a breath,/Until this meditation end with Death." The verses "Mad am I, I mock my own mad error!/Slow round in my chamber I turn in my terror!" recall Edgar Allan Poe's "madmen" (and compare "rapping at my chamber door" in "The Raven") in its spooky fear: the "monsters" which assail Ginsberg's imagination were inspired by the Madrid Codex. Ginsberg's commentary on the codex is noteworthy not only for its illumination of the psychologically disturbed imagery in his "Denver Doldrums"—composed during his severe depression over his frustrating love affair with Neal Cassady (Ginsberg's poem "Green Valentine" composed in Chiapas, Mexico, in 1954 also expressed his loneliness and erotic desire for Cassady)—but also for the light it sheds on his relationship with Burroughs. Already by the mid-forties, Burroughs had begun formulating his theory concerning the role of the Maya priesthood in the "control" of their society, and Ginsberg was also aware that the Maya cities had vanished. There are many theories including ecological destruction, warfare, drought, and overpopulation as to why Maya civilization fell, to which Ginsberg alludes in "an exploration of certain Mayan cities depopulated but intact, like ghost ships." In this passage on the Madrid Codex, Ginsberg also refers to Alfred Korzybski, whose theories of language were adumbrated in *Science and Sanity*, one of the books Burroughs had shared with Ginsberg and Kerouac during the mid-forties.

Another influence on Ginsberg's early relationship to Mexico was his mentor William Carlos Williams, who had Hispanic roots, spoke Spanish as a child, and translated several poems from Spanish, including Aztec works under the title "Three Nahuatl Poems," the first of which is vivid with Williams-like imagery: "One by one I proclaim your songs:/I bind them on gold crabs as if they were anklets:/like emeralds I gather them./Clothe yourself in them: they are your riches./Bathe in feathers of the quetzal,/your treasury of birds' plumes black and yellow, the red feathers of the macaw." Williams traveled to Mexico in 1950, discussing the country in his *Autobiography* and *In the American Grain*.[5] In Williams's poem "Desert Music" we also discover the precise, photographic images the Beats would employ in their depictions of Mexico: "paper flowers (para los santos)/baked red-clay utensils daubed/with blue, silverware,/dried peppers, onions, print goods, children's/clothing the place deserted all but/for a few Indians squatted in the/booths."[6]

Williams contributed the introduction to Ginsberg's first book, *Empty Mirror*, and in a poem from November 1949 titled after Williams's epic poem "Paterson," Ginsberg began to launch into a new style, for in his earlier work he had been imitating Andrew Marvell and Thomas Wyatt in conventional rhyme and meter. He broke out into celebratory, manic dithyrambs: technical proficiency increased as he discovered how to pack striking images into each verse. In the first half of the poem, the speaker intones a series of comic, absurdist, rhetorical questions in the style of T. S. Eliot's "The Love Song of J. Alfred Prufrock" (which also influenced Gregory Corso's "Marriage"): "What do I want in these rooms papered with visions of money? How much can I make by cutting my hair? If I put new heels on my shoes/bathe my body reeking of masturbation and sweat,/layer upon layer of/excrement/dried in employment bureaus, magazine hallways, statistical cubicles, factory/stairways,/cloakrooms of the smiling gods of psychiatry." He then invokes "the presumption of department store supervisory employees,/old clerks in their asylums of fat, the slobs and dumbbells of the ego with/money and power/to hire and fire and make and break."[7] This entire opening section paints a Dantesque portrait of American bureaucracy and capitalism, reminiscent of the world condemned by Henry Miller in *Tropic of Capricorn*. American society is ruled by money and fear. The population is kept under control by "the smiling gods of psychiatry"—surely an allusion to Ginsberg's own collision with the mental health establishment when he spent time in the asylum.

The speaker's disgust with this tableau of American life is such that he offers an ecstatically agonizing alternative to this death-by-conformity: "I would rather go mad, gone down the dark road to Mexico, heroin dripping/in my veins,/eyes and ears full of marijuana,/eating the god Peyote on the floor of a mudhut on the border/or laying in a hotel room over the body of some suffering man or woman;/jar my body down the road, crying by a diner in the Western sun;/rather crawl on my naked belly over the tincans of Cincinnati;/rather drag a rotten railroad tie to a Golgotha in the Rockies;/rather, crowded with thorns in Galveston, nailed hand and foot in Los/Angeles, raised up to die in Denver,/pierced in the side in Chicago."[8] The poem is a trial run for "Howl" with the immediate confession of "madness" coupled with drugs. As we have seen in chapter 3, Philip Lamantia had introduced peyote from Mexico into the San Francisco countercultural scene, and Ginsberg composed the second "Moloch" section of "Howl," in his own words, "on peyote." He also contributed a section of his *Journal* to the Autumn 1960 issue of Tuli Kupferberg's journal *Birth* in which he described taking peyote in April 1952: "After awhile, when sickness passed—first thing I noticed: eyes closed toward light leaves in eye a golden glow hue—which darkens when you pass hand over lidded eye. It made me feel like a very transparent sort of organism. . . . Peyote is not God—but is a powerful force—can see, if everybody on, how they would organize their lives once every year, communicating with each other."[9] Here in "Paterson" however, peyote is described as a kind of communion-taking which involves—instead of the bread symbolizing the body of Christ consumed in a church—the poet "taking the god Peyote on the floor of a mudhut on the border." The sacred ritual of peyote takes place "on the border"—the liminal realm between the United States and Mexico—and peyote itself is apostrophized as a god, capitalized "Peyote." The poem continues Thomas Wolfe's and William Saroyan's tradition of hymning the vast American continent in lyrical prose-poetry, a style Jack Kerouac would also learn from the two authors. And Ginsberg's use of anaphora—the repetition of "rather"—anticipates his mastery of the technique in "Howl": "who poverty and tatters"; "who bared their brains to Heaven"; "who passed through universities with radiant cool eyes." And there is an insistent pattern of Christian imagery with "suffering," "naked," "Golgotha," "crowded with thorns," "nailed hand and foot," "tombed," "resurrected," "streetcorner Evangel," and "agonized."

The speaker in "Paterson" would rather live "madly" and fully, participating in a peyote ceremony in a "mudhut" on the Mexico border than endure the "sane" living death of contemporary America. The poem is also remarkable because of its use of slang and "obscenity" in a series of words usually forbidden to poetry: "masturbate," "fart," "prick," "shit," as well as references to heroin, marijuana, and peyote. Ginsberg combines the lofty, ecstatic, and sacred with the doomed and profane in a way never before accomplished in American poetry. The poem thus becomes a way to counter the repressive taboos of American culture, to challenge the hegemony of the machine in favor of a primal, atavistic connection to the Mexican earth. Ginsberg told Edward Lucie-Smith: "What I'm interested in is states of altered perception, widened consciousness, deepened feeling. In writing a poem, I'm composing a memento during the time of ecstasy. . . . In our society, ecstasy is considered 'immoral' . . . the highly organized conditions of modern civilization preclude certain free sexual and emotional responses basic to human physiology, basic to human desire."[10] The idea of traveling to Mexico unleashes a flood of images from the visionary unconscious which also connects the suffering Christ with the "dark road to Mexico." As we have seen, for many of the Beats, the depiction of Christ in the iconography of Mexican churches emphasizes the physical agony Christ endured, rather than presenting the sanitized versions of the crucifixion often on view in many churches.

In another poem, "Ready to Roll" from *Reality Sandwiches,* Ginsberg registers his anticipation concerning traveling outside of the United States: "To

Mexico! To Mexico! Down the dovegrey highway, past/Atomic City police, past the fiery border to dream/cantinas! . . . Music! Taxis! Marijuana in the slums! Ancient sexy parks!"[11] For Ginsberg as well as Kerouac, the "highway" is the route to freedom, and it is here given a Homeric epithet, "dovegrey"—we think of "grey-eyed Athena"—which will lead the young hipsters to a visionary experience. They are leaving behind the constrictions of American life to enjoy marijuana unfettered by the threat of the police. Again the "border" for Ginsberg is not merely a physical place, a demarcation on the map separating two countries, but also a liminal space: when you cross that invisible line, you pass through not only a national boundary but into a new interior psychological and spiritual territory. Beat Mexico literature thus becomes the record of both the physical act of moving from one geographical location to another and the means by which one may—this is not by any means guaranteed—uncover new aspects of the self and identity.

While these early poems were imagined versions of Mexico, based on Ginsberg's relationship with Burroughs and his desire to escape America, in August 1951, Ginsberg drove with his friend Lucien Carr to Mexico City for the first time, intending to visit. Burroughs, who was out of town travelling with Lewis Marker.[12] Instead, Ginsberg embarked on a hair-raising automobile journey across Mexico with Joan Vollmer and a daredevil, speeding Lucien Carr at the wheel. However, two years later he planned a more extended visit, and in his November 24, 1953, letter to Neal and Carolyn Cassady revealed that he wanted to take from Havana "a cheap Mexican Freighter for another $10 to Merida, Yucatan (Mexico) then by bus to the Jungle archeological sites of Mayan civilization—which I've always been interested in and have been reading about and must see as Byron saw Ruins of Athens & Rome (& Egypt?)."[13] Ginsberg notes his desire to "look up Professor Stromswich for info on Mayapan ruins," and in one of the several bibliographies listed in his journals dated "April 16—Good Friday '54" his plans included reading about "volcanoes & earthquake geology Book on basic botany Morley and Blom's work." These notes allude to Sylvanus Griswold Morley, author of *The Ancient Maya* (1946), and Frans Blom's *The Conquest of Yucatan* (1936), the Danish archeologist Ginsberg would meet in San Cristobal. Ginsberg also lists under the rubric "Reading Jan 1—'54/June/July" an ambitious educational program including Thomas Merton's *The Seven Story Mountain*, selections from Immanuel Kant, D. H. Lawrence's *Studies in Classic American Literature*, Plato's *Symposium*, articles from the *Encyclopedia Britannica* on "Hermetic types and sects," as well as "Guidebooks Uxmal & Merida." Upon arriving in Palenque, in order to orient himself, Ginsberg even sketched out a careful map, depicting the surrounding towns including Tumbala, Hidalgo, Yajalon, Chilon, and San Cristobal.[14]

Ginsberg's curiosity about Mexico was not only due to the influence of William S. Burroughs. We should remember that this first extended journey to Mexico occurred just a few years after Ginsberg's vision of William Blake in Harlem in 1948. As Ginsberg declares at the end of part 1 of "Siesta in Xbalba": "I thought, five years ago/sitting in my apartment,/my eyes were opened for an hour/seeing in dreadful ecstasy/the motionless buildings/of New York rotting/under the tides of Heaven." This epiphany was thus still relatively fresh in his memory, and Ginsberg was embarking on a quest for what Richard M. Bucke, the biographer of Walt Whitman, called "cosmic consciousness" in his book *Cosmic Consciousness: A Study of the Evolution of the Human Mind* (1901): the overwhelming sensation of unity with time, eternity, and the universe that poets and mystics throughout the ages have experienced. Ginsberg was thus also reading not only guidebooks and historical texts about Mexico but also a variety of mystical literature during this period. After traveling to Merida for three days—it took twenty years for the conquistador Francisco de Montejo with his superior weapons to crush the Maya resistance and colonize Merida in 1542, known as *Tiho* to the Maya—Ginsberg went to Chichen Itza where he spent time at night in his hammock looking at the stars and beheld the great pyramid temple. Arriving in Palenque, Ginsberg reports in February 1954 reading *The Cloud of Unknowing* and considers becoming "a monk"; however he decides "no need to do that, can develop anywhere and such agitations are passing. What hung me up on Cloud of Un. [*sic*] was the lovely and obviously true idea that a contemplative doesn't have to do anything but what he feels like, sit and think or walk and think, don't worry about work, life, money, no hangups, his job is to have no job but the unknown Abstraction & its sensations, & his love of it."[15] The phrase "the darkness of unknowing" came into English literature as "the cloud of unknowing" from the title of a treatise composed by an anonymous fourteenth century English author which recounts the conceptions of Pseudo-Dionysius the Areopagite, who as we have seen influenced Philip Lamantia. *The Cloud of Unknowing* advises one to find God through interior contemplation and love rather than through the intellectual faculties, and is in the tradition of the "negative theology" of Pseudo-Dionysius: God is beyond the human ability to describe, beyond language, essentially ineffable. Both the *Cloud of Unknowing* and the *Mystical Theology* of Pseudo-Dionysius became essential texts for several of the Beats including Lamantia, Ginsberg, Kerouac, McClure, and Diane di Prima. Thus Mexico allowed Ginsberg some distance from his native land—he revealed that he needed to escape the confines of New York City—as well as solitude, time for contemplation, and writing, all of which propelled his evolution as a poet.

An important moment in Ginsberg's Mexican itinerary was his visit to Uxmal in the Puuc hills where he observed: "The ruins here present from many points a splendid spectacle of white courtyards, complicated latticework and crude sculptures, temple roof-combs rising out of mounds, rubbled Mayan arched entranceways to unexcavated vast flat plazas, pyramids covered with trees, vistas of jungle and mountain perhaps 20 miles away in brilliant sunlite. . . . Directly east, the *House of the Magician* symmetrically facing me with balance and proportion unthinkable for this continent—I'd never realized the vast sophistication of Pre-Columbian America."[16] Ginsberg's close visual appreciation of the great complex of buildings and their elaborate formation is apparent, and one of Frederick Catherwood's celebrated drawings of Uxmal depicts the "Ornament over the Gateway of the Great Teocallis" (1844)—*teocalli* signifies "God-house" in Nahuatl and is a pyramid surmounted by a temple. Echoing Charles Olson, who believed American writers should turn to the history, culture, language, and myth of the Indigenous peoples of the Americas for inspiration rather than exclusively to Europe, Ginsberg asserted: "While I was in Chichen Itza and Palenque, cities of the old Maya empire on the Yucatan peninsula, I thought that [it] would be interesting to treat them as if they were the great ruins of Greece that Shelley and Keats wrote about. Why couldn't Americans use those Central American ruins for the same nostalgia and classical reference, the same sense of the eternal, time in eternity?"[17] These insights into the cultural achievements of the Maya would propel Ginsberg toward a new burst of creativity, for he would indeed turn to "those Central American ruins" for inspiration when he moved on to visit Palenque, located about thirty-one kilometers from the Usumacinta River. Nine hundred and ninety-seven kilometers in length, the Usumacinta was an important trade route, for other major Maya sites were situated directly on its banks such as Yaxchilan and Piedras Negras, which lies about forty-five kilometers downstream on the other side of the river in Guatemala.

Ginsberg's extroverted, kindly, generous, gregarious personality and his ability to easily make friends proved helpful, since one day he "was walking around Palenque & ran into a woman who grew up around here—the edge of the most inaccessible jungle area of South Mexico."[18] Her name was Karena Shields, an amateur archaeologist and author of *The Changing Wind* (1959)—a book about life in the Chiapas jungle—who had spent her childhood on a

Ginsberg in Palenque, courtesy of the Allen Ginsberg Estate

large *finca,* had played "Jane" in the early Tarzan movies, and claimed, according to Ginsberg, that she "was the only person in the world who knew of a lost tribe of Mayans living in Guatemala on a . . . river who still possibly could interpret codices & were specially on a mission to keep alive Mayan flame—and she told me all sorts of secrets, beginning with outline of Mayan Metaphysics & mystical lore & history & symbolism, that would have delighted Bill, who doesn't know—that it is all still extant."[19] "Bill" here is of course William Burroughs, and we also note here the belief—held for example by D. H. Lawrence—that there exists "secret" hidden lore possessed by the Maya as well as a circle of worldwide "initiates" into ancient esoteric knowledge. Shields invited Ginsberg to stay in her *finca,* and he explains that the "Cocoa Finca (or plantation)" was situated in the middle of the jungle: it would take a day on horseback to reach Palenque. Ginsberg traveled seven hours "thru beautiful dark jungle—soldier ants, anthills, lianas, orchids, vast trees covered with parasite cactus and fern, big leaved plantain trees, parrots screeching and wild deep roar of howler monkeys in trees sounding like Tarzan Jungle."

Ginsberg conveys a palpable sense of the seeming endlessness of the Mexican jungle and is alert to the lush proliferation of plant and animal life to be seen with every step. Some of Ginsberg's best travel writing about Mexico—fluent, exact, and often amusing—is in his letters and journals. His time with

Karena Shields led to Ginsberg's major accomplishment while in Mexico: "Siesta in Xbalba" (properly spelled "Xibalba"), a long poem in two parts. The first section was composed during his stay at Shields's *finca* and the second before Ginsberg's departure from Mexico.[20] "Siesta in Xbalba" took shape during Ginsberg's travels in Chiapas and the Yucatan and was largely drafted between April and May 1954. The poem—which had its sources in twenty pages of Ginsberg letters and approximately fifty pages of his *Journal*—underwent revisions until 1955, and was mimeographed to be circulated for the first time at the end of July 1956. The poem has made an impact beyond the literary world, for the distinguished Mayanists David Stuart and George Stuart in their monograph *Palenque: Eternal City of the Maya* quote verses from Ginsberg's poem at the opening of chapter 8, "Gods and Rulers"—"Palenque, broken chapels in the green/basement of a mount."[21]

The title "Siesta in Xbalba" contains the word many associate with a classic stereotype of life in Mexico—taking a restful nap in the afternoon—intentional on Ginsberg's part, for the poem explores the links between sleep, dream, change, eternity, and the hypnagogic zone between life, death, and time. Ginsberg was now in the midst of one of the greatest Maya cities—Palenque—where learned mathematicians and astronomers known for their intellectual wizardry pondered the mystery of Time, which they conceived in terms of the great cycles of Sun, Moon, and Venus. The Maya took time seriously, carefully chronicling in the *Book of the Katun* the events of each 7,200 days or twenty years: these written records were then kept securely in their temple archives. Surrounded by the remains of a lost culture, hemmed in all around by dense jungle, Ginsberg was compelled to consider the existential solitude of the human self apart from superfluous trappings of "civilization" and the immensity of time and space. The poet kept his notes while in Mexico in a lively journal and refashioned several passages from these observations for use in his poem. In another work inspired by ruins Ginsberg would compose during his 1963 visit to Cambodia—"Angkor Wat"—he also relied on notes taken down in Siem Reap, located outside the site of the great temple of Angkor Wat. Xibalba is a region extending from Tabasco through Palenque to the border of Guatemala, known to the Maya as the Underworld, the "Area of Limbo, or Place of Obscure Hope, Purgatory": the word *Xibalba* derives from the root *xib*, meaning, "fear, terror, trembling with fright."

The Maya, as Inga Clendinnen has observed, believed that beneath "the world lay the nine levels of the Underworld, a chill, bleak, shadowy place, where all Maya, save those fortunate few whose manner of death—in war, childbirth or sacrifice—exempted them, were doomed to wander endlessly."

In the Quiché Maya epic *Popol Vuh* which chronicles the creation of the world, the twins—Hunahpu and Xbalanque, both splendid ballplayers and blowgunners—make a journey to Xibalba to conquer the lords of death and avenge their father. They succeed through a variety of subterfuges in defeating the rulers of the Underworld and arise to become the moon and the sun. Ginsberg visited the large cave believed by the Maya to be an entrance to Xibalba.[22] As we have seen, caves were significant to the Indigenous peoples of Mexico, for "caves were valued as the place of origin of ancestral peoples who were identified with the life-giving forces found in seeds, water, and terrestrial beings. Caves were also 'passageways' to the underworld, and rituals performed in caves would symbolically transport human beings into the realm of the world below." Ginsberg spent an entire month working five to ten hours a day on "Siesta in Xbalba" and rightly considered that the poem marked a great advance from his earlier poetry.

He composed the poem while sitting at the foot of Mount Don Juan surrounded by ruins and was aiming at replicating the tradition of Shelley and Byron on the "ruins of time" as we see in the following letter written to Neal and Carolyn Cassady from Salto de Agua, May 12, 1954. Ginsberg seeks to evoke "the natural observations of palmtrees eerie appearance followed by some high poetic abstraction—all falling together in a kind of perfect sequence like a Wordsworth meditation—and best of all, the central thing, of course, naturally, and really fortunately, the locale—the ruins of Palenque and remembrance of others worked in artfully—so that it is in this new form, an approach such as the romantic Shelley or Byron, to the subject of the ruins of time—a subject otherwise impossible to write about nontritely."[23] "Siesta in Xbalba" also reflects Ginsberg's readings in *The Cloud of Unknowing*; as we saw above, he was struck in the text by "the lovely and obviously true idea that a contemplative doesn't have to do anything but what he feels like, sit and think," and in the first section of "Siesta" he muses: "One could pass valuable months/and years perhaps a lifetime/doing nothing but lying in a hammock/reading prose with the white doves/copulating underneath/and monkeys barking in the interior/of the mountain."[24] The "siesta"—virtually unknown in America—allows one to avoid the heat of the midday sun, to interrupt the workday's tedium with restful slumber. Ginsberg's retreat into archaic Mexican time surrounded by doves and monkeys is a way back to the sacred: as he exclaims near the end of part 1, "There is a god/dying in America," and as did D. H. Lawrence, he seeks in Mexico to resurrect the old gods, to find a way back to the "dark blood" of the primal world.[25]

In the first section of the poem, Ginsberg lists the great ruins he has visited in a stately hymn: "Pale Uxmal,/unhistoric, like a dream,/Tuluum shimmering on the coast in ruins;/Chichen Itza naked/constructed on a plain;/Palenque, broken chapels in the green/basement of a mount;/lone Kabah by the highway;/Piedras Negras buried again/by dark archaeologists;/Yaxchilan/resurrected in the wild,/and all the limbo of Xbalba still unknown." It is a striking catalogue, illustrating Ginsberg's close observations of the architecture and history of the Maya, each description a brief, cinematic snapshot preserving the memory of his perceptions. When Ginsberg shifts his gaze from buildings to the surrounding landscape, he is equally visually precise: "the long shade of the mountain beyond/in the near distance,/its individual hairline of trees/traced fine and dark along the ridge/against the transparent sky light,/rifts and holes in the blue air/and amber brightenings of clouds/disappearing down the other side/into the South."[26] Ginsberg hopes to find some transcendent vision "in the bleak flat night of Yucatan/where I come with my own mad mind to study alien hieroglyphs of Eternity."[27] His mind is still "mad" after his 1948 Blakean epiphany in Harlem—when he was seeking the cosmic connection to Eternity—and the "hieroglyphs" here are Maya glyphs, which had not yet been fully deciphered. The mystery of the meaning of the "writing" Ginsberg sees on the stone ruins is emphasized by a repeated pattern of phrases such as "High dim stone portals, entablatures of illegible scripture," "bas-reliefs of unknown perceptions," "indecipherable head-dresses of intellect/scattered in the madness of oblivion/to holes and notes of elemental stone" which indicate his desire to unlock the secrets hidden in the ancient writing.[28]

Ginsberg opens "Siesta in Xbalba" with an allusion to his recent visit to Uxmal: "Late sun opening the book,/blank page like light,/invisible words unscrawled,/impossible syntax/of apocalypse—Uxmal: Noble Ruins /No construction—." The meaning here is ambiguous: Is the "book" that is "opened" here with its "blank page" the composition book in which Ginsberg is about to inscribe his poem, or is it the "book of the "World" upon which the "late sun" sheds its light and which contains an inscrutable message, or finally, perhaps an open Mayan Codex which has yet to be interpreted? The Maya have left in their ruins undeciphered clues to an as yet uninterpretable language with "blank page," "invisible words unscrawled," "impossible syntax."[29] "Hieroglyph," in Ginsberg's "alien hieroglyphs of Eternity," represents for him its literal etymology: "holy writing" (ancient Greek *hieros* = sacred; *glyph* = carving). Perhaps in this ancient culture he can find the secret to the meaning of human existence for which he hungers and intimations of which he experienced six years previously during his Blake epiphany. Ginsberg is lost "in the/abandoned/labyrinth of Palenque/measuring my fate/wandering solitary in the wild." The "labyrinth" of the ancient Mexican site mirrors the mazelike complexities of Ginsberg's own selfhood. It has been argued that in "Siesta in Xbalba," Ginsberg employs a number of key words—such as "obscure," "madness," "mystical," "nakedness," and "wild"—which reappear in "Howl" and provide the insistent, propelling power of its music.[30] And perhaps the omnipresent dogs of Mexico and their sad, emaciated, starved yowling may also have impressed upon the poet the title for his most famous poem, aptly titled "Howl.". Just as "Siesta in Xbalba" seeks to find eternity among the vanished civilization of the ancient Mayan civilization, so too in "Howl" Ginsberg seeks—as did T. S. Eliot—a redemptive vision, fragments to shore up against the ruins of the modern world.

"Siesta in Xbalba" is a meditation on time, mortality, and eternity. Ginsberg notes the "pillars and corridors/sunken under the flood of years:/Time's slow wall overtopping/all that firmament of mind,/as if a shining waterfall of leaves and rain/were built down solid from the endless sky/through which no thought can pass." Ginsberg's verses bear more than a passing resemblance to the opening of Percy Bysshe Shelley's "Mont Blanc": "The everlasting universe of things/Flows through the mind, and rolls its rapid waves,/Now dark—now glittering—now reflecting gloom—/Now lending splendor, where from secret springs/The source of human thought its tribute brings/Of waters"; and a few lines later: "Where waterfalls around it leap for ever." Shelley's awe before Mont Blanc—the highest peak of the Alps on the border between Italy and France—invokes a universal "mind" to which the poet connects, as Ginsberg also makes contact with "all that firmament of mind." As Ginsberg strolls through the ruins of Mayan civilization, he peers into the underworld of the *Popol Vuh*: "I alone know the great crystal door/to the House of Night,/a legend of centuries/—I and a few Indians./And had I mules and money I could find/the Cave of Amber/and the Cave of Gold/rumored above the cliffs of Tumbala."[31] We hear echoes of Samuel Taylor Coleridge's putatively opium-induced mystical experience recorded in "Kubla Khan"—"caverns" and the repeated "caves of ice"—as well as Arthur Rimbaud's "*J'ai seul la clef de cette parade sauvage*": "I alone hold the key to this savage parade," from *Les Illuminations*. And as in "Kubla Khan," Ginsberg listens while in Chiapas to "ancestral voices prophesying war" as he turns from the moss-covered stones before him toward his native land threatened by the "ultimate" apocalypse of nuclear war: "Yet these ruins so much/woke me to nostalgia/for the classic stations/of the earth,/the ancient continent I have not seen/and the few years/of memory left/before the ultimate night of war."[32]

In part 2, Ginsberg recalls his travels throughout Mexico scene by scene: taking a logboat down Rio Michol; observing Lake Catemaco from the bus; being spooked by the mummies in Guanajuato's El Museo de Las Momias, which contains the mummified remains of people who perished during the cholera outbreak of 1833: "grasping their bodies/with stiff arms, in soiled/funeral clothes;/twisted, knock-kneed,/like burning/screaming lawyers—/what hallucinations/of the nerves?—indecipherable-sexed." Here the memento mori theme returns, and we also catch a hint of the style of "Howl" with the sudden surreal humor of the simile "like burning/screaming lawyers" and the Blakean ("The Tyger") exclamation "what hallucinations/of the nerves?" The science fiction author Ray Bradbury (1920–2012) was so horrified following his visit to the Guanajuato mummies, "the experience so wounded and terrified me, I could hardly wait to flee Mexico. I had nightmares about dying and having to remain in the halls of the dead with those propped and wired bodies. In order to purge my terror, instantly, I wrote 'The Next in Line.' One of the few times that an experience yielded results almost on the spot." Ginsberg ends his travelogue with his journey to San Miguel de Allende, where he witnesses through the keyhole of his hotel room joyful scamperings of young lovers: he arrives finally in Mexicali, the capital of Baja California on the U.S. border. Ginsberg closes "Siesta in Xbalba" with a return to threats of apocalypse. A notable feature of Maya literature is the frequent appearance of prophecy: the *Chilam Balam* contains—as well as calendrical and medical data—warnings of famine, floods, earthquakes, hurricanes, plague, and epidemics, predictions of future catastrophe. Indeed, it is the *Chilam Balam* which prophesied that one day the Spaniards would arrive: "Receive your guests, the bearded men, the men of the east, the bearers of the sign of God." When Ginsberg turns his attention to his own homeland, he draws parallels between the fate of the Maya and that awaiting his own country: "The nation over the border/grinds its arms and dreams/of war: I see/the fiery blue clash/of metal wheels/clanking in the industries/of night, and/detonation of infernal bombs."[33] The language of "Howl's" "the starry dynamo in the machinery of night" is again prefigured by "industries/of night." Ginsberg beheld in these great Mayan ruins submerged beneath the jungle a warning of what may happen to our world beset by the nuclear arms race, and the mood of "Siesta in Xibalba" is elegiac. Like Margaret Randall's "Quetzalcoatl: 1961" or Philip Lamantia's "Ceylonese Tea Candor (Pyramid Scene)" and "Lava,"

Ginsberg's poetry is replete with warnings of apocalypse and Armageddon. So too Jack Kerouac in *On the Road* counterpointed the impoverished "fellahin" of Mexico to contemporary humanity, musing that they "didn't know that a bomb had come that could crack all our bridges and roads and reduce them to jumbles, and we would be as poor as they someday, and stretching out our hands in the same, same way." Bidding farewell to Mexico, Ginsberg contemplates an uncertain future for himself as well as for his native land.

After Ginsberg's return to the United States, he reflected upon his earlier experiences in Mexico. Ginsberg learned about Burroughs's killing of Joan after he had missed seeing Burroughs in Mexico City and had returned to the United States in 1951. He composed the poem—like "Siesta in Xbalba," included in *Reality Sandwiches*—"Dream Record: June 8, 1955" upon Joan Vollmer's death. Ginsberg notes that he spent a drunken night in San Francisco with a boy. He sleeps and dreams: "I went back to Mexico City/and saw Joan Burroughs leaning/forward in a garden-chair, arms/on her knees. She studied me with/clear eyes and downcast smile, her/face restored to a fine beauty/tequila and salt had made strange/before the bullet in her brow." The two reminisce about Burroughs, Kerouac, and Herbert Huncke, and Ginsberg asks her, "What kind of knowledge have/the dead? can you still love/your mortal acquaintances?" Her image then fades away from him and momentarily he beholds "her rain-stained tombstone/rear an illegible epitaph/under the gnarled branch of a small/tree in the wild grass/of an unvisited garden in Mexico."[34] Joan was buried in the Panteon Americano cemetery, her gravestone reading: "Joan Vollmer Burroughs, Loudonville, New York, 1923, Mexico D.F. Sept. 1951." Ginsberg's poem attempts to make sense of Joan's death in Mexico City and recalls the meetings in the underworld we find in classical literature such as Virgil's *Aeneid* and Homer's *Odyssey.* In later comments and interviews, Ginsberg went even further in attempts to soften and rationalize Joan's death—in a bizarre example of Beat misogyny—suggesting that Joan's murder was actually an act of suicide: Vollmer had always wanted to die and Burroughs in pulling the trigger had simply fulfilled her wish.

Ginsberg did not make many trips to Mexico, but he did visit again prior to a trip to Cuba, arriving in Mexico City on January 15, 1965, when he spent time with Margaret Randall. Ginsberg remarks upon the green bounty of the Zocalo, noting the loveliness of "the colored tile houses set up under the snaky boughed palms. And the light in the trees transparent green trembling sharp leaves," returning to the exact descriptions of nature of "Siesta in Xbalba." He walks to the Calle Guerrero, eats a sausage and tacos, drinks

Papaya juice. The next day he reports: "Museum Modern Art Chapultepec Magic surrealism Frida Kahlo, combines Alberto Gironella, big black rat by Coronel, Alchemical math by Carrington, black sweater selfportrait Montoya then 13 funny historic gems by Antonio Ruiz (El Corzo) 1897–1964."[35] The telegraphic style is typical of Ginsberg's journals, noting the surrealistic works he enjoyed in the museum, including Leonora Carrington's alchemical paintings. As we saw in chapter 2, Philip Lamantia shared with Carrington—who also composed stories as well as novels including *The Hearing Trumpet* (1976) and *The Stone Door* (1977)—an interest in the occult, and esoteric themes pervade her oeuvre. Ginsberg goes on in this passage—like his friend Kerouac—to envisage Mexico as a place where he can live the life of a "bearded sage and eat tortillas for a year." Ginsberg is sometimes considered—by those who have not read him closely—an exclusively serious writer, but his sense of humor is omnipresent. He also refers to "Acapulco Gold," which is invoked by a character in Michael McClure's novel *The Adept* (1970). "Acapulco Gold" was presumably high-quality marijuana grown in the Guerrero Mountains outside of Acapulco, and the term is first attested in 1964. Like Burroughs, Ginsberg made long, scrupulous studies over decades of psychotropic substances, carefully recording the results in his poems and journals. Indeed, Ginsberg was central in the nexus between academia and the counterculture in the exploration of entheogens, a role, as we shall see in the next chapter, which Michael McClure continued in his search for mushrooms in Mexico. American universities including Harvard, Berkeley, and Stanford all instituted programs to explore scientifically the effects of these substances regarding creativity, spiritual awareness, and mental illness.

In the final paragraph, Ginsberg notes the magnificent Sun Stone—the subject of a famous poem by Octavio Paz in circular form, concluding with the identical lines with which it begins, "Piedra de sol" (1957)—and Coatlicue, both on display in the Museo Nacional de Anthropologia, the renovation of which was completed in September 1964 just before Ginsberg's visit. The Coatlicue sculpture was discovered on August 13, 1790, in the Zocalo of Mexico City, and four months later on December 19, the Aztec Sun Stone—the great calendar stone, 141 inches in diameter and 39 inches thick, weighing approximately twenty-four short tons—was found. Ginsberg is struck by the sublimity of these great sculptures as well as by the new museum, falling into a "high trance" listening to a recording of a "Curander [*sic*]" chanting in a "Magic Mushroom" ceremony—this is likely Maria Sabina of Huautla de Jimenez in Oaxaca.[36] This visit to the national museum swiftly encapsulates many of the Mexican themes of both Ginsberg and the Beats: the role of surrealism; the desire to find in Mexico a place of spiritual—and culinary—restoration; the significance of consciousness-expanding substances such as Acapulco Gold and Magic Mushrooms; the fascination with the power and beauty of the masterpieces of Aztec and Maya culture; and finally the engagement with shamanistic practices.

We have explored in this chapter how Mexican themes appear in several Ginsberg poems including "Paterson," "Ready to Roll," and most importantly "Siesta in Xbalba" composed in Palenque. Ginsberg followed William S. Burroughs in his curiosity concerning the Maya, visiting several archaeological sites in Mexico. Although he did not study Maya glyphs, the trope of glyphs/hieroglyphs and undeciphered writing, the riddle of the code of the universe, is a major theme in "Siesta in Xbalba."[37] Ginsberg's visionary quest in Mexico—a continuation of his initial ecstatic encounter with the spirit of William Blake in 1948—found expression in his evocations of the ruins of the great Maya civilization as well as his experiments with entheogens. Ginsberg's poetic evolution while in Mexico prepared the way for "Howl," and his connection to Mexico continued over the decades: in August 1981, he traveled to Mexico again for the Primer Festival Internacional de Poesia held in Morelia, Michoacan, appearing with Homero Aridjis, Andrei Voznesenski, Jorge Luis Borges, W. S. Merwin, and Gunter Grass. Finally, in later works such as the recently published *Iron Curtain Journals* (2018), Ginsberg continued his close attention to Mexican culture in his observations concerning the Museo Nacional de Anthropologia. Mexico was—along with India—the most important destination on his lifelong quest for enlightenment.

# 7 ✻ BONNIE BREMSER

## *Troia: Mexican Memoirs*

Although often neglected by the academy, Margaret Randall and Joanne Kyger made significant contributions to Beat literature about Mexico. Another important work in this canon—which has received comparatively greater attention, considered by Ronna C. Johnson "a lost classic of Beat experimental writing"—is *Troia: Mexican Memoirs* by Bonnie Bremser.[1] Born in Washington, D.C., in 1939, Brenda Frazer—while a student at Sweet Briar College—met the Beat poet Ray Bremser at George Washington University, where Bremser, LeRoi Jones (later Amiri Baraka), Gregory Corso, Allen Ginsberg, and Peter Orlovsky all read their poetry. Bonnie married Ray three weeks after meeting him at age nineteen on March 21, 1959.[2] Ray Bremser spent time in jail for offenses including armed robbery, and his work was published in LeRoi Jones's *Yugen*. Bob Dylan acknowledged Bonnie's husband as an influence in his "Eleven Outlined Epitaphs" on the jacket sleeve of *The Times They Are a-Changin'*: "Love songs of Allen Ginsberg/an' jail songs of Ray Bremser."[3] Ray's incarceration on drug charges and subsequent legal troubles led the couple to flee to Mexico. So too, William S. Burroughs—and later Ken Kesey, author of *One Flew over the Cuckoo's Nest*, and fellow "Merry

Prankster" traveler on the bus "Furthur" with Neal Cassady, an episode chronicled in Tom Wolfe's *The Electric Kool-Aid Acid Test* (1968)—was escaping prosecution when he journeyed to Mexico. Ray and Bonnie borrowed money from Elaine de Kooning, and Bonnie began working as a prostitute to support Ray, herself, and their baby daughter Rachel, who was born in 1960. Bonnie recalled that "the exact term we used in describing our alienated condition in Mexico . . . was 'fugitives from justice.'" "Troia" in the title *Troia: Mexican Memoirs* in one putative etymology is said to derive from the designation for Helen of Troy—hence a sexually faithless woman. *Troia* is composed of four books: book 1, "Mexico City to Veracruz and Back to Texas"; book 2, "Mexico to Laredo: Getting Ray Out of Jail"; book 3, "Mexico City and Rural Excursions: Losing Rachel"; book 4, "Mexico City and Back to New York." Bremser originally wrote *Troia* as a series of two-page letters to Ray between March and November 1963—Bremser estimates that she produced four to five hundred pages of text—which were later edited by Michael Perkins, who organized the material in its present form. Perkins published the work in 1969 as *Troia: Mexican Memoirs* and in Britain as *For Love of Ray* (1971).

As we have seen earlier, the tendency of a writer like Jack Kerouac to turn Mexico and Mexicans into imaginative versions of his own heart's desire has been critiqued.[4] Kerouac's "romantic" hymning of Mexico as a lost paradise nevertheless influenced Bremser's musical style. Bremser's poetics is both hip and lofty. She acknowledged the centrality of jazz musicians John Coltrane, Thelonious Monk, Ray Charles, and Bessie Smith to her style, and in her poem "banjopome/scat on suspenders" published in *Yowl* in 1963, Bremser imitates the sounds of a snare drum, piano, bass, and xylophone, playing pleasurably with the sounds of words syncopated in Beat jazz style: "In view of snare shuffle/drum-drum/which dda da dit/can't no one say no/different/plunk/plunk . . . fatback whacka do/mistah play that/bass-fiddle." When Bremser sings the landscape of Mexico—Amy Friedman has accurately described her development of "a rhythmic, flowing poetic prose"—she also creates a musical prose-poetry and brings, as does Kerouac, the divine and the earthly together in lyrical fashion: "I look out and God drops from his hand the myriad stars and constellations I have never seen before, plumb to the horizon flat landed out beneath the giant horoscopic screen of the Mexican heaven." During Kerouac's trips to Mexico in 1955 and 1956, he worked on *Tristessa*, and again his prose *moves*: "here I am in Mexico City, rainy Saturday night, mysteries, old dream sidestreets with no names reeling in, the little street where I'd walked through crowds of gloomy Hobo Indians wrapped in tragic shawls enough to make you cry."[5] So too in *Troia*, Mexico City—which

Bremser habitually abbreviates as "Mexcity"—becomes for her, as for Kerouac, a central location. Mexico City is named in the titles of three of the four "Books" of *Troia*, and Bremser hymns its name, emphasizing its designation as a "federal district": "Mexcity, D.F., hot morning and I have slept a couple of hours of exhausted sleep"; "Mexico City, distrito federal, Mexico D.F., Mexcity, dome-topped rocknrolls the whole day from five in the morning or so building up to a crush at several points in the day." Jack Kerouac, William S. Burroughs, and Philip Lamantia all spent extended periods in Mexico City and created several of their most important works there; thus Bremser in making the megalopolis a central character in her book is continuing a well-established Beat tradition.

The notion of the journey as spiritual allegory also informs *On the Road*: the title itself calls to mind Lao Tzu's *Tao Te Ching*, and the *Tao* signifies the Path, Way, or Road toward balance with the cosmos. Bremser casts her travels in Mexico, chronicled in *Troia*, after Kerouac's model, announcing from the outset her quest for self-realization through romantic love: "The first time that Ray was taken away from me by New Jersey I was fresh out of college, married to Ray only six months, a rebel, yes, but still investigating just the outermost bounds of myself. I didn't know much of what anything was about, had only the confidence to accept Ray's love and marry him." Bremser employs the religious language of "hope," "despair," "abandonment," "faithfulness," "believed," and "repentance": "The hope of a dream had long since died in my cynicism, and despair had taken over, enabling me to live in abandon without even knowing what abandon was. But the dream had grown freshly when I met Ray, and when they took him from me the first time, I abandoned my hope and gave up the faithfulness and the dream I had so implicitly believed in. . . . So, blame me! I can't blame myself anymore, for the repentance is done in the act and working through it." Bremser celebrates the dream of romantic love as a kind of "redemption" from the fallen state of individual solitude.

In her essay "Poets and Odd Fellows," Bremser returns to this religious imagery in a description of her lovemaking with Ray: "In the diffused sunlight we could see each other. His long body looked like a naked Jesus, stretched out in undershorts," suggesting the sacramental nature of their erotic love. Just as the characters in *On the Road* are named Sal Paradise and Dean Moriarty, so too Bonnie and Ray are a duo in search of salvation. Sal's name invokes both Salvatore and Salvation, and at the very opening of *Troia*, Bremser reveals: "Yes, funny, you who know me, Bonnie of the streets, of the hard touch, of the frantic spiritual judgment come to coerce you, you remember, jazz, soul, bebop, and well along the straight road to salvation." More words associated with religious life—"devotion," "sacrifice, " and "purity"—appear later in book 2 when Bremser confesses: "I had thought it was my devotion, that my sacrifice in Mexico had kept us alive, and now in Texas it became clearly dependence on poetry, and poetry has lofty words to describe a purity I had a long time been on vacation from."[6] Bremser thus sets the stage in the opening pages of her struggle with the twin poles of flesh and spirit, alienation and salvation, silence and speech. *Troia* is indeed an "experimental" work given the fluidity and speed of Bremser's prose, the odd disjunctions in chronology, her idiosyncratic and often striking veering of thought (one is reminded at times of Virginia Woolf), her surprising and original turns of phrase. The reader is also confronted with her vacillation between accepting her role as prostitute and rebelling against it, her surrender to the passive role as supporter of her family and her reclaiming of agency as a writer, her past life in America and present adventures in Mexico. She is, like Kerouac's characters, "mad to live," and like them bounces back and forth between a manic ecstasy—Bremser ingested a variety of drugs including Benzedrine, heroin, and peyote while in Mexico—and a depressive ennui. The cover of the 2007 Dalkey Archive Press edition of *Troia* features a drawing by Alice Neel depicting a mysteriously half-smiling Bremser with both hands holding her cheeks in an Expressionist pose of tortured, visionary intensity.

Bremer's style sometimes directly mimics Kerouac's, as when we encounter her declaration: "*I will moan and groan in misery no more.*"[7] In *On the Road*, Kerouac invents a kind of Biblical mantra: "go moan, go groan, go groan alone go roll your bones, alone; go thou and be little beneath my sight."[8] And finally, like Kerouac, Bremser keeps the narrative lively and swift by commencing her book in medias res: "Once across, we were quickly tired of Matamoros and purchased tickets to Mexico City."[9] She follows the highway south through Mexico—the 775-mile stretch of the Pan American Highway connecting Laredo, Texas, with Mexico City was completed in July 1937, allowing American tourists access to the country in their automobiles—and chimes off the place names with musical pleasure: Padilla, Abasolo, Guemez, Ciudad Victoria, Ciudad Monte, Valles, Ixmiquilpan, Actopan, Pachuca. She lingers on the names of these places, creating a kind of litany, a kind of slow initiation into an alien culture which is at once beckoning and strange. The Nahuatl origin of some of these locations explains the—to an Anglophone visitor—odd yet alluring proliferation of the letters *x* and *q*. Several English words have Nahuatl roots, including *coyote, mesquite,* and *ocelot* as well as *avo-*

*cado*, *tomato*, *chocolate*, *chili*, and *guacamole*. Bremser describes details of her experiences with food (eating huevos rancheros); the indigenous plants (mesquite bushes); and the animals (a profusion of mangy dogs). For an unpracticed writer—*Troia* was her first effort at sustained literary composition—Bremser is adept at evoking the sights, sounds, and atmosphere of Mexico as she first travels across the border from Texas.

As we discussed in chapter 4, Margaret Randall was an important figure in the Beat contingent along with Philip Lamantia in Mexico City. Bremser's connection with Lamantia—she abbreviates his name as "P"—is also established at the opening, for Bonnie and Ray are "on our way to make the scene at P's." For Bremser—as for Randall and Lamantia—Mexico City holds out the promise of becoming a center where American expatriates can create a literary and spiritual community. Her excitement on the road is palpable as she erupts in an operatic apostrophe: "Mexico, Mexico, your sun crashes me in the head obliterating all bodily care, all shame, shameless Mexico, I am your child, and you have my child as the token."[10] *Troia*'s narrative structure, as we have noted, is not strictly chronological, and Bremser moves back and forth in time as the book progresses. Arriving at Lamantia's apartment, there is a flashback as we are informed that she first encountered Lamantia the year she met Ray—which was 1959—in San Francisco, "having just aired our souls on the Mojave Desert." She recalls her response to Lamantia's surrealistic poetry: "He took us to his room in the B Hotel and, handing us one enormous reefer, proceeded to read stuff that will knock you out, poetry that can't fail to hit you in your own personal cause of it all, and therefore we love him." It was during this time with Lamantia that Ray composed many of the "jazz poems'" which were later collected in his volume *Blowing Mouth*.

Bremser also meets Lamantia's "blonde stage-managing wife" whom she abbreviates as "L.": this is Lucille Dejardin. Dejardin translated two texts by Antonin Artaud about opium, "A Letter to the Legislator of the Law on Narcotics" and "General Security—The Liquidation of Opium," both appearing in Philip Lamantia's *Narcotica* (1959). In "Mexico City and Rural Excursions: Losing Rachel," Bremser reveals that she and Ray listened to Lamantia "talk of Indian pyramids. P. has been held at nighttime superstitious bay by nearby Teotihuacan pyramid of the sun and tells us of hidden spearheads . . . and shifts right from that story to tell us of the magic mushroom people in the hills (mountains) of Oaxaca."[11] One of the characteristics of the literature of the Beat movement, as we have emphasized, is the way works by each individual author often comment on and respond to other authors in the group. Thus Jack Kerouac provides a chronicle of virtually every Beat in his novels, employing a variety of pseudonyms: "Bull Lee" for William S. Burroughs; "Carlo Marx" for Allen Ginsberg; "Francis de Pavia" for Philip Lamantia. So too, Bremser includes Lamantia within her narrative, and her reference to the "hidden spearheads" Lamantia encountered on Teotihuacan confirm the "arrowsharp rock juttings" which Lamantia had described in his poem analyzed in chapter 3 regarding his visit to the pyramid, "Ceylonese Tea Candor (Pyramid Scene)." Bremser confirms the episode when Lamantia confronted Aztec ghosts at Teotihuacan. Bremser also learns from Lamantia of the existence of Maria Sabina, the famed *curandera* of Huautla de Jimenez in the Sierra Mazateca in Oaxaca, who became a central heroine for the counterculture, inspiring Anne Waldman's poem "Fast Speaking Woman." In her chronicling of her meetings with fellow Beats such as Lamantia, Bremser emphasizes the fact that Mexico by the late fifties had become an important destination in the search for alternatives to the stultifying conformity and repression of life in the United States.

In *Troia*, Bremser's personal quest appears in a repeated cycle of imagery which hymns the places of Mexico in terms which suggest sacred precincts: "The sun rises, Veracruz rises, some altar on this Easternmost coast, the morning of Mexico, Veracruz rises beyond the sugar fields."[12] Bremser is again alluding to the sacred place of the sun in Aztec and Maya religious ceremonies—Veracruz is compared to an "altar"—and there is a hint of irony since it was at Chalchihuecan near Veracruz on the Totonacan coast that Hernan Cortes landed on November 21, 1519, with five hundred and eight soldiers and ten cannons: thus began the destruction of the Indigenous cultures of Mexico. Later in book 3, Bremser exhibits her knowledge of Mexican history and geography in a passage in which Cortes is explicitly mentioned: "Mexico is a basin within a circle of mountains which is punctuated by the two volcanoes on the eastern side. Between the volcanoes is the easiest, most level pass, a natural entrance from Veracruz, Cortes found it and named it, but superstitions prevent it from being used." Cortes is mentioned again in a passage in which Bremser describes a trip she made with a client to Mexico City: "and we drive there in his distinguished black car in the hot Mexcity, *Zocalo* heat of open pavements and uncontrollable dust from the evaporated lakes—Cortes' biggest mistake, Mexcity is a nightmare of the dream it must have been of lakes and straight solid standing rock houses simple with the primal worshipping fervor; it has now become Spanish trash and dust and shame." Bremser refers to the canals the Aztecs built at Teotihuacan and how the city degenerated once the conquistadors arrived. Later, Bremser invokes Popocatepetl and subtly alludes to D. H. Lawrence's *Mornings in Mexico* (1927)—

"the morning of Mexico, Veracruz rises beyond the sugar fields"—in which Lawrence reflected upon the Indigenous cultures of Old and New Mexico in eight classic essays.[13]

Another sequence of religious imagery follows: "a prophetic bus ride" and "oh, the universe I am to grow accustomed to in Mexico. I am redeemed!"; two pages later, her daughter Rachel is described as "an object of worship, our white baby."[14] Yet Bremser is not limited to the lyrical mode: she is also capable of rendering vivid and accurate descriptions of specific places in Veracruz. She exhibits her virtuosic technique in her painterly—*ut pictura poesis*—evocation of the Palacio Gobierno: "Two men across the corner wash the pavement of the Plaza in front of the Palacio Gobierno which is a Spanish dream of balconies and underwalking intrigues only now honored by slick shipping clerks on the make—the square-shaped park of the plaza slices into immaculate pie sections of bench backs and miniature trees twisting with symmetrical bald branches, houses a tiny fountain with colored tiles which is every morning emptied and cleaned for public use, for the cruisers' comfort, for drunken *borracheros'* collapse, and subsequent edification of tourists to the glory of Spain"[15] In addition to describing the architecture and layout of Mexican towns such as Veracruz, Bremser delights in tempting recitals of Mexican cuisine: "I go beyond the grocery store into the courtyard where there is a line long as at the unemployment office waiting to buy *gordas*, tortillas fried big and fat with black beans inside. They are truly delectable with coffee. . . . Little Mexican chicks knock on our door with plates of some kind of tortilla concoction with tomatoes and onions, they all have different names, depending on how they are cooked, *panuchos* and *gordas* were the best though." Bremser praises "black coffee, black beans, tortillas well baked—you never know what a feast of pleasure eating can be till you have accustomed yourself to this black Veracruz food," and sings a gastronomic aria: "Cry me strawberries, or silent fresas arriving into town from mud-walled vicinities of barefoot Indians. I am in awe, eat as many strawberries as I can."[16] Among all the Beat travelers to Mexico, Bremser is the most ebullient and appealing in her open joy in sharing the delights of Mexican food. While *Troia* falls within the genre of autobiographical memoir devoted to the most personal and private issues, it is also a travel book and packs a good deal of culinary, mythological, geographical, architectural, and ethnographic information about Mexico within its pages.

Yet Mexico for the Beats as we have emphasized was also the scene of death, destruction, and suffering. For Bremser, Mexico becomes a place of spiritual and physical testing, and although the pleasures of Mexico are intense, Bremser earns her money—we are reminded—through her labor as a sex worker: "All day my mind shrinks from the understanding of what I have to do at night."[17] Indeed, Allen Ginsberg contacted Margaret Randall to help Bonnie and Ray when they arrived in Mexico. Randall commented in her recently published autobiography *I Never Left Home: Poet, Feminist, Revolutionary* (2020) that Bremser had thought Randall to be "a naïve and bourgeois woman. . . . I was certainly naïve in many ways, and clearly bourgeois compared with Ray and Bonnie. But I'd supported Ray's evasion of prison time, played a part in putting them in contact with people south of the border, and don't remember making a judgment about Bonnie's decision to prostitute herself if it was the only way they could survive. I did wonder if it might not be coercion on Ray's part, rather than Bonnie's choice." Margaret Randall's intuition that it was Ray's *coercion* and not an independent decision on Bonnie's part to support her family in such a manner would be in accord with the tradition of Beat misogyny, and Bonnie wrestles throughout with questions of her own agency.

Bremser plays with the reader from the opening, revealing and concealing, projecting an adventurous self and retreating into the fact that she is "inscrutable, too, even to myself." In the introduction, she evokes the ancient practice of sacred prostitution in a precipitous, startling aside: "Or should I cite history about the temple prostitutes?" However, she immediately undercuts this with: "No, that would be a downright lie." There are indeed accounts by the Greek historian Herodotus and other ancient sources concerning sacred sexual rites which took place in temples. Herodotus claimed that in Babylon there was a custom "which is wholly shameful: every woman who is a native of the country must once in her life go and sit in the temple of Aphrodite and there give herself to a strange man. . . . When she has lain with him, her duty to the goddess is discharged and she may go home, after which it will be impossible to seduce her by any offer, however large." Sir James George Frazer in *The Golden Bough* offers a similar example: "In Cyprus it appears that before marriage all women were formerly obliged by custom to prostitute themselves to strangers at the sanctuary of the goddess, whether she went by the name of Aphrodite, Astarte, or what not. Similar customs prevailed in many parts of Western Asia. Whatever its motive, the practice was clearly regarded, not as an orgy of lust, but as a solemn religious duty performed in the service of that great Mother Goddess of Western Asia whose name varied, while her type remained constant from place to place."[18] However, Bremser's purpose is not to attain historical "truth" but to suggest at the opening her own confusions and unreliability as a narrator, signaling that

*Troia* is about *our*—the *readers'*—reactions to her story. The question for us is to decide how we might interpret her struggles with patriarchy, autonomy, sexuality, and power as she travels in Mexico.

This allusion to the ancient world is part of a pattern of imagery sustained throughout *Troia*. Bremser also refers to Egypt—as we have seen, an ancient civilization that fascinated Burroughs, Lamantia, and Corso as well—and her opening pages end with an invocation: "My soul is black to its depth and the heart shines through like a beacon, or that powerful Egyptian self-induced light which moves all material things effortlessly. The pacified ghost roams at leisure within the pyramid, takes on the countenance of its own sphinx, expresses itself inwardly, and that pretty much excludes you."[19] These are cryptic lines, yet this is an encoded allusion to the fact that Egypt is known to students of the occult as the birthplace of alchemy, and Bremser's black soul evokes the etymology of alchemy as *al-chemia*, the "black land," the name for ancient Egypt. And the "powerful Egyptian self-induced light which moves all material things effortlessly" recalls the powers of the Egyptian gods such as Ptah, who brought the universe into being merely by speaking. Bremser returns to Egyptian imagery in book 3 when she and Ray have arrived in Valles in San Luis Potosi and make a trip to the river: "The river's edge is muddy, we have walked down ivy Grecian steps to get to the river, step the Egyptian prow of one of the ferry canoes, the driver is silent and does not speak; he collects 20 centavos. We move down the silent river, the world moves above in reflections, oh look up at the Mexico—oh sky!"[20] The Mexican river induces her to ponder Egyptian rivers, and these repeated allusions to Egypt and the implied connection to the Mexican landscape are no accident. Bremser in "The Village Scene"—one of the fragments of her continued memoir which has yet to be published in full—describes a visit she and Ray made to the Museum of Natural History: "He explained to me about Cleopatra's obelisk, which was in the gardens to the south of the museum. We spent long hours looking at the exhibits, especially the ones about ancient Egypt."[21] Ray Bremser's poem "Follow the East River," packed with Egyptian allusions, appeared in his volume *Poems of Madness* (1965): "Aquarius carried plague & water/Germans hepatitis & the crud/from over Europe/carried the westerlies of queen Hat Shepsut/squatting the dismal width of the delta of Nile . . . /We couldn't find Memphis knowing it always was there." The poem goes on to allude to the Nile, the Valley of the Kings, Thebes, Amun, Nefertiti, Hathor, and Anubis.[22] It is evident that there is an intertextuality here between wife and husband—Bonnie responding to Ray's earlier time in New York City's Museum of Natural History where he contemplated the artworks memorializing Hatshepsut (d. 1458 B.C.E.), the fifth pharaoh of the 18th Dynasty of Egypt, and Nefertiti, queen and Great Royal Wife of Akhenaten, and his subsequent poem "Follow the East River"—and her current time in Mexico. Bonnie observes, "[we] felt as though our marriage was somehow being reconsecrated in this mythological setting." This is clearly the manner in which she imagines the landscape of Mexico, which she often "mythologizes" as the place where her love for her husband is both celebrated and tested.

Egypt and Mexico are further conflated in Bremser's imagination when she discusses several trips to Coatzacoalcos—the name in Nahuatl means "where the snake hides"—a port city in the southern part of the state of Veracruz. She dances on the beach with Ray: "Or, flash ahead to Coatzacoalcos, a strain of pure music floats over the chilly breeze, we are both sunburned and have been writing human hieroglyphs of bodily dance on the beach the whole day."[23] Hieroglyphs are of course the writing of ancient Egypt, while the Maya are invoked in book 3 in a passage in which Bonnie and Ray argue concerning Bonnie's "hustling": "It was straight action, either I was out hustling, busy, or we were spending the money and then went out again, and everything that was not business was supposed to be pleasure, sacred, necessary, but the moment any irritation comes up between us the whole story comes out in very personal glyphs and the arguments take longer and longer and it gets so that we both can't even stand to enter the argument anymore knowing the enormity of involvement beforehand, and begin to concentrate it. I tell Ray to 'beat it' or 'get off my back.'"[24] Bremser's phrase regarding "very personal glyphs" is revelatory. Glyphs compose the writing system developed by the Maya and thus Bonnie at this point in the narrative conceives her personal conflicts with her husband in terms of the pre-Conquest culture of the Maya. A "glyph" to someone not trained to interpret it is of course mute and untranslatable, like the complex, contradictory feelings Bonnie experiences in the untenable position she occupies throughout *Troia* of at once loving deeply her husband yet at the same time resenting the fact that she must sleep with other men to support her family. Bonnie acknowledges her extreme introversion: "I have always been shy. . . . Maybe that shyness has always been an armor for the great darkness within me, truly matching in fact Ray's Neptunian depths."[25] Mexico on one level has become the backdrop for an intense psychodrama—"the great darkness within me." Her plight often seems as inscrutable as the "glyphs" which adorn the Maya temples of Chichen Itza, Uxmal, and Palenque.

The Indigenous peoples of Mexico play a major role in *Troia,* culminating in Bremser's pilgrimage to Huautla de Jimenez to meet Maria Sabina. In the opening sections, these encounters are chronicled from a distance: "Beyond the morning's darkness yet things begin to move about in the market. I have awakened to change Rachel's diapers and move to watch the nighttime Indians fade into the distance drunken, collapse up some alley, up many alleys as they filter away just at the end of night, there is a half-hour pause where nothing moves."[26] As in the United States, the Native population has been dispossessed and condemned to lives of poverty and alcoholism. Later in book 1, Bremser describes an Indigenous woman who plies the same trade as Bonnie: "Play me a danzon-flute lighted thump the Indian heart trip light across the snake-veiled dance floor. An Indian whore, her hair braided with ribbons and runs in her stockings, red shoes—the taxicab driver loves her—she only costs five pesos."[27] Bremser wants the Indigenous peoples of Mexico to take back their land: "I delight in glee in the Indians all around in the hill—ha! they have us surrounded—give it back to yourselves Indians! It is as easy as that—how I hate the American Spanish . . . no need to tell the rest of Acapulco, anyone who has ever been to Acapulco knows the rest and, if not, the travel folders on Third Avenue are adequate enough information, reckless tourism.[28] Bremser delights in the fact that, for the moment, Indians "have us surrounded," rather like the Native Americans in Hollywood Western movies who encircle the white pioneers hiding within their circle of Conestoga wagons, firing their rifles. She also associates the poverty and oppression of native peoples with an influx of American "reckless tourism" which already by the early sixties had begun to transform Mexico into a favored travel destination. By the seventies, the Mexican government set out to reshape the northeastern coast of Quintana Roo in the Yucatan into an extensive, gaudy strip of hotels which would transform Cancun into a blight of international mass tourism. Bremser identifies with the oppressed people of Mexico, and urges them to "give it back to yourselves Indians!" Just as Henry David Thoreau opposed the Mexican-American War and spent a night in jail for refusing to pay his poll tax, which would have contributed both to the War as well as slavery—this political stance led to his great essay *Civil Disobedience* (1849)—so too the Beats opposed the incursions of American colonialism into Mexico and identified with the oppressed, not the oppressors. Bremser recognizes this aspect of her relationship to Mexico, acknowledging in an interview: "It was almost as though the people in Mexico are so open to their poverty, or so open to the oppression of being down-trodden or something like that.

That's what I was identifying with, that darkness in myself as, okay, now the worst has happened to me, yet these people can accept me."[29] Bremser returns to her earlier self-analysis—"the great darkness within me"—when she describes "that darkness in myself," which takes on a double meaning in this context: her inner spirit, her psyche is dark and obscure and threatening, but the people of Mexico also have dark bodies, and Bremser's interior darkness answers to their exterior darkness.

This examination of "Indians"—Bremser does not specify Maya, Aztec, or "mestizo"—continues in the narrative of Bonnie and Ray's encounter with Maria Sabina (1894–1985). Sabina, who spoke only Mazatec and did not learn how to read or write or how to speak Spanish, was a *curandera*, a female shaman, living in *Cerro Fortin*—Fortress Mountain—high above the village of Huautla de Jimenez.

During the sixties, the hippies continued the Beat fascination with shamanism, and as we shall see in chapter 8, musician and poet Jim Morrison would adapt shamanic practices for his performances. Studies such as Mircea Eliade's *Shamanism: Archaic Techniques of Ecstasy*—originally published in French in 1951—which survey the ways ancient cultures sought contact with the transcendent to cure body and soul, sometimes with the aid of entheogens, also appealed to members of the counterculture. The concept of shamanism united in the poet the function of tribal leader and healer/doctor and also, as with the ancient Greeks and Romans, emphasized the notion of inspiration as central to the creative act. However, the role of the female shaman—the *curandera*—has often been obscured in histories of shamanism. Barbara Tedlock has researched the role of the *curandera*, who also often performs the role of midwife: "Within the long Christian tradition of branding shamanic practitioners as witches and sorcerers, midwives have been singled out over and over again as particularly evil. These women were perceived by many men as not only interfering with God's realm but as a direct threat to the male monopoly on medical knowledge and practice. In this way women's shamanic knowledge, including healing, birthing, trancing, dreaming, and prophecy, became hidden." One of the significant achievements of *Troia* is its memorable portrait of Maria Sabina.

R. Gordon Wasson achieved international recognition when *Life* magazine, on May 13, 1957, published the article "Seeking the Magic Mushroom," and Huautla de Jimenez in Oaxaca gradually became a unique site for countercultural pilgrimages. As Bremser reports: "One half of the people I know who have gone to Mexico have made the thirty-hour trip up into the mountains to get to Huautla, everyone knows about it"[30] Mexican poet Homero

Maria Sabina, photograph by Gusmano Cesaretti/Arte Povera Foto Books Inc., 2021

Aridjis created a novel based on Maria Sabina's life entitled *Carne de Dios—Flesh of the Gods*—a translation of the Nahuatl word for the psychedelic mushrooms, *Teonanacatl*: John Lennon, Allen Ginsberg, William S. Burroughs, Jack Kerouac, and Philip Lamantia all make appearances in the narrative. Aridjis describes Sabina's *veladas*—mushroom eating ceremonies—and her naming of the mushrooms as her *Saint Children.* Terence McKenna in *The Archaic Revival* pointed out that "the mushroom cults of Mexico were destroyed by the coming of the Spanish conquest. The Franciscans assumed they had an absolute monopoly on theophagy, the eating of God; yet in the New World they came upon people calling a mushroom *teonanacatl,* the flesh of the gods. They set to work, and the Inquisition was able to push the old religion into the mountains of Oaxaca so that it only survived in a few villages when Valentina and Gordon Wasson found it there in the 1950s." In book 2 of *Troia: Mexican Memoirs,* Bremser drops hints of things to come: "South of us back down and beyond Tehuacan, Indian mushroom people live each day as if their lives were gifts which they in turn dedicate to the mountain and the mushroom. Directly beyond Veracruz rises a mirage above the insurmountable Popocatepetl."[31] To live each day as a gift is a goal advocated by Henry David Thoreau in *Walden*—"only that day dawns to which we are awake"—and just as Thoreau admired the Native Americans for their ability to live close to Nature without desecrating it, so Bremser looks to the natives of Mexico for wisdom in how to live her life fully and reverently.

As in Lamantia, the great volcano Popocatepetl is described as "insurmountable," and we are tantalized by news of a group of "Indian mushroom people" who live their lives in correspondence with the rhythms of the cosmos and who may have something to teach visitors from more "advanced" societies. However, as Bremser and Ray approach the village and begin their stay there, she acknowledges the gulf between herself and its inhabitants: "Huautla made me know that we were no more than tourists, really. So distant from the Indians, we were not able to talk to anyone. Most of the people seldom speak Spanish there anyway, this is an Indian village."[32] Although Bremser feels separated from the villagers due to differences in language and culture, she is nevertheless amazed by what she encounters: "And we walk circles of dirt road ambush and pass Indians pitter-pat on the road with things on their heads wrapped in rags, and it is no shame, they don't even look at us. I am overawed."[33] Bremser remains suspended between two worlds: the America she has left behind and the exotic land of Mexico where she does not speak the languages of its native peoples. As John Lardas in *Bop Apocalypse: The Religious Visions of Kerouac, Ginsberg, and Burroughs* has observed: "Along with other Americans during the 1950s, Beats faced incessant cultural pressure to progress, leave the past behind, and become new. Given the Faustian nightmare at the heart of the American Dream as it was popularly conceived, they dreamed of a different America that was new yet approachable.

Living in Mexico enabled them to begin thinking about their ideal America." Bremser would like—as did many members of the counterculture—to leave behind the titanic struggles of modernity and re-enter the timeless world of archaic humanity. Yet for the contemporary person, this retreat ultimately proves impossible, and the "ideal America"—like the "ideal Mexico"—is precisely that: an ideal which one strives to achieve in one's imagination but which often escapes one in reality.

Bremser describes the mushrooms—"Big and small, their thin heads project from the center like dried flowers, but more organic, brownish black, they look like the earth itself"—and proceeds to "eat about a pound of them while we are in Huautla."[34] *Troia* shifts back and forth chronologically, and ingesting the mushrooms in the heart of Mexico leads to the climax of the book. Bremser returns in memory to her time in New York where she sampled another Mexican import—peyote:

> "THERE IS SALVATION. I wrote it on the ceiling once, not even my own wall. . . . But it was legitimate, I mean sincere, and spontaneous. And I will explain: It was in New York City in the summer of 1959, late in August. Ray and I had already been to San Francisco and had a couple of dried peyote buttons which Wally dug out of some abandoned satchel in his cellar. . . . I am thrown in to a void, try to distinguish his figure departing the doorway. . . . Till then I muse, my eyes slowly grasp the candle and focus the luminous upper wax, not even grown warm yet, it glows waiting the flame, the destruction travels downward, the flame aspiring upwards. What is reality, where the means to grasp this, the flame's even power is fed by gases from the core of action, the wax sapping upwards from the rooted wick, the wick, look at the wick, it is a monk with his head bowed in prayer, the huge dignity of him upright standing in the middle of it, giving of himself, and allowing that he be the means of connecting everything with everything. . . . And I grabbed up the candle quick and wrote on the ceiling THERE IS SALVATION, for the candle, the wick, the monk, Ray. . . . That is what is known as seeing the light."[35]

"Wally" is Wallace Berman—editor of *Semina*—who also supplied Michael McClure with the peyote for his first trip, which resulted in McClure's famous "Peyote Poem." The religious quest which as we have seen forms a central theme of *Troia* is reasserted now in relation to psychotropic substances from Mexico—both peyote and mushrooms—which became central to the Beats in their search for the transcendent. The style here again is Kerouacian—

"salvation, "void," "secret out of time"—and Bremser literally *sees the light,* scrawling on the ceiling that she has indeed found freedom from the psychological conundrums which have troubled her.

Anne Waldman—co-founder of the Naropa Institute's Jack Kerouac School of Disembodied Poetics, now Naropa University in Boulder, Colorado—was also influenced by Maria Sabina. Waldman's well-known poem "Fast Speaking Woman" is a thirty-page text described by Waldman as a "list chant," replicating the style of Maria Sabina's utterances during her therapeutic sessions with psychedelic mushrooms. Sabina has described her experience of inspiration: "At times the Wise Man sang, sang, and sang. I didn't understand the words exactly, but they pleased me. It was a different language from what we speak in the daytime. It was a language that without my comprehending it attracted me. It was a language that spoke of stars, animals, and other things unknown to me." Waldman also published texts on chant and performance poetry which explore the interrelationship between Beat poetics and the practices of shamans in Indigenous Mexican cultures. Waldman listened to the recording which R. Gordon Wasson made of Maria Sabina on the night of July 21–22, 1956, and realized she could employ Sabina as a source for her own poetry. Jerome Rothenberg in *Shaking the Pumpkin: Traditional Poetry of the Indian North Americas* includes a section from "The Chants" of Maria Sabina: "Ah, Jesu Kri/I am a woman who shouts/I am a woman who whistles/I am a woman who lightnings, says/Ah, Jesu Kri/Ah, Jesusi/Ah, Jesusi/Cayetano Garcia." One may see how Waldman created her own poem "Fast Speaking Woman" based on Sabina's chants. Rothenberg observed that Waldman performed "Fast Speaking Woman" in a variety of venues, including "poetry readings and even, if memory doesn't fail me, as part of Bob Dylan's short-lived Rolling Thunder Revue or of his film *Renaldo and Clara*: 'I'm a shouting woman/I'm a speech woman/I'm an atmosphere woman/I'm an airtight woman' in distinct reflection of the other's: 'I am a spirit woman, says/I am a lord eagle woman, says—' which the North American poet acknowledges formally as her 'indebtedness to the Mazatec Indian Shamaness in Mexico.'" Waldman's poem surveys the innumerable roles, identities, and selves of "Woman" as had Diane di Prima in her epic poem *Loba.* Composed during the early seventies, Waldman's poem, in converging the energies of American second-wave feminism with Mexico's archaic shamanic traditions, uncovers primal roots and analogues in the shape-shifting and multiplicity which are incarnated in Maria Sabina's spiritual voyages. Waldman has said of the genesis of her poem: "'Fast Speaking Woman' is still going on, it's interminable. It began as a journal work, a list, fill in the blanks around the word 'woman' piece, but constantly playing with the sound of other words in my head. It began in South America and later Michael Brownstein gave me a copy of the Maria Sabina recording, which was completely relevant. The piece is a re-working of how this Mazatec Shamaness handles language. I feel close to shaman energy, but anyway, I was writing this poem on airplanes, in hotels, at home, and so on." In "adapting" oral chanting into a written "text," Waldman continues the tradition of Beat ethnopoetics. Maria Sabina would become world-renowned, and her role in the development of both Bonnie Bremser's and Anne Waldman's evolutions as writers and the wisdom they would derive from their journeys in Mexico was of central significance.

We have seen the myriad ways Mexico left a profound impression on the life and work of Bonnie Bremser. From the outset, Bremser acknowledged that the real struggle of her time in Mexico would be, "How to be myself in such a different place? Put it all in a sieve and squash your personality through into a new diversified you." As M. Christine Anderson observes in "Women's Place in the Beat Movement: Bonnie Bremser Frazer's *Troia: Mexican Memoirs*": "Rather than seeking escape from contradictions, *Troia* was Bonnie Frazer's effort to integrate the forces that threatened to pull her apart, to reconstitute the range of her experiences and longings into literary expression." Her contacts with Philip Lamantia in 1961 consolidated the tradition of an abiding Beat presence in Mexico during the decade of the sixties. After leaving Mexico, Bremser went to New York City and moved to Allen Ginsberg's East Hill Farm in Cherry Valley in upstate New York, where she regained her health and worked on the land, ultimately earning a degree in biochemistry and obtaining a position at the USDA.

During her time with Ginsberg, Bremser began a turn toward Buddhism, and Ginsberg loaned her the book *The Life of Milarepa,* the celebrated Tibetan saint.[36] Intending to travel to South America with Ray in 1970, she and Ray had only gotten as far as Guatemala when their money ran out. She wrote "Artista in Guatemala," recently published along with other uncollected work in *Some American Tales* (2020), under the name Brenda Frazer. We are told that with what is left from a royalty check from *Troia,* she purchased a copy of "the first book of the Mayan Codices for $8" in Guatemala City, leaving her with just $5 from her royalties—another testament to Beat mad love for Mexico.[37] In many ways, Bonnie's time in Mexico became emblematic of the themes which we have been developing: the struggle of Beat women to free themselves from patriarchy; the desire to flee an oppressive, materialistic, increasingly technocratic America; an interest in shamanism and entheogens

Bonnie Bremser with three-year-old Georgia, East Hill Farm, summer 1970. Photograph by Gordon Ball. Copyright Gordon Ball

as routes toward the transcendent; and the life of poetry and the arts as a means of living a self-realized life. If she did not find "the Answer"—a final philosophical conclusion to her queries about existence—while in Mexico, she paved the way, however, for a generation of independent, thoughtful women who sought a rejuvenation of mind and spirit outside the confines of traditional social expectations of their supposedly "natural" roles in American society.

# 8 ✻ MICHAEL MCCLURE AND JIM MORRISON

## Break On Through to the Other Side

MICHAEL MCCLURE WAS born in 1932 in Marysville, Kansas, and shared Kansas roots with other figures connected with the Beats such as writer Charles Plymell and actor Dennis Hopper. McClure was a classmate at Wichita High School of founder of the Auerhahn Press of San Francisco Dave Haselwood, and artist Bruce Conner. As a young man, McClure read widely in Emmanuel Swedenborg, Charles Baudelaire, Ezra Pound, T. S. Eliot, e. e. cummings, and Rainer Maria Rilke, discovering William Blake at seventeen and composing poems in Blake's style.[1] Like Allen Ginsberg, who as we have seen in chapter 6 experienced a mystical vision of Blake in Harlem in 1948, as an adolescent McClure also "dreamed I was Blake. Blake seemed as real a presence as an automobile."[2] In his novel *The Mad Cub*, McClure recalls: "I dream I am William Blake . . . I have a long white beard."[3] In early 1955, McClure met Ginsberg at a party in San Francisco for W. H. Auden at Ruth Witt-Diamant's, and McClure noted that one of Ginsberg's "gifts" to him during this period was "showing me the stanzas of *Mexico City Blues* that Jack was sending him in 1955."[4] Kerouac included McClure in his vast epic of Beat novelistic mythology as Pat McLear in *The Dharma Bums* and *Big Sur*.

Mexico appears in several of McClure's poems and became for him a place of pilgrimage and of spiritual discovery, and his readings in Antonin Artaud influenced his explorations of shamanism. Artaud's "To Have Done with the Judgment of God" was published in City Lights's *Journal for the Protection of All Beings* in 1961 along with McClure's essay "Revolt." Finally, the ecology of Mexico would be of great significance to McClure; he was extremely sensitive to the country's landscape and natural wonders. This chapter covers several key McClure poems incorporating Mexican themes; his explorations of peyote and travels to Oaxaca; his treatment of Aztec mythology in his poem "Quetzalcoatl Song"; as well as his relationship with Jim Morrison, who although not a Beat writer was greatly influenced by their example. Morrison's immersion in shamanism and Aztec imagery—the Doors played concerts in Mexico City in June 1969, allowing Morrison the opportunity to visit Teotihuacan—emerges in Morrison's philosophy and song lyrics and thus provided a conduit of Beat conceptions about Mexico into the sixties hippie generation.

It is noteworthy that the Beats who were born in California—Joanne Kyger and Philip Lamantia for example—or who moved to California and remained there, such as Michael McClure and Lawrence Ferlinghetti as well as musicians such as Jim Morrison, would develop a more sustained relationship to Mexico than other American authors: it was an accessible travel destination due to its physical proximity to the Golden State. They viewed Mexico as a neighbor, as well as an intriguing land, and were thus able to visit more frequently. Furthermore, they were aware that California was once Mexican territory. The Beats were deeply interested in and protective of Indigenous cultures, siding with the oppressed colonized rather than the European aggressors. Indeed, all of California bears the marks of Spain's colonialist enterprise: the names of its great cities—San Diego, Los Angeles, Santa Barbara, San Francisco, San Jose—are of course all Spanish. And California schoolchildren were once taught that Father Junipero Serra (1713–1784) was a great man because he spread along *El Camino Real*—the Royal Road—the missions which set out to "civilize" the "savage and primitive" Native Americans, to turn them away from their "devilish," "pagan" beliefs toward the True Light of Christianity. Of course, this is no longer the accepted version of what actually happened when the Spaniards met original Californians, bringing with them disease, oppression, and cruel "educational systems," as contemporary historians have amply demonstrated.

A key moment in McClure's evolution as a writer was his encounter in 1957 with biologist Sterling Bunnell (1932–2015). Indeed, on the bookshelf of his personal library, the interplay between McClure's scientific, historical, spiritual, botanical, and literary interests is palpable. For example, on the top shelf of one of McClure's bookcases we find *The Poems of Percy Bysshe Shelley*; L. A. Borradile's *The Invertebrata*; Paul A. Meglitsch's *Invertebrate Zoology*; *Biopoesis* by Harvey Bialy; *The Wild Flowers of California* by Mary Parsons; *Speaking of Siva*, translated by A. K. Ramanujan; *Energy Flow in Biology* by Harold Morowitz; William Gray's *Magical Ritual Methods*; *The Evolution of Individuality* by Leo Buss; and *The Complete Poems of Hugh MacDiarmid, Volume 2*. McClure acknowledged that before he met Bunnell, he had "thought in terms of biology or natural history or physiology or morphology. Sterling introduced the concept of ecology to me. So I would say it was a concern since 1957. Since then Sterling became and remained one of my best friends."[5]

This devotion to an ecology of nature also encompassed an "ecology of mind," for in 1962, McClure and Bunnell participated in research psychologist Frank Barron of the University of California at Berkeley was conducting at the Institute of Personality Assessment and Research concerning the ways entheogens affect creativity. Barron published *Creativity and Human Freedom* (1968), *Creative Person and Creative Process* (1969), and also contributed an essay to the volume *LSD, Man and Society* (1967) entitled "LSD and Religious Experience," as did Walter N. Pahnke. Pahnke was one of the pioneers in the study of the relationship between the use of entheogens and mystical experience—a central concern of the Beats—as well as the employment of these substances in the treatment of mental illnesses: an area of inquiry which has recently undergone a resurgence. In June 1962, McClure and Bunnell—encouraged by Barron to locate psilocybin mushrooms for his research—traveled to the mountains of Oaxaca where they met Maria Sabina and located seven species of psychedelic mushrooms. The report on their findings was presented at the American Psychological Association Conference in 1962.[6] It is noteworthy the central role Mexico began to play in the fifties and sixties as a realm where entheogens had been employed in sacred ceremonies for centuries and where the suppressed powers of the unconscious might be recovered through a new understanding of the cultures of "preliterate" peoples who might restore sanity and balance to the "rational" and technologized Western world.

In his introduction to the 2013 edition of *Ghost Tantras*—first published in 1964—McClure discusses his 1962 trip to see Mexico and Maria Sabina with Sterling Bunnell and documents how he composed the poems. *Ghost Tantras* is written entirely in "beast language," McClure's attempt to replicate the speech of animals. As Gregory Stephenson has observed: "*Ghost Tantras* is a return to the earliest poetry, to primitive song that summons healing or helping powers and induces states of trance or vision. The poems are shamanistic invocations, incantations, evocations of the beast spirit, of mammal consciousness." It is thus appropriate that McClure composed several of the poems on his way to Mexico in search of its shamanistic wisdom. McClure explains that it is was as he departed San Francisco for Mexico City that he composed Tantra 15b in his notebook which begins "HRAHH! GRAHHR! WRAH! GROOOOOOOOOOO!" As the plane flew "over central California at dusk," he composed Tantra 16, while Tantra 17 was written "o'er central California at night-beginning." McClure arrived in Los Angeles where Tantra 18 was composed and Tantras 19 and 20 are dated respectively "landing in Mex City—morn" and "Mex City—eve." Tantra 19 bears the marks of its Mexican composition: "GRAHH GRAH GROOR DANN HEER./Cloud down bed volcano peak. Sharks' backs/swimming in eternity tooo!"—thus the allusion to neighboring volcano Popocatepetl. McClure describes driving through the desert and stopping periodically with Bunnell to study the "roadside botany." Arriving in Huautla de Jimenez, they "carefully make cultures of *psilocybes*, sterilizing the instruments with a portable burner, propping a tarp of waterproof canvas over our heads, and our sterilized instruments make clean cuts in the small mushrooms. In the early afternoon the *curandera* María Sabina allows us into her chanting ceremony. Lightning is flashing and thunder booming through the uncovered windows of her home on a high road."[7]

McClure thus replicated a journey novelist John Steinbeck made with his much-admired biologist friend Edward Ricketts in 1940—whose studies greatly influenced Steinbeck's Weltanschauung—to the Gulf of California to collect marine specimens which Steinbeck described in *Sea of Cortez* (1941). So too McClure viewed Bunnell as a mentor, and more than fifty years following this time in Mexico, composed a poem in tribute to him appearing in *Persian Pony* (2017) entitled "Ivory Statuette." McClure recalled his explorations with Bunnell: "MEMORY PERFECT/envisioning surface of stones/in the lightning storm of Oaxacan mountains/as he drives in rain-crumbling mud tracks/to bring back sacred mushrooms/and psychedelic salvia for research./A YOUTHFUL TRIP." "Psychedelic salvia" refers to *Salvia divinorum*—also known as "sage of the diviners" or "seer's sage"—which possesses psychoactive properties. It grows in the cloud forest of the Sierra Mazateca of Oaxaca and has been used by shamans to induce states of visionary consciousness and for healing. McClure revealed that he met "a *curandero* of the Leaves of the Good Shepherdess, in his hacienda." This was Isauro Nave, from whom McClure and Bunnell obtained the *hojas de la Pastora*—the "leaves of the Shepherdess," *Salvia divinorum*.

*Ghost Tantras*—with its genesis during McClure's voyage to Mexico with Bunnell to bring psychedelic mushrooms back to California—records the quest to anchor one's body in the primal experiences of Earth. Indeed, this became a central quest of the Beat and subsequently the hippie generation, and in the same year *Ghost Tantras* was published, 1964, the essay "The Hallucinogenic Drugs" appeared in *Scientific American* in April, authored by Frank Barron, Murray E. Jarvik, and Sterling Bunnell. This text is noteworthy for placing the nascent interest of the counterculture in Mexican entheogens within a scientific context. Frank Barron was noted for his studies in creativity, and indeed, writers began to be employed as human guinea pigs in the research into entheogens. Gregory Bateson at Stanford, Timothy Leary at Harvard, and Barron at Berkeley were eager to explore the ways these substances might inspire the creative mind. William S. Burroughs, Charles Olson, Philip Lamantia, and Allen Ginsberg participated in these experiments. According to Marcus Boon in *The Road of Excess: A History of Writers on Drugs*: "Ginsberg's first experience with LSD took place in 1959 at the invitation of the anthropologist Gregory Bateson at the Mental Research Institute at Stanford University." And of course, it was Mexico which was the matrix of some of the most vital research being conducted. During the fifties and sixties, the Beats were an important force in re-evaluating the interpretation of the meaning of entheogens. On the one hand, they worked with researchers to explore the scientific understanding of these substances, and on the other, they also in their studies of traditional cultures in Mexico began to fathom the role throughout history of entheogens in the sacred and ritual life of humanity.

It was the early explorations of R. Gordon Wasson into the mushrooms of Oaxaca which led to Timothy Leary's travels to Mexico and eventually to the explosion of interest in peyote—*peyotl* in Nahuatl—and "magic mushrooms." As the authors of "The Hallucinogenic Drugs" point out: "Among the Aztecs there were professional diviners who achieved inspiration by eating either peyote, hallucinogenic mushrooms (which the Aztecs called *teo-nanacatyl*, or 'god's flesh') or other hallucinogenic plants. *Teonanacatyl* was said to have been distributed at the coronation of Moctezuma II (1466–1520) to make the ceremony appear more spectacular. In the years following the conquest of Mexico there were reports of communal mushroom rites among the Aztecs and other Indians of southern Mexico. The communal use has almost died out today, but in several tribes the medicine men or women (*curanderos*) still partake of *Psilocybe* and *Stropharia* in their rituals." Allen Ginsberg would compose the "Moloch" section of "Howl" after ingesting peyote, while Ken

Kesey (1935–2001) wrote the opening pages of *One Flew over the Cuckoo's Nest* under its influence.[8]

One of McClure's best-known works, "Peyote Poem," derives from his peyote sessions. Peyote—*Lophophora williamsii*—is a cactus which flourishes in northern Mexico as well as north of the border in Texas, and was documented as we have seen in chapter 3 by the early Norwegian explorer in Mexico, Carl Lumholtz. McClure's "Peyote Poem" was the only text Wallace Berman included in the third issue of *Semina* published in 1958, and the cover illustration features two dried peyote buttons. Francis Crick (1916–2004)—co-discoverer with James Watson of the structure of DNA and winner of the Nobel Prize for Medicine in 1962—quoted two lines from "Peyote Poem" in the second lecture "The Simplest Living Things" in his book *Of Molecules and Men*: "THIS IS THE POWERFUL KNOWLEDGE/We smile with it."[9] "Peyote Poem" is divided into three numbered sections which recount in focused detail McClure's experiences with the hallucinogen. McClure practices a phenomenological method in which precise description and a scientific approach are valued. McClure declares that "I hear/the music of myself and write it down": a lovely way of expressing a sense of experiencing the complex, mysterious beauty of his interior self. He goes on to exclaim: "And the Indian thing. It is true!/Here in my Apartment I think tribal thoughts." Ingesting peyote places McClure in contact with the ritual and sacramental ceremonies of the Indians, and he achieves a state of blessed being: "I know/all that I need to know. There is no hurry." As he settles into a euphoric sense of unity with the cosmos, he has reveries of Mexico: "There is nothing/in the night but fast clouds. No stars. Smokey gray/and black the rooms are the color of blue Mexican glass/and white": peyote transforms his San Francisco apartment into a dream of Mexico. In the "Symposium on McClure" issue of *Margins* (1975), Francis Crick describes being in Berkeley in the summer of 1959 and discovering McClure's "Peyote Poem" at City Lights bookstore. Crick was impressed with "how well it conveys the effects of the hallucinogen" and was also "fascinated by its radiant quality and also by its unexpectedness." He went on to observe: "What I did not know, or even guess, at that time was Michael's profound and very personal interest in science... Michael McClure is so at home in the fantastic world that science has conjured out of ourselves and our surroundings—a world which makes that of other cultures seem contrived and pedestrian—that he takes it all in his stride.... If I were a poet I would write like Michael McClure—if only I had his talent."[10]

In his essays and poetry about both mushrooms and peyote, McClure connects the entheogens with his knowledge and experiences of Mexico. In his essay "The Mushroom" from *Meat Science Essays*, McClure asserts: "The mushroom high isn't like any other. All of the hallucinogens—peyote or mescaline, lsd, and psilocybin (the Mexican mushroom) lift you to an Olympian universe. Everything is timeless, huge, and bright and you're free to walk in it and do what you want to do. Each of the highs is a different continent in the Olympian universe. Peyote takes you to lands of religiosity and physical matter." And in "Drug Notes," McClure describes peyote with his accustomed particularity: "Lophophora Williamsii is a small spineless cactus. It is divided radially by a number of ridges. Small gray hair tufts (probably atrophied spines) prickle in circular bans on the dark green flesh. Sometimes peyote grows in a clump, several plants converging on one root or a group of joined roots. I've seen seven plants in one cluster. Peyote grows around Laredo and southwards into Northern Mexico." McClure has stated, "I have always considered myself to be a biologist as well as a poet," and in his novel *The Mad Cub* declared: "Peyote teaches me the separate consciousness of my being and I am aware of the creature that is stomach and the one that is solar plexus. . . . In reading biology I hope to make the discoveries that will liberate man to exist in timelessness and state of superconsciousness." Thus peyote, mescaline, which is derived from the peyote cactus and the effects of which Aldous Huxley celebrated in *The Doors of Perception* (1954)—the French poet Henri Michaux also ingested mescaline and reported on his experience in *Miserable miracle* (1956)—and psilocybin synthesized from the mushroom all derive from Mexico, hence, as we have argued, placing the country at the center of the American counterculture's quest for what McClure calls a "state of superconsciousness."[11]

During his many travels to Mexico, McClure developed a profound devotion to its land and people. In his work of the early seventies, we witness his disgust at the ways Americans view Mexico. In "Baja—Outside Mexicali" from *September Blackberries* (1974), McClure bemoans the incursion of privileged Americans tourists rampaging across the California border into Baja, Mexico: "AMERICANS PASS BY,/WORLD LORDS,/hauling huge land vans/and campers behind/trucks pulling/dune buggies and power boats/of hallucination./Great timid Gypsy Lords/of plastic objects/and shining metals/roar at 85 miles per—/out of their secret/walled strongholds/in Orange County/where safe/from commy Blacks/and Chicanos/they pile up/mickey mouse/treasure." McClure portrays prosperous, Caucasian Americans as they barrel across the border in their campers. They emerge from Orange County, a politically conservative area of Los Angeles, where they attempt to insulate themselves from the African American and Mexican American populations who represent to them a political, revolutionary threat—they are "commies"—Communists who threaten the capitalist world symbolized by Mickey Mouse and Disneyland. McClure describes the building of Boulder Dam which was intended "to make power/and give water to thirsty/Los Angeles./Mexico was paid off/with a diddy bop/irrigation project/and a market for cheap/agriculture./The Rio Colorado/power is and was used/to build the art-/ifacts on wheels/that thunder by./Mexicans watch/from dust drenched adobe/under palm thatch/or sometimes/from/a purple and yellow house/and they envy./The wind-moved tamarisk/trees are beautiful/as graygreen chinchilla fur."[12] Again we note McClure's eye for botanical detail: tamarisk—or salt cedar—exists in New Mexico as well as Mexico. Mexico has been doubly exploited: its land stolen by the United States to create California and Texas and its migrants exploited who came to work in the grape fields of the great San Joaquin Valley of California where the charismatic Cesar Chavez (1927–1993) took on the long struggle to unionize farmworkers. McClure notes the poor Mexicans observing the American intruders from simple "dust drenched adobe" dwellings.

The allusion to the tamarisk tree indicates that even in one of his most polemical poems about Mexico, McClure's readings in biology and ecology are evident. As McClure remarked in a 1975 interview with Roland Husson: "The great problem is to make young people aware of the degradation of our planet by pollution and by overpopulation. . . . My only hope is that the young see with their own eyes what is about to happen." McClure devotes close attention to the botanical and animal life he encountered during his travels amid the fragile ecosystems of Mexico. Unesco declared the Sian Ka'an area near the ruins of Muyil in Quintana Roo a protected biosphere and a World Heritage Site in 1987. Other protected areas include the Rio Lagartos Biosphere where one may visit the magnificent flamingos of Celestun. While traveling and swimming with his wife Amy Evans McClure along the Tulum coast in 2001, McClure composed an unpublished poem in the front of a photo album memorializing their journey in honor of the great frigate birds—*Fregata magnifcens*—which patrol the coast. The birds with their splendid wingspans recall to the poet the great pterodactyls of dinosaur times, yet the poem closes in a threnody: "green breakers/green breakers/the color of chips/of wave-worn/plastic/on the white sand/where/whiskey bottles/are edged/with pearly/barnacles." Ocean pollution has made terrible inroads upon the once pristine habitat of these lordly birds.

Along with Gary Snyder, McClure was the earliest Beat American environmentalist, and he read both "Point Lobos: Animism" and "For the Death of

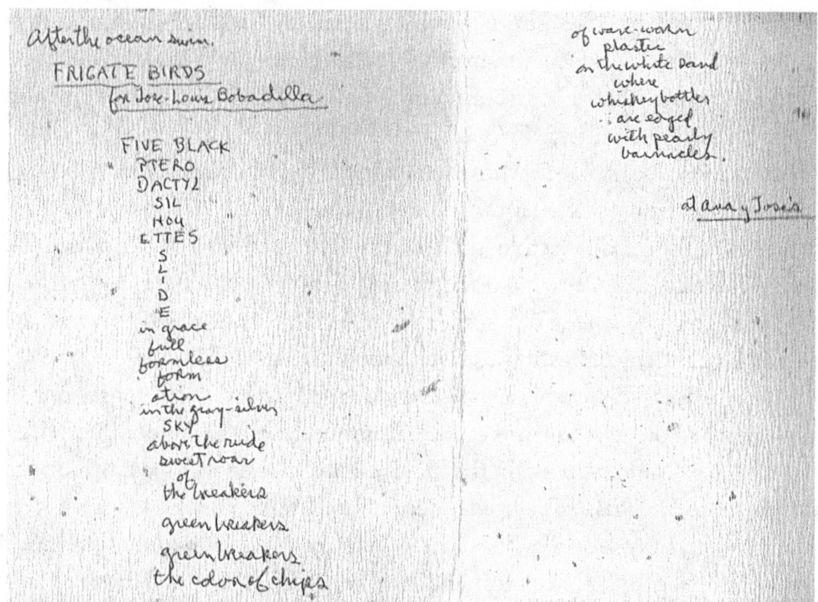
After the ocean swim.
FRIGATE BIRDS
for Jose-Louis Bobadilla

FIVE BLACK
PTERO
DACTYL
SIL
HOU
ETTES
S
L
I
D
E
in grace
full
formless
form
ation
in the gray-silver
SKY
above the rude
sweet roar
of
the breakers
green breakers
green breakers
the color of chips
of wave-worn
plastic
on the white sand
where
whiskey bottles
are edged
with pearly
barnacles.

at Ana y Jose's

McClure poem, courtesy of Amy Evans McClure

100 Whales" at the celebrated 6 Gallery event in San Francisco where Allen Ginsberg performed "Howl" for the first time. McClure quotes D. H. Lawrence in the poem, again illustrating the Beat devotion to the great British author who possessed such a preternatural sensitivity to birds, beasts, and flowers. In his volume *Simple Eyes and Other Poems* (1994), "Field 6" contains the verses: "A/POOL/that organizes life/turns walls to shapes like pollywogs/and morning glories into trees/and desert mud to melting glass." In his footnote, McClure clarifies: "In Sonora, Mexico, there are thirty-foot-tall morning glory plants that have evolved woody trunks: these large smooth-barked trees, with whiplike branches, bear morning glory flowers and are visited by hummingbirds. Deer come and eat the fallen blossoms in the morning."[13] The Sonoran desert—the world's most biodiverse—is home to a range of plants and animals including ocotillo, saguaro cactus, owls, antelopes, and bighorn sheep.[14] McClure's extensive research in Sonora appears in Richard Felger's *The Trees of Sonora* (2001), and McClure's careful attention to small details of botanical knowledge—size ("thirty-foot-tall morning glory plants"), texture ("smooth-barked trees"), and shape ("whiplike branches")—is typical of his Mexico poems. So too, McClure observes the hummingbirds and deer who visit the morning glory—*Ipomoea arborescens,* known in Mexico by the Nahuatl name *Cazahuatl* or *Cazahuate.*

McClure devotes the entire second section of *Simple Eyes and Other Poems*—entitled "Mexican Mountains"—to his experiences south of the border. Five poems feature Mexican themes including "Mexico Seen from the Moving Car," "The Butterfly," "Quetzalcoatl Song," "Reading Frank O'Hara in a Mexican Rainstorm," and "Mirroring Flame in the Fireplace." "Quetzalcoatl Song" was composed after McClure discovered the tale of Quetzalcoatl in "Legends of the Suns" as retold in *A Guide to Mexican Poetry* by Irene Nicholson. Quetzalcoatl is known among the Maya as *K'uk'ulkaan,* a name from the Yucatecan language: *k'uk'* = quetzal; *k'uk'ul* = plumed; *kaan* = serpent. A quetzal bird is depicted eating a snake in the Dresden Codex, and the coat of arms of Mexico—*Escudo Nacional de Mexico*—depicts an eagle consuming a snake perched on a prickly pear cactus. This is based on the Aztec legend that Tenochtitlan would be built on the place where an eagle was seen devouring a snake on top of a lake. The frontispiece of the Codex Mendoza (1529–1553) also shows an eagle atop a cactus plant. Quetzalcoatl was god of the wind and sky worshipped by the Toltecs, and one of their priests or kings named Topiltzin also took the name Quetzalcoatl—henceforth, there has been a confusion in both history and myth concerning whether Quetzalcoatl refers to a god or a man.[15] As we have seen, Quetzalcoatl dramatically enters the narrative of the collision between Hernan Cortes and Moctezuma. Claude Levi-Strauss has pointed out: "When Quetzalcoatl, the civilizing god of the Toltec (from whom the Aztec, who arrived in the region of Mexico in the thirteenth century, acquired their culture) was persecuted by a rival god and had to leave his people, he announced that the day would come when, across the sea, from the place where the sun rises, would appear beings similar to himself. The Indians imagined them in the form of a tall man, with white skin, wearing a long and rounded beard. Thus said the chronicles, and when the Indians saw the Christians, they took them for gods—brothers and sons to Quetzalcoatl. The Maya were aware of the same prophecy: 'Welcome your guests,' we can read in one of their sacred books, 'who are bearded and come from the country of the East.'"

In the *Anales Cuauhtitlan,* which is part of the Codex Chimalpopoca, it is reported that the four hundred sons of Mixcoatl—the cloud serpent, or the Milky Way—killed Quetzalcoatl's father when Quetzalcoatl was nine years old. Quetzalcoatl goes in search of his father and is urged by dark magicians to engage in the practice of human sacrifice. He stands firm against these attempts to lead him astray, but Tezcatlipoca who is the god of the "smoking mirrors"—obsidian mirrors were employed in sorcery—shows him his own image and Quetzalcoatl is horrified to find that he possesses inflamed eyelids, shrunken eyes, and a wrinkled face and thus his people will now flee when they behold him. McClure returns to this image of the mirror in a later poem, "Swirls in Asphalt" section 9, with the verses: "Like Mayan/kings and queens/whose/dwarfs stare/*into obsidian mirrors*" (McClure's emphasis). Tezcatlipoca then creates for Quetzalcoatl a garment made of the plumes of the quetzal, a turquoise mask, reddens his lips with red dye, paints yellow squares on his forehead, and gives him serpent teeth. He makes him a wig, creates a blue-feathered beard, and arranges red feathers to fall behind his back. Now when Quetzalcoatl sees himself in the mirror, he is astonished and "came out of his retirement where he had been in vigil and retreat." Tezcatlipoca gives him pulque until Quetzalcoatl becomes inebriated: he now summons his sister Quetzalpetlatl to spend the night with him. When he wakens from the night's debauchery, Quetzalcoatl becomes penitent and asks his workers to create a stone coffin. He lies alone there for four days and nights and then leaves for the seashore, dresses himself in his fancy wardrobe, and sets himself on fire. As his ashes rise into the sky, "all the fine-feathered birds appeared to watch how they went up aloft. . . . When the ashes had ceased to burn, Quetzalcoatl's heart rose up. . . . They say it was raised to heaven and entered there. The old men say it became the morning star which appears at dawn."[16]

McClure creates out of this marvelous narrative a dramatic poem which opens with capital letters, a favorite stylistic device of McClure's: "QUETZALCOATL, PUT ON YOUR MASK/OF TURQUOISE,/paint checkered squares/of yellow and black/on your forehead." McClure shows us Quetzalcoatl's "hideous wrinkles," "sunken red eyes," as well as his "capes of feathers" and "blue feather veils." The poem gathers energy: "Paint your lips with scarlet!/That is not you in the smoking mirror./Here, this is you in the deep clear pool./This is you in the music the rattlesnake sings . . . /This is you as you walk/where the deer/eat the fallen white flowers."[17] The detail concerning the deer who "eat the fallen white flowers" is echoed in the footnote we considered above to "Field 6" which informs us that the morning glory flowers "are visited by hummingbirds. Deer come and eat the fallen blossoms in the morning." McClure enriches his poem with botanical knowledge which he gathered during his trips to Sonora, Mexico. The poem closes with Quetzalcoatl's self-immolation and transformation into a star: "You are the child in your heart,/grown halfway into a god./Now you sleep in your stone coffin./Now you burn yourself and rise in flames./You are a star in the sky,/a star in the sky,/with the murderers of your father." While Margaret Randall, as we have seen in chapter 4, employs Quetzalcoatl as a symbol of the dangers of nuclear war, McClure retells the myth, creating a "version" in his own poetic style. Jerome Rothenberg devotes a chapter to the myth in *Technicians of the Sacred* while the anthropologist Laurette Sejourne—who was part of the literary circle in Mexico City which included Randall and Philip Lamantia—includes a close analysis of Quetzalcoatl in her study *Burning Water: Thought and Religion in Ancient Mexico.*[18]

In "Mexico Seen from the Moving Car" we also find a subtle allusion to Quetzalcoatl: "Hawks with pale bellies/perch on the cactus,/their bodies are portholes/to other dimensions./This might go on forever./I am a snake and a tiptoe feather/at opposite ends of the scales/as they balance themselves/against each other./This might go on forever." The balance and tension of soaring hawk and earthbound snake symbolize eternally the yin-yang dialectical structure of the universe: as Heraclitus declares, "harmony comes from the tension of the bow and the lyre." The feathered serpent also perches on the cactus, as does the hawk, and Quetzalcoatl is invoked with "I am a snake and a tiptoe feather." As he drives through the Mexican countryside, the verse "This might go on forever" refers both to the Kerouacian road where he is traveling and the poem itself which he is writing. The title of McClure's poem—"Mexico Seen from the Moving Car"—is in the tradition of Kerouac's *On the Road* and Gregory Corso's "Mexican Impressions": "Through a moving window/I see a glimpse of burros." McClure closes with an unattributed quotation—"The everlasting universe/of things/flows through the mind/and rolls/in rapid waves,/Now dark—now glittering—now reflecting gloom"—the opening of Percy Bysshe Shelley's "Mont Blanc," which also influenced Allen Ginsberg's "Siesta in Xbalba."[19] In ending with Shelley—another Beat favorite and Corso's hero—McClure compares his reaction to the sublimity of the Mexican countryside to Shelley's awed response to the great peak in the Alps.

McClure admired Mexico's rich Indigenous mythological traditions and incorporated the theme of Quetzalcoatl into his poetry; he was also fascinated by the ecological diversity and beauty of the country, which supplied his poetry with a rich source of imagery. McClure located in the energies of the body an avenue toward the regeneration of society. As Richard Candida Smith in *Utopia and Dissent: Art, Poetry, and Politics in California* remarks: "Like many of his colleagues, McClure assumed that historical forces forcefully intervened into the psyche in order to reproduce the existing, unequal power relationships and that art, as an analogue of natural creative process, provided the only basis for countering the colonization of the soul. McClure went further than most in emphasizing the biological aspect of human being as fundamental to the liberatory potential claimed for the arts."[20] It was this emphasis on the body as source of mystical illumination, the impulse towards Blakean vision, and an awareness of Mexico as a place of magical potentialities which fired the friendship which developed between McClure and musician and poet Jim Morrison (1943–1971).

McClure met Jim Morrison in 1968 and spent time with him in Los Angeles. As an adolescent, Morrison was a voracious reader, requesting as a high school graduation present from his parents the complete works of Friedrich Nietzsche. His relationship with McClure was easily predictable, for Morrison already had become knowledgeable about Beat authors. When he moved with his family to Alameda, California, in 1957, Morrison frequented during high school the bohemian cafes of San Francisco and City Lights bookstore and read Kenneth Rexroth, Lawrence Ferlinghetti, and Jack Kerouac. According to his friend Fud Ford, Morrison was impressed by "the travel. Reading *On the Road* was great for a young mind to fantasize about." As a film student at UCLA, Morrison created a movie entitled *HWY: An American Pastoral*, which chronicles a hitchhiker played by Morrison in his own version of *On the Road*. Near the end of the film, he makes a phone call to Michael McClure, revealing that the man with whom he hitched a ride gave him some trouble, so he "wasted him." He ends his trip at the Whisky a Go Go on the Sunset Strip in West Hollywood. Much of the film involves automobiles and highways. As Yasue Kuwahara has observed, travel by car pervades Morrison's poetic imagery. In *The Lords and the New Creatures*, he muses: "Modern life is a journey by car," while "End of the Night" tells us to "take the highways to the end of the night," and "Roadhouse Blues" exhorts the listener to "keep your eyes on the road, your hand upon the wheel/Yeah, we're goin' to the Roadhouse/We're gonna have a real/Good time." Cars and roads and America's great Interstate Highway System initiated by Dwight D. Eisenhower in 1956 are the legacies Morrison inherited from Jack Kerouac, and McClure's friendship with Jim was a continuation of Morrison's early familiarity with the Beat scene. Furthermore, like McClure, Morrison was primarily a literary man who was drawn to music. As the sixties progressed, many of the Beats became increasingly involved in the music scene. Just as the Beats of the fifties loved jazz, so too the evolution of rock 'n' roll and folk music through the Beatles and Bob Dylan would become central to the poetry of Allen Ginsberg. Michael McClure met Bob Dylan, who gave him an autoharp, and in turn, McClure would dedicate his book *Hail Thee Who Play* (1974) "for Jim Morrison." Following Morrison's death, McClure collaborated with Ray Manzarek—keyboardist for the Doors—in giving poetry readings

McClure composed a novel—*The Adept* (1971)—and worked with Morrison in June of 1969 on a film script based on ideas from the book under the title *Saint Nicholas.* Allen Ginsberg knew of McClure's project with Morrison, for he mentions it in an interview from 1970 with Robert Head, editor of the underground New Orleans newspaper *NOLA.* Morrison described the plot as "a contemporary story about a couple of dope dealers that go to the desert to make a score," and when his interviewer noted the similarities to the film *Easy Rider* (1969), Morrison responded: "Yeah, I know but there's nothing I can do about it . . . this story was written before *Easy Rider* was made, you know and it's just superficial similarities." Like *Easy Rider,* the narrative of the McClure-Morrison script features a motorcycle-riding cocaine dealer. *Easy Rider* opens at *La Contenta* bar where Wyatt and Billy meet Mexicans who sell them drugs. The first words spoken in the film are in Spanish as Wyatt says "*Buenos dias.*" So too, in *The Adept* the main characters Nicholas and Rark fly to Mexico and go to the desert where they meet a "half-breed" Indian to make a drug deal. Rark notes: "That is Mexico below us—coming in!" and McClure emphasizes throughout the novel (as he had in his poetry) the landscape of the Sonoran desert: saguaros, ocotillo—"a skinny cactus like plant used for making fences before barbed wire"—barrel cactus, cottonwood, Palo Verde trees, yellow wildflowers.

Richard Evans Schultes and Albert Hoffmann in *Plants of the Gods: Origins of Hallucinogenic Use* observe that Mexico is reputed to possess "the world's richest area in diversity and use of hallucinogens in aboriginal societies." Indeed, Rark goes on to note in his rhapsody about Mexico, "the finest samples of the greatest marijuana, hashish, bhang, ololiuqui." The entheogen ololiuqui in the Nahuatl language—or *Turbina corymbosa*—is a species of morning glory which McClure notes in his poetry and with which Charles Olson was also familiar. The seeds are known as *semilla de la Virgen,* "seeds of the Virgin Mary," and were used as psychedelics by the Aztecs and associated with Xochipilli—whose name means "Flower Prince"—god of pleasure, flowers, feasting, game playing, painting, and dancing. In a famous masterwork sculpture of Xochipilli from the Late Postclassic period (1450–1500 C.E.), the god is depicted in an ecstatic pose, head adorned with heron feathers and tilted back, jaguar claws about his neck, cross-legged, sitting on a drum: several psychotropic plants festoon his body, including morning glory, sinicuichi, and mushroom flowers. R. Gordon Wasson speculated that the statue depicts Xochipilli "absorbed by *temicxoch,* 'dream flowers,' as the Nahua say describing the awesome experience that follows the ingestion of an entheogen. I can think of nothing like it in the long and rich history of European art:

Xochipilli absorbed by *temicxoch*." Rark continues his list, declaring: "Everyone got to get high on any dope they chose from Acapulco Gold to Mexican Sacred Mushrooms." In their work together on the film script of *Saint Nicholas*, McClure and Morrison were channeling the same cultural power symbolized by Mexico which defined the sixties Zeitgeist and which also surfaced in *Easy Rider*.

Morrison made several trips to Mexico, and during these travels closely observed his surroundings; he was capable of creating pleasing, imagistic poems, as with the following: "Mexican parachute/Blue green pink/Invented of Silk/& stretched on grass/Draped in the trees/of a Mexican Park/T-shirt boys in their/Slumbering art." Here each line of the verse contains—as often in McClure's Mexican poems—a discrete, photographic image which brings vividly to life the Mexican milieu. Morrison continued his trips to Mexico when, in late June 1969, the Doors flew to Mexico City where they had been originally scheduled to perform in the city's largest bullring, the Plaza Monumental. However, due to the student revolt which had taken place in Mexico City, the Mexican government was concerned that too many young people would be gathered again in their capital city, and it was arranged instead for the musicians to play in a large nightclub. However, this did not prevent Morrison from pursuing his interests in ancient Mexican culture, and he replicated the Beat fascination with—and pilgrimages to—the pyramids. According to Stephen Davis in *Jim Morrison: Life, Death, Legend*: "During the daytime, Jim and the band went sightseeing, climbing the sacrificial steps of nearby Aztec pyramids . . . and visiting the Museo de Anthropologia." The museum was opened especially for the Doors to visit on Monday, June 30—a day when the museum was usually closed to the public.[21] A photograph taken during the trip he took to Teotihuacan depicts a bearded, hair-to-his-shoulders Morrison reaching out to touch Quetzalcoatl.

Snake, serpent, and lizard imagery pervades Morrison's writings such as *The Celebration of the Lizard* section of *The American Night*. The lyrics to "The End" are equally serpentine. Here Morrison speaks of riding a snake to an "ancient lake" which likely alludes to Lake Texcoco, where the Aztecs built Tenochtitlan. These repeated invocations of the Earth's chthonic powers in the form of the reptile—which symbolizes both phallic and lethal energy—clearly have one source in Morrison's fascination with Mexican culture.

Like McClure and the Beats, Morrison was influenced by Antonin Artaud and the inspiration he derived from the Tarahumara Indians of Mexico. The distinguished scholar of French literature Wallace Fowlie—Morrison had written to Fowlie to express his gratitude for his translations of Arthur

Jim Morrison at Teotihuacan, copyright Jerry Hopkins/Reelin' in The Years Productions LLC on behalf of the Doors Property LLC

Rimbaud—devoted his book *Rimbaud and Jim Morrison: The Rebel as Poet* to a consideration of the spiritual search of the French and American artists, and quotes Morrison as saying: "I'm interested in anything about revolt, disorder, and chaos." Fowlie goes on to argue that "these are words of Rimbaud, Artaud (Theatre of Cruelty), and possibly Lautreamont." Furthermore, in "Artaud's *The Theatre and Its Double,* Jim had read that each performance should be a risk. The audience should be shaken out of its complacency."[22] For Morrison, the rock concert should be not just an amusing night's entertainment but rather the place where a Dionysian ritual of ecstasy is performed. The references in Morrison's song lyrics and poetry form a consistent pattern of imagery in which psychoactive substances, death, the night, sexual ecstasy, Mexican place names, and the desire to "break on through to the other side"—to achieve a state of unbridled cosmic consciousness—recur. Morrison's affinity for Indigenous cultures and for Mexico had its roots in his childhood. When he was four years old, his family was driving in the desert between Santa Fe and Albuquerque, New Mexico. The young Jim then witnessed a grisly car accident—chronicled in a voice-over in his movie *HWY: An American Pastoral*—in which a vehicle filled with Native Americans crashed, and Morrison was horrified to see their bleeding bodies on the roadway. He later claimed that "possibly, the soul of one of those Indians, maybe several of them, just ran over and jumped into my brain. . . . It's not a ghost story, man. It's something that really means something to me." The scene was dramatized in Oliver Stone's film *The Doors* (1991) and is memorialized yet again in Morrison's lyrics for "Dawn's Highway" in which he recalls bleeding "Indians" dying on the road.

Mexico represented for Morrison a land where shamanism was still practiced in its primal form, and where poet, healer, and Dionysian ecstatic were united in one tribal figure. As Jeroen W. Boekhoven in *Genealogies of Shamanism: Struggles for Power, Charisma and Authority* points out: "For their 1969 album *The Soft Parade* the Doors recorded the song 'Shaman's Blues.' A year before, famous rock critic Richard Goldstein had portrayed Morrison as 'The Shaman as Superstar' in New York Magazine. Morrison told him: 'The shaman, he was a man who would intoxicate himself. See, he was probably already an unusual individual. And, he would put himself into a trance by dancing, whirling around, drinking, taking drugs—however. Then, he would go on a mental travel and describe his journey to the rest of the tribe.'"[23] Morrison's *The Lords: Notes on Vision* begins "Look where we worship," and it becomes clear that Morrison is embarked on a philosophical quest in which shamanism is central. Morrison declares: "In the seance, the shaman led. A sensuous panic, deliberately evoked through drugs, chants, dancing, hurls the shaman into trance. Changed voice, convulsive movement. He acts like a madman. These professional hysterics chosen precisely for their psychotic leaning, were once esteemed. They mediated between man and spirit-world. Their mental travels formed the crux of the religious life of the tribe. . . . The cure is culled from ecstasy."[24] Morrison's description replicates quite precisely the account given by Anatole Lewitzky in his dossier for Georges Bataille's Le College de Sociologie, arguing that "among Turko-Mongolians, Finno-Ugrics, Asian Tunguso-Manchurians and Palearctics, as well as among the Tibetans and the North American Indians, we encounter magico-religious practices that show numerous common characteristics. Note the presence of the *drum*, widespread from the Lapps to the Eskimo of Greenland, ecstatic *dances*, the clearly pathological nature of the shaman's personality, and finally the idea of a profoundly intimate contact with the representatives of the spirit world, the notion of levitation and more generally, of penetration into other worlds." The shaman thus was indeed preoccupied with the desire to "break on through to the other side." Allusions to Indians and shamanism appear throughout Morrison's works such as *The American Night*: "Watch them dance/an indian mile"; "I have an/ancient Indian crucifix around/my neck." A close friend of Morrison's, Rich Linnell, when asked during an interview, said: "Oh yeah, he would do the little dance, the little Indian dance a number of times. I probably wasn't close enough to it at the time to be clear on where Jim was coming from in that respect, as to what motivated him to do that, but certainly there was this Indian thing going on, the dance he would do on the one foot and hopping around in circles was always reminiscent of an Indian dance."[25]

Morrison became more deeply involved with shamanism and entheogens through his friendship with Philip O'Leno when the two were film students at UCLA in 1964. Carlos Castaneda was at UCLA during this period and came to fame with his books about the Mexican shaman, Don Juan. Furthermore, living in Los Angeles, Morrison was already steeped in Mexican American culture, for by 1928, Los Angeles possessed the largest population of Mexican immigrants of any American city. In the late forties, Octavio Paz arrived in Los Angeles and in *The Labyrinth of Solitude* described "a city inhabited by over a million persons of Mexican origin. At first sight, the visitor is surprised not only by the purity of the sky and the ugliness of the dispersed and ostentatious buildings, but also by the city's vaguely Mexican atmosphere, which cannot be put into words or concepts." Los Angeles was founded in 1781, and Olvera Street—Calle Olvera or Placita Olvera—forms part of El Pueblo de Los Angeles Historic Monument. Olvera Street is a much-visited destination where an island of Mexican culture—created with tourists in mind—still exists today. Morrison's friend O'Leno traveled to Mexico as part of his spiritual quest: he had been studying the history of religions and read a number of texts including Carl Jung, Hermann Hesse's *Siddhartha,* W. Y. Evans-Wentz's *Tibetan Yoga and Secret Doctrines,* Joseph Campbell's *The Hero with a Thousand Faces,* and Erich Neumann's *The Origins and History of Consciousness.* The two friends discussed these books together, and Morrison also read William S. Burroughs's *Naked Lunch* and *The Yage Letters.* O'Leno traveled to Oaxaca in the summer of 1965 where he sampled mushrooms, and in early 1966, Morrison, O'Leno, and their mutual friend Felix made a trip—as O'Leno recalled—"to go to the desert to get high, you know, find some Indians, eat some peyote." When O'Leno returned from one of his journeys to Mexico, Morrison asked him: "'Well, have you ever broken through?' And I answered, 'Yes,' because I had. Some of the experiences I had on mushrooms up there in the mountains, I was completely transcended out." By the mid-sixties, Morrison was associating Mexico with the secret of "breaking through" into higher states of consciousness.

In addition, Morrison's studies of Aztec culture pervade his work as well as allusions to Mexican places and references concerning journeys to Mexico. In *The New Creatures,* poem 3, we find: "Call out of the Wilderness/Call out of fever, receiving/the wet dreams of the Aztec King." Ensenada, a popular tourist town about four hours south of Los Angeles, was less than appealing to Lawrence Ferlinghetti, who noted that even "the dogs can't stand it—they lie around stretched out with flies all over them in the gutters, a curious race apart. . . . Three days here, and I can't stand it any longer, I'll leave in the morning, Dirt streets of shitcity!" The town appears several times in Morrison's poetry, which contains—as with Ferlinghetti's—dark imagery: "Ensenada/the dead seal/the dog crucifix/ghosts of the dead car sun./Stop the car. Rain. Night./Feel." Located in Baja California, Ensenada boasted beaches for surfing—hence "the dead seal"—and Morrison spent time in the San Miguel Bar which featured, according to one source, "cheap Mexican beer, good tacos and friendly company." Michael McClure admired Morrison's Ensenada poem, observing that it "reminded me of William Carlos Williams' 'The Red Wheelbarrow,' one of the great objectivist poems. Jim and I talked a lot of putting his poem on a billboard on Sunset Boulevard. With no signature. Just the poem."[26]

One may observe the way Morrison fuses the various aspects of his fascination with Mexico in a passage from *Wilderness, Volume 1* in the poem "Lamerica": "Hitchhiker drinks: 'I call again on the dark hidden gods of the blood.'" The "dark hidden gods of the blood" is a direct allusion to D. H. Lawrence's concept of the "dark gods"—the forces of the primal, instinctive unconscious which pulse through our bodies. In a later section of *Wilderness* titled "Explosion," we discover again a rich texture of Mexican imagery, the poem invoking at the outset "The Voice of the Serpent." We next encounter "old books in/ruined/Temples/The pages break like ash." Next, "an Old man appears &/moves in tired dance/amid the scattered dead/gently they stir." The poem concludes in an epiphany: "I received an Aztec wall/of vision/& dissolved my room in/sweet derision/Closed my eyes, prepared to go/A gentle wind inform'd me so/And bathed my skin in ether glow."[27] The Serpent is of course the omnipresent Quetzalcoatl, while the "old books in ruined/Temples" allude to the codices burned by Bishop de Landa, for "the pages break like ash." An "Old Man" appears, a shaman moving in a "tired dance." Finally, "an Aztec wall/of vision" is invoked as the poem again turns into a version of a William Blake quatrain with rhymes on "vision," "derision," and then "go," "slow," and "glow." There is also a Blake echo in the archaic, "A gentle wind inform'd me so."

We have explored the centrality of Blake for the counterculture, and he was a favorite of Michael McClure and Allen Ginsberg. Blake's famous apothegm from *The Marriage of Heaven and Hell*—"If the doors of perception were cleansed, every thing would appear to man as it is: Infinite. For man has closed himself up, till he sees all things thro' narrow chinks of his cavern"—supplied the title of Aldous Huxley's book on psilocybin, *The Doors of Perception,* as well as Morrison's rock group the Doors. Morrison created a visionary poetics rooted in the myths of Mexico and powered by an ecstatic sexual energy. Both McClure and Morrison were profoundly inspired by Mexico. Morrison had grown up as a young man already familiar with Beat authors and had known of Kerouac's journeys as well as William Burroughs's and Allen Ginsberg's experiments with entheogens to achieve higher states of consciousness. Before he met McClure, Morrison had already traveled to Mexico several times, and would return again in 1969 with the Doors. McClure and Morrison continued the Beat preoccupation with Mexico during the decade of the sixties, propelling the curiosity of a new generation of seekers to venture across the border, to attempt to break on through to the other side.

# 9 ❋ JOANNE KYGER

## Phenomenological Mexico

JOANNE KYGER (1934–2017) MAJORED in philosophy as an undergraduate at the University of California at Santa Barbara, taking courses on Ludwig Wittgenstein and Martin Heidegger with Paul Weinpahl. Hugh Kenner introduced her to T. S. Eliot, Ezra Pound, William Carlos Williams, and W. B. Yeats. However, she left the university just one unit short of completing her degree.[1] Kyger also studied René Descartes's *Discourse on Method,* seeking to challenge his notions of "rationality" and the mind-body dualism in her six-part "poem-script" "Descartes and the Splendor Of," employed as the basis for a fascinating experimental film which aired on the PBS television station KQED in November 1968.[2] She read Joseph Campbell's *The Hero with a Thousand Faces* (1949), which led her to C. G. Jung and the conception of human experience as an archetypal journey: this is when Kyger "understood that it was possible to have this narrative, this old narrative that could go through your life that was common to all humans. And you saw your life in terms of that." Arriving in San Francisco in 1957, Kyger attended the poetry group convened on Sunday afternoons by Robert Duncan and Jack Spicer.[3] Both Duncan and Spicer studied Native American cultures—Duncan experimented with shamanism—and as we have seen, Antonin Artaud's writings about the Tarahumara Indians of Mexico were widely disseminated among Beat writers in San Francisco during the fifties. Kyger's *Up My Coast* (1981) is composed of Kyger's retelling of Miwok myths based on C. Hart Merriman's *The Dawn of the World: Myths and Tales of the Miwok Indians of California*. Along with Margaret Randall, Bonnie Bremser, Joan Vollmer, and ruth weiss, Kyger was one of the few women to venture to Mexico, yet from the beginning she asserted her claim to visibility within the male-dominated Beat movement. As Ronna C. Johnson has observed: "Claiming authorial literary status, women Beat poets such as Kyger protested the explicit sexism and misogyny of male-centered, male-authored Beat writing, resisting their exclusion from cultural and literary salience in the movement and in the global literary history it charted."[4]

One may note Kyger's sense of exclusion from the Beat orbit in a poem such as "The Pigs for Circe in May" from *Places to Go* (1970), where male privilege is sarcastically lampooned: "They rise/taking their way, the struggle of heads, walking/strong and oblivious, with pomp and rich robes saying/we are the minds of this century." It is not difficult to detect an echo here of Allen Ginsberg's famous declaration in "Howl" concerning the "best minds of my generation." And in "Poison Oak for Allen," dated September 2, 1996, Kyger sarcastically and humorously reflects: "Here I am reading about your trip to India again,/with Gary Snyder and Peter Orlovsky. Period./Who took cover picture of you three/with smart Himalayan mountain backdrop/The bear?" Kyger was, however, strongly attracted to the Beat movement as it emerged into national notoriety. She recalled the "Howl" obscenity trial in the spring of 1957, visits to City Lights bookstore where she would purchase a copy of "Howl" and "fall in love with the writing, the tone, the truth." She also read *On the Road* during an automobile trip from San Francisco to the Russian River and the redwoods: "I look out the window occasionally but I am too busy reading this wild adventure to notice much my first trip north." Kyger goes to "hear Kenneth Rexroth and Lawrence Ferlinghetti read with jazz at The Cellar. My friend Nemi Frost has moved up from Santa Barbara. Nemi has lived in Mallorca and met Robert Creeley and the painter John Altoon, and tells me mad stories of her adventures there. I am starting to get a picture of a certain kind of world." It is evident that Kyger, although spending her early apprenticeship in the orbit of Jack Spicer, Robert Duncan, and Charles Olson, was also beginning to "get a picture of a certain kind of world" which included the visionary declamatory genius of "Howl"—Kyger would compose an elegy for Ginsberg entitled

Joanne Kyger, © 1970, Elsa Dorfman

"Wide Mind" on April 6, 1997, the day after Ginsberg's death—as well as the hunger for adventure, travel, and spiritual illumination represented by *On the Road*, a novel in which Mexico plays a major role. In 1991, Kyger summarized Kerouac's influence on her own life and work: "His terrific use of words, bubbling away. His wonderful tone. The great ability to tell a story. Especially about friends I knew. The excitement of the truth, of the times. The Beat Generation Energy."

Kyger studied meditation with the Zen master Shunryu Suzuki—the teacher as well of Diane di Prima—and experimented with the expansion of consciousness through ingesting peyote. When Gary Snyder visited Kyger in 1958, they took peyote together: "It was horrendous. It ripped the Christianity right off my back . . . this huge rush of animal energy, and I didn't know how to relate myself to it. I finally saw this wild boar as my totem animal, and I followed it through India and into the Eleusinian mysteries."[5] A year later in 1959 in New York City, Diane di Prima first ingested peyote—which would break her style open to the new long-line poetry represented by her book *The New Handbook of Heaven* (1963)—and di Prima reported that she "found other levels in my head. Later I wanted to get to the same places without the peyote." It is noteworthy that years before her first journeys to Mexico, Kyger had already taken a trip on peyote, experiencing a vision characteristic of the shamanistic journey: an encounter with her "totem animal" which serves as a tutelary spirit. For the Beats, shamanism became central, for the shaman's power is in words, in language, in images, in poetry. As Kyger observed, the responsibility of the shaman "is to activate the strength of words, because sound is transformational and transformation manifests in terms of power. A shaman goes to another world to find cures, she has to be very very careful to get there and to get back." After moving to Bolinas in 1969, Kyger participated in peyote gatherings with a group of women in a large, open-air house. "Peyote has its own truth," Kyger came to believe, and she "was able to experience this wonderful expanded sense of self in the world. I mean you become aware of the interconnectedness of everything. It could be a very wonderful, magical, intuitive experience." Kyger spent the years 1960–1964 with Gary Snyder in Japan, and in addition to her experiences with peyote, another connection to the ritual practices of ancient Mexico occurred following her return from Japan when she met the anthropologist Carlos Castaneda—whose book *The Teachings of Don Juan: A Yaqui Way of Knowledge* (1968) concerning a Yaqui Indian shaman became popular among the counterculture—as well as Michael Harner, the distinguished scholar of shamanism.

Joanne Kyger's experiences in Mexico—as well as her poetic practice—were influenced by Charles Olson's travels to Campeche and his celebrated "Projective Verse" manifesto which she read in 1957 upon arriving in San Francisco: the essay helped her decide "how to structure my words on the page." Kyger met Olson at the Berkeley Poetry Conference, where she gave a reading with Ron Loewinsohn and Lew Welch on July 24, 1965. Olson's fascination with the Maya—he believed that world culture was interpreted in ways that were claustrophobically Eurocentric—would provide a stimulus for Kyger's own travels to Mexico. Kyger recalled that Olson gave her "a poetics which contained history as memory of time and place. Growing up in the U.S. with Western history being taught as an extension of the Greek and Roman Empire—learning Latin, and Greek and Roman mythology as a source of contemporary culture, I welcomed Olson's expanded sense of world history. Especially that of America which he understood did not stop at the border of the U.S. It included the many nation states of Mexico, especially the Mayan, (which as an informal archaeologist he personally experienced) which are often, unaccountably, not included in our 'Western' cultural inheritance—even from a post 1519 invasion point of view."[6]

It was following her move to the small town of Bolinas north of San Francisco in 1969—where a literary community had evolved including Robert Creeley, Bill Berkson, Tom Clark, and David Meltzer—that Kyger began to experience "the cultural emptiness of the place." The native Coast Miwok peoples had been destroyed after the gold rush of the nineteenth century and had left no architectural remains. Kyger "knew that at one time in California's early and short history it had been part of Mexico. I started to think 'north' and 'south,' this hemisphere." Kyger made her first trip to Mexico in 1972 when she visited San Cristobal de las Casas in Chiapas, which created a seismic shift in her awareness of her own geographical and cultural sense of self and identity: "After that first trip to Mexico I understood how little 'Americans' actually know about what lies south of the border, the United States of Mexico. How in terms of the history of indigenous tribal movement, there is no border. How a sense of who I am culturally, geographically, has to do with the heritage of this continent." In her writings over the next decades, Kyger repeatedly explored the consequences of this expanded sense of history which she had first encountered in her relationship to the work of Charles Olson.

Indeed, Kyger had in her youth considered becoming an archaeologist, and like many Beats was enamored of travel. Born in 1934 in Vallejo, California, the daughter of a U.S. Navy captain, she experienced a peripatetic youth in China, Illinois, Florida, Pennsylvania, and Santa Barbara. Several of her books are devoted to journeys, including *Strange Big Moon: The Japan and Indian Journals, 1960–1964* (1981; 2000) describing time in the Far East with Gary Snyder; *Desecheo Notebook* (1971), chronicling a voyage to a small island off the coast of Puerto Rico; and *Trip Out and Fall Back* (1974) concerning her brief residence in New York City from 1966 to 1967 when she met poet Anne Waldman, became affiliated with the Yippies, and took part in the Central Park "Be-In." From September 11 to 19, 1978, Kyger was in Amsterdam for the One World Poetry Conference and recorded the experience in a poem written in collaboration with Bill Berkson. However, by far the majority of Kyger's travel writings have been devoted exclusively to her times in Mexico, including *Mexico Blonde* (1981), *Phenomenological* (1989), *Patzcuaro* (1999), *God Never Dies: Poems from Oaxaca* (2004), and *On Time: Poems 2005–2014*. *Not Veracruz* (2007)—although the title is a famous Mexican city—contains no poems about the country.

Kyger's three trips to Chiapas in 1972, 1976, and 1981 comprised her earliest forays into Mexico. A sequence of poems entitled "Visit to Maya Land" dated "Fall 1976, Chiapas" opens with the poem "Marian Lopez Calixto's Story." The ethnopoetics movement gained momentum during the sixties when American writers began to translate, adapt, or otherwise transform poetry and mythology from "pre-literate" cultures into English and to employ allusions to these sources for their own literary purposes. Gary Snyder spoke of the "genius" of the great French anthropologist Claude Levi-Strauss and employed Native American coyote mythology in his poetry. As we have seen in chapter 4, Margaret Randall turned to the myth of Quetzalcoatl to comment on the terrors of the nuclear age. And Charles Olson, at the close of his essay "Human Universe," retells a Maya myth: "Or to be a man and a woman as Sun was, the way he had to put up with Moon, from start to finish the way she was, the way she behaved, and he up against it because he did have the advantage of her, he moved more rapidly, in the beginning he was only young and full of himself, and she, well, she was a girl living with her grandfather doing what a girl was supposed to be doing, making cloth." At the close of the two-page narrative, Olson ends with his celebrated peroration to the intense passion for life displayed by the Maya: "O, they were hot for the world they lived in, these Maya, hot to get it down the way it was—the way it is, my fellow citizens." Kyger continued Olson's desire to transmit they ways the Maya were able "to get it down the way it was," here adapting an anthropogonic myth from the Tzotzil Maya of Chiapas. Kyger tells us that during "the time of the ancients" for five days the earth became dark and many pots were broken. The pots were able to speak and demons came forth from the pots: the lion, the snake and the jaguar. People perished. Then there was a transformation of the people and they became good again:

    The sun came out
In soft white radiance.
    And our father in heaven came down
To make some other people
    First from clay

But they couldn't move well
And he destroyed them again
Pulverized the clay
And prepared the clay
And made the clay alive

Kyger's swift narrative cleaves closely to the original version by Marian Lopez Calixto. Calixto's description of the creation of mankind is as follows:

> As so it was that Our Father in Heaven came down to earth to create men anew: To prepare mankind. When Our Father in Heaven made the people, it was from clay that he first made them; From which he created the people. But they could not move very well at all. Quite incorrectly they stood there like stumps. "What shall I do?" said Our Father in Heaven. And he destroyed them once again. Our Father was going to create another kind, one that had just occurred to him. He broke apart all the clay. He shook the clay all about. He commenced to pulverize the clay. And he prepared the clay. When Our Father had created them, he spoke to them. He pulsed their wrists.

Because the Beats were dissatisfied with the biblical creation story, they turned with great fasciation to cosmogonies from other cultures as well as to the early Gnostics, who, rather than the Hebrew Yahweh, posited a demiurge who bungled the creation, hence our sorry state of affairs on Planet Earth. It is noteworthy that Kyger fails to capitalize "Our Father in Heaven" as in the original version, suggesting that Christian influence on Mexican myth had resulted in the obvious echo of the Bible which Kyger seeks to minimize.

Nine years later, Kyger again traveled to Mexico: *Phenomenological* is her account of this 1985 Yucatan journey. *Phenomenological* was published as volume 24 in a series of texts by a variety of authors including John Wieners, Robert Duncan, Alice Notley, Robin Blaser, Ed Sanders, Michael McClure, and Kyger herself. The series was inspired by Charles Olson's ideas which he had named "A Plan for the Curriculum of the Soul."[7] *Phenomenological* is graced with a cover featuring a figure from a Maya codex. Kyger states that in February 1985 she "traveled with Donald Guravich and Diana Middleton-Quaid, our neighbor in Bolinas, to the Yucatan Peninsula to visit the pyramids of antiquity and to acquaint ourselves with contemporary culture."[8] Kyger met Guravich at Naropa University in Boulder, Colorado, in 1977: he had already traveled frequently in Mexico and created several illustrations included in *Phenomenological.*[9] The book is divided formally into a series of journal entries beginning February 14, and concluding on March 29, 1984. Resembling other Kyger travel sequences such as *Mexico Blonde* (1981), it provides a day-by-day account of her activities including cuisine, dreams, books she is reading, visits to archaeological sites, and evocations of friends and acquaintances.

The form of Kyger's Mexico chapbooks is arresting. They are a blending of lines arranged as prose interspersed with verses intended to be read as poetry. Kyger is working in a long tradition of the Japanese *nikki bingaku*—the poetic journal—such as Matsuo Basho's *Oku no Hosomichi.* Kyger composed a journal while in Japan, later published as *Strange Big Moon*; keeping journals and notebooks was established Beat practice. Gary Snyder, Allen Ginsberg, Jack Kerouac, and Diane di Prima were all copious journal-makers, and Kyger also employs the journal as a place to record ideas and impressions, describe reactions to books she was reading, and generate ideas for her poetry. Yet Kyger began to conceive of the journal as a distinct literary genre and—more specifically—as the form best suited to cast her experiences while traveling in Mexico. Kyger considered the poetic journal as a form which features "a kind of movement back and forth from prose-like descriptive narrative bridges into shorter poem-like lines. Like the haibun style. And the element of time, happening in the moment, aware of the moment. Tight, spare." As Jane Falk has argued: "Because Kyger thought that the poem should be a direct transcription of the experiences of daily life and the mind's movements, which made it somewhat like a journal entry, the journal, by bridging the gap between writing and life, provided her with both the substance and style of her poetry, and allowed for the following of the mind in the moment of its spontaneity." We note in Falk's analysis the phrase "the mind's movements" which recalls the Buddhist practice of mindfulness as well as Philip Whalen's famous description of poetry as "a picture or graph of a mind moving." Kyger blurs the distinction between "poem"/"prose," "fiction"/"non-fiction," "dream"/"reality," "extraordinary"/"ordinary," "significant"/"insignificant." The word *journal* derives from French *jour*, or "day," and Kyger points out that her journals "record incidents, voices, what the weather is doing, what's happening in the land outside the door. And yes, they are truly what is going on. But they feel significant, important, even though they are ordinary. The more ordinary the better." In her Mexico books, Kyger does this quite intentionally in order to bring the reader directly into the experience of Mexico's people, landscape, traditional myths and rituals, literary history, flora and fauna, as well as the seemingly mundane details of her daily life which draw the observer into a world at once transcendent and "ordinary."

We may observe this method at work in *Phenomenological.* Kyger leaves Bolinas, California, on February 14, 1984, arriving in Merida the following day, and we are plunged in medias res: "Just sitting down/at café in front of the Hotel Caribe/First time alive in evening Merida./Cervezas on top terrace/Romantic full moon accompanied by frenzied/jack hammers/drowning out conversation./Diana loses her bag/(with everything in it)/but finds it back by the table/we all vow to be more/Careful."[10] Seemingly insignificant or trivial details such as the sound of construction workers or a friend losing her belongings would usually be excluded from accounts of travels to "exotic" destinations such as Mexico, yet Kyger is devoted to a Buddhist attention to seemingly insignificant objects, events, and happenings. As Michael Davidson has observed in *The San Francisco Renaissance: Poetics and Community at Mid-Century*, Kyger's verses "resolutely refuse to editorialize." A famous Zen saying is "chop wood, carry water"—which indicates one must pay as much attention to the practical, simple, and "ordinary" as to the supposedly "higher" metaphysical aspects of life. Kyger in a lecture delivered on June 6, 1984, at the Boise Gallery of Art quoted with approval Soetsu Yanagi's—founder of the Japanese craft movement—description of the celebrated Kizaemon Tea-bowl: "A good Tea-bowl, Yes. BUT HOW ORDINARY! So simple, no more ordinary thing could be imagined. There is not a trace of ornament, not a trace of calculation. . . . But that was as it should be. The plain and unagitated, the uncalculated, the harmless, the straightforward, the natural, the innocent, the humble, the modest: where does beauty lie if not in these qualities. . . . Why should beauty emerge from the world of the ordinary? The answer is, ultimately, because that world is natural. In Zen there is a saying that at the end of the road lies effortless peace." Kyger's admiration for this aestheticism of the daily as represented by Japanese craftsmanship is a clear influence on her Mexico poetics.

Kyger spends time in Santa Lucia Park, and on February 19, travels to the port town of Progreso, about thirty-two kilometers from Merida. On the following day, she makes an extended entry regarding Sor Juana Inés de la Cruz (1648–1695), celebrated as Mexico's greatest poet and admired as we have seen by both Margaret Randall and Philip Lamantia. "Born of a Spanish father and a/Creole mother in the middle 1600s near/Popocatepetl," Sor Juana is "the first truly Mexican/poet of New Spain, blending the Old World/ and the New." Kyger emphasizes Sor Juana's insights in her play *The Divine Narcissus* concerning the similarities between Indigenous ritual practices and the symbolism of the Catholic Church which she declares—switching to colloquial language—"was a big no-no" in the eyes of the ecclesiastical authorities.[11] Kyger returns here to a frequent Beat trope of solidarity with the pre-Christian sacred practices of the Indigenous peoples, and Kyger views Sor Juana as her Mexican predecessor in the fight for equal rights for women. Indeed, in her poem *The Tapestry and the Web* (1965), Kyger reimagines the plot of Homer's *Odyssey* so that Penelope—rather than simply waiting patiently and chastely among her suitors for Odysseus to return from his thrilling and amorous ten-year voyage back to Ithaca—is portrayed as an independent woman who is self-directed, seeking her own fulfillment and pleasures rather than living as a faithful martyr to her absent husband. Thus, Sor Juana of Mexico spoke directly to Kyger in her own struggles as a woman for literary visibility within the male Beat literary establishment.

On February 21, Kyger travels to Uxmal. Perhaps the only way to account for the stupendous nature of Uxmal was to invent an etiological myth to explain its wonders. As we have seen in chapter 3, Margaret Randall tells the tale in her poem "Uxmal" of the Dwarf who challenged the King. Kyger refers in a later entry of March 24 to her reading "Allen Ginsberg on the Adivino," which is a reference to Ginsberg's discussion of the famous Pyramid of the Magician. This is another example of the intertextual nature of much of the Beat writing about Mexico, for it is frequently the case that the Beats had not only read books on Mexican literature, history, and religion but had also communicated with each other either through letters or through their books. Kyger then goes on to describe the exotic flora she encounters in the jungle: "ferns, cactus/gumbo limbo, bromiliads, mimosa, and gold/flowers on dark unleafed branches/Chac gives us some afternoon rain." Kyger interweaves within her Mexican texts her knowledge of Aztec and Maya myth and archaeology: *Chac* is the Maya god of rain.

Already, Kyger's method becomes clear: she describes what she sees, and we begin to understand that indeed, the book is "phenomenological." In this sense, Kyger's Mexican writings differ markedly from a writer like Jack Kerouac, who tends to "romanticize" Mexico as "the magic land at the end of the road." Kyger has cited Olson's *Maya Letters* where Olson declares about the Maya: "I guess these people had a very ancient way of NOT IMPROVING on nature . . . and with an attention that did not include 'improvement.'" The Maya incarnated a "phenomenological realism which strums the strings of time without touching them." Phenomenology is the philosophical method expounded by Edmund Husserl (1859–1938) and developed more fully by his student Martin Heidegger (1889–1976) which aims to allow us an encounter with "the things themselves" by "bracketing" our preconceptions. This disciplined mode of perception faces the "phenomena" of the world as they appear to us—in ancient Greek, the word *phainomenon* signifies "that which appears or is seen"—rather than as we believe "reality" ought to be. Dan Coffey points out that many of Kyger's writings "have been phenomenological in nature—using that discipline to reflect on the thought processes that are involved in observing the material world." Indeed, Kyger playfully titles one of her poems "Narrative as Attention on a Rainy Sunday's Phenomenology." Mexican scholars, such as Artur Rivas Sainz in his book *Fenomenologia de lo Poetico* (1950), have explored a phenomenological poetics, and Mexico becomes the ideal place "for Kyger to carry out her experiment involving the poetic use of the phenomenological method." In her *Desecheo Notebook,* Kyger declares: "Concepts promise protection/from experience/The spirit does/not dwell in concepts." This is the challenge of both phenomenology and Zen Buddhism as well: to free the mind of intellectual structures and systems in order to attempt to strip the self of its conditionings.

Kyger had informed David Chadwick in a 1995 interview: "My own interest in Zen came about because in the late '50s I had been studying Wittgenstein and Heidegger when a student at U.C. Santa Barbara. Heidegger had come to the study of 'nothing.' Then I found D.T. Suzuki's book on Japanese Zen and I thought oh! This is where you go with this mind. This 'nothing' is really 'something.'" Kyger asserted that "for me, Suzuki had asked questions about identity and about the self in a language that provided accessible answers."[12] Kyger's philosophy professor Paul Weinpahl—author of *Zen Diary* (1970)—also published an essay entitled "Zen and the Work of Wittgenstein" in which he pursued the connections between Buddhist thought and Wittgensteinian mysticism. The Beats were interested in *consciousness,* and Kyger saw herself as going her own independent way, evolving naturally from philosophy to Buddhism: "I'd started out in philosophy, and Buddhism was of interest to me, and consciousness. What goes on in your mind—where does it come from? What are you supposed to do with your life? And things like that. Identity. And I didn't find too many women, or men, at that point, let's put it that way, who were interested in those questions. So I was already off the mainstream in some way."

One can see how travel to Mexico was a seductive activity for exploring the philosophical ramifications of arriving at the "nothing" of the "self," of the phenomenological method, for as Kyger visits countless sites in Mexico, her "ego" is compelled to take a "back seat" and the emphasis shifts to the immediate perception, the immediate registering of the particular fact which confronts consciousness. As Jonathan Skinner remarks in "Joanne Kyger's Travel Poems": "Poetry stages a centered retreat from ego. If travel, in these poems, involves the cliched quest of self, it is without any of the false identification, the posturing that so often marks such a journey." In leaving America and a galaxy of habitual prejudices and reactions and habits behind, she is forced—or reduced—to become a recording mind which "tells us what is there" in Mexico. One may see this method at work in her entry for Thursday, February 23:

"We are on the way to Dzibilchaltun, a very/large and very partially restored site of/approximately 20 square miles, occupied/continuously from 1000 B.C. until the Spanish/conquest. Dzibilchaltun means 'where there/is writing on flat rocks.'" This entry is straight reportage, material which sounds as if it might be partially gathered from the entry on Dzibilchaltun from *The Blue Guide to Mexico,* leavened with quotidian remarks. Kyger ends this section with: "Iridescent green snakes in that scrub won't/kill you, but they'll make you very sick,/Says fat American lady carrying a stick."[13]

Kyger's final, seemingly nonchalant couplet reminds us that as prosy as the book appears, poetry is also its domain, rhyming "sick" with the "stick" borne by that "fat American lady," the sort of comical, deflationary rhyme favored by Kyger's friend, Philip Whalen. It is a collage of styles, but detached, a voice without a "voice" which observes and records as it perceives the beauties of the Yucatan: places "where there is writing on flat rocks," green snakes, mysterious cenotes. The world is open before one at all times and is there to be *seen,* and here the Mexican landscape invades Kyger's senses and perceptions. Maurice Merleau-Ponty declares in the preface to his *Phenomenology of Perception* (1945): "The world is not an object such that I have in my possession the law of its making; it is the natural setting of, and field for, all my thoughts and all my explicit perceptions. Truth does not 'inhabit' only 'the inner man,' or more accurately, there is no inner man, man is in the world, and only in the world does he know himself." One may observe the influence of Martin Heidegger's *Being and Time* as well, for in *Phenomenological* Kyger opens herself up to being itself, noting the experience of each moment, and always carefully notates the time and dates—as did Philip Whalen—of her experiences, thus observing and recording phenomenological movement and duration. In her collection *Joanne* (1970), Kyger encodes Heidegger in the verses: "what I wanted to say/was in the broad/sweeping/form of being there." Heidegger's key term in *Being and Time* is *Dasein,* which means "being there." And the titles of Kyger's poetry collections alone should alert us to the centrality of time in her work: *On Time; About Now; As Ever.*

Literary allusions proliferate throughout *Phenomenological,* and Kyger carried along several books during her Mexican journeys. She re-reads Charles Olson's *Mayan Letters,* which leads her to "muse about the Yucatan 30 years ago, when Olson was here. So much emptier, no big tours from Florida." On Friday, February 24, she takes up *Serenade,* a novella set in Mexico by James M. Cain, "a fast-moving classic, which has the famous/iguana stew recipe. And worry about my funky/wardrobe falling apart." This sudden oddball humor—informing the reader about Cain's novel, obviously brought on the trip due to its Mexican setting, the quirky shift to a dish featuring the omnipresent reptile of Mexico, the iguana, and the final concern about her fashionableness phrased in the hip word "funky"—lends Kyger's writing about Mexico a charming, often whimsical humor which serves to deflate any claims to pretentiousness. In Philip Whalen's poem "'Home Again, Home Again . . .'"—dated "20.vi.71"—he describes a lady possessed of "voice and beauty and total batty logical inexorability," assumed by some to be a portrait of Kyger. It was Philip Whalen among the Beats with whom Kyger formed the closest friendship, and his own poetry often features the same "batty" style, quick shiftiness of sensibility, darting from one topic to the next, and the same gentle playfulness: it was Whalen who saw poetry as "a picture or graph of a mind moving."[14]

Memories of her earlier encounters with Maya civilization recur in the entry for Tuesday, February 28: "To go to Chichen Itza. First read about/in Richard Halliburton's book in Upper/Darby Pennsylvania Junior High School 1940s/when he jumps in the Sacrificial Pool and/is knocked deaf and dumb for three days." Kyger alludes to Richard Halliburton's (1900–1939) *New Worlds to Conquer* (1929) recounting his journeys to Mexico and dramatic descent into what he calls the "Mayan Well of Death," the sacred cenote at Chichen Itza. Cenotes were of central usefulness to the Maya, for the entire Yucatan peninsula is a limestone shelf. A ready water supply could be found only where the crust of the earth had broken to form sinkholes, or cenotes. This memory serves to illustrate that Mexico had long been a part of Kyger's consciousness, going all the way back to her days in junior high school—as with Jack Kerouac, whose time in Mexico City recalled the Lowell, Massachusetts, of his childhood—and these recollections resurface during her present time in the country. The alluring aura of mystery which has long drawn travelers to Mexico is sounded in Kyger's sudden invocation of Halliburton, a long-forgotten writer who however influenced authors as diverse as Thomas Wolfe, F. Scott Fitzgerald, Ernest Hemingway, Jim Harrison, and Susan Sontag.

Kyger again imitates throughout *Phenomenological* the Japanese *haibun* and *nikki* daybook genre, mixing prose with lines arranged in verse form as in the description which follows of the great pyramids at Chichen Itza.[15] Kyger chronicles the mad, absurd scene of the overrun tourist trap which Chichen Itza has become. Earlier she pointed out that it was Sylvanus Morley (1883–1948) and the Maya scholar J. Eric S. Thompson (1898–1975) who were able to convince both the Mexican government and the Carnegie Institute to restore the ruins (1924–1937), with the "labor coming from the Mayan Chamkom." Kyger is cognizant that Chichen Itza was built up both through the interventions of

American scholars and institutions and through hard labor by the Indigenous Maya themselves. Robert Redfield, the distinguished anthropologist, published with Alfonso Villa Rojas *Chan Kom: A Mayan Village* (1934) which explores this group of Maya—spelled variously as "Chan Kom" and "Cham Kom"—who lived not far from the town of Valladolid and who rebuilt Chichen Itza. Kyger illustrates the ways U.S. imperialism and the tourist industry proliferate today in her striking image: "Teenagers of U.S. galloping/up and down on/history's past conquests." She recapitulates the argument of Beat authors who condemned the role of the United States in continuing the colonialism first imposed on Mexico by the Spaniards. However, perhaps there is a hint of redemption for America, since Kyger provocatively adds the gnomic phrase: "Like human karma chain/with U.S. Help in restoring/the greatest of Mayan Toltec attractions." Is Kyger implying that the United States has ameliorated its "bad karma" through the beneficent act of helping in the archaeological recovery of this ancient site, or does she mean ironically that American "karma" has been made worse by an act of cultural intervention? The "constant flow up and down" of tourists on the pyramid may symbolize a kind of "human karma chain" in which both past and present are caught up in both the literal and figurative action—*karma* denotes "action" in Sanskrit—of the chain of history as it proceeds through time, the "galloping teenagers" continuing the careless depredations of "history's past conquests" of Mexico.

Continuing her survey of the ruins of Chichen Itza, Kyger beholds the Platform of the Jaguars and Eagles: its "stone carvings of the famous eagle with heart/in his talons, and jaguar with heart in his/claws, and on top of the hearts, a flower." She moves on to the Nunnery, where she encounters the poet Leslie Scalapino with her "blue and white flowered dress and webbed plastic/shoes." She asks her to send greetings to friends, "to say hello to/Alice Notley and Anne Waldman." Kyger weaves into her Mexico books her relationships with other artists—in the manner of Frank O'Hara or Diane di Prima in her experimental *The Calculus of Variation* (written 1961–1964; published 1972)—bringing her friendships into her transcriptions of daily life. She then travels by train to Palenque, where she spends Tuesday, March 6, through Thursday, March 8, visiting the Temple of the Foliated Cross "with all its flowering fecundity—/etched on stone in the back wall panel/is the Young Corn God." Earlier Kyger had referred in her section on Sor Juana to the power of the Corn God in Maya ritual. Here, Kyger refers to the masterful artwork which depicts king K'inich Kan Bahlam as a youth as well as an old man. In the center of the Tablet is a wildly proliferating maize plant atop which sits a huge, mythical bird.

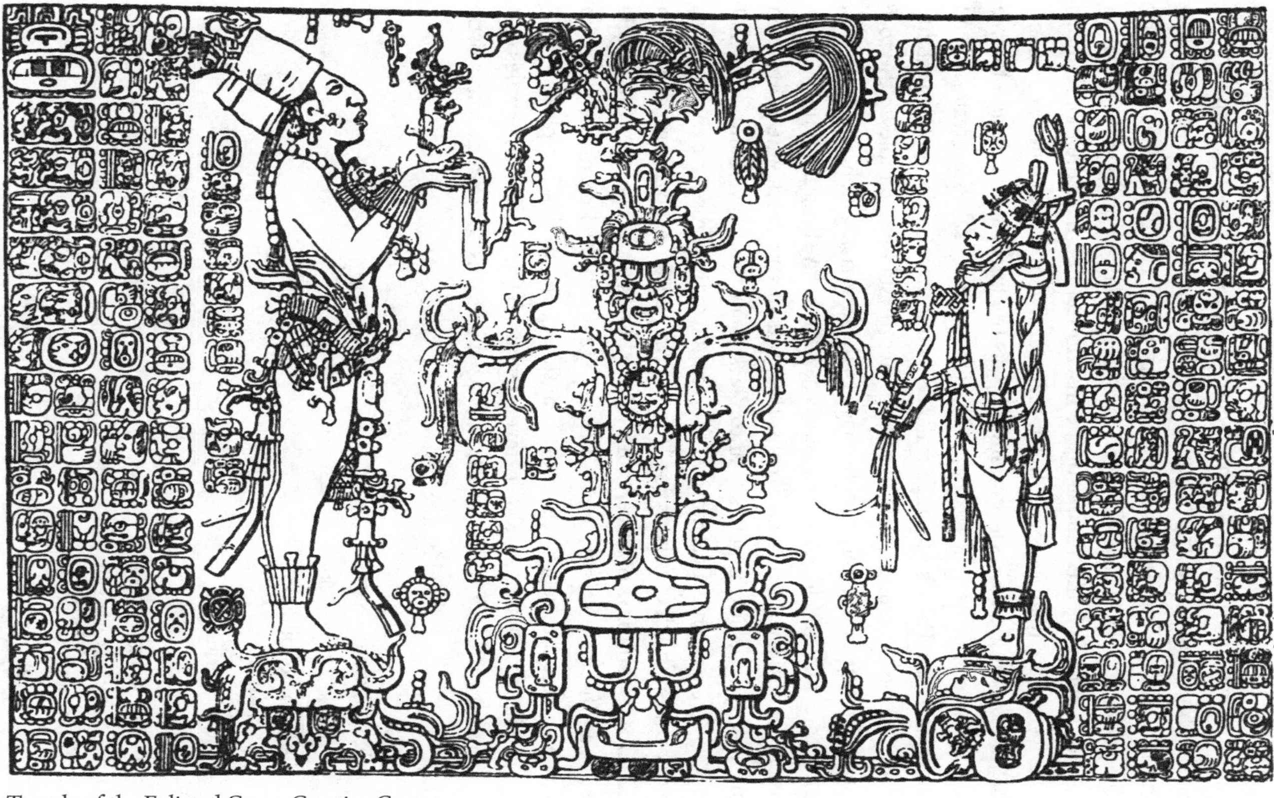

Temple of the Foliated Cross, Creative Commons

Just as Allen Ginsberg was entranced by the stone carvings of Palenque memorialized in "Siesta in Xbalba," Kyger is also struck by the immensity of the site. She visits the burial tomb of ruler Pacal (615–683 C.E.)—also spelled "Pakal"—in the Temple of the Inscriptions which was discovered in 1952 by Alberto Ruz. As David and George Stuart observed: "Looming over the main plaza of Palenque is the Temple of the Inscriptions, perhaps the most famous funerary temple of all Maya civilization. Its renown must have been considerable during the Late Classic era, since it was the burial structure and temple dedicated to the life and legacy of K'inich Janab Pakal, the greatest of all Palenque kings. Pakal's presence was keenly felt through the monumentality of this 'house,' dwarfing nearly all of the other freestanding temples in the core of the city." Kyger not only pays homage to these amazing stone creations but, as in earlier trips to Mexican ruins, she is dazzled by the flora and fauna: "Monster, birds nest fern,/bromeliad, ceiba tree, and an arm/thick vine"; "fourteen toucans/fly by black in gray sky and/Black head, white eye band/Chestnut back, gold chest/Insect catcher." At the Temple of the Cross, she encounters a lovely butterfly which stands for "the continuing embellishment/of Life in this ancient/Epitome of grace/Our eyes are blown up." Kyger sees the nimble insect as "friend butterfly," and notes its return at the close of their trip "in brown and red and yellow/the most beautiful guard/of this Temple."

On Monday, March 12, Kyger travels by bus to Chicxulub, three miles east of Progeso on the Yucatan coast. She again returns to a precise, imagistic style:

Bright white sand
    Dark blue sky
Thin band of blue
        green
    aqua marine
On horizon
            & light green
        olive stretches
Soft low waves
            at our feet are white
And long white streaks
    in the sky.[16]

Here the landscape of the Mexican coast is invoked in a striking sequence of nearly all monosyllabic words chiming in repetition, "white," "green," "blue," with three two-syllable words, "aqua," "marine," "stretches," and just one trisyllabic word: "horizon." It is noteworthy that the only relatively long word is "horizon," which stretches in length of sound to suggest the length of the wide horizon of Chicxulub. Kyger paints all the colors of earth, water, and sky while simultaneously picturing the waves which mirror in their whiteness the white of the clouds above. In an interview conducted at Kent State University during its annual Creative Arts Festival, April 22, 1974, Kyger contributed her thoughts along with Joel Oppenheimer and Ed Dorn to a discussion of "Three Versions of the Poetic Line":

> The line to me is a physical body. It meant a landscape. You lay out your physical body and your physical body goes thru your hand, and you lay that out on the page. It was like a landscape line. Now, I don't feel that precious or exact about handling the line that way because I'm more into a voice line, and the poem gets to be more like a score, a score for the voice though. And I'm not trying to make it that exact. Didn't Williams say that: if you get it exactly on the page any voice can play it.[17]

The influence of Charles Olson's "Projective Verse" is evident: the muscular, energetic physical body which gives voice to the line through the breath. During Olson's time in Campeche—about which Kyger wrote so eloquently—Olson engaged in actual fieldwork, digging up a variety of Maya artifacts and recording his findings. This experience shaped Olson's emerging poetics. As Dylan J. Clark remarked, a "concept that is central to anthropological and archaeological practice, as well as Olson's projective verse, is the notion of fieldwork—being in 'the field' as the site of production. For Olson, 'composition by field,' the methodology of projective verse, stresses the kinetics of poetics as opposed to the structure of form, the 'inherited line, stanza, overall form,' which grows out of the energy transferred, as needed: it is first-hand and action-oriented."[18] So too, Kyger in her lyrical evocation of Chicxulub sees the line as "a physical body. . . . You lay out your physical body and your physical body goes thru your hand, and you lay that out on the page." Olson's aesthetic theory—born at least in part through his sensory connection to Mexico's people and culture—is impressively carried on by Kyger in *Phenomenological.* Jane Falk confirms the link between Olson and Kyger, for Kyger also conceived of Mexico and "the world, itself, being one huge space, and the poet the recorder through the viewfinder of the eye."

On Isla Mujeres, Kyger takes pleasure in huevos rancheros, coffee in the mornings, and swimming at Garrafon Reef "with mask and snorkel / and fins on coral reef in clear/glass like water to see/gold and striped fish/flit by./We find our own little niche of sand/and coral amid the masses of snorklers/on this tiny famous reef." She visits "the remains of the little Mayan temple/to Ixchel, moon goddess/this morning in the rain—/a dramatic perch on the southernmost/end of the island." The women of the Yucatan would undertake pilgrimages to Ixchel's shrines at both Isla Mujeres and Cozumel, for she was the goddess of fertility, pregnancy, and childbirth. Ixchel is also the patroness of weaving, and William S. Burroughs in *Ah Pook Is Here* pays tribute to her as the "Spider Web That Catches the Dew of Morning." On the bus returning to Merida, Kyger notes "the cunningly thatched Mayan houses,/with sweet little doors—walls of sticks/neatly lined up, stone or white plaster,/set in palm groves;/chickens, pigs, little/gardens; and Mayan ladies in white skirts/and overblouses embroidered round the neck./Long dark hair never cut. Rebozos/with woven flecks of white." The trip finally concluding, they depart on Thursday, March 29, to Mexico City, Puerto Vallarta, Zihuatanejo, then back to San Francisco and, finally, Bolinas and "house as we left it."[19]

*Mexico Blondé* (1981)—a holograph reproduction of Kyger's manuscript again illustrated by Donald Guravich—is a briefer text than *Phenomenological* and is attractive due to the immediacy which Kyger's shapely handwriting lends to its appearance. As in *Phenomenological*, the entries are dated. On February 6, Kyger and Guravich arrive in Guadalajara: "This city mucho polluted. We plan to get out soon." On the train to Mexico City, Kyger dreams that poet Bill Berkson and Shunryu Suzuki—her Zen teacher of times past—and the Zen scholar D. T. Suzuki are all in the room next to her on the train: "Great gusty winds in/mountain monastery forest drive me/in temple door, red tori under arm/to find Suzuki Roshi pounding/great prajnaparamita sutra drum./I join in hesitantly because I can't/remember it all. But the vibrations/feel so good."[20] The *Prajnaparamita*—"The Perfection of Transcendent Wisdom"—sutra is a central text in Mahayana Buddhism and was often invoked by the Beats. Thus, memories of Kyger's time in Japan during the early sixties merge with her Zen practice, again drawing parallels with the ways Beat authors found sustenance in both Buddhist practice and in Mexico's ancient cultures. These lofty spiritual sensations are followed swiftly by the entry for February 9, which finds Kyger "in the elegant/city of Oaxaca. A beer in the evening/zocolo watching the many gringos./So many of them. This must be a/tourist town!/One guy has a very/small mouth and several plates of/food. It takes him hours to eat!" At Santa Domingo Church, Kyger views the artifacts housed in the museum from Tomb Seven at Monte Alban including skeletons, bone carvings, jade necklaces, and bead work—"3500 years of continuous/

human history"—and visits the basilica of Our Lady of Soledad. February 18 is spent doing laundry "in this one room domesticity," but later that day she tours Zaachila, the last Zapotec capital after the fall of Monte Alban, located about six-and-a-half kilometers from the city of Oaxaca. In this area, evidence of the earliest writing in Mesoamerica was found in glyph inscriptions dating to 600 B.C. Kyger views the famous tombs discovered there in 1962, describing the "7 carved reliefs in the walls, over each niche, where offerings were placed," and alludes to the last Zapotec king Cosijoeza (1450–1504). An ingratiating entry from Monday, February 23, returns us to the pleasures of the flesh: "How nice it is/to have a 4 o'clock shower, a change/of clothes, smoke a little grass, a sip/of mezcal with a lime squeeze. And sit/down and think about interior/decorating."

In *Mexico Blondé,* this method is employed to great effect. One entry reads in toto: "The animals we saw today:/pigeons, 1 dead cat, four black/birds, two lizards, flies, two great/danes, 1 small boxer." And the following entry reads: "Each person was bound to earth/by his totemic animal and bound to/heaven by the positions of Sun,/moon, stars, planets and constellations/at his birth."[21] "Below" and "Above" are of course symbolized in their interdependent relationship by the myth of Quetzalcoatl, a creature who is at once bird and snake, Sky and Earth. In these accounts of quotidian existence in Mexico—here, a list of animals she has seen during the day—followed immediately by a deeper insight, Kyger sets the microcosm and the macrocosm immediately against each other: the small, seemingly insignificant counterpointed with the large philosophical questions of human meaning and identity in relation to the cosmos. The latter quotation indeed reads as if it might have been taken from a guidebook to Mexican religion, and this pastiche/collage method is typical of Kyger's technique throughout her Mexican writings. As we have seen earlier, when Kyger first ingested peyote, she reported experiencing "this huge rush of animal energy, and I didn't know how to relate myself to it. I finally saw this wild boar as my totem animal." When Kyger reports noting that in ancient Mexico "each person was bound to earth/by his totemic animal," she is returning to a theme which she had experienced in her own spiritual adventures in San Francisco several decades previously.

Thomas Merton in his essay on Monte Alban entitled "The Sacred City" noted that Claude Levi-Strauss had revealed "the extraordinary sophistication of totemic thought." Merton argues that in North and Central America, Indigenous peoples' "elaborate symbolic association of the human person with cosmic animals represents something much more intimate than an 'alienated' subjection to external forces. . . . What we have here is in fact not a matter of alienation but of identity. But it is obviously a conception of identity which is quite different from our subjective and psychological one, centered on the empirical ego regarded as distinct and separate from the rest of reality." In her Mexico books, Kyger seeks—like Merton—a connection to what is *there*, to the physical cosmos in order to overcome precisely our contemporary "alienation." Kyger believed that "ideas are dime a dozen. Ideas are something called our European structure of mind which sucks in the world, which our education has given us very freely and very generously. I don't want that. I want to see how you live *in* your environment or in your compassion for place. One thing I realized teaching at Naropa Institute this summer, as the class was reading Jaime de Angulo, was that I was really trying to get people over to this space where they have some animal-spirit connection. To realize that the tree is in a simultaneous breath with ourselves, and it's not a *difference* of consciousness."[22] In teaching the anthropologist Jaime de Angulo, who had familiarized the counterculture with Native American mythology and shamanism through his books and lectures, Kyger returns to the desire for an "animal-spirit connection," to avoid the state of being "which sucks in the world" and leaves the soul empty. What is significant about Kyger's insights into the Aztecs and Maya is that they were simultaneously rooted in the Earth through their connection to their "totemic animal" and to the cosmos through a mathematical understanding of the movements of the heavenly bodies, "the positions of Sun,/moon, stars, planets and constellations/at his birth."

*Patzcuaro* (1999)—the third of Kyger's Mexican books—is also the result of an expedition she undertook with Donald Guravich. She notes in her preface that she had visited Patzcuaro several times over the past ten years with him and that the book was written during the winter of 1997–1998. Kyger described her method: "I wanted to attempt to compose some words that were more 'precise.' I approached this formally at a certain time every day, and excerpted journal entries that I had written over the past weeks—a collage portrait of events, including dreams that seemed prescient. I gave myself lots of space on the page using a 9X12 water color sketchbook. I did this periodically over our 40-day stay and the poems in the book resulted." She informs us that "Patzcuaro, Michoacan, Mexico, a beautiful small colonial city located on the edge of a high mountain lake, was built upon the pyramids and dwellings of the Purepecha people who still live and speak their Purepecha language there today." She had been given Pablo Neruda's *Memoirs*, which she took with her on the trip and was "deeply impressed by the warmth of the feelings and language for his fellow poets, a wholehearted brotherhood."[23] *Patzcuaro* opens with a striking descriptive passage: "If you think you are responsible/for an entire institution, time to go/to Mexico./A car sinks in a muddy pothole,/disappears. Neat rows of roses. Lagoon baby/crocodiles, yellow fish exotica. The painting/of rabbit and coyote by Oaxaca's Francisco Toledo."[24] As Mary Paniccia Carden observes in her essay "Joanne Kyger's Travel Chapbooks: A Poetics of Motion," the poem is rich in "sensory detail" describing the exotic flora and fauna of Mexico as well as its great artists as represented by Francisco Toledo (1940–2019), the Zapotec sculptor and painter born in Oaxaca. Beat authors often allude to Mexican artists in their writing: for example, both Ted Joans and Margaret Randall recorded their admiration for Frida Kahlo, and here Kyger invokes Toledo, creator of a painting depicting the myth of Rabbit and Coyote originating in the town of Juchitan in Oaxaca.[25] The narrative concerns a rabbit who comes to a chile farm and eats all the chiles: the farmer makes a scarecrow made of beeswax to catch the invader. The natural landscape and artistic and mythic traditions are rendered by Kyger immediately and palpably.

In the second poem, "The News from Patzcuaro," Kyger gives the history of the area, informing us the news "begins about 1500 years ago when ground/is broken for a ceremonial pyramid, by a now/forgotten kingdom/ with strong trade routes/Eight hundred years later the Purepecha arrive/ from the north—the people of today/who lived and continued on thru the conquest/by Spain during which time/they were finally helped/by the enlightened compassion of Father/Vasco de Quiroga/who modeled their villages/after Thomas More's Utopian principles/of self-sufficiency and equality of wealth./Their old Mother God was transformed/into the Virgin of Health—de la Salud—/fashioned from corncob/and orchid honey paste/ and dwells still in her towering pyramid rebuilt/as a basilica." Vasco de Quiroga, a judge and lawyer from Mexico City, came to ameliorate the squalid living conditions of the Purepecha, who had been severely mistreated by the brutal conquistador Nuno de Guzman after his arrival in 1529. Quiroga created cooperatives for the villagers modeled on Sir Thomas More's ideas which he promulgated in his classic book *Utopia* (1516). December is also the month when the people of Patzcuaro celebrate the Virgin of Health, a revered figure throughout Michoacan. In an interview conducted two years following her trip to Patzcuaro, Kyger spoke of how this event is then "followed by the celebration for the Virgin Guadalupe, the Empress of Mexico. The outpouring of worship and petitioning given to these two deities moved me deeply. Worshippers cared in a deep and fundamental spiritual way, they *believed*."

Again, Kyger supplies us the history of the area she is visiting, letting the words speak for themselves. She also juxtaposes the metaphysical with the earthly two pages later when the entire entry features just seventeen words: "Could be/anywhere/on Earth and Time focused completely/focused/on chopping/the tomatoes, chilies, and onions."[26] As we have seen previously, the desire to maneuver the ego into the place where one is able to experience "time focused completely" is the subtext of Kyger's Mexico poems, and here the Zen moment involves the Holy Trinity of Mexican cuisine: tomato, chile, onion.

While Kyger devotes several fine passages to the pleasures of life in Mexico, she is, like all of the Beats, fully cognizant of the political struggles of the Indigenous people of Chiapas, referring in one poem to the time—as we saw earlier in Margaret Randall's writings—when "the identity of Subcomandante Marcos/was announced and the peso devalued." Subcomandante Marcos—Rafael Sebastian Guillen Vicente (1957–)—turned to radical politics following the massacre of the students on October 2, 1968, at Tlatelolco in Mexico City, and became head of the movement to liberate Chiapas from capitalist hegemony. Jeff Conant in *A Poetics of Resistance* memorably described the insurgence of January 1, 1994: "In remoter Chiapas, an invisible army had gathered in the mist of highland villages, uniformed in dark colors, faces masked, some armed, with bolt-action rifles, some with sticks, some armed only with their rage and shielded only with their dignity." In the third poem of the sequence, "Dead in Acteal, Chiapas," Kyger recounts the massacre on December 22, 1997, by the right-wing paramilitary group *Mascara Roja*, or "Red Mask," noting: "Seven men, twenty women, eighteen children/Forty-five Tzotzil souls/'Immense majority shot in the back/with high-caliber weapons'/December 22, 1997/With an attempt made to 'cover up'/the events . . . /Indigenous agrarian economy/barely holds on/The Pope 'prays'/for the suffering victims/implores the 'Lord'/to comfort their families."[27] The Tzotzil are Maya of the Chiapas highlands—whose treasury of myth Kyger features in her poem "Marian Lopez Castillo's Story"—and Kyger's disgust at the hypocrisy and false pieties of "Christians" when faced with the poverty and struggles of the Tzotzil is palpable.

Kyger continues the theme of the collision between Indigenous beliefs and the Spanish conquistadors in the poem "Under the Roof of the Archangels." The celebrated narrative which Kyger memorializes concerns Our Lady of Guadalupe—*Nuestra Senora de Guadalupe*—in which the Virgin Mary appeared four times before a Mexican peasant named Juan Diego Cuauhtlatoatzin, beginning on December 9, 1531, on the Hill of Tepeyac near Mexico

City, and spoke to him in Nahuatl, his native language. Kyger documents this historic moment: "The sirens/go off, it is the day for the Empress of Mexico Guadalupe in which the indigena/weds the Maria of Spain's conquest, 1531, and Juan/Diego perceives an apparition on an Ancient Goddess's/hilltop and finds roses in barren soil/which he gathers in his cloak. They imprint/an image of the sacred new Virgin of now/Catholic Mexico. God did it."[28] Kyger refers to the fact that the location of Juan Diego's vision—Tepeyac Hill—was the place where the Aztec earth goddess Tonantzin was worshiped. Tonantzin in Nahuatl means "little mother," and she was revered as the benevolent mother of humanity. However, after accurately transcribing the historical account of this dramatic event, Kyger undercuts the positive interpretation placed on Juan Diego's vision with the three final words of the poem: "God did it." Is it the fact that this historical turn in the ways Christianity was syncretized with local Indigenous beliefs happened because "God did it"? Rather, Kyger would agree with Judith Friedlander, who observed in *Being Indian in Hueyapan: A Study of Forced Identity in Contemporary Mexico*: "It is often noted that the Catholics were so successful in converting the Indians because they were flexible enough in their interpretations of the dogma to be able to incorporate into Catholicism many of the customs of the people they came to convert."[29] Kyger does not see the hand of "God" in the process by which the Indigenous peoples of Mexico were enslaved by a foreign conqueror; rather, it is clear that Kyger links the violent uprisings in Chiapas with the centuries of Spanish domination and subsequent incursion of capitalism and oppression into the rural economies of Mexico, as well as with the domination of the Catholic church.

*God Never Dies: Poems from Oaxaca, December 7, 2003–January 9, 2004*—the fourth and final chapbook devoted to Kyger's Mexican travels—is a testament to the strength and longevity of the impact of Mexico on her imagination. The title, we are told, is taken from the celebrated waltz by Macedonia Alcala "Dios Nunca Muere"—"God Never Dies"—which "is known as the Hymn of Oaxaca." The chapbook contains sixteen dated poems, and the poem for Tuesday, December 23, is entitled "Here in Oaxaca It's the Night of the Radishes." Kyger has noted in her correspondence with Dale Smith that "Night of the Radishes is celebrated at Christmas Eve in Oaxaca. Everyone grows these gigantic turnip sized radishes, covered with red skin like the little ones, and gather in the main zocalo to carve them into the most intricate shapes—making manger scenes, big figures of Guadalupe, secular scenes with lots of action figures. Big dioramas of churches and figures, bull fights. They are then judged by a panel and win lots of money. It's a big deal and you have to see it to believe it. The red and white pieces held together by little pieces of toothpick. 'Heaven' only knows where this practice came from. But lots of 'room for fun' to see the carving through the red skin."[30] Kyger typically integrates several of the techniques we have hitherto examined in this poem: she notes the plant life, "gardenia"; she tells us what she is wearing, "shoes without socks"; we are informed about the weather, "the sun is frankly generous"; we learn of her Buddhism with a gently humorous reference to the fact that the buddha "doesn't mind being 'catholic'/in Mexico"; and finally the allusion to the ritual which will take place that night, "carving through the red skin."[31]

Finally, the double meaning of the title of Kyger's last volume containing Mexican poems, *On Time: Poems 2005–2014*—to be punctual, but also a poetic disquisition on the meaning of time—alerts us again to Kyger's phenomenological themes. She includes a section entitled "Dreaming Poets in Mexico with the *I Ching*: A Oaxaca Notebook October 2011." This begins a sequence of eleven poems composed during her October stay in Oaxaca. Consistent with Beat practice, Kyger integrates her knowledge of Buddhism and of texts such as the *I Ching* with her Mexican experiences. In the poem for October 5, Kyger begins: "It's not as if I was a wanderer—really holding to domestic stability/When the latter is a bit like holding onto a toothpick in the sea." At the close, we learn the deeper significance of being a "wanderer." She relates quotidian events, going to the internet café in Oaxaca and having trouble "trying to log on/to a critically unfamiliar machine." Meanwhile, news from America filters through as she learns that "Texas Governor, Rick Perry, suggests Mexico's drug wars may need/deployment of US Troops./Mexico remembers the Mexican-American War. No way/for armed incursion." Four days later in a poem dated Saturday, October 8, the political troubles signaled by the allusion to "Texas Governor, Rick Perry" return: "'Mexico needs no enemies with friends/like the US Bureau of Alcohol Tobacco & Firearms'/US federal agents conceived operations/which has Mexico's 'bad guys' well armed and arrogant./'The ATF is there to impede,/yet seems to supervise gun running into Latin America.'" This again seems a bit of "found poetry," an article taken from a newspaper or magazine which again suggests the ongoing "war on drugs" and the impossible political situation caused by the American government.

Kyger's mind then shifts to the *I Ching* of the title of the sequence: "This thing called 'patience' as a practiced virtue results in a clear/unmolested mind./Random opening to the *I Ching* #56 The Wanderer—/'Persistently conscious of being a stranger in a strange land—'"[32] Thus we subtly return to the "wandering" woman of the opening of the poem. Kyger seamlessly combines her concerns about "domestic stability," getting used to an unfamiliar internet system in Oaxaca, the "drug wars" happening between the United States and Mexico, and the *I Ching*. Like Diane di Prima, Michael McClure, and Bob Dylan, Kyger was also fascinated by the *I Ching*, which she encountered through her readings of Jung. As she pointed out in an interview: "I first encountered Jung when I was at the University of California in Santa Barbara, during 1952–56—probably in some of my classes or reading on my own. I realized later that he did the introduction to the *I Ching*, the Bollingen edition with the English translation by Cary Baynes, who was Jaime de Angulo's first wife. That connection interested me a great deal. However, I realized at a certain point that the introduction was more complicated than I need to get into this particular text."[33] In the poem, she opens the *I Ching* at "random," emphasizing the Jungian "synchronicity" of her own putative existence as a "wanderer" in Mexico and the wisdom of *I Ching* number 56, which has as its title "The Wanderer." Kyger quotes an actual section from the Bollingen edition of the *I Ching*: "He is persistently conscious of being a stranger in a strange land."[34]

Finally, on Sunday, October 16, Kyger narrates a curious event involving a "relic" from Pope John Paul II who had recently died. The "relic" was conveyed to the Oaxaca zocalo where it was put on display in the main cathedral, and thousands came to behold it. Newspapers had published photographs of the pope "in his casket with a glass top,/laid out in all his ceremonial robes of red and black and gold./Like he's newly dead./I find out today that the Pope/Was a life size replica made of wax."[35] Although Kyger is skeptical of the role Christianity has played in Mexico, she remains in awe of the power of faith and returns to the theme of devotion which we encountered above in her reaction to the celebrations in Patzcuaro: "I'm always overcome by other people's devotion—because it seems to be this reference point where all this yearning and hope can rest and ask and petition. Certainly in that way of just asking, something happens, is revealed. So just to see religion in its basic bhakti practice of devotion is always amazing to me. You can feel the strength that comes from it. A part of the life of religion. It's fascinating."[36] *Bhakti* is a Hindu term meaning "devotion to one god with all of life's activities directed to the god's service," and Kyger admires these expressions of sincere belief. We recall from chapter 4 the moment in Margaret Randall's "The Boy with the Mayan Face" when the Boy says to her, "*Estoy de pedido*"—"I am asking." In Spanish the "petition" of which Kyger speaks is "*pedido*," and the revelatory moments are quite similar: in both cases one *asks for* something in a spirit of humility and vulnerability. The vulnerability calls out to us to answer, which, to fulfill our true humanity, we are required to do.

We have seen in this chapter how central Mexico was to Joanne Kyger in her life as a poet and the ways she transformed her experiences within the context of her relationship with the Beat movement and background in philosophy, especially phenomenology. Kyger was alert to the complexities of life in Mexico, counterpointing the glories of its archaeological treasures with the poverty and inequality which were the fate of many of its people. She was also fascinated by the mythology of the Maya, and we may see the rich narrative traditions of the Maya in her poetry. Kyger—like Margaret Randall—emphasized the struggle for equality for women and identified with the great Mexican poet Sor Juana de la Cruz, who fought against patriarchy. Kyger perceived her Mexico books as a way to at once honor this great country and its traditions and to continue her explorations of the mysteries of identity and selfhood through the camera eye of phenomenology.

# EPILOGUE

*THE BEATS IN MEXICO* endeavors to demonstrate the centrality of Mexico's people, history, mythology, sacred rituals, landscape, and literature to authors of the Beat generation, as well as to the larger counterculture of the United States. Mexico remains for many Americans a collection of stereotypes: a cartoon with the caption "*manana*" depicting a sleeping man sitting in the shade with a sombrero tilted over his face; Pancho Villa; the folk song "La Cucaracha"; piñatas; Mexican jumping beans. And *norteamericanos* are familiar with some odd forms of supposedly Mexican cuisine due to the influx of fast food establishments such as Taco Bell and Chipotle. Americans know little of the culture of Mexico, and the situation has now worsened with the proliferation of tribal, racist, and hateful rhetoric spouted by ignorant politicians over the past several years. These prejudices are of long standing, as we witness with the nineteenth century newspaperman George Wilkins Kendall, who complained about Mexico in his *Narrative of the Texan Santa Fe Expedition* (1847):

> Strange that with a country as fair as any upon the face of the earth, abounding in every species of soil and climate, fruit and mineral, the Mexicans will not

> profit from the lessons and adopt the systems of their Saxon neighbors. They pertinaciously cling to the customs of their forefathers, and are becoming every year more and more impoverished—in short, they are morally, physically, and intellectually distanced in the great race of improvement which is run in almost every other quarter of the earth. Give them but tortillas, frijoles, and chile colorado to supply their animal wants for the day, and seven-tenths of the Mexicans are satisfied; and so they will continue to be until the race becomes extinct or amalgamated with Anglo-Saxon stock; for no political change, no revolution, can uproot that inherent indolence and antipathy to change, which in this age of improvement and advancement must sooner or later work their ruin and downfall. In these wonder-working days of steam, to stand still is to retrograde.[1]

We note that it is precisely this clichéd view of the Mexican character—"indolence," a reluctance to immediately embrace the transcendent glory of the steam engine, the delight taken in simple "animal" pleasures such as "tortillas, frijoles and chile colorado"—which the Beats extol. It was the putative "scientific progress" of the modern world that the British Romantics from William Blake to D. H. Lawrence and the American Transcendentalists Henry David Thoreau and Ralph Waldo Emerson also mightily opposed. There is also of course in Kendall's critique more than a hint of racism: the Mexicans refuse to learn from the great wisdom "of their Saxon neighbors," and furthermore, unless their "race" combines with the superior "Anglo-Saxon stock," they shall be condemned forever to their frijoles and tortillas.

For Jack Kerouac, Mexico was "the magic land at the end of the road," and the Beats sought in Mexico a revivification of their own capacity for wonder and joy. Gordon Brotherston remarked that both D. H. Lawrence and Antonin Artaud believed that a real "revolution was impossible without the discovery of 'living culture' and Mexico was one of the last places, if not the last, to find it." Lawrence and Artaud also "dreamed of a fuller society in which the blood-sun-wisdom of the Mexican Indians, knowable through their literature, would redeem man."[2] So too for the Beats, Mexico became a place of spiritual pilgrimage as well a kind of mirror to America and the Western world, reflecting back to us ourselves and the ways we might improve our inner and outer lives. The fact that Mexico would so thoroughly engage the imaginations of so many of the members of the American counterculture is a testament to its continuing mesmerizing power as a replenishing source of inspiration and wisdom. Indeed, it was precisely to the degree that Mexico was different from the United States that the Beats found it attractive.

As we have emphasized, the Beat response to Mexico was far from monolithic. They considered different topics and experimented with a variety of literary forms to shape their experiences. Lawrence Ferlinghetti, like Joanne Kyger, often employed the journal form and was fond of a pastiche method in which he constantly wove within the texture of his prose and poems direct quotations or allusions to prior visitors to Mexico such as Malcolm Lowry and D. H. Lawrence. William S. Burroughs turned primarily to the novel and short story to invoke a darkness-light polarity which symbolized for him both the promise of Mexico as well as the tragic dimensions which unfolded in his personal life. Burroughs also pursued—with compulsive energy—a lifelong fascination with the Maya Codices. Philip Lamantia—arguably America's greatest Surrealist author—translated poetry by Sor Juan de la Cruz, studied seriously the language of the Cora people, and recorded his mystical experiences while living in Mexico. Margaret Randall founded one of the most important literary magazines in Mexico—*El Corno Emplumado*—sought equal rights for women, and registered the inequities she perceived in society, communicating through the genres of autobiography, fiction, poetry, and photography. Jack Kerouac, in both his novels and poetry collection *Mexico City Blues*, explored Aztec myth and dreamed of establishing an adobe monastery where he could pursue a Buddhist, contemplative life. Allen Ginsberg composed in both poetry and journal form, following in many ways the example of Burroughs in his engagement with Maya culture, and created one of his best pre-"Howl" poems while in Mexico, "Siesta in Xbalba." Bonnie Bremser's original autobiographical prose text *Troia: Mexican Memoirs* introduced a new and bold voice from a woman's perspective into Beat discourse. Michael McClure in his *Ghost Tantras* experimented formally with a new poetics rooted in mammalian consciousness and exhibited the most interest among the Beats for the rich ecosystems of Mexico. McClure also earned the respect of the great scientist Francis Crick for his ability to translate his experiences ingesting peyote into poetry. His friend Jim Morrison—who studied the Beats as an adolescent—through his songs and lyrics carried the Beat relationship to Mexico into the sixties' hippie generation, making a trip to Teotihuacan to visit the Pyramid of the Sun. Finally, Joanne Kyger created a unique hybrid genre of journal and poetry, and due to her training in philosophy, phenomenology, and Zen Buddhism, strove to record her experiences in Mexico moment by moment without "privileging" the "spiritual" over the "material," noting: "The basis of Zen meditation, any meditation, is prana which is understanding the breath. . . . If you can slow your breath down, you can slow your thoughts down. If you slow your thoughts down, as Lew Welch said, Buddhism is really useful because it hones the mind."

The Beats undoubtedly sought a variety of pleasures in Mexico—most travelers to new lands are in search of adventure and joy—yet they also sought to address (if not resolve) a number of interior and exterior polarities: America/Mexico; rationality/unconscious; repression/freedom; technology/nature; modern/archaic; clock-time/timelessness and eternity; patriarchy/empowerment for women. There was also a sense of identification with what Jack Kerouac called the "fellaheen"—the oppressed peoples of Mexico who represented a massive silent protest against the modern technocracy. Aldous Huxley in *Beyond the Mexique Bay* (1934) responded to D. H. Lawrence's desire to "go back" to the time before modernity by resuscitating the Aztec religion. Huxley develops these themes in *Brave New World* (1932), in which the character John—the "Savage"—exemplifies this struggle between contemporary and "primitive." Huxley asserted that Lawrence himself was uncertain about whether the "dark gods" could be revivified and that his ambivalence is on display in the stark contradictions at the heart of his Mexico novel *The Plumed Serpent* (1926). Huxley also discusses *Mexico: A Study of Two Americas* (1931) by Stuart Chase, arguing that the importance of Chase's book lies in the fact that he raises "the problem of reconciling the primitive with the civilized. . . . The question which confronts us is this: can we evolve a new society which shall combine the virtues of primitives with those of the civilized, but exhibit the vices of neither? Mr. Chase poses this general question in a particular form: how much of what is good in North American civilization can Mexico import and still remain Mexico?" Huxley argues that the "civilized" person "can take, or at least they can try to take, the primitive's human wholeness. A primitive is forced to be whole—a complete man, trained in all the skills of the community, able to fend for himself in all circumstances: if he is not whole, he perishes. A civilized man, on the contrary, is under no external necessity to be whole."[3] Today we would abjure the words "civilized" to describe ourselves and "primitive" to describe the inhabitants of other cultures. And as we have seen, an author like Jack Kerouac has been rightly criticized for his "essentializing" of the "Other"—Margaret Randall charts a more sensitive response to the "Other" in her Mexico writings—and his failure to resolve his own romanticizing of racial and ethnic "difference." However, Huxley raises a question relevant to the Beats, for they too in their journeys to Mexico were attempting to find if there was something they could bring back to America from Mexico, whether there was a secret to living a fuller, whole, complete life which was missing in modern American "civilization."

Indeed, another major theme I have explored in *The Bests in Mexico* is the role of Mexico in the countercultural turn toward the expansion of consciousness through both psychotropic substances—a theme Aldous Huxley himself explored in *The Doors of Perception*—and shamanism. Both Joanne Kyger and Bonnie Bremser ingested peyote and recorded their experiences in their writings. We also saw in Allen Ginsberg's "Paterson" his desire to leave behind the constrictions of death-in-life in the United States: "I would rather go mad, gone down the dark road to Mexico, heroin dripping/in my veins,/eyes and ears full of marijuana,/eating the god Peyote on the floor of a mudhut on the border." This cri de coeur indicates his profound need to descend into the dark truths of the unconscious as symbolized by Mexico, where the soul can—in Jim Morrison's words—"break on through to the other side." Ginsberg's invocation of peyote in his poem from 1949 signals the role Mexico would play for the Beats in their experimentation with the expansion of consciousness. The employment of sacred mushrooms—*Teonanacotyl, Carne de Dios,* or "God's Flesh"—by the Aztecs was widespread, and Michael McClure returned from Oaxaca with psilocybin samples to be employed in scientific research, while peyote brought to San Francisco by Philip Lamantia from San Luis Potosi would be a central moment in turning the Beats on to psychedelics. William S. Burroughs explored entheogens in Mexico, traveled to Colombia in quest of *ayahuasca*—yage—and exchanged letters with Allen Ginsberg on the subject, subsequently published as *The Yage Letters* (1963). The Beat exploration of marijuana, peyote, "magic mushrooms," mescaline, and *ayahuasca*—all retrieved from their trips to Mexico and South America—would pave the way for Timothy Leary at Harvard and other academic researches into the possibilities of employing these substances not only for spiritual illumination but for the treatment of mental illness. Most recently, William A. Richards in his *Sacred Knowledge: Psychedelics and Religious Experiences* as well as Michael Pollan's *How to Change Your Mind* both bear witness to the pioneering efforts of the Beats during their travels in Mexico.[4]

It is fitting that it is a Mazatecan woman *curandera* who so beautifully described the ultimate spiritual quest of the Beats in Mexico. Maria Sabina declared: "There is a world beyond ours, a world that is far away and nearby, both invisible and seen. And there is where God lives, the spirits and the saints, a world where everything has already happened and everything is known. That world talks. It has a language of its own. I report what it says. The sacred mushrooms take me by the hand and bring me to the world where everything is known. It is them, the sacred mushrooms, that speak in a way I can understand. I ask them and they reply to me. When I return from the journey I say what they have said to me, what they have shown me."[5] The contribution of women to the development and evolution of Beat literature is one area which I have emphasized in *The Beats in Mexico*. Rightly accused of misogyny, the male Beats often marginalized Beat women, and women's own "journeys" of the mind and spirit were excluded from anthologies. Both Diane di Prima and Joanne Kyger were not included in Don Allen's important collection *The New American Poetry*. Margaret Randall is a central figure whose work is only now beginning to garner the attention it deserves. And as we have seen, the Beat fascination with shamanism was central to Joanne Kyger's poetry as well as Anne Waldman's work which was influenced by the visionary poetry/chant of Maria Sabina, as we may see in Waldman's poem "Fast Speaking Woman." Bonnie Bremser journeyed to Oaxaca to observe Maria's healing rituals, which she recorded in *Troia: Mexican Memoirs*. Thus, female Beat authors were central to the recovery of this important spiritual tradition. The process of canon formation is fraught with political and social prejudices, which affected not only female Beat authors but also African American authors such as Ted Joans and Bob Kaufman. Kaufman's work has finally been admitted to the canon of twentieth-century poetry, while Joans has also been accorded greater critical attention as the epitome of the transnational Beat. Although Joans did not write extensively about Mexico, we have seen in several of his poems the ways he incorporated Mexico within the context of the struggle for African American social justice. The Beats learned much during their travels in Mexico. Indeed, Mexico still has many things to teach us. Given the threats posed by the often ignorant, reactionary political climate in the United States, it is essential to emphasize our sense of kinship with this great country and its people, and to celebrate the humanitarian values which the Beats—not always perfectly—sought to affirm.

# ACKNOWLEDGMENTS

I am grateful to many people who helped me in a variety of ways during the composition of *The Beats in Mexico*. I have learned a great deal from lively discussions concerning many of the issues raised in this book with students in my Beat Literature course at Eastern Michigan University. Many thanks to the librarians and interlibrary loan staffs at the University of Michigan and Eastern Michigan University. I am grateful to Betty Ferber for her information regarding her husband Homero Aridjis and his relationship with Beat authors, and for granting permission to include her lovely photograph of Aridjis and Lawrence Ferlinghetti. Elaine Katzenberger of City Lights Books also provided helpful information concerning Ferlinghetti. I enjoyed immensely my email correspondence and telephone conversations with Malcolm McNeill, who was extremely generous discussing his collaboration with William S. Burroughs on *Ah Pook Is Here*. Garrett Caples at City Lights Books was of great help regarding Philip Lamantia. Thanks to the librarians at the Bancroft Library at University of California at Berkeley for their magnificent archive of the Philip Lamantia Papers, and to Nancy Peters for granting permission to include a page from Lamantia's journals which he kept during his travels in Mexico. Margaret Randall kindly responded to my queries, and I benefited greatly from her immense knowledge of everything Mexican. Thanks to Paul M. Pearson at the Thomas Merton Center, Bellarmine University. Peter Hale of the Allen Ginsberg Estate responded generously to my questions concerning Ginsberg's time in Mexico. My gratitude to Gordon Ball for his memoir *East Hill Farm: Seasons with Allen Ginsberg* and for his wonderful photograph of Bonnie Bremser. Amy Evans McClure in both emails and phone conversations provided me invaluable assistance regarding her travels with her late husband Michael McClure in Mexico. Margot Kempers and John Reuters assisted me regarding Elsa Dorfman's portrait of Joanne Kyger. Thanks to Penelope Rosemont for sending me her hard-to-find book on Mexico and Surrealism. Catherine Nuckols-Wilde of Tulane University patiently shared her knowledge of the Madrid Codex.

I owe a great debt of gratitude to Nicole Solano, editor at Rutgers University Press, for making the production of this book a joy. Nicole has been everything any author hopes for: responsive, open with her own ideas, and unfailingly supportive. My thanks to Sonia Tam for her work in bringing my manuscript to completion. Thanks to Maria Beye, my indefatigable companion during our travels through Mexico. I thank William Byrd, whose music continues to inspire my hours at the piano. Finally, I thank the people of Mexico, who have made my travels in their stupendous country a high point of my life over the past several decades.

# NOTES

## INTRODUCTION

1. Frederick Luis Adama, *The Routledge Concise History of Latino/a Literature* (London: Routledge, 2013), 87; Daniel Belgrad, "The Transnational Counterculture: Beat-Mexican Intersections," in *Reconstructing the Beats*, ed. Jennie Skerl (New York: Palgrave Macmillan, 2004), 27.
2. Glenn Sheldon, *South of Our Selves: Mexico in the Poems of Williams, Kerouac, Corso, Ginsberg, Levertov and Hayden* (Jefferson, NC: McFarland and Company, 2004), 7.
3. Denise Levertov, "Pleasures," in *Collected Poems*, ed. Paul A. Lacey and Anne Dewey (New York: New Directions, 2013), 96.
4. Jill Leslie McKeever Furst, *The Natural History of the Soul in Ancient Mexico* (New Haven: Yale University Press, 1995), 1; Levertov, "Xochipilli," in *Collected Poems*, 124; Levertov, "The Sense of Pilgrimage," in *The Poet in the World* (New York: New Directions, 1973), 73.
5. Bob Kaufman, *Collected Poems*, ed. Neeli Cherkovsky, Raymond Foye, and Tate Swindell (San Francisco: City Lights, 2019), 166; Hart Crane, "The Circumstance," in *The Complete Poems of Hart Crane*, ed. Marc Simon (New York: Liveright, 2000), 150. On Crane's residence in Mexico, see Suzanne E. Hall, "Hart Crane in Mexico: The End of a New World Poetics," *Mosaic: A Journal for the Interdisciplinary Study of Literature* 46, no. 1 (March 2013): 135–149.
6. On Olson and Black Mountain, see Martin Duberman, *Black Mountain College: An Exploration in Community* (New York: E. P. Dutton, 1972); on Olson and the counterculture, see Stephen Fredman, "The Contemporaries: A Reading of Charles Olson's 'The Lordly and Isolate Satyrs,'" in *Contemporary Olson*, ed. David Herd (Manchester: Manchester University Press, 2015), 185–186; Charles Olson, "A Bibliography on America for Ed Dorn," in *Additional Prose: A Bibliography on America, Proprioception and Other Notes and Essays*, ed. George F. Butterick (Bolinas, CA: Four Seasons Foundation, 1974), 5; Ed Dorn, "Twenty-Four Love Songs," in *Way More West: New and Selected Poems* (New York: Penguin Books, 2007), 125; and Joseph Rickey, ed., *Ed Dorn Live: Lectures, Interviews, and Outtakes* (Ann Arbor: University of Michigan Press, 2007), 126; see also Edward Dorn and Gordon Brotherston, *The Sun Unwound: Original Texts from Occupied America* (Berkeley: North Atlantic Books, 1999), which contains texts translated from Nahuatl and Mayan.
7. Elyssa East, "Hunting among Stones," Poetry Foundation, August 14, 2013, https://www.poetryfoundation.org/articles/70038/hunting-among-stones.
8. Gordon Brotherston, *Image of the New World: The American Continent Portrayed in Native Texts* (London: Thames and Hudson, 1979), 24; Dylan J. Clark, "An Archaeologist of the Morning in the Mayab," in *Staying Open: Charles Olson's Sources and Influences*, ed. Joshua S. Hoeynck (Wilmington, DE: Vernon Press, 2019), 229.
9. Tom Clark, *Charles Olson: The Allegory of a Poet's Life* (Berkeley: North Atlantic Books, 2000), 191.

10. Clark, *Charles Olson*, 194–195.

11. Dennis Tedlock, *The Olson Codex: Projective Verse and the Problem of Mayan Glyphs* (Albuquerque: University of New Mexico Press, 2017), 45; Gabrielle Vail and Anthony Aveni, eds., *The Madrid Codex: New Approaches to Understanding an Ancient Maya Manuscript* (Boulder: University of Colorado Press, 2009), 3; Dennis Tedlock, description of his undergraduate course on the Maya, http://www.buffalo.edu/cas/english/undergraduate-programs/undergraduate-course-list.html, accessed February 21, 2015: the link is no longer active; Charles Olson, "Human Universe," in *Collected Prose*, ed. Donald Allen and Benjamin Friedlander (Berkeley: University of California Press, 1997), 159; Charles Olson, "The Kingfishers," in *Selected Writings*, ed. Robert Creeley (New York: New Directions, 1967), 171; Mary Miller and Karl Taube, *An Illustrated Dictionary of the Gods and Symbols of Ancient Mexico and the Maya* (New York: Thames and Hudson, 2015), 60–61; Philip Ainsworth Means, "The Philosophic Interrelationship between Middle American and Andean Religions," in *The Maya and Their Neighbors* (New York: D. Appleton-Century Company, 1940), 431; on Olson and this text, see Tedlock. *The Olson Codex*, 56.

12. Mary Ellen Miller and Megan E. O'Neill, *Maya Art and Architecture* (London: Thames and Hudson, 2014), 15; Marjorie I. Ingle, *The Mayan Revival Style: Art Deco Mayan Fantasy* (Salt Lake City: Peregrine Smith Books, 1984); Helen Delpar, *The Enormous Vogue of Things Mexican: Cultural Relations between the United States and Mexico, 1920–1935* (Tuscaloosa: University of Alabama Press, 1992), 130–131, 87, 89–90; Erik Davis, *The Visionary State: A Journey through California's Spiritual Landscape* (San Francisco: Chronicle Books, 2006), 108–111; Stephen Park, "Mesoamerican Modernism: W. C. Williams and the Archaeological Imagination," *Journal of Modern Literature* 34, no. 4 (Summer 2011): 24; *The First Inter-American Writers' Conference of the University of Puerto Rico, April 14–23, 1941* (Rio Piedras: University of Puerto Rico, 1941), 44; Benjamin Keen, *The Aztec Image in Western Thought* (New Brunswick: Rutgers University Press, 1971), 551; Carrie Gibson, *El Norte: The Epic and Forgotten Story of Hispanic North America* (New York: Grove Press, 2019), 350; Patrick Lepetit, *The Esoteric Secrets of Surrealism: Origins, Magic, and Secret Societies* (Rochester, VT; Inner Traditions, 2012), 70; André Breton, Leon Trotsky, and Diego Rivera, "Manifesto: Towards a Free Revolutionary Art," in *Modernism: An Anthology of Sources and Documents*, ed. Vassiliki Kolocotroni, Jane Goldman, and Olga Taxidou (Chicago: University of Chicago Press, 1998), 597–601; Rene Prieto, *Miguel Angel Asturias's Archaeology of Return* (New York: Cambridge University Press, 1993), 31; Asturias also edited *Poesia precolumbina* (Buenos Aires: Compania General Fabril Editore, 1960); André Breton, "Recuerdos de Mexico/Remembrance of Mexico," in *Mexico Through Foreign Eyes 1850–1990*, ed. Carole Naggar and Fred Ritchin (New York: W.W. Norton and Company, 1993), 113.

13. Georges Bataille, "L'Amerique disapure," in *L'art precolombien*, ed. Jean Babelon et al. (Paris: Les Beaux Arts, 1930), 5–14; an English translation, "Extinct America," appeared in *October* 36 (Spring 1986): 3–9. On Bataille, see James Clifford, *The Predicament of Culture: Twentieth-Century Ethnography, Literature, and Art* (Cambridge: Harvard University Press, 1988), 125–127; Louise Tythacott, *Surrealism and the Exotic* (London: Routledge, 2003), 215–229; Margaret Astrov, *The Winged Serpent: American Indian Prose and Poetry* (Boston: Beacon Press, 1946; reprinted 1992); on the *Evergreen Review*, see Loren Glass, *Counterculture Colophon: Grove Press, the Evergreen Review, and the Incorporation of the*

*Avant-Garde* (Stanford: Stanford University Press, 2013), 61–62. For William Carlos Williams's "Three Nahuatl Poems," see Thomas Mabry Cranfill, ed., *The Muse in Mexico: A Mid-Century Miscellany* (Austin, University of Texas Press, 1959)90–91, and Jerome Rothenberg, ed., *Technicians of the Sacred: A Range of Poetries from Africa, America, Asia and Oceania* (New York: Anchor Books, 1969), 222–223; Tuli Kupferberg, *Beating* (New York: Birth Press, 1959), n.p.

**14.** On Nezahualcoyotl, see Francis Gillmor, *Flute of the Smoking Mirror: A Portrait of Nezahualcoyotl, Poet King of the Aztecs* (Tucson: University of Arizona Press, 1968). Ernesto Cardenal, "Netzahualcoyotl," in *Homage to the American Indians* (Baltimore: Johns Hopkins University Press, 1973), 69–85; Kenneth Rexroth, *An Autobiographical Novel*, ed. Linda Hamalian (New York: New Directions, 1991), 309–319.

**15.** Rexroth, *Autobiographical Novel*, 317, 318, 320; Charlene Spretnak, "Gary Snyder: On Biocentric Wisdom," in *Conversations with Gary Snyder*, ed. David Stephen Calonne (Jackson: University Press of Mississippi, 2017), 116. On Austin, see also James Ruppert, "Discovering America: Mary Austin and Imagism," in *Studies in American Indian Literature: Critical Essays and Course Designs* (New York: Modern Language Association, 1983), ed. Paula Gunn Allen, 243–258.

**16.** Kenneth Rexroth, "American Indian Songs: The United States Bureau of Ethnology Collection," in *Assays* (New York: New Directions, 1961), 55.

**17.** Edward Dorn, *Interviews*, ed. Donald Allen (Bolinas, CA: Four Seasons Foundation, 1980), 51; Anne Waldman and Laura Wright, "Some Questions for Jerome Rothenberg," in *Cross Worlds, Transcultural Poetics: An Anthology* (Minneapolis: Coffee House Press, 2014), 119. For online issues from 1970 to 1980 of *Alcheringa*, see https://jacket2.org/reissues/alcheringa/; see also Gary Snyder, "The Politics of Ethnopoetics," *Alcheringa* 2, no. 2 (1976): 13–22; on Allen Ginsberg's experiences in Australia with "Aboriginal song men," see Stuart Coupe, "Allen Ginsberg: The Last Australian Interview," in *Conversations with Allen Ginsberg*, ed. David Stephen Calonne (Jackson: University Press of Mississippi, 2019), 189; Philip Whalen, "Letter to Joanne Kyger," *Rocky Ledge* 7 (February/March 1981): 18.

**18.** Jose Coronel Urtecho and Ernesto Cardenal, *Antologia de la Poesia Norteamericano* (Madrid: Aguilar, 1963); see also Stefan Baciu, "Beatitude South of the Border: Latin America's Beat Generation," *Hispania* 49, no. 4 (December 1966): 733–739.

**19.** Ernesto Cardenal, *Homage to the American Indians* (Baltimore: Johns Hopkins Press, 1973); David Stephen Calonne, *Diane di Prima: Visionary Poetics and the Hidden Religions* (New York: Bloomsbury, 2019), 148–149; Di Prima commented in a 1976 interview: "When I think of new people writing I think of Leslie Silko, Simon Ortiz, some of the West Coast street oral poetry that has no written technique to it, Chicano poets, and so on." See Bill Tremblay, Kate Mele, and Russ Derickson, "An Interview with Diane di Prima," *Colorado State Review* 5, no. 1 (Spring 1977): 11; Brotherston, *Image of the New World*, 61–62; Joanna O'Connell, "Pre-Columbian Literatures," in *Mexican Literature: A History*, ed. David William Foster (Austin: University of Texas Press, 1994), 7; Antonio de Ciudad Real, quoted in Inga Clendinnen, *Ambivalent Conquests: Maya and Spaniard in Yucatan, 1517–1570* (New York: Cambridge University Press, 1989), vi; for a reproduction of the "Be-In" poster, see Sherry L. Smith, *Hippies, Indians, and the Fight for Red Power* (New York: Oxford University Press, 2012), 44; Michael Coe, Dean Snow, and Elizabeth Benson, *Atlas of Ancient America* (New York: Facts on File, 1989), 148; for Anzaldua's feminist reading of

Aztec myth, see Gloria E. Anzaldua, *Interviews/Entrevistas*, ed. AnaLouise Keating (New York: Routledge, 2000), 200; Richard F. Townsend, *The Aztecs* (London: Thames and Hudson, 1992), 58, 60. See also David Carrasco and Roberto Lint Sagarena, "The Religious Vision of Gloria Anzaldua: *Borderlands/La Frontera* as a Shamanic Space," in *Mexican American Religions: Spirituality, Activism, and Culture*, ed. Gaston Espinosa and Mario T. Garcia (Durham, NC: Duke University Press, 2008), 223–241.

20. Juan Bruce-Novoa, *Chicano Poetry: A Response to Chaos* (Austin: University of Texas Press, 1982), 48, 71; David Carrasco, "Aztec Moments and Chicano Cosmovision: Aztlan Recalled to Life," in *Moctezuma's Mexico: Visions of the Aztec World, Revised Edition*, ed. David Carrasco and Eduardo Matos Moctezuma (Boulder: University Press of Colorado, 2003), 175–198; Furst, *The Natural History of the Soul in Ancient Mexico*, 11; Graham Greene, *Another Mexico*, 13, quoted in Drewey Wayne Gunn, *American and British Writers in Mexico 1556–1973* (Austin: University of Texas Press, 1974), x. Alberto Escobar de la Garma, "The Beat Presence in Mexican Literature," in *The Routledge Handbook of International Beat Literature*, ed. A. Robert Lee (New York: Routledge, 2018), 30.

21. Jack Kerouac, *Desolation Angels* (New York: Riverhead Books, 1995), 261; Tom Clark, *Edward Dorn: A World of Difference* (Berkeley: North Atlantic Books, 2002), 239–247.

## 1. LAWRENCE FERLINGHETTI

1. Larry Smith, "Lawrence Ferlinghetti," in *Dictionary of Literary Biography Volume Sixteen, The Beats: Literary Bohemians in Postwar America* (Detroit: Gale Research Company, 1983), 201; Neeli Cherkovski, *Ferlinghetti: A Biography* (Garden City, NY: Doubleday and Company, 1979), 24.

2. Lawrence Ferlinghetti, "Mexico, Again, May 1972," in *Writing across the Landscape: Travel Journals 1960–2010*, ed. Giada Diano and Matthew Gleeson (New York: Liveright, 2015), 232.

3. Ernesto Cardenal, *From Nicaragua with Love* (San Francisco: City Lights, 1986); *Volcan: Poems from Central America* (San Francisco: City Lights (2001); *First World, Ha Ha Ha! The Zapatista Challenge*, ed. Elaine Katzenberger (San Francisco: City Lights, 2001); R. Gordon Wasson, *The Wondrous Mushroom: Mycolatry in Mesoamerica* (San Francisco: City Lights, 2015).

4. Jesse Tangen-Mills, interview with Lawrence Ferlinghetti, Guernica, November 1, 2010, https://www.guernicamag.com/ferlinghetti_11_1_10/; Sean Wilentz, *Bob Dylan in America* (New York: Anchor Books, 2011), 69; Larry Smith, *Lawrence Ferlinghetti: Poet-at-Large* (Carbondale: Southern Illinois University Press, 1983), 169.

5. Lawrence Ferlinghetti, *The Mexican Night: Travel Journal* (New York: New Directions, 1970), 1.

6. Steven Belletto, *The Beats: A Literary History* (New York: Cambridge University Press, 2020), 246.

7. See Alicja Piechucka, "Black Suns of Melancholy: Hart Crane's Treatment of the Sun Motif in the Light of Mircea Eliade's Study of Solar Cults," *European Journal of American Studies* 8, no. 1 (Spring 2013): 5.

8. Malcolm Lowry, *Selected Poems of Malcolm Lowry*, ed. Earle Birney (San Francisco: City Lights, 1964); Ferlinghetti, *The Mexican Night*, 22, 23; Lowry, *Selected Poems*, 26.

9. Barry Silesky, *Ferlinghetti: The Artist in His Time* (New York: Warner Books, 1990), 98, 100; Cherkovski, *Ferlinghetti*, 133.
10. Ferlinghetti, *The Mexican Night*, 3, 4, 6; Jack Kerouac, *Lonesome Traveler* (New York: Grove Press, 1982), 27.
11. Ferlinghetti, *The Mexican Night*, 7; Ferlinghetti, "The Dog," in *Writing across the Landscape*, 342.
12. Ken Winkler, "The Man Who Bought Cuchama: Walter Evans-Wentz and the Holy Mountain," *San Diego Reader*, June 26, 1980, https://www.sandiegoreader.com/news/1980/jun/26/cover-the-man-who-bought-cuchama/.
13. Ferlinghetti, *The Mexican Night*, 9.
14. Kerouac, *Lonesome Traveler*, 21, 9–10.
15. Kerouac, *Lonesome Traveler*, 13; Malcolm Lowry, *Under the Volcano* (Harmondsworth: Penguin Books, 1962), 132, 235; Chris Ackerley and Lawrence J. Clipper, *A Companion to Under the Volcano* (Vancouver: University of British Columbia Press, 1984), 189, 190, 311–312. One scholar argues that Lowry possessed a deeply ecological sensibility, another reason for Ferlinghetti's affinity for his works. The sign concerning our "eviction" in the Garden indicates that Lowry believed "Earth may be Eden, but there is no reason why earth should be the exclusive domain of a single species that so ignorantly describes itself as *Homo sapiens*. We may be evicted by nuclear winter or by environmental collapse, or, more subtly, by continuing to promote world over earth, we will inevitably evict ourselves from our own souls, the ground of our being." See J. Douglas Porteous, "A Loving Nature: Malcolm Lowry in British Columbia," in *A Few Acres of Snow: Literary and Artistic Images of Canada*, ed. Paul Simpson-Housley and Glen Norcliffe (Toronto: Dundurn Press, 1992), 265.
16. Ferlinghetti, *The Mexican Night*, 13, 17, 18, 19 (emphasis added).
17. Ferlinghetti, *The Mexican Night*, 21; Maria de Los Angeles Romero Frizzi, "The Indigenous Population of Oaxaca from the Sixteenth Century to the Present," in *The Cambridge History of the Native Peoples of the Americas Volume II, Mesoamerica Part 2*, ed. Richard E. W. Adams and Murdo J. MacLeod (New York: Cambridge University Press, 2000), 302; on the history of Oaxaca, see also Gary M. Feinman, "Oaxaca," in *The Oxford Encyclopedia of Mesoamerican Cultures: The Civilizations of Mexico and Central America, Volume 2*, ed. David Carrasco (New York: Oxford University Press, 2001), 395–399; Ross Parmenter, *Lawrence in Oaxaca: A Quest for the Novelist in Mexico* (Salt Lake City: Peregrine Smith Books, 1984); Joanne Kyger, *Mexico Blondé* (Bolinas, CA: Evergreen, 1981), n.p.
18. *Selected Letters of D. H. Lawrence*, ed. James T. Boulton (Cambridge: Cambridge University Press, 1997), 287.
19. T. Philip Terry, *Terry's Guide to Mexico: The New Standard Guidebook to the Mexican Republic* (Boston: Houghton Mifflin, 1923), 529; Lawrence Ferlinghetti, *Life Studies/Life Stories* (San Francisco: City Lights Books, 2003), 141, 162–163, 165, 167.
20. http://www.friendsofdhlawrence.org/ferlinghetti/visit.html; Lawrence Ferlinghetti, "The Man Who Rode Away," in *Open Eye, Open Heart*, (New York: New Directions, 1973), 35.
21. Dennis Tedlock, *The Olson Codex: Projective Verse and the Problem of Mayan Glyphs* (Albuquerque: University of New Mexico Press, 2017), 25; Michael Coe and Mark Van Stone, *Reading the Maya Glyphs*, 2nd ed. (New York: Thames and Hudson, 2015), 7; Mary Miller and Karl Taube, *An Illustrated Dictionary of The Gods and Symbols of Ancient Mexico and the Maya* (New York: Thames and Hudson, 2015), 198; see also John Collis and

David M. Jones, "Uxmal," in *Blue Guide: Mexico* (New York: W. W. Norton, 1997), 827–833; Ferlinghetti, *The Mexican Night*, 41–42.

22. Allen Ginsberg, "Siesta in Xbalba," *Reality Sandwiches* (San Francisco: City Lights, 1974), 21.

23. Mircea Eliade, "Spirit, Seed, Light," in *Occultism, Witchcraft and Cultural Fashions: Essays in Comparative Religions* (Chicago: University of Chicago Press, 1976), 93–119; "An Interview with Pierre Delattre," in *Beat Angels: Volume 12 of The Unspeakable Visions of the Individual*, ed. Arthur and Kit Knight (California, PA: Arthur and Kit Knight, 1982), 75; Ferlinghetti, *The Mexican Night*, 45, 52.

24. Pierre Delattre, "The Last Beatnik Casualty Is Brought to My Door," in *Episodes* (Saint Paul, MN: Gray Wolf Press, 1993), 103, 104; Silesky, *Ferlinghetti*, 175.

25. Lawrence Ferlinghetti, "Carnaval de Maiz," in *Open Eye, Open Heart*, 112.

26. Ferlinghetti, "Carnaval de Maiz," 112–113.

27. Miller and Taube, *An Illustrated Dictionary*, 113; Margaret Randall, *My Life in 100 Objects* (New York: New Village Press, 2020), 32, 33; William S. Burroughs, *Naked Lunch: The Restored Text* (New York: Grove Press, 2001); Cherkovski, *Ferlinghetti*, 225.

28. Lawrence Ferlinghetti, "Adieu a Charlot; Second Populist Manifesto," in *City Lights Journal* no. 4 (San Francisco: City Lights Books, 1978), 65.

29. Ferlinghetti, "Adieu a Charlot," 68, 69, 70. On Carlos Castaneda, see Christopher Partridge, *High Culture: Drugs, Mysticism, and the Pursuit of Transcendence in the Modern World* (New York: Oxford University Press, 2018), 308–318.

30. Lawrence Ferlinghetti, "Looking at a Map of Mexico," in *Writing across the Landscape*, 243.

31. Ferlinghetti, "Looking at a Map of Mexico."

32. Richard F. Townsend, *The Aztecs* (New York: Thames and Hudson, 1995), 118–119, 211; Lawrence Ferlinghetti, "Through the Labyrinth into the Sun: August 1982," in *Writing Across the Landscape: Travel Journals 1960–2010* (New York: Liveright, 2015), 265, 266. On the archeological discoveries Ferlinghetti describes, see Roger Atwood, "Under Mexico City," *Archaeology*, July/August 2014, https://www.archaeology.org/issues/138-1407/features/2173-mexico-city-aztec-buried-world.

33. Ferlinghetti, "Through the Labyrinth into the Sun," 268, 407.

34. Ferlinghetti, "Through the Labyrinth into the Sun," 270–271.

35. Jack Hirschman, *The Xibalba Arcane* (Washington: Azul Editions, 1994),8.

36. Jack Kerouac, *Pomes All Sizes* (San Francisco: City Lights, 1992), 78.

37. Ferlinghetti, *Writing across the Landscape*, 403, 409, 425, 436–438, 439.

## 2. WILLIAM S. BURROUGHS

1. Jorge Garcia-Robles, *The Stray Bullet: William S. Burroughs in Mexico* (Minneapolis: University of Minnesota Press, 2013), 47–50; Carl Weissner, *Burroughs: Eine Bild-Biographie* (Berlin: Nishen, 1994), 40; Ted Morgan, *Literary Outlaw: The Life and Times of William S. Burroughs* (New York: W. W. Norton, 2012), 186; William S. Burroughs, *Naked Lunch: The Restored Text* (New York: Grove Press, 2001), 14, 287–288; Barry Miles, *Call Me Burroughs: A Life* (New York: Twelve, 2013), 186. See also Michael Spann, *William S.*

*Burroughs' Unforgettable Characters: Lola 'La Chata' & Bernabe Jurado* (Providence: Inkblot Publications, 2013).

2. Oliver Harris and Ian MacFadyen, eds., *Naked Lunch @ 50: Anniversary Essays*, (Carbondale: Southern Illinois University Press, 2009), 11; Linda Schele and Mary Ellen Miller, *The Blood of Kings: Dynasty and Ritual in Maya Art* (Fort Worth, TX: Kimball Art Museum, 1986); Michael Stevens, *The Road to Interzone: Reading William S. Burroughs Reading* (Archer City, TX: Suicide Press, 2009), 264. See also John Lyons, "Life Scripts: Aspects of the Maya in the Work of Ernesto Cardenal and William S. Burroughs," *The Crane Bag* 6, no. 2 (1982): 89–96.

3. Paul H. Wild, "William S. Burroughs and the Maya Gods of Death: The Uses of Archaeology," *College Literature* 35, no. 1 (Winter 2008): 41; Miles, *Call Me Burroughs*, 68.

4. Jack Kerouac, *On the Road* (New York: Penguin, 2011), 134.

5. Allen Ginsberg, *The Book of Martyrdom and Artifice: First Journals and Poems, 1937–1952*, ed. Juanita Liebermann-Plimpton and Bill Morgan (Cambridge, MA: Da Capo Press, 2006), 163.

6. Rob Johnson, *The Lost Years of William S. Burroughs: Beats in South Texas* (College Station: Texas A and M University Press, 2006), 20; Bill Morgan, *The Beats Abroad: A Global Guide to the Beat Generation* (San Francisco: City Lights, 2015), 227; Oliver Harris, ed., *The Letters of William S. Burroughs, 1945–1959* (New York: Viking, 1993), 69, 63; William S. Burroughs, "Remembering Jack Kerouac," in *The Adding Machine: Selected Essays* (New York: Arcade, 1993), 178; Eric Strand, "The Last Frontier: Burroughs's Early Work and International Tourism," *Twentieth Century Literature* 59, no. 1 (Spring 2013): 8; Weissner, *Burroughs: Eine Bild-Biographie*, 40; Harris, *The Letters of William S. Burroughs*, 71; Brian Schottlaender, *Anything but Routine: A Selectively Annotated Bibliography of William S. Burroughs*, vol. 4, iii, https://cloudfront.escholarship.org/dist/prd/content/qtoxj4d6bm/qtoxj4d6bm.pdf?t=o58984; William S. Burroughs, *Queer* (New York: Penguin Books, 1987); William S. Burroughs, *Port of Saints* (Berkeley: Blue Wind Press, 1980), 20, 137; William S. Burroughs and Brion Gysin, *The Third Mind* (New York: Viking, 1978), 191; Maria Damon, "Beat Poetry," in *The Princeton Encyclopedia of Poetry and Poetics*, 4th ed., ed. Roland Greene et al. (Princeton: Princeton University Press, 2012), 130; Johnson, *The Lost Years of William S. Burroughs*, 91; William S. Burroughs, *Naked Lunch: The Restored Text*, ed. James Grauerholz and Barry Miles (New York: Grove Press, 2001), 14; Ian MacFadyen, "dossier one," in *Naked Lunch @ 50*, 5; Jack Kerouac, *Visions of Cody* (New York: Penguin Books, 1972), 379; Tom Clark, *Edward Dorn: A World of Difference* (Berkeley: North Atlantic Books, 2002), 241; Oswald Spengler, *The Decline of the West, Volume 2, Perspectives of World—History*, trans. Charles Atkinson (New York: Alfred A. Knopf, 1928), 84; Morgan, *The Beats Abroad*, 228; Allen Ginsberg, introduction to William S. Burroughs, *Junky* (New York: Penguin, 1977), v; Burroughs, *Junky*, 111, 128, 149, 124, 151; William S. Burroughs, introduction to *Queer* (New York: Penguin, 1987), v; Loni Reynolds, "'The Final Fix' and 'The Transcendent Kingdom': The Quest in the Early Work of William Burroughs," in *Hip Sublime: Beat Writers and the Classical Tradition*, ed. Sheila Murnaghan and Ralph M. Rosen (Columbus: Ohio State University Press, 2018), 63; Burroughs, *Queer*, 49, 50; Victor Bockris, *With William Burroughs: A Report from the Bunker* (New York: St. Martin's Griffin, 1996), xx; William S. Burroughs, *The Cat Inside* (New York: Penguin, 1992), 17.

7. Miles, *Call Me Burroughs*, 187; Burroughs, *Junky*, 123; William S. Burroughs, "The Name Is Burroughs," in *The Adding Machine: Selected Essays*, 10; Hibbard, ed., *Conversations with William S. Burroughs* (Jackson: University Press of Mississippi, 1999), 59–60. Burroughs often returns to his disgust with Diego de Landa's "barbarous" destruction of the Mayan codices. See Daniel Odier and William S. Burroughs, *The Job: Interviews with William S. Burroughs* (New York: Penguin, 1989), 40.

8. Paul H. Wild, "William S. Burroughs and the Maya Gods of Death: The Uses of Archeology," *College Literature* 35, no. 1 (Winter 2009): 42; for the book burning depicted in the Tlaxcala Codex, see Gordon Brotherston, *Painted Books from Mexico: Codices in UK Collections and the World They Represent* (London: British Museum Press, 1995), 10; Alfred M. Tozzer, ed., *Landa's "Relacion de las Cosas de Yucatan,"* Peabody Museum Papers, vol. 18 (Cambridge: Harvard University, 1941), 169; William S. Burroughs, *Ah Pook Is Here and Other Texts: The Book of Breeething, Electronic Revolution* (London: John Calder, 1979), 17; Claude Levi-Strauss, *Anthropology Confronts the Problems of the Modern World* (Cambridge: Harvard University Press, 2013), 17; Howard Campbell, "Beat Mexico: Bohemia, Anthropology and 'the Other,'" *Critique of Anthropology* 23, no. 2 (June 2003): 217; William S. Burroughs, "Lack," in *American Poets Say Goodbye to the Twentieth Century*, ed. Andrei Codrescu and Laura Rosenthal (New York: Four Walls Eight Windows, 1996), 51; Robert Redfield, *The Folk Culture of Yucatan* (Chicago: University of Chicago Press, 1941), 391; Robert A. Sobieszek, *Ports of Entry: William S. Burroughs and the Arts* (Los Angeles and New York: Los Angeles County Museum of Art and Thames and Hudson, 1996), 122; John Tytell, "The Beat Legacy," in *Beat Culture: The 1950s and Beyond*, ed. Cornelius A. van Minnen, Jaap van der Bent, and Mel van Elteren (Amsterdam: VU University Press, 1999), 270–271; Patricia Allmer and John Sears, *Taking Shots: The Photography of William S. Burroughs* (Munich: Prestel, 2014), 7, 39; William S. Burroughs, *Nova Express* (New York: Grove Press, 1964), 42; Byron Ellsworth Hamann, "How Maya Hieroglyphs Got Their Name: Egypt, Mexico, and China in Western Grammatology since the Fifteenth Century," *Proceedings of the American Philosophical Society* 152, no. 1 (March 2008): 3; John T. Irwin, *American Hieroglyphics: The Symbol of the Egyptian Hieroglyphics in the American Renaissance* (New Haven: Yale University Press, 1980); Burroughs, *Junky*, 112; Ginsberg, "Siesta in Xbalba,"in *Reality Sandwiches* (San Francisco: City Lights, 1974), 27; Burroughs, *Naked Lunch: The Restored Text*, 194; E. J. Michael Witzel, *The Origins of the World's Mythologies*, 172; Wild, "William S. Burroughs and the Maya Gods of Death," 44; Jorge Luis Borges, "The Writing of the God," in *Collected Fictions*, trans. Andrew Hurley (New York: Penguin, 1998), 253; Schele and Miller, *The Blood of Kings*, 265.

9. Burroughs, *Naked Lunch*, 137.

10. Lydia H. Liu, "Writing," in *Critical Terms for Media Studies*, ed. W.J.T. Mitchell and Mark B. N. Hansen (Chicago: University of Chicago Press, 2010), 314.

11. Jennie Skerl, *William S. Burroughs* (Boston: Twayne Publishers, 1986), 55; William S. Burroughs, *The Soft Machine* (New York: Grove Press, 1961), 82–83; Gordon Brotherston, *Image of the New World: The American Continent Portrayed in Native Texts* (London: Thames and Hudson, 1979), 126; Elizabeth Hill Boone, *Cycles of Time and Meaning in the Mexican Books of Fate* (Austin: University of Texas Press, 2007), 13; Michael D. Coe and Justin Kerr, *The Art of the Maya Scribe* (New York: Harry N. Abrams, 1997), 177–178; Miles, *Call Me Burroughs*, 187.

12. Hamann, "How Maya Hieroglyphs Got Their Name," 4. Hamann quotes J. Eric S. Thompson, *Maya Hieroglyphic Writing* (Washington, D.C.: Carnegie Institution of Washington, 1950), 155, 295.

13. Heathcote Williams, "Burroughs in London," *The White Review*, March 2014, http://www.thewhitereview.org/feature/burroughs-in-london/. William S. Burroughs, *The Revised Boy Scout Manual*, ed. Geoffrey D. Smith and John M. Bennett (Columbus: Ohio State University Press), 4; Diane di Prima, "Notes on the Solstice," *Alcheringa, New Series* 1, no. 2 (1975): 84; Bonnie Bremser, "Dreams," *Coldspring Journal* 1 (September 1974): 11; Burroughs, *Ah Pook Is Here*, 24; Burroughs, *The Revised Boy Scout Manual*, 67; Matthew Levi Stevens, *The Magical Universe of William Burroughs* (Oxford: Mandrake of Oxford, 2014), 99–100; Boone, *Cycles of Time and Meaning*; Odier and Burroughs, *The Job*, 44.

14. Anthony Enns, "Burroughs's Writing Machines," in *Retaking the Universe: William S. Burroughs in the Age of Globalization*, ed. Davis Schneiderman and Philip Walsh (London: Pluto Press, 2004), 103; William S. Burroughs, "The Bay of Pigs," in *The Burroughs File* (San Francisco: City Lights, 1991), 136–144; Mary Miller and Karl Taube, *An Illustrated Dictionary of the Gods and Symbols of Ancient Mexico and the Maya* (New York: Thames and Hudson, 2015), 164; Joe Maynard and Barry Miles, *William S. Burroughs: A Bibliography, 1953–73* (Charlottesville: University Press of Virginia, 1978), 166, 167. On *Cyclops*, see entries C281, C290, C294, and C295 for bibliographical information; on Burroughs, McNeill, and *Ah Pook Is Here*, see James Reich, "'The Elvis of Letters' Has Left the Building: An Interview with Malcolm McNeill," *International Times*, http://internationaltimes.it/the-elvis-of-letters-has-left-the-building/.

15. Malcolm McNeill, *The Lost Art of Ah Pook Is Here: Images from the Graphic Novel* (Seattle: Fantagraphics Books, 2012).n.p.

16. Hibbard, *Conversations with William S. Burroughs*, 59.

17. David Carrasco, *Religions of Mesoamerica: Cosmovision and Ceremonial Centers* (New York: Harper and Row, 1990), 113, 114; Malcolm McNeill, "Information on the Artwork," *Rush* 1, no. 3 (December 1976); David Bowles, *Tales of the Feathered Serpent: Illustrated by Charlene Bowles* (El Paso, TX: Cinco Puntos Press, 2020), 62; Gabrielle Vail and Anthony Aveni, eds., *The Madrid Codex: New Approaches to Understanding an Ancient Maya Manuscript* (Boulder: University Press of Colorado, 2004),, 3; Dennis Tedlock, *2000 Years of Mayan Literature* (Berkeley: University of California Press, 2010), 146; Tedlock, *The Olson Codex* (Albuquerque: University of New Mexico Press, 2017), 50.

18. Peter Conners, *White Hand Society: The Psychedelic Partnership of Timothy Leary and Allen Ginsberg* (San Francisco: City Lights, 2010), 152. See also Joseph J. Downing, "Zihuatanejo: An Experiment in Transpersonative Living," in *Utopiates: The Use and Users of LSD 25*, ed. Richard Blum (New York: Atherton Press, 1964), 142–177; W. J. Rorabaugh, *American Hippies* (New York: Cambridge University Press, 2015), 40.

19. William S. Burroughs, *Cities of the Red Night* (New York: Henry Hold, 2001), xvii–xviii.

20. Miller and Taube, *An Illustrated Dictionary*, 99; Claude Levi-Strauss, *The Origin of Table Manners: Introduction to a Science of Mythology 3* (New York: Harper and Row, 1979), 145, 146; Tedlock, *2000 Years of Mayan Literature*, 99.

21. Miles, *Call Me Burroughs*, 556; William S. Burroughs, *The Place of Dead Roads* (London: Grafton Books, 1983), 248; William S. Burroughs, *The Western Lands* (New York: Penguin Books, 1987), 70–71; on Aztec warfare, see Richard F. Townsend, *The Aztecs*

(New York: Thames and Hudson, 1995), 24; see also Frederick A. Peterson, *Ancient Mexico: An Introduction to Pre-Hispanic Cultures* (New York: G. P. Putnam's Sons, 1959), 163; Burroughs, *The Cat Inside*, 8, 48, 76; William S. Burroughs, *Last Words: The Final Journals of William S. Burroughs*, ed. James Grauerholz (New York: Grove Press, 2000), 247, 248.
22. Burroughs, introduction to *Queer*, xxii; Jack Kerouac, letter to John Clellon Holmes, December 9, 1952, in Jack Kerouac, *Selected Letters 1940–1056*, ed. Ann Charters (New York: Penguin Books, 1995), 388–389.
23. Kerouac actually drew a portrait of Emily Dickinson in his notebooks, and during a summer 1957 trip to Mexico City, composed a rather ribald, comic poem addressed to her. See Isaac Gewirtz, *Beatific Soul: Jack Kerouac on the Road* (New York and London: The New York Public Library and Scala Publishers, 2007), 175, 199.

## 3. PHILIP LAMANTIA

1. Alberto Escobar de la Garma, "The Beat Presence in Mexican Literature," in *The Routledge Handbook of International Beat Literature*, ed. A. Robert Lee (New York and London: Routledge, 2018), 30; Aridjis in February 1985 responded to the increasingly unbearable air pollution in Mexico City by collecting signatures from writers including Gabriel Garcia Marquez and Octavio Paz and created the "Grupo de los Cien" to combat ecological destruction. See Carlos Fonseca, "A Poet of Mythologies: Homero Aridjis at 80," *Los Angeles Review of Books*, September 9, 2020, https://lareviewofbooks.org/article/a-poet-of-mythologies-homero-aridjis-at-80/; see also "Philip Lamantia: el poeta beatifico," http://www.revistadelauniversidad.unam.mx/9011/aridjis/90aridjis.html; Kenneth Rexroth—an influence on the Beats and, along with Robert Duncan, the major figure in the "San Francisco Renaissance"—praised Aridjis: "Few poets better demonstrate the spread of an international style throughout the world as well as the reduction and synthesis of the great writers of the heroic age of modern poetry to an international, negotiable idiom." See "Kenneth Rexroth on Homer Aridjis," in *Mutual Impressions: Writers from the Americas Reading One Another*, ed. Ilan Stavans (Durham: Duke University Press, 1999), 267; Franklin Rosemont, "Surrealist, Anarchist, Afrocentrist: Philip Lamantia Before and After the 'Beat Generation,'" in *Are Italians White? How Race Is Made in America*, ed. Jennifer Guglielmo and Salvatore Salerno (New York: Routledge, 2003), 126, 124; Martica Swain, *Surrealism in Exile and the Beginning of the New York School* (Cambridge: MIT Press, 1995), 346.
2. Kenneth Rexroth, *American Poetry in the Twentieth Century* (New York: The Seabury Press, 1973), 165; Robert Duncan, *Collected Essays and Other Prose*, ed. James Maynard (Berkeley: University of California Press, 2019), 348. An excerpt from Artaud's *To Have Done with the Judgment of God* also appeared in Ferlinghetti's *Journal for the Protection of All Beings*, no. 1 (San Francisco: City Lights Books, 1961), 18–20. On Artaud, see also David Stephen Calonne, *The Spiritual Imagination of the Beats* (New York: Cambridge University Press, 2017), 30–31.
3. Antonin Artaud, *The Peyote Dance*, trans. Helen Weaver (New York: Farrar, Straus and Giroux, 1976).
4. Stuart, Kendall, *Georges Bataille* (London: Reaktion Books, 2007), 68; on Bataille and Mexico, see also Joseph Defalco Lamperez, "The Aztecs and Urban Form in Georges

Bataille, Diego Rivera, and J.G. Posada," *Mosaic* 49, no. 4 (December 2016): 145–166; David Hopkins, *Dada and Surrealism: A Very Short Introduction*, 23–24; on Breton and Mexico, see Gerard Durozoi, *History of the Surrealist Movement* (Chicago: University of Chicago Press, 2002), 348–349; Elliott H. King, "Surrealism and Counterculture," in *A Companion to Dada and Surrealism*, ed. David Hopkins (Malden, MA: John Wiley and Sons, 2016), 418; see also Anna Balakian, *André Breton: Magus of Surrealism* (New York: Oxford University Press, 1971), 170–172. French intellectual fascination with Mexico has long been intense. Nobel Prize–winner J.M.G. Le Clézio speaks three pre-Columbian languages and learned Maya while living in a Yucatecan village during the seventies. Le Clézio translated Maya texts—*Les Prophéties due Chilam Balam* (1976)—and has also published *In the Eye of the Sun: Mexican Fiestas* (1996) and *The Mexican Dream: Or, The Interrupted Thought of Amerindian Civilizations* (1993). See Jake Watts, "Peripatetic Nobel with a Heart in Mexico," https://web.archive.org/web/20090107094600/http://www.unasletras.com/v2/articulo/literatura_8/Peripatetic-Nobel-with-a-Heart-in-Mexico_691/.

5. The interest of Mexican writers in Surrealism was also widespread. See Octavio Paz, "André Breton or the Quest of the Beginning," in *Alternating Current*, trans. Helen Lane (New York: Arcade Publishing, 1990), 54. See also Rita Eder, "Benjamin Péret and Paul Westheim: Surrealism and Other Genealogies in the Land of the Aztecs," in *Surrealism in Latin America: Vivisimo Muerto*, ed. Dawn Ades, Rita Eder, and Graciela Speranza (Los Angeles: Getty Research Institute, 2012), 77–94; See Ted Joans, *Teducation: Selected Poems of Ted Joans, 1949–1999* (Minneapolis: Coffee House Press, 1999), 97, 135, 191. On Joans, see A. Robert Lee, "Black Beat: Performing Ted Joans," in *Reconstructing the Beats*, ed. Jennie Skerl (New York: Palgrave Macmillan, 2004), 117–132.

6. Henry Miller, *Big Sur and the Oranges of Hieronymus Bosch* (Norfolk, CT: New Directions, 1957), 345.

7. Garrett Caples, "Philip Lamantia and André Breton," in *Retrievals* (Seattle and New York: Wave Books, 2014), 100; see "Mount Diablo" in Philip Lamantia, *Meadowlark West*, reprinted in *The Collected Poems of Philip Lamantia* (Berkeley: University of California Press, 2013).

8. Andrew Schelling, *Tracks along the Left Coast: Jaime de Angulo and Pacific Coast Culture* (Berkeley: Counterpoint Press, 2017), 196; Garrett Caples, ed., "High Poet," in *The Collected Poems of Philip Lamantia*, xxxiv; Jose Garcia-Robles, *At the End of the Road: Jack Kerouac in Mexico* (Minneapolis: University of Minnesota Press, 2014), 50; Allen Ginsberg noted in an interview with David Widgery in 1965: "You'll find all the young intellectuals in America affected to a great extent by influences from South American Indians, Mexican peyotl and mushroom Indians." See *Conversations with Allen Ginsberg*, ed. David Stephen Calonne (Jackson: University Press of Mississippi, 2019), 34.

9. Philip Lamantia, *Preserving Fire: Selected Prose*, ed. Garrett Caples (Seattle: Wave Books, 2018), 43–44; Gerard de Cortanze, *J.M.G. Le Clezio: Le nomade immobile* (Paris: Gallimard, 1999), 157; Carl Lumholtz, *Unknown Mexico* (New York: Scribner's, 1902), 311.

10. Lumholtz, *Unknown Mexico*, 357.

11. Lumholtz, *Unknown Mexico*, 358; Thomas Albright, "Reestablishing Contact with the 'Beat' Esthetic," in *On Art and Artists: Essays by Thomas Albright*, ed. Beverly Hennessey (San Francisco: Chronicle Books, 1989), 42.

12. Caples, "High Poet: The Life and Work of Philip Lamantia," in *The Collected Poems of Philip Lamantia*, xxxiv.

**13.** David Meltzer, ed., *San Francisco Beat: Talking with the Poets* (San Francisco: City Lights, 2001), 143.
**14.** On the Cora, see Joseph E. Grimes and Thomas B. Hinton, "The Huichol and Cora," in *Handbook of Middle American Indians: Ethnology, Part Two*, ed. Evon Z. Vogt (Austin: University of Texas Press, 1969), 792–813; Lamantia, *Preserved Fire*, 73.
**15.** Philip Lamantia, "Notes from my visit with Cora: April-May, 1955," Bancroft Library, University of California at Berkeley, BANC MSS 2002/179, carton 5, folder 28; Lamantia, "Triple V: The Day Non-surrealism Became Surrealist," in *The Collected Poems of Philip Lamantia*, 427.
**16.** Lamantia, "Cora," in *The Collected Poems of Philip Lamantia*, 172.
**17.** Frank Waters, *Book of the Hopi* (New York: Penguin Books, 1977), 116–117; Mary Miller and Karl Taube, *An Illustrated Dictionary of the Gods and Symbols of Ancient Mexico and the Maya* (New York: Thames and Hudson, 2015), 60; Dennis Tedlock, *2000 Years of Mayan Literature* (Berkeley: University of California Press, 2010), 146; Caples, "High Poet," in *The Collected Poems of Philip Lamantia*, xxxvii; John Suiter, *Poets on the Peaks: Gary Snyder, Philip Whalen and Jack Kerouac in the North Cascades* (New York: Counterpoint, 2002), 304, 151.
**18.** Lamantia, "The night is a space of white marble," in *The Collected Poems of Philip Lamantia*, 197.
**19.** Pseudo-Dionysius, *The Complete Works*, trans. Colm Luibheid (Mahwah, NJ: Paulist Press, 1987), 136, 137.
**20.** Suiter, *Poets on the Peaks*, 151.
**21.** Meltzer, *San Francisco Beat*, 143; Lamantia, *Preserved Fire*, 39, 38; http://content.cdlib.org/view?docId=kt409nb28g&doc.view=entire_text.
**22.** Philip Lamantia, *Tau by Philip Lamantia and Journey to the End by John HoffmanT* (San Francisco: City Lights, 2008), 104, 101.
**23.** Gordon Brotherston, *Image of the New World: The American Continent Portrayed in Native Texts* (London: Thames and Hudson, 1979), 122; Garrett Caples, "A Note on John Hoffman and *Journey to the End*," in Lamantia, *Tau by Philip Lamantia*; Allen Ginsberg, "Howl" in *Collected Poems: 1947–1980* (New York: Harper and Row, 1984); ruth weiss, *Can't Stop the Beat: The Life and Words of a Beat Poet* (Studio City, CA: Divine Arts, 2011), 96, 97.
**24.** Michael Duncan and Kristine McKenna, ed., *Semina Culture: Wallace Berman and His Circle* (New York: DAP/Distributed Art Publishers, Inc, 2005), 206, 207; *Semina 1955–1964: Art Is Love Is God* (New York: Boo-Hooray, 2014), 99; Asuncion Lavrin, "Women in Colonial Mexico," in *The Oxford History of Mexico*, ed. William H. Beezley and Michael C. Meyer (New York: Oxford University Press, 2010), 260, 261; Stanley T. Williams, *The Spanish Background of American Literature, Volume One* (New Haven: Yale University Press, 1955), 121–122, 356; Sor Juana Inés de la Cruz, "On Men's Hypocrisy," in *The Mexico Reader: History, Culture, Politics*, ed. Gilbert M. Joseph and Timothy J. Henderson (Durhan: Duke University Press, 2002), 156; Sor Juana Inés de la Cruz, "Reply to Sor Filoleta de la Cruz," in *A Woman of Genius: The Intellectual Autobiography of Sor Juana Inés de la Cruz*, trans. Margaret Sayers Peden (Salisbury, CT: Lime Rock Press, 1982); Gordon Brotherston, *Latin American Poetry: Origins and Presence* (Cambridge: Cambridge University Press, 1975), 8, 201.

**25.** Lamantia, *Collected Poems,* 212, 356.
**26.** *Semina: Art Is Love Is God,* 98; Lamantia, *The Collected Poems of Philip Lamantia,* 111.
**27.** Frederick Frost and Channing Arnold, *The American Egypt: A Record of Travel in the Yucatan in 1909* (London: Hutchinson, 1909).
**28.** Harris Feinsod, *The Poetry of the Americas: From Good Neighbors to Countercultures* (New York: Oxford University Press, 2017), 180; Lamantia, "Ceylonese Tea Candor (Pyramid Scene)," in *The Collected Poems of Philip Lamantia,* 143.
**29.** Aymon de Roussy de Sales, "The Fifth Sun," *Borderlands* 50, no. 4 (1994): 2, 9, 10; D. H. Lawrence, *The Plumed Serpent* (New York: Vintage Books, 1959), 195; Lamantia, "Morning Light Song," in *The Collected Poems of Philip Lamantia,* 199.
**30.** Dennis Tedlock, *The Olson Codex* (Albuquerque: University of New Mexico Press, 2017), 5; De Sales, "The Fifth Sun," 12.
**31.** De Sales, "The Fifth Sun," 15.
**32.** Lamantia, "Ceylonese Tea Candor (Pyramid Scene)," 144.
**33.** De Sales, "The Fifth Sun," 4. See also Richard F. Townsend, *The Aztecs* (New York: Thames and Hudson, 1992), 119.
**34.** Miller and Taube, *An Illustrated Dictionary,* 161–162; D. H. Lawrence, *Mornings in Mexico* (London: Penguin Books, 1986), 10–11.
**35.** Michel de Montaigne, *The Complete Essays,* trans. M.A. Screech (London: Penguin Books, 2003), 1035; Lamantia, "Opus Magnum," in *The Collected Poems of Philip Lamantia,* 192; D. H. Lawrence, *The Symbolic Meaning: The Uncollected Versions of Studies in Classic American Literature,* ed. Armin Arnold (New York: Viking Press, 1964), 18; E. J. Michael Witzel, *The Origins of the World's Mythologies* (New York: Oxford University Press, 2012), 89; Yuri V. Knorozov, *Selected Chapters from the Writing of the Maya Indians* (Cambridge: Peabody Museum, 1967), 17; Jose Arguelles, *The Mayan Factor: Path Beyond Technology* (Rochester, VT: Bear and Company, 1996); Jose and Miriam Arguelles, *Mandala* (Berkeley: Shambhala, 1972); Raphael Girard, *Esotericism of the Popol Vuh: The Sacred History of the Quiché-Maya* (Pasadena: Theosophical University Press, 1979).
**36.** Lamantia, "Ceylonese Tea Candor (Pyramid Scene)," 145.
**37.** Inga Clendinnen, "'Fierce and Unnatural Cruelty': Cortes and the Conquest of Mexico," in *The Cost of Courage in Aztec Society: Essays on Mesoamerican Society and Culture* (New York: Cambridge University Press, 2010), 52. William H. Prescott writes: "The monuments at San Juan Teotihuacan . . . were found by the Aztecs, according to their traditions, on their entrance to the country, and when Teotihuacan the habitation of the gods, now a paltry village, was a flourishing city, the rival of Tula, the great Toltec capital"; *History of the Conquest of Mexico* (New York: Random House, 2010), 607–608; Miller and Taube, *An Illustrated Dictionary,* 170; Ian Hamilton, *Robert Lowell: A Biography* (New York: Random House, 1982), 371–373; Gordon Brotherston, *Book of the Fourth World: Reading the Native Americas through Their Literature* (New York: Cambridge University Press, 1992), 156; Denise Levertov, "The Artist," in *Collected Poems,* ed. Paul A. Lacey and Anne Dewey (New York: New Directions, 2013), 91; Robert Lowell, *Notebook* (New York: Farrar, Straus and Giroux, 1970), 101, 102–103.
**38.** Louise M. Burkhart, "Spain and Mexico," in *The Cambridge History of Magic and Witchcraft in the West,* ed. David J. Collins, S.J. (New York: Cambridge University Press,

2018), 432; Manuel Leon-Portilla, *Aztec Thought and Culture: A Study of the Ancient Nahuatl Mind*, trans. Jack Emory Davis (Norman: University of Oklahoma Press, 1963), 177; Lamantia, "The Beat Generation: August 30, 1961," in *Preserving Fire*, 47, 48; Lamantia, "Ceylonese Tea Candor (Pyramid Scene)," 146; Lamantia would read the poem to his friends Homero Aridjis and Ernesto Cardenal, who were struck by the poem's apocalyptic vision. See "Philip Lamantia," in *The Beats: A Graphic History*, ed. Paul Buhle (New York: Hill and Wang, 2009), 144.

39. Ted Joans, "Another Dream Deferred? A take-off on Langston's famous poem," in *Teducation: Selected Poems 1949–1999* (Minneapolis, MN: Coffee House Press, 1999), 7; Langston Hughes, "Harlem," *in The Collected Poems of Langston Hughes*, ed. Arnold Rampersand (New York: Vintage, 1995), 426.

40. For the depiction of Cortes in the *Florentine Codex*, see Gordon Brotherston, *Painted Books from Mexico: Codices in UK Collections and the World They Represent* (London: British Museum Press, 1995), 39; Susanne Klengel, "Vulcanism between the Old and New World," in *El Surrealismo entre la Viejo y Nuevo Mundo* (Centro Atlantico de Arte Moderno: Las Palmas de Gran Canaria, Spain, 1989–90); Charles Frankel, *The End of the Dinosaurs: Chicxulub Crater and Mass Extinctions* (Cambridge: Cambridge University Press, 1999), 88; Robert Lee Hotz, "New Clues Emerge of Dinosaurs' Final Day," *Wall Street Journal*, September 10, 2019, A1, A5; Wolfgang Paalen, "The Volcano-Pyramid," in *Form and Sense* (New York: Wittenberg and Company, 1945), 55; Lamantia, "Advent," in *The Collected Poems of Philip Lamantia*, 110, 111.

41. Lamantia, "Mexico City Central Moon," in *The Collected Poems of Philip Lamantia*, 338.

42. Curt Muser, *Facts and Artifacts of Ancient Middle America* (New York: E. P. Dutton, 1978), 98, 132; Theodor-Wilhelm Danzel, *Mexiko und das Reich Des Inka* (Hamburg: Deutsche Hausbucherei, 1925), 52; C. A. Burland, *Magic Books from Mexico* (Mexico City, 1966), 28–29, plate 14 is a reproduction of the depiction of Mayahuel in the Codex Laud; Bernardino de Sahagun, quoted by Rebecca Earle, "Indians and Drunkenness in Spanish America," in *Cultures of Intoxication*, ed. Phil Withington and Angela McShane (New York: Oxford University Press, 2014), 84.

43. Bill Morgan and David Stanford, eds., *Jack Kerouac and Allen Ginsberg: The Letters*, (New York: Penguin, 2010), 163, 551. For a description of the pulque feasts, see Gordon Brotherston, *Feather Crown: The Eighteen Feasts of the Mexica Year* (London: The British Museum, 2005), 61–65.

44. Lamantia, "Mexico City Central Moon," 338. Ted Joans, *Teducation*, 135; on Pancho Villa and the Surrealists, see Gerard Durozoi, *History of the Surrealist Movement* (Chicago: University of Chicago Press, 2002), 372–373, 386.

45. Lamantia, "Mexico City Central Moon," 339; Frank Waters, *Mexico Mystique: The Coming Sixth World of Consciousness* (Chicago: Swallow Press, 1975).

## 4. MARGARET RANDALL

1. On Randall in Albuquerque, see https://plaza.sbs.arizona.edu/754; Margaret Randall, "The Poet's Annotated Chronology," in *Time's Language: Selected Poems 1959–2018* (San Antonio, TX: Wings Press, 2018), xxii.

2. Randall, "Elaine," in *Time's Language*, 287–288; Garrett Caples, "Beyond Borders," Poetry Foundation, July 2, 2019, https://www.poetryfoundation.org/articles/150404/beyond-borders.
3. Margaret Randall, *I Never Left Home: Poet, Feminist, Revolutionary* (Durham: Duke University Press, 2020), 307; Margaret Randall, *The Morning After: Poetry and Prose in a Post-Truth World* (San Antonio, TX: Wings Press, 2017), 121; Randall, *I Never Left Home*, 117–118; Randall, *The Morning After*, 123.
4. For anthologies and books on Beat women, see Richard Peabody, ed., *A Different Beat: Writings by Women of the Beat Generation* (London: Serpent's Tail, 1997); Brenda Knight, *Women of the Beat Generation: The Writers, Artists and Muses at the Heart of a Revolution* (New York: MJF Books, 2000); Nancy M. Grace and Ronna C. Johnson, *Breaking the Rule of Cool: Interviewing and Reading Women Beat Writers* (Jackson: University Press of Mississippi, 2004); Anne Waldman and Laura Wright, eds., *Beats at Naropa: An Anthology* (Minneapolis: Coffee House Press, 2009); see also Ronna C. Johnson and Nancy M. Grace, *Girls Who Wore Black: Women Writing the Beat Generation* (New Brunswick, NJ: Rutgers University Press, 2002); Isabela Castelao-Gomez and Natalia Carbajosa Palmero, *Female Beatness: Mujeres, genero y poesia en la generacion Beat* (Valencia: Publicacions de la Universitat de Valencia, 2019); Eleanor Elson Heginbotham, "Witnessses, Wanderers, and Writers: Women on the 'Beat' Road," in *Hit the Road, Jack: Essays on the Culture of the American Road*, ed. Gordon E. Slethaug and Stacilee Ford (Montreal: McGill-Queen's University Press, 2012), 100; Margaret Randall, "Notes from Mexico," *Wild Dog* 14 (February 12, 1965): 30; Bill Morgan, *I Celebrate Myself: The Somewhat Private Life of Allen Ginsberg* (New York: Viking Press, 2006), 398; Allen Ginsberg, *Iron Curtain Journals: January–May 1965*, ed. Michael Schumacher (Minneapolis: University of Minnesota Press, 2018), 8; Angus Stuart, "Merton and the Beats," in *Thomas Merton: Monk on the Edge*, ed. Ross Labrie and Angus Stuart (North Vancouver, BC: Thomas Merton Society of Canada, 2012), 79–100; Thomas Merton, *The Courage for Truth: The Letters of Thomas Merton to Writers*, ed. Christine M. Bochen (New York: Farrar, Straus and Giroux, 1993), 260; Margaret Randall, *Poesia Beat*, trans. Jeronimo-Pablo Gonzalez Martin (Madrid: Visor, 1977), 7, translation mine. Margaret Randall, *Los Beat: Poesia de la Rebellion*, trans. Edelmis Anoceto (Matanzas: Cuba, 2019); Randall, "I Am Waiting," in *Time's Language*, 375–377; Margaret Randall, *I Never Left Home*, 285; Harris Feinsod, *The Poetry of the Americas: From Good Neighbors to Countercultures* (New York: Oxford University Press, 2017), 4–5. See also "*El Corno Emplumado*," in *A Secret Location on the Lower East Side: Adventures in Writing, 1960–1989*, ed. Steven Clay and Rodney Phillips (New York: New York Public Library and Granary Books, 1998), 146–147; Luis H. Pena, "Literary Reviews: A Bibliographical Essay," in *Mexican Literature: A History*, ed. David William Foster (Austin: University of Texas Press, 1994), 379.
5. Merton, *The Courage for Truth*, 215; Rudolf Frieling and Gary Garrels, *Bruce Conners: It's All True* (Berkeley: University of California Press, 2016), 83; Margaret Randall, "*El Corno Emplumado*, 1961–1969: Some Notes in Retrospect, 1975," *Triquarterly* 43 (Fall 1978): 407; Margaret Randall, ed., *Selections from El Corno Emplumado/The Plumed Horn 1962–1964*, Lost and Found: The CUNY Poetics Document Initiative, Series 2, No. 1, Spring 2011), 1–2; Caples, "Beyond Borders," https://www.poetryfoundation.org/articles/150404/beyond-borders. For additional information on her relationship with Philip Lamantia in Mexico City, see Randall's *I Never Left Home*, 125–127.

6. Marisol Luna Chavez, "The Plumed Horn," in *Defying Stability: Artistic Processes in Mexico 1952–1967*, ed. R. Eder (Mexico City: Universidad Nacional Autonoma, 2014), 185; Randall, "*El Corno Emplumado*," 407; on Margaret Randall and *El Corno Emplumado*, see also Alberto Escobar de la Garma, "The Beat Presence in Mexican Literature," in *The Routledge Handbook of International Beat Literature*, ed. A. Robert Lee (New York: Routledge, 2018), 31.

7. Margaret Randall and Stephanie Anderson, "An Interview with Margaret Randall," *Chicago Review* 59, no.1/2 (Fall 2014/Winter 2015): 92.

8. Jerome Rothenberg, *The Flight of Quetzalcoatl* (Brighton: Unicorn, 1967); Benjamin Péret, *Anthologie des mythes, legends et contes populaires d'Amerique* (Paris: Albin Michel, 1960), 32, translation mine; Randall, "*El Corno Emplumado*," 410.

9. Margaret Randall, "Quetzalcoatl: 1961," in *El Corno Emplumado*, no. 1 (January 1962): 15; Laurette Sejourne, "In Search of the Lost Culture," in *El Corno Emplumado*, no. 5 (January 1963): 23; Margaret Randall, *More Than Things* (Lincoln: University of Nebraska Press, 2013), 13–14; Margaret Randall, *My Life in 100 Objects* (New York: New Village Press, 2020), 30; Margaret Randall, *Ruins* (Albuquerque: University of New Mexico Press, 2011), 76, 77; Lawrence Ferlinghetti, *The Mexican Night: Travel Journal* (New York: New Directions, 1970), 24, 28.

10. See Elena Poniatowska, "The Student Movement in 1968," in *The Mexico Reader: History, Culture, Politics*, ed. Gilbert M. Joseph and Timothy J. Henderson (Durham: Duke University Press, 2002), 553–569. See also Elena Poniatowska, *Massacre in Mexico*, trans. Helen R. Lane (New York: Viking Press, 1975).

11. Lawrence Ferlinghetti, *Love in the Days of Rage* (New York: Dutton, 1988), 16.

12. Margaret Randall and Robert Cohen, "Concerning the Suppression of *El Corno Emplumado*," in *The Mexican Night*, 32, 33, 35; Margaret Randall, "Words for El Corno Emplumado," in *First Laugh: Essays 2000–2009* (Lincoln: University of Nebraska Press, 2011), 136. Anne Mette Nielsen and Nicolenka Beltran created a documentary entitled *El Corno Emplumado: Una historia de los sesenta*, which is available at https://www.youtube.com/watch?v=wc37Nal2EOI.

13. Margaret Randall, "Feet Still Run," in *Time's Language*, 268–269, 271; Margaret Randall, *To Change the World: My Years in Cuba* (New Brunswick, NJ: Rutgers University Press, 2009), 258; Margaret Randall, "A Day Like This," in *She Becomes Time: New Poems* (San Antonio, TX: Wings Press, 2016), 14–15.

14. Margaret Randall, *Los "Hippies": Expresion de una crisis* (Mexico City: Siglio XXI, 1968; reprinted 2010); Randall, "Through Broken Shards of Earth," in *She Becomes Time*, 101; Randall, *I Never Left Home*, 165–166; Justino Fernandez, *A Guide to Mexican Art*, trans. Joshua C. Taylor (Chicago: University of Chicago Press, 1969), 109, 322; Whitney Chadwick, *Women, Art and Society*, 5th ed. (New York: Thames and Hudson, 2012), 345; Catriona McAra and Jonathan P. Eburne, "*Mujeres conciencia* (Women's Awareness): Leonora Carrington's Agit-prop," July 26, 2019, https://vavoresearch.wordpress.com/2019/07/26/mujeres-conciencia-womens-awareness-leonora-carringtons-agit-prop-by-catriona-mcara-and-jonathan-p-eburne/; Randall, "Angelita, little angel," in *Time's Language*, 198.

15. Margaret Randall, "The Boy with the Mayan Face," in *Part of the Solution: Portrait of a Revolutionary* (New York: New Directions, 1973), 124–126.

**16.** Randall, "The Boy with the Mayan Face," 126.
**17.** Randall, "The Boy with the Mayan Face," 127, 128–129.
**18.** Allen Ginsberg, "Sakyamuni Coming Out from the Mountain," in *Collected Poems, 1947–1980* (New York: Harper and Row, 1984), 90; Charles J. Friedrich, *The Philosophy of Hegel* (New York: Random House, 1954), 399–410; Emmanuel Levinas, *Totality and Infinity: An Essay on Exteriority*, trans. Alphonso Lingis (Pittsburgh: Duquesne University Press, 1969), 197–198.
**19.** Joanna O'Connell, "Pre-Columbian Literatures," in *Mexican Literature: A History*, ed. David William Foster (Austin: University of Texas Press, 1994), 1; Randall, *I Never Left Home*, 115; Ruth Hubbard and Margaret Randall, *The Shape of Red: Insider/Outsider Reflections* (San Francisco: Cleis Press, 1988); Randall, "The Difference," in *Time's Language*, 32–33; Noam Chomsky, "Time Bombs," in *First World, Ha Ha Ha! The Zapatista Challenge*, ed. Elaine Katzenberger (San Francisco: City Lights, 1994), 176.
**20.** Randall, *She Becomes Time*, 99, 128; Diane di Prima, "Montezuma," in *Pieces of a Song: Selected Poems* (San Francisco: City Lights, 1990), 39. "What we should lament is not the loss of houses or of land, but the loss of men's lives. Men come first; the rest is the fruit of their labor." See Thucydides, *The Peloponnesian War*, book 1, trans. Rex Warner (London: Penguin Books, 1975), 122.
**21.** Margaret Randall, *Stones Witness* (Tucson: University of Arizona Press, 2007), 34, 36; Randall, *She Becomes Time*, 102.
**22.** Randall, *She Becomes Time*, 105.
**23.** John Lloyd Stephens, *Incidents of Travel in Central America, Chiapas, and Yucatan* vol. 2 (New York: Harper and Brothers, 1841), 423–425.
**24.** John Collis and David M. Jones, *Blue Guide: Mexico* (New York: W. W. Norton, 1997), 828.
**25.** Randall, "Uxmal," in *She Becomes Time*, 105–107.
**26.** Randall, *My Life in 100 Objects*, 214; Margaret Randall, *Against Atrocity: New Poems* (San Antonio, TX: Wings Press, 2019), 105.
**27.** Louise M. Burkhart, "Spain and Mexico," in *The Cambridge History of Magic and Witchcraft in the West*, ed. David J. Collins, S.J. (New York: Cambridge University Press, 2018), 430; David Carrasco, ed., *The Oxford Encyclopedia of Mesoamerican Cultures: The Civilizations of Mexico and Central America, Volume 2* (New York: Oxford University Press, 2001), 144.
**28.** https://plaza.sbs.arizona.edu/754.
**29.** Margaret Randall, *Women Brave in the Face of Danger: Photographs of and Writings by Latin and North American Women* (Trumansburg, NY: The Crossing Press, 1985), n.p.; on the statue, see Justino Fernandez, *A Guide to Mexican Art: From Its Beginnings to the Present* (Chicago: University of Chicago Press, 1969).

## 5. JACK KEROUAC

**1.** Rachel Adams, *Continental Divides: Remapping the Cultures of North America* (Chicago: University of Chicago Press, 2009), 154; David Stephen Calonne, *Bebop Buddhist Ecstasy: Saroyan's Influence on Kerouac with an Introduction by Lawrence Ferlinghetti* (San Francisco: Sore Dove Press, 2020); Jack Kerouac, *Selected Letters, 1940–1956*, ed. Ann Charters (New

York: Penguin, 1996), 381, 382; Douglas Brinkley, ed., *Windblown World: The Journals of Jack Kerouac 1947–1954*, (New York: Penguin, 2004), 338–339. Kerouac drew meticulous maps as he worked on the manuscript of *On the Road* showing his itinerary. See Huw Lewis-Jones, ed., *The Writer's Map: An Atlas of Imagination* (Chicago: University of Chicago Press, 2018), 60–61. For a map of Kerouac's spring 1950 journey to Mexico from New York via Denver, see http://www.dennismansker.com/otroad/ontheroadmap4.htm.

2. William S. Burroughs, *The Letters of William S. Burroughs, 1945–1959*, ed. Oliver Harris (New York: Penguin, 1993), 53.

3. Jack Kerouac, *Desolation Angels* (New York: Riverhead Books, 1995), 248.

4. Jack Kerouac, *Sur le Chemin*, in *The Unknown Kerouac: Rare, Unpublished and Newly Translated Writings*, ed. Todd Tietchen (New York: Library of America, 2016), 174–237; Jack Kerouac, *Heaven and Other Poems* (Bolinas: Grey Fox Press, 1977), 51; Neal Cassady, *The First Third and Other Writings* (San Francisco: City Lights, 1981), 204, 205.

5. Jack Kerouac, *On the Road* (New York: Penguin Books, 2011), 263, 264.

6. Kerouac, *On the Road*, 266, 272.

7. Charles Olson, "Human Universe," in *Selected Writings*, ed. Robert Creeley (New York: New Directions, 1966), 57; Kerouac, *On the Road*, 267–268.

8. Erik R. Mortenson, "Beating Time: Configurations of Temporality in Jack Kerouac's *On the Road*," in *The Beat Generation: Critical Essays*, ed. Kostas Myrsiades (New York: Peter Lang, 2002), 68–69; Kerouac, *On the Road*, 268.

9. Manuel Luis Martinez, *Countering the Counterculture: Rereading Postwar American Dissent from Jack Kerouac to Tomas Rivera* (Madison: University of Wisconsin Press, 2003). On Kerouac's perceived tendency to reduce "minority" groups to stereotypes, see also Jon Panish, "Kerouac's *The Subterraneans*: A Study of 'Romantic Primitivism,'" MELUS 19, no. 3, *Intertextualities* (Autumn 1994): 107–123. Cecil Robinson, *The Mexican in American Literature* (Tucson: University of Arizona Press, 1963), 215.

10. Kerouac, *Lonesome Traveler* (New York: McGraw-Hill, 1960), 27.

11. Oswald Spengler, *The Decline of the West, Volume 2, Perspectives of World-History*, trans. Charles Atkinson (New York: Alfred A. Knopf, 1928), 84.

12. Edouard Glissant, *Poetics of Relation* (Ann Arbor: University of Michigan Press, 1997), 190; Kevin J. Hayes, ed., *Conversations with Jack Kerouac* (Jackson: University Press of Mississippi, 2005), 4.

13. The Editors, "The Ways of Alcheringa,," *Alcheringa, New Series* 1, no. 1, 1975, 3; Albert Keiser, *The Indian in American Literature* (New York: Oxford University Press, 1933), 209; Jane Goodall, *Artaud and the Gnostic Drama* (New York: Oxford University Press, 1994), 150; James Clifford, *The Predicament of Culture: Twentieth-Century Ethnography, Literature and Art* (Cambridge: Harvard University Press, 1988), 127; William Plummer, *The Holy Goof: A Biography of Neal Cassady* (New York: Prentice-Hall, 1981), 66.

14. Isaac Gewirtz, *Beatific Soul: Jack Kerouac on the Road* (New York and London: New York Public Library and Scala Publishers, 2007), 155; Jack Kerouac, "About the Manuscript," in *Some of the Dharma* (New York: Penguin Books, 1997), n.p.

15. Kerouac, *Some of the Dharma*, 124. Allen Ginsberg, *Iron Curtain Journals: January-May 1965*, ed. Michael Schumacher (Minneapolis: University of Minnesota Press, 2018), 9.

16. *Tao Te Ching*, trans. Stephen Mitchell (New York: Harper and Row, 1991), n.p.; Kerouac, *Selected Letters*, 547.

**17.** Lew Welch, "In Answer to a Question from P.W.," in *Ring of Bone; Collected Poems*, ed. Donald Allen (San Francisco: City Lights/Grey Fox, 2012), 56; Jack Kerouac, "Heaven," in *Heaven and Other Poems* (Bolinas, CA: Grey Fox Press, 1977), 23; Curt Muser, *Facts and Artifacts of Ancient Middle America* (New York: E. P. Dutton, 1978), 186; Alan Jacobs, "Thomas Merton, the Monk Who Became a Prophet," *The New Yorker*, December 28, 2018, https://www.newyorker.com/books/under-review/thomas-merton-the-monk-who-became-a-prophet.

**18.** Paul Wilkes, ed., *Merton by Those Who Knew Him Best* (San Francisco: Harper and Row, 1984), 35.

**19.** Wilkes, *Merton by Those Who Knew Him Best*, 38.

**20.** Allen Ginsberg, introduction to *Pomes All Sizes*, by Jack Kerouac (San Francisco: City Lights,1992), ii; Sam Shepard, *Rolling Thunder Logbook* (New York: Viking Press, 1977), 96; Bob Dylan, "Romance in Durango," in *Bob Dylan: The Lyrics 1961–2012* (New York: Simon and Schuster, 2016), 365–366.

**21.** Ted Joans, "The Wild Spirit of Kicks," in *Teducation: Selected Poems, 1949–1999* (Minneapolis: Coffee House Press, 1999), 97; on Joans, see A. Robert Lee, "Black Beat: Performing Ted Joans," in *Reconstructing the Beats*, ed. Jennie Skerl (New York: Palgrave Macmillan, 2004), 117–132; Sean Wilentz, *Bob Dylan in America* (New York: Anchor Books, 2011), 81; Jack Kerouac, *Mexico City Blues* (New York: Grove Weidenfeld, 1990), 207. On Dylan and Mexico, see Christopher Rollason, "*'Solo Soy Un Guitarrista'*: Bob Dylan in the Spanish-Speaking World—Influences, Parallels, Reception, and Translation," *Oral Tradition* 22, no. 1 (2007): 112–133.

**22.** Kenneth Rexroth, "Discordant and Cool," *New York Times Book Review*, November 29, 1959, 14; Kerouac, *On the Road*, 160–161; Jack Kerouac, *Book of Sketches: 1952–57* (New York: Penguin, 2006), 413; Kerouac, *Mexico City Blues*, 12; Mary Miller and Karl Taube, *An Illustrated Dictionary of the Gods and Symbols of Ancient Mexico and the Maya* (New York: Thames and Hudson, 2015), 92, 93, 172.

**23.** Kerouac at the close of *Dr. Sax* appends a note, "Written in Mexico City, Tenochtitlan, 1952 Ancient Capital of Azteca."

**24.** Kerouac, "13th Chorus," in *Mexico City Blues*, 13.

**25.** Dennis Tedlock, "Parallel Verse, Translation, *The Popol Vuh*," in *Cross Worlds, Transcultural Poetics: An Anthology*, ed. Anne Waldman and Laura Wright (Minneapolis: Coffee House Press, 2014), 73; Marcus Boon, *The Road of Excess: A History of Writers on Drugs* (Cambridge: Harvard University Press, 2002), 160, 161; James T. Jones, *A Map of Mexico City Blues: Jack Kerouac as Poet* (Carbondale: Southern Illinois University Press, 1992), 93. See also Nancy M. Grace, *Jack Kerouac and the Literary Imagination* (New York: Palgrave Macmillan, 2007), 188.

**26.** Luis Mario Schneider, *Mexico y el surrealismo, 1925–1950* (Mexico: Arte y Libros, 1978), 103–104; Antonin Artaud, "Le Popocatepetl," *Les Temps Modernes*, no. 177 (December/January 1960/61): 686–687; Kerouac, "14th Chorus," in *Mexico City Blues*, 14.

**27.** Kerouac, *Desolation Angels*, 268, 269, 272; Jimmy Fazzino, *World Beats: Beat Generation Writing and the Worlding of U.S. Literature* (Hanover, NH: Dartmouth College Press, 2016), 52.

**28.** Kerouac, "Execrable Spanish America," in *The Unknown Kerouac*, 245–256, 257.

29. Jack Kerouac, *Tristessa* (New York: Penguin Books, 1992), 7; Nancy McCampbell Grace, "A White Man in Love: A Study of Race, Gender, Class, and Ethnicity in Jack Kerouac's *Maggie Cassady, The Subterraneans,* and *Tristessa,*" in *The Beat Generation*, 117; Kerouac, "Mexico Fellaheen," in *Lonesome Traveler*, 33, 34, 35, 36.

30. Louise M. Burkhart, "Spain and Mexico," in *The Cambridge History of Magic and Witchcraft in the West*, ed. David J. Collins (New York: Cambridge University Press, 2018), 433; Georges Bataille, "Extinct America," in *October* 36, trans. Annette Michelson (Spring 1986), 7. Bataille's original text, "L'Amerique Disparue," appeared in *L'Art Precolombien: L'Amerique Avant Christophe Colomb* (Paris: Les Beaux-Arts, 1930), 12. See also Beatrice Pire, "'If You Could Die': Hart Crane's 'Accursed Share' in Mexico," *European Journal of American Studies* 13, no. 2 (Summer 2018): 1–11.

31. Joanne Kyger, *Phenomenological* (Canton, NY: Grover Publishing, 1989), entry for February 20, 1985, n.p.

32. Diane di Prima, "Notes on the Solstice," *Alcheringa, New Series,* Vol.1, No. 2, 1975, 86.

## 6. ALLEN GINSBERG

1. On the relationship between Ginsberg and Burroughs, see Jeffrey Dunn, "A Conversation: Ginsberg on Burroughs," in *Conversations with Allen Ginsberg*, ed. David Stephen Calonne (Jackson: University Press of Mississippi, 2019), 134–143; Allen Ginsberg, *The Book of Martyrdom and Artifice: First Journals and Poems, 1937–1952*, ed. Juanita Liebermann-Plimpton and Bill Morgan (Cambridge, MA: Da Capo Press, 2006), 401; David S. Willis, *World Citizen: Allen Ginsberg as Traveller* (UK: Beatdom Books, 2019), 9–10.

2. Ginsberg, *The Book of Martyrdom*, 130; Hart Crane, "Voyages," in *The Collected Poems of Hart Crane* (New York: Liveright, 1933), 102.

3. Ginsberg, *The Book of Martyrdom*, 163; Michael D. Coe and Justin Kerr, *The Art of the Maya Scribe* (New York: Harry N. Abrams, 1998), 169, 181.

4. Gabrielle Vail and Anthony Aveni, eds., *The Madrid Codex: New Approaches to Understanding an Ancient Maya Manuscript,* (Boulder: University of Colorado Press, 2009), 3; Ginsberg, *The Book of Martyrdom*, 212.

5. Mary Ellen Miller and Megan E. O'Neil, *Maya Art and Architecture*, 2nd ed. (London: Thames and Hudson, 2014), 232, and see figure 227; Susan Milbrath, *Star Gods of the Maya: Astronomy in Art, Folklore, and Calendars* (Austin: University of Texas Press, 1999), 264; Allen Ginsberg, "Denver Doldrums," in *The Book of Martyrdom*, 463, 464; Stephen Park, "Mesoamerican Modernism: W.C. Williams and the Archaeological Imagination," *Journal of Modern Literature* 34, no. 4 (Summer 2011): 21–47.

6. William Carlos Williams, "Three Nahuatl Poems," in *Technicians of the Sacred*, ed. Jerome Rothenberg (New York: Anchor Books, 1969), 222; William Carlos Williams. "The Desert Music," in *Pictures from Brueghel and Other Poems* (New York: New Directions, 1962), 111.

7. Allen Ginsberg, "Paterson," in *Collected Poems: 1947–1980* (New York: Harper and Row, 1984), 40.

8. Ginsberg, "Paterson," in *Collected Poems*.

9. Allen Ginsberg, "From *Journals*, Sunday, April 19, 1952," in *Birth* no. 3, book 1 (Autumn 1960): 71, 76; this section of the *Journals* was later published in Allen Ginsberg, *Journals: Early Fifties, Early Sixties*, ed. Gordon Ball (New York: Grove Press, 1977), 7–13.

10. Edward Lucie-Smith, *Mystery in the Universe: Notes on an Interview with Allen Ginsberg* (London: Turret Books, 1965), 5.

11. Allen Ginsberg, "Ready to Roll," in *Reality Sandwiches* (San Francisco: City Lights, 1974), 64.

12. John Tytell, *Writing Beat and Other Occasions of Literary Mayhem* (Nashville: Vanderbilt University Press, 2014), 94.

13. Barry Gifford, ed., *As Ever: The Collected Correspondence of Allen Ginsberg & Neal Cassady*, (Berkeley: Creative Arts Book Company, 1977), 159.

14. Gifford, *As Ever*, 164; Allen Ginsberg, *Journals: Early Fifties, Early Sixties*, ed. Gordon Ball (New York: Grove Press, 1992), 52, 86, 87, 50.

15. Allen Ginsberg, "Siesta in Xbalba," in *Reality Sandwiches*, 32–33; Gifford, *As Ever*, 169.

16. Ginsberg, *Journals*, 38, 40.

17. Ginsberg, *Best Minds*, quoted in Willis, *World Citizen*, 66.

18. Michael Coe, Dean Snow, and Elizabeth Benson, *Atlas of Ancient America* (New York: Facts on File, 1989), 121, 122; Gifford, *As Ever*, 166.

19. Bill Morgan, *I Celebrate Myself: The Somewhat Private Life of Allen Ginsberg* (New York: Viking, 2006), 167; Gifford, *As Ever*, 167; Jonah Raskin, *American Scream: Allen Ginsberg's Howl and the Making of the Beat Generation* (Berkeley: University of California Press, 2004), 118.

20. Gifford, *As Ever*, 166–167; Bill Morgan, *The Beats Abroad: A Global Guide to the Beat Generation* (San Francisco: City Lights, 2015), 259.

21. Franca Bellarsi, "'Alien Hieroglyphs of Eternity' and 'Cold Pastorals': Allen Ginsberg's 'Siesta in Xbalba' and John Keats's Great Odes," *Comparative American Studies* 11, no. 3 (September 2013): 248; Glen Burns, *Great Poets Howl: A Study of Allen Ginsberg's Poetry, 1943–1955* (Frankfurt am Main: Peter Lang, 1983), 258; David Stuart and George Stuart, *Palenque: Eternal City of the Maya* (New York: Thames and Hudson, 2008), 185.

22. Maud Worcester Makemson, *The Book of the Jaguar Priest: A Translation of the Book of Chilam Balam of Tizimin, with Commentary* (New York: Herny Schuman, 1951), 97–98; Curt Muser, *Facts and Artifacts of Ancient Middle America* (New York: E. P. Dutton, 1978), 86; *The Norton Anthology of World Literature, Volume C*, Fourth Edition, ed. Martin Puchner (New York: W.W. Norton, 2018), 516; Mary Miller and Karl Taube, *An Illustrated Dictionary of the Gods and Symbols of Ancient Mexico and the Maya* (New York: Thames and Hudson, 2015), 177–178; Muser, *Facts and Artifacts*, 184; Coe, Snow, and Benson, *Atlas of Ancient America*, 138; Inga Clendinnen, *Ambivalent Conquests: Maya and Spaniard in Yucatan, 1517–1570* (Cambridge: Cambridge University Press, 1987), 145.

23. David Carrasco, *The Aztecs: A Very Short Introduction* (New York: Oxford University Press, 2012), 28; Gifford, *As Ever*, 182; Paul Portugues, *The Visionary Poetics of Allen Ginsberg* (Santa Barbara: Ross-Erikson, 1978), 75.

24. Ginsberg, "Siesta in Xbalba," in *Reality Sandwiches*, 21.

25. Ginsberg, "Siesta in Xbalba," in *Reality Sandwiches*, 33.

26. Ginsberg, "Siesta in Xbalba," in *Reality Sandwiches*, 27–28, 24–25.

27. Ginsberg, "Siesta in Xbalba," in *Reality Sandwiches,* 27.
28. Ginsberg, "Siesta in Xbalba," in *Reality Sandwiches,* 25, 26.
29. Ginsberg, "Siesta in Xbalba," in *Reality Sandwiches,* 21.
30. Jonah Raskin, *American Scream: Allen Ginsberg's Howl and the Making of the Beat Generation* (Berkeley: University of California Press, 2004), 118; John Tytell, *Beat Transnationalism* (Beatdom Books, 2017), 120.
31. Ginsberg, "Siesta in Xbalba," in *Reality Sandwiches,* 28, 29.
32. Ginsberg, "Siesta in Xbalba," in *Reality Sandwiches,* 30.
33. Ray Bradbury, "The Next in Line," in *The Stories of Ray Bradbury* (New York: Knopf, 1980), xvii; Ralph L. Roys, "The Prophecies for the Maya Tuns or Years in the Books of Chilam Balam of Tizimin and Mani," in *Contributions to American Anthropology and History* 10, nos. 48–51 (Washington: Carnegie Institution of Washington, 1949), 157; Makemson, *The Book of the Jaguar Priest*; Ginsberg, "Siesta in Xbalba," in *Reality Sandwiches,* 34–39.
34. Kerouac, *On the Road,* 285; Ginsberg, "Dream Record: June 8, 1955," in *Reality Sandwiches,* 48–49.
35. Allen Ginsberg, *Iron Curtain Journals: January–May 1965,* ed. Michael Schumacher (Minneapolis: University of Minnesota Press, 2018), 9.
36. See *National Museum of Anthropology: Great Museums of the World,* ed. Carlo Ludovico Ragghianti (New York: Newsweek, 1977).
37. Bill Morgan, *The Beats Abroad,* 238–239.

## 7. BONNIE BREMSER

1. Ronna C. Johnson, "Beat Transnationalism under Gender: Brenda Frazer's *Troia: Mexican Memoirs,*" in *The Transnational Beat Generation,* ed. Nancy M. Grace and Jennie Skerl (New York: Palgrave Macmillan, 2012), 51. An excerpt from *Troia: Mexican Memoirs* is included in *The Portable Beat Reader,* ed. Ann Charters (New York: Penguin Books, 1992), 465–471.
2. Nancy M. Grace and Ronna C. Johnson, *Breaking the Rule of Cool: Interviewing and Reading Women Beat Writers* (Jackson: University Press of Mississippi, 2004), 109. Bremser is said to have contemplated a sequel to *Troia,* but thus far only excerpts from this projected work have been published. "Poets and Odd Fellows" and "The Village Scene" appeared in *Beat Down to Your Soul: What Was the Beat Generation?,* ed. Ann Charters (New York: Penguin, 2001), 18–35. "Breaking out of D.C." appeared in *A Different Beat: Writings by Women of the Beat Generation,* ed. Richard Peabody (London: Serpent's Tail, 1997), 60–64. Bill Morgan, *The Typewriter Is Holy: The Complete, Uncensored History of the Beat Generation* (New York: Free Press, 2010), 160.
3. Bob Dylan, "Eleven Outlined Epitaphs," https://beatpatrol.wordpress.com/2010/04/05/bob-dylan-11-outlined-epitaphs-1963/. On Dylan's relationship to the Beats, including Ray Bremser, see Anne Waldman, "Bob Dylan and the Beats: Magpie Poetics, an Investigation and Memoir," in *Highway 61 Revisited: Bob Dylan's Road from Minnesota to the World,* ed. Colleen J. Sheehy and Thomas Swiss (Minneapolis: University of Minnesota Press, 2009), 249–259. See also Simon Warner, *Text and Drugs and Rock 'n' Roll: The Beats and Rock Culture* (New York: Bloomsbury, 2014).

4. Kurt Hemmer, "The Prostitute Speaks," *Paradoxa*, no. 18 (2003): 101, 102; Mary Paniccia Carden, *Women Writers of the Beat Era: Autobiography and Intertextuality* (Charlottesville: University of Virginia Press, 2018), 64; Grace and Johnson, *Breaking the Rule of Cool*, 122; Manuel Luis Martinez, "'With Imperious Eye': Kerouac, Burroughs, and Ginsberg on the Road in South America," *Aztlan: A Journal of Chicano Studies* 23, no. 1 (Spring 1998): 43.

5. Grace and Johnson, *Breaking the Rule of Cool*, 116; Bonnie Bremser, "banjo pome/scat on suspenders," *Yowl* 4 (1963): 5; Amy L. Friedman, "'I say my new name': Women Writers of the Beat Generation," in *The Beat Generation Writers*, ed. A. Robert Lee (London: Pluto Press, 1996), 202; Jack Kerouac, *Tristessa* (New York: Penguin, 1992), 7. Frazer Bremser had read Kerouac's *On the Road* when it was published in 1957 and told Nancy Grace that *Troia* was influenced by him: "Even now, the way he [Kerouac] fit words together—the sweetness of it, the way things expand when you look at it. If I try to keep those things in mind, if I try to keep the transcendent quality in mind when I'm writing, which I have a really hard time doing now, but then I was able to do it. . . . He had the knack of the long sentence, which is carried by emotional weight fueled by transcendent flashes of realization. . . . The closest I come now is Genet, and then I can get excited, or Melville." On the influence of jazz, see Grace and Johnson, *Breaking the Rule of Cool*, 115, 116.

6. Bonnie Bremser, *Troia: Mexican Memoirs* (Champaign, IL: Dalkey Archive Press, 2007), 96, 123, 2, 3, 4, 116; between 1949 and 1968, other characters affiliated with the Beats lived or visited Mexico City, including David Kammerer, Lucien Carr, Kells Elvins, Joan Vollmer, Neal Cassady, Bill Garver, Hal Chase, and Howard Hart. See William T. Lawlor, ed., *Beat Culture: Lifestyles, Icons, and Impact* (Santa Barbara, CA: ABC-CLIO, 2005), 232–233; Bremser, "Poets and Odd Fellows," in *Beat Down to Your Soul*, 24.

7. Bremser, *Troia*, 5.

8. Kerouac, *On the Road* (New York: Penguin, 2011).

9. Bremser, *Troia*, 9.

10. Lawlor, *Beat Culture*, 233; Bremser, *Troia*, 12, 13.

11. Bremser, *Troia*, 14; Philip Lamantia, *The Collected Poems*, ed. Garrett Caples (Berkeley: University of California Press, 2013), xlii; Bremser, *Troia*, 126. Arnold Moodnik and Mikhail Horowitz, "Ray Bremser," in *Dictionary of Literary Biography Volume 16, The Beats: Literary Bohemians in Postwar America*, ed. Ann Charters (Detroit: Gale Research, 1983), 37. In "The Village Scene," Bremser gives the background of the trip out West from New York which she and Ray had contemplated. See Bremser, "The Village Scene," in *Beat Down to Your Soul*, 33. In another prose piece, Bremser returns to this meeting with Lamantia and Berman in San Francisco. See Bremser, "I Hear a Trane, I Hear You: For John Coltrane (Who's Been Dead for Years)," in *The Unspeakable Visions of the Individual Volume 10*, ed. Arthur and Kit Knight (California, PA: 1980), 96.

12. Bremser, *Troia*, 16.

13. Vitus Huber, *Die Konquistadoren: Cortes, Pizarro und die Eroberung Amerikas* (Munich: C. H. Beck, 2019), 39; Bremser, *Troia*, 156–157, 64; for a map and description of the Valley of Mexico, see Manuel Leon-Portilla, *Aztec Thought and Culture: A Study of the Ancient Nahuatl Mind*, trans. Jack Emory Davis (Norman: University of Oklahoma Press, 1963), xvii–xxiii.

14. Bremser, *Troia*, 17, 19.

15. Bremser, *Troia*, 26.
16. Bremser, *Troia*, 33, 34, 39, 124.
17. Bremser, *Troia*, 41.
18. Margaret Randall, *I Never Left Home: Poet Feminist, Revolutionary* (Durham and London: Duke University Press, 2020), 117; Bremser, *Troia*, 5; Herodotus, *The Histories*, trans. Aubrey de Selincourt (Middlesex: Penguin, 1974), 121, 122; Sir James George Frazer, *The Golden Bough: A Study in Magic and Religion* (London: Oxford University Press, 1994), 312. Some modern scholars have doubted the existence of sacred prostitution. See Stephanie Budin, *The Myth of Sacred Prostitution in Antiquity* (New York: Cambridge University Press, 2008).
19. Bremser, *Troia*.
20. Bremser, *Troia*, 124.
21. Bremser, "The Village Scene," in *Beat Down to Your Soul*, 29, 30, 31.
22. Ray Bremser, "Follow the East River," in *Beat Down to Your Soul*, 35–40.
23. Bremser, *Troia*, 40.
24. Bremser, *Troia*, 150.
25. Bremser, *Troia*, 116.
26. Bremser, *Troia*, 27.
27. Bremser, *Troia*, 42.
28. Bremser, *Troia*, 53.
29. Grace and Johnson, *Breaking the Rule of Cool*, 124.
30. Barbara Tedlock, "Hidden Female Shamanic Traditions," in *Cross Worlds, Transcultural Poetics: An Anthology*, ed. Anne Waldman and Laura Wright (Minneapolis: Coffee House Press, 2014), 89; R. Gordon Wasson, "Seeking the Magic Mushroom," *Life Magazine*, May 13, 1957; Michel Pharand, "The Mythophile and the Mycophile: Robert Graves and R. Gordon Wasson," *Gravesiana: The Journal of the Robert Graves Society* 1, no. 2 (1996): 211; on Maria Sabina and the counterculture, see also Christopher Partridge, *High Culture: Drugs, Mysticism, and the Pursuit of Transcendence in the Modern World* (New York: Oxford University Press, 2018), 295–297; Piers Vitebsky, *Shamanism* (Norman, OK: University of Oklahoma Press, 2001), 87; Bremser, *Troia*, 136–137.
31. https://brooklynrail.org/2019/02/fiction/Excerpt-of-Carne-de-Dios; Terence McKenna, *The Archaic Revival* (New York: HarperCollins, 1991), 40; Bremser, *Troia*, 92.
32. Bremser, *Troia*, 130.
33. Bremser, *Troia*, 132.
34. John Lardas, *Bob Apocalypse: The Religious Visions of Kerouac, Ginsberg, and Burroughs* (Urbana: University of Illinois Press, 2001), 187; Bremser, *Troia*, 133.
35. Bremser, *Troia*, 134, 135, 136.
36. Anne Waldman, *Fast Speaking Woman: Chants and Essays* (San Francisco: City Lights,1996), 37, 39–40; Jerome Rothenberg, ed., *Maria Sabina: Selections* (Berkeley: University of California Press, 2003), xii; Jerome Rothenberg, *Shaking the Pumpkin: Traditional Poetry of the Indian North Americas*, Revised Edition (Albuquerque: University of New Mexico Press, 1991), 52. The recording Waldman refers to which chronicles Maria Sabina's ceremony is "Mushroom Ceremony of the Mazatec Indians of Mexico," recorded by Z. P and R. G. Wasson on the Folkways label, 1966. Anne Waldman and Marilyn Webb, eds., *Talking Poetics from Naropa Institute: Annals of the Jack Kerouac School of Disembodied Poetics,*

*Volume Two* (Boulder, CO: Shambhala, 1979), 31; Bremser, *Troia*, 20–21; M. Christine Anderson, "Women's Place in the Beat Movement: Bonnie Bremser Frazer's *Troia: Mexican Memoirs*," *Women's Studies International Forum* 26, no. 3 (May/June 2003): 255; Brenda Knight, "Memory Babes: Joyce Johnson and Beat Memoir," in *The Cambridge Companion to the Beats*, ed. Steven Belletto (New York: Cambridge University Press, 2017), 147; Gordon Ball, *East Hill Farm: Seasons with Allen Ginsberg* (Berkeley: Counterpoint, 2011), 437.

37. Bonnie Bremser, "Artista in Guatemala," in *Some American Tales* (Manchester, UK: Death of Workers Whilst Building Skyscrapers, 2020).

## 8. MICHAEL MCCLURE AND JIM MORRISON

1. Rod Phillips, *"Forest Beatniks," and "Urban Thoreaus": Gary Snyder, Jack Kerouac, Lew Welch and Michael McClure* (New York: Peter Lang, 2000), 8. David Meltzer, *San Francisco Beat: Talking with the Poets* (San Francisco: City Lights, 2001), 151.

2. Michael McClure, *Scratching the Beat Surface: Essays on New Vision from Blake to Kerouac* (New York: Penguin, 1994), 138.

3. Michael McClure, *The Mad Cub* (New York: Bantam Books, 1970), 26. On the influence of Blake on McClure and Jim Morrison, see Stephen F. Eisenman, *William Blake and the Age of Aquarius* (Princeton: Princeton University Press, 2017), 103–104, 56–59.

4. William R. King, "Michael McClure," *Dictionary of Literary Biography Volume 16: The Beats: Literary Bohemians in Postwar America*, ed. Ann Charters (Detroit: Gale Research Company, 1983), 384; Meltzer, *San Francisco Beat*, 184.

5. See Rose Marie Beebe and Robert M. Senkewicz, *Junipero Serra: California, Indians, and the Transformation of a Missionary* (Norman: University of Oklahoma Press, 2015); Elias Castillo, *A Cross of Thorns: The Enslavement of California Indians by the Spanish Missions* (Fresno, CA: Craven Street Books, 2015). Many thanks to Amy Evans McClure for supplying me with a photograph of Michael's bookshelf. On Sterling Bunnell, see http://www.cuke.com/Cucumber%20Project/interviews/bunnell-sterling.html; Meltzer, *San Francisco Beat*, 158.

6. King, "Michael McClure," *Dictionary of Literary Biography*, 390; Frank Barron, "Motivational Patterns in LSD Usage" and Walter N. Pahnke, "LSD and Religious Experience," in *LSD, Man and Society*, ed. Richard C. Debold and Russell C. Leaf (Middletown, CT: Wesleyan University Press, 1967), 3–19, 60–84; Bill Morgan claims that, rather than seven, "McClure and Bunnell discovered five varieties of mushrooms and brought them back for experimentation." See Bill Morgan, *The Beats Abroad: A Global Guide to the Beat Generation* (San Francisco: City Lights, 2015), 256–257.

7. Gregory Stephenson, *The Daybreak Boys: Essays on the Literature of the Beat Generation* (Carbondale: Southern Illinois University Press, 1990), 114; Michael McClure, "Introduction to the 2013 Edition," *Ghost Tantras* (San Francisco: City Lights/Grey Fox, 2013), n.p.; Harris Feinsod reports that while in Mexico, "McClure recited the *Ghost Tantras* 'in a corrida.'" See Feinsod, *The Poetry of the Americas: From Good Neighbors to Countercultures* (New York: Oxford University Press, 2017), 193; McClure, "Introduction," *Ghost Tantras*, n.p.

8. Gunn, *American and British Writers in Mexico, 1556–1973* (Austin: University of Texas Press, 1974), 197–198; Michael McClure, *Persian Pony* (Victoria, B.C.: Ekstasis Editions,

2017), 33; In *September Blackberries* (New York: New Directions, 1974), McClure included a poem "Off Effect" which was "for Sterling Bunnell," 11; Marcus Boon, *The Road of Excess: A History of Writers on Drugs* (Cambridge: Harvard University Press, 2002), 261; Frank Barron, Murray E. Jarvik, and Sterling Bunnell Jr., "The Hallucinogenic Drugs," *Scientific American* 210, no. 4 (April 1964): 30, 32; Robert Faggen, "Ken Kesey," in *Beat Writers at Work: The Paris Review*, ed. George Plimpton (New York: The Modern Library, 1999), 217. Kesey was arrested on marijuana charges and fled to Mexico in 1966 where he spent time in Puerto Vallarta, Mazatlán, and Manzanillo, which he chronicles in his three-act play *Over the Border*. See Ken Kesey, *Over the Border*, in *Ken Kesey's Garage Sale* (New York: Viking Press, 1973), 39–169.

9. J. S. Slotkin, "The Peyote Way," in *Teachings from the American Earth: Indian Religion and Philosophy*, ed. Dennis Tedlock and Barbara Tedlock, (New York: Liveright, 1992), 96; Francis Crick, opening of second lecture in "The Simplest Living Things" (Seattle: University of Washington Press, 1966), 29.

10. Michael McClure, "Peyote Poem," in *Of Indigo and Saffron: New and Selected Poems* (Berkeley: University of California Press, 2011), 34–35, 39. On McClure's peyote poem, see also Richard Candida Smith, *Utopia and Dissent: Art, Poetry, and Politics in California* (Berkeley: University of California Press), 247ff.; Francis Crick, "The Poetry of Michael McClure: A Scientist's View," in *Margins* 18, "A Symposium on McClure," ed. John Jacob (March, 1975): 23, 24. On McClure's poem "Double Moire for Francis Crick," see Stefan Benz, "Sing[ing] of the Middle Way: Michael McClure's Venture for a New Mode of Thought between Natural Science and Mysticism," *Current Objectives of Postgraduate American Studies* 19, no. 1 (2018): 1–24.

11. McClure, *Meat Science Essays* (San Francisco: City Lights, 1963), 15, 23; Leslie Iversen, *Drugs: A Very Short Introduction* (New York: Oxford University Press, 2001), 17, 94–95; Sarah Shortall has observed in her essay "Psychedelic Drugs and the Problem of Experience" that during the fifties and sixties, "countercultural leaders styled the drugs as religious sacraments offering an experience of transcendence. In doing so, they drew upon the precedent set by Huxley as well as a growing fascination with Native American traditions that had long employed peyote and psilocybin for religious purposes." See Sarah Shortall, "Psychedelic Drugs and the Problem of Experience," in *Cultures of Intoxication*, ed. Phil Withingon and Angela McShane (New York: Oxford University Press, 2014), 195.

12. McClure, *Lighting the Corners: On Art, Nature, and the Visionary, Essays and Interviews* (Albuquerque: University of New Mexico Press, 1993), 299; McClure, *The Mad Cub*, 91; Michael McClure, "Baja—Outside Mexicali," in *September Blackberries* (New York: New Directions, 1974), 127–128.

13. On Cesar Chavez, see Kevin Starr, *Coast of Dreams: California on the Edge, 1990–2003* (New York: Vintage Books, 2006), 145; Roland Husson, "Gahr, Groooor, Grayohh: Pour Une Poésie de la Viande, Un Entretien avec Michael McClure," in *Entretiens: Beat Generation*, ed. Yves Le Pellec (Rodez: Editions Subervie, 1975), 211 (translation mine); Michael McClure, *Simple Eyes and Other Poems* (New York: New Directions, 1994), 32, 131.

14. Michael Benanav, "The Forbidding Reputation and Hypnotic Scenery of the Devil's Highway," *New York Times*, April 29, 2019. Richard Felger, *The Trees of Sonora* (New York: Oxford University Press, 2001). In the acknowledgments, McClure's "field work" is cited.

**15.** Irene Nicholson, *A Guide to Mexican Poetry: Ancient and Modern* (Mexico City: Minutiae Mexicana, 1968); McClure's poem is closely based on Nicholson's text, 15–20; David Carrasco, *Quetzalcoatl and the Irony of Empire: Myths and Prophecies in the Aztec Tradition* (Boulder: University Press of Colorado, 2000), 33; Joseph Campbell, *Historical Atlas of World Mythology, Vol II: The Way of the Seeded Earth, Part I, The Sacrifice* (New York: Harper and Row, 1988), 41; on *K'uk'ulkaan,* see Dennis Tedlock, *2000 Years of Mayan Literature* (Berkeley: University of California Press, 2010), 139; Stuart B. Schwartz, ed., *Victors and Vanquished: Spanish and Nahua Views of the Conquest of Mexico* (Boston: Bedford/St. Martin's, 2000), 9.

**16.** Claude Levi-Strauss, *The Story of Lynx* (Chicago: University of Chicago Press, 1996), 221; Nicholson, *A Guide to Mexican Poetry,* 19; McClure, "Swirls in Asphalt," in *Of Indigo and Saffron,* 209.

**17.** McClure, "Quetzalcoatl Song," in *Simple Eyes,* 14.

**18.** McClure, "Quetzalcoatl Song," in *Simple Eyes,* 15; Jerome Rothenberg, *Technicians of the Sacred: A Range of Poetries from Africa, America, Asia and Oceania* (New York: Anchor Books, 1969), "The Flight of Quetzalcoatl," 92–97; Laurette Sejourne, *Burning Water: Thought and Religion in Ancient Mexico* (New York: Grove Press, 1960), 53–79.

**19.** McClure, "Mexico Seen from the Moving Car," in *Simple Eyes,* 11, 12.

**20.** Smith, *Utopia and Dissent,* 301.

**21.** Fud Ford, "Teenage Beatniks," in Frank Lisciandro, *Jim Morrison: Friends Gathered Together,* ed. Steven Wheeler (Middletown, DE: Vision Words & Wonders, 2014), 14, 15, 21; Yasue Kuwahara, "Apocalypse Now!: Jim Morrison's Vision of America," in *The Doors Companion: Four Decades of Commentary,* ed. John M. Rocco (New York: Schirmer Books, 1997), 99; "Jim Morrison: Unpublished Film Script Written with Michael McClure, *Saint Nicholas,*" https://recordmecca.com/item-archives/doors-st-nicholas/; *Conversations with Allen Ginsberg,* ed. David Stephen Calonne (Jackson: University Press of Mississippi, 2019), 40; Jerry Hopkins, *The Lizard King: The Essential Jim Morrison* (London: Plexus, 2010), 290; Peter Fonda, Dennis Hopper, and Terry Southern, *Easy Rider* (New York: Signet, 1969), 41; Richard Evans Schultes and Albert Hofmann, *Plants of the Gods: Origins of Hallucinogenic Use* (New York: McGraw Hill, 1979), 27; Michael McClure, *The Adept* (New York: Delacorte, 1971), 62, 63, 101, 111; http://www.getty.edu/art/exhibitions/aztec/interactive/index.html; Mary Miller and Karl Taube, *An Illustrated Dictionary of The Gods and Symbols of Ancient Mexico and the Maya* (New York: Thames and Hudson, 2015), 190; R. Gordon Wasson, *The Wondrous Mushroom: Mycolatry in Mesoamerica* (New York: McGraw-Hill, 1980), 58; Jim Morrison, *Wilderness, Volume 1: The Lost Writings of Jim Morrison* (New York: Vintage Books, 1988, 112; Hopkins, *The Lizard King,* 122; Stephen Davis, *Jim Morrison: Life, Death, Legend* (New York: Gotham Books, 2004), 342; http://newdoorstalk.proboards.com/thread/1685/doors-mexico-city-june-1969.

**22.** Jim Morrison, *Celebration of the Lizard,* in *The American Night: The Writings of Jim Morrison, Volume 2* (New York: Vintage, 1991), 44, 45, and "The End," 112; Wallace Fowlie, *Rimbaud and Jim Morrison: The Rebel as Poet* (Durham: Duke University Press, 1993), 78, 86, 124.

**23.** Davis, *Jim Morrison,* 8; Jeroen W. Boekhoven, *Genealogies of Shamanism: Struggles for Power, Charisma and Authority* (Groningen: Barkhuis, 2011), 194. On Morrison and

shamanism, see also Laurence Coupe, *Beat Sound, Beat Vision: The Beat Spirit and Popular Song* (Manchester: Manchester University Press, 2007), 169–174.
**24.** Jim Morrison, "Notes on Vision" in *The Lords and the New Creatures, Poems,* 11, 71, 72.
**25.** Aaron Lewitzky, "Shamanism," in *The College of Sociology 1937–39,* ed. Denis Hollier (Minneapolis: University of Minnesota Press, 1988), 251; Jim Morrison, *The American Night,* 13, 124; Rich Linnell, "Unpredictable," in *Jim Morrison,* 77.
**26.** George J. Sanchez, *Becoming Mexican American: Ethnicity, Culture, and Identity in Chicano Los Angeles, 1900–1945* (New York: Oxford University Press, 1990); Octavio Paz, *The Labyrinth of Solitude* (New York: Grove Weidenfeld, 1985), 13; Philip O'Leno, "Little Brother," in *Jim Morrison,* 29–63; Lawrence Ferlinghetti, *The Mexican Night: Travel Journal* (New York: New Directions, 1970), 3, 6, http://newdoorstalk.proboards.com/thread/1685/doors-mexico-city-june-1969; Hopkins, *The Lizard King,* 106.
**27.** Morrison, *Wilderness,* 46, 75–77.

## 9. JOANNE KYGER

**1.** Bill Morgan, *Beat Atlas: A State by State Guide to the Beat Generation in America* (San Francisco: City Lights Books, 2011), 231; Bill Berkson, "Joanne Kyger," in *Dictionary of Literary Biography 16, The Beats: Literary Bohemians in Postwar America,* ed. Ann Charters, 325.
**2.** The film may be viewed at https://archive.org/details/kqed-tape-8013_13487_pm0035059.
**3.** Nancy M. Grace and Ronna C. Johnson, *Breaking the Rule of Cool: Interviewing and Reading Women Beat Writers* (Jackson: University Press of Mississippi, 2004), 144; Joanne Kyger, "Letters To & From: 'Communication Is Essential,'" ed. Ammiel Alcalay and Joanne Kyger. *Lost and Found; The CUNY Poetics Documents Initiative* 3, no. 7 (Fall 2012): 1–2.
**4.** Ronna C. Johnson, "The Beats and Gender," in *The Cambridge Companion to the Beats,* ed. Steven Belletto (New York: Cambridge University Press, 2017), 167. An example of the literary politics with which Kyger had to contend is the fact that she was excluded from Don Allen's groundbreaking *The New American Poetry* (1960; 1969); however, later, her poems were included in Allen's *The Postmoderns: The New American Poetry Revised* (1982).
**5.** Joanne Kyger, "The Pigs for Circe in May," in *Places to Go* (Los Angeles: Black Sparrow Press, 1970); Joanne Kyger, "Poison Oak for Allen," in *About Now: Collected Poems* (Orono, Maine: National Poetry Foundation, 2007), 618. There are several other Kyger poems in which she takes issue with Beat misogyny including "October 29, Wednesday" and "Town Hall Reading with Beat Poets." See Mary Paniccia Carden, "'A New Consciousness': Women's Creative Nonfiction in Beat Literature Courses," in *The Beats: A Teaching Companion,* ed. Nancy McCampbell Grace (Croydon: Clemson University Press, 2021), 137; Joanne Kyger, introduction to "Communication is Essential" in *Joanne Kyger: Letters To & From,* 1; Joanne Kyger, "Wide Mind," in *As Ever: Selected Poems* (New York: Penguin Poets, 2002), 284; Joanne Kyger, "Memories of Kerouac," in *There You Are: Interviews, Journals and Ephemera,* ed. Cedar Sigo (Seattle: Wave Books, 2017), 30; Deborah Baker, *A Blue Hand: The Beats in India* (New York: Penguin Books, 2008), 73; Berkson, "Joanne Kyger," 326.

**6.** Phyllis Stowall, "My Work Is My Life: An Interview with Diane di Prima," *City Miner* 13 4, no. 2, (1979): 21; Kyger, *There You Are*, 100; Paul Watsky, "A Conversation with Joanne Kyger," *Jung Journal: Culture & Psyche* 7, no. 3 (2013): 108, 109, 102; Ralph Maud, *Charles Olson's Reading: A Biography* (Carbondale: Southern Illinois University Press, 1996), 170; Joanne Kyger, "The Community of the Curriculum of the Soul," https://www.poetryfoundation.org/harriet/2012/08/the-community-of-the-curriculum-of-the-soul.

**7.** On Kyger and Bolinas, see Lytle Shaw, "Presence in the Poets' Polis: Hippie Phenomenology in Bolinas," in *Among Friends: Engendering the Social Site of Poetry*, ed. Anne Dewey and Libbie Rifkin (Iowa City: University of Iowa Press, 2013), 67–86; Kyger, *There You Are*, 124–125; Grace and Johnson, *Breaking the Rule of Cool*, 143. For Kyger's time in Amsterdam, see Bill Berkson and Joanne Kyger, "Amsterdam Memoirs of the Sex Life of Lewis MacAdams," in *P78 Anthology: Mandala 1112*, ed. Harry Hoogstraten and Jos Knipscheer (Haarlem: Mandala, 1979), 87–97; a slightly different version of the text was published as *Amsterdam Souvenirs* (Santa Cruz, CA: Blue Press, 2016); Charles Olson, "Human Universe," in *Collected Prose*, ed. Donald Allen and Benjamin Friedlander (Berkeley: University of California Press, 1997), 164, 166; Joanne Kyger, *Up My Coast* (Point Reyes Station, CA: Floating Island Publications, 1981) and *About Now*, 348–352; G. H. Gossen, *Chamulasin the World of the Sun: Time and Space in a Maya Oral Tradition* (Prospect Heights, IL: Waveland Press, 1984), 150–151; Kyger, *About Now*, 348–349; for Kyger's explanation of the history of the "Curriculum" and her own *Phenomenological*, see Joanne Kyger, https://www.poetryfoundation.org/harriet/2012/08/the-community-of-the-curriculum-of-the-soul.

**8.** Joanne Kyger, *Phenomenological* (Canton, NY: Glover Publishing, 1989), n.p. All further references are to this edition.

**9.** Watsky, "A Conversation with Joanne Kyger," 109.

**10.** Kyger's conception of the journal is included in *For the Time-Being: The Bootstrap Book of Poetic Journals*, ed. Tyler Doherty and Tom Morgan (Lowell, MA: Bootstrap Productions, 2007), 30–33; Kyger, *There You Are*, 137; Jane E. Falk, "Journal as Genre and Published Text: Beat Avant-Garde Writing Practices," *University of Toronto Quarterly* 73, no. 4 (Fall 2004): 997; Hailey Higdon, "Everyone Counts: Some Questions for Joanne Kyger," https://queenmobs.com/2017/02/everyone-counts-questions-joanne-kyger/; Kyger, *Phenomenological*, n.p.

**11.** Michael Davidson, *The San Francisco Renaissance: Poetics and Community at Mid-Century* (Cambridge: Cambridge University Press, 1989), 188; Joanne Kyger, "Lecture," in *When Poetry Began It Practically Included Everything: Selections from Poetry Readings and Talks at the Boise Gallery of Art 1984–1985*, ed. Gail Kirgis and Norman Weinstein (Idaho Humanities Council, 1986), 34; Kyger, *Phenomenological*, n.p.

**12.** Dennis Tedlock, *The Olson Codex: Projective Verse and the Problem of Mayan Glyphs* (Albuquerque: University of New Mexico Press, 2017), 25; Michael Coe and Mark Van Stone, *Reading the Maya Glyphs*, 2nd ed. (New York: Thames and Hudson, 2015), 7; Mary Miller and Karl Taube, *An Illustrated Dictionary of the Gods and Symbols of Ancient Mexico and the Maya* (New York: Thames and Hudson, 1997), 198; see also "Uxmal," in John Collis and David M. Jones, eds., *Blue Guide: Mexico* (New York: W. W. Norton, 1997), 827–833; https://www.poetryfoundation.org/harriet/2012/08/the-community-of-the-curriculum-of-the-soul. Kyger slightly alters and truncates Olson's passage: "I'd guess that this people had a very ancient way of *not improving on nature,* that is, that it is not a question of either intelligence or spirituality, but another thing, something Americans have a hard time getting their minds around, a form or bias of attention which does not include *improvements*." Olson, *Mayan Letters* in Charles Olson, *Selected Writings,* ed. Robert Creeley (New York: New Directions, 1966),, 92; Dan Coffey, "'My Phenomenology Waits': Death and Rebirth in Joanne Kyger's *Phenomenological,*" http://jacketmagazine.com/11/kygger-coffey.html. "Joanne Kyger Looks Back: From an Interview with David Chadwick, September 29, 1995 in Her Bolinas Home," *Beat Scene* no. 77 (Summer 2015): 41; Ravi Singh, "Entretien Avec Joanne Kyger, Bolinas, California, 10 Octobre 2015," in *Beat Generation: New York, San Francisco, Paris,* ed. Philippe-Alain Michaud (Paris: Centre Pompidou, 2016), 259, translation mine. This interview was published in French, and Kyger's comment reads: "Pour moi, beaucoup de questions sur l'identité, de soi, etc. y étaient posées dans un langage qui apportait des réponses accessibles."

13. Paul Weinpahl, "Zen and the Work of Wittgenstein," *Chicago Review* 12, no. 2 (Summer 1958): 67–72; Grace and Johnson, *Breaking the Rule of Cool,* 141–142; Jonathan Skinner, "Generosity and Discipline: Joanne Kyger's Travel Poems," http://jacketmagazine.com/11/kyger-skinner.html. Kyger, *Phenomenological,* n.p.

14. Inga Clendinnen, *Ambivalent Conquests: Maya and Spaniard in Yucatan, 1517–1570* (Cambridge: Cambridge University Press, 1987), 27; Maurice Merleau-Ponty, preface to *Phenomenology of Perception* in *The Essential Writings of Merleau-Ponty,* ed. Alden L Fisher (New York: Harcourt, Brace & World, 1969), 31; Joanne Kyger, *Joanne* (Bolinas, CA: Angel Hair, ca. 1970), n.p., reprinted in *About Now,* 211; Philip Whalen, *The Collected Poems,* ed. Michael Rothenberg (: Middletown, CT; Wesleyan University Press, 2007), 659; Berkson, "Joanne Kyger," 328; Linda Russo, "How You Want to Be Styled: Philip Whalen in Correspondence with Joanne Kyger, 1959–1964," in *Among Friends: Engendering the Social Site of Poetry,* ed. Anne Dewey and Libbie Rifkin (Iowa City: University of Iowa Press, 2013), 21–42. Whalen sent Kyger a fascinating letter dated "Thursday 19:IX:68 in the middle of the afternoon" containing a suggested reading list which includes two anthologies, Margaret Astrov's *The Winged Serpent* (New York: John Day, 1946) and A. Grove Day's *The Sky Clears: Poetry of the American Indians* (New York: Macmillan, 1951). Whalen cautions that "both are rather feeble books of translations. . . . Miss Astrov's is the better." See Philip Whalen, "Letter to Joanne Kyger," in *Rocky Ledge* no. 7 (February/March 1981): 15–21.

15. Kyger, *Phenomenological,* n.p.

16. David Stuart and George, *Palenque: Eternal City of the Maya* (London: Thames and Hudson, 2008), 200, 166; Kyger, *Phenomenological,* n.p.

17. Joanne Kyger, "Three Versions of the Poetic Line," *Credences* 4, vol. 2, no. 1 (March 1977): 64.

18. Dylan J. Clark, "An Archaeologist of the Morning in the Mayab, 1951," in *Staying Open: Charles Olson's Sources and Influences,* ed. Joshua Hoeynck (Wilmington, DE: Vernon Press, 2019), 246.

19. Jane Falk, "Joanne Kyger 'Descartes and the Splendor Of': Bridging Dualisms through Collaboration and Experimentation," in *The Philosophy of the Beats,* ed. Sharin N. Elkholy (Lexington: University Press of Kentucky, 2012), 125; Kyger, *Phenomenological,* n.p.

20. Joanne Kyger, *Mexico Blonde* (Bolinas, CA: Evergreen, 1981), n.p.

**21.** Joanna O'Connell, "Pre-Columbian Literatures," in *Mexican Literature: A History*, ed. David William Foster (Austin: University of Texas Press, 1994), 6; Kyger, *Mexico Blonde*, n.p.

**22.** Kyger, *Mexico Blondé*, n.p.; Thomas Merton, "The Sacred City," *The Catholic Worker* 34, no. 1 (January 1968): 4; Kyger, *There You Are*, 99.

**23.** Kyger, *There You Are*, 124; Joanne Kyger, *Patzcuaro: December 17, 1997–January 26, 1998* (Bolinas, CA: Blue Millennium Press: 1999), 5.

**24.** Kyger, *Patzcuaro*, 7.

**25.** Mary Paniccia Carden, "Joanne Kyger's Travel Chapbooks: A Poetics of Motion," *Journal of Beat Studies* 6 (2018): 26.

**26.** Kyger, *Patzcuaro*, 8, 10; Kyger, *There You Are*, 124.

**27.** Kyger, *Patzcuaro*, 13; Jeff Conant, "From *A Poetics of Resistance*," in *Roots and Routes: Poetics at New College of California*, ed. Patrick James Dunagan, Marina Lazzara, and Nicholas James Whittington (Wilmington, DE: Vernon Press, 2020), 221. A useful anthology regarding the Zapatista Army and the revolt in Chiapas is *First World, Ha Ha Ha! The Zapatista Challenge*, ed. Elaine Katzenberger (San Francisco: City Lights, 1995).

**28.** Kyger, *Patzcuaro*, 15.

**29.** Judith Friedlander, *Being Indian in Hueyapan: A Study of Forced Identity in Contemporary Mexico* (New York: St. Martin's Press, 1975), 102–103.

**30.** Joanne Kyger, *God Never Dies: Poems from Oaxaca, December 7, 2003–January 9, 2004* (Santa Cruz, CA: Blue Press, 2004), n.p.; on this festival, see Peter Kuper, *Diario de Oaxaca: A Sketchbook Journal of Two Years in Mexico* (Oakland, CA: PM Press, 2017), 52–53; Dale Smith, "Joanne Kyger and the Narrative of Every Day," *Jacket*, October 34, 2002, http://jacketmagazine.com/34/kyger-by-smith.shtml.

**31.** Kyger, *God Never Dies*, n.p.

**32.** Joanne Kyger, *On Time: Poems 2005–2014* (San Francisco: City Lights, 2015), 84.

**33.** Watsky, "A Conversation with Joanne Kyger," 95.

**34.** *The I Ching, or Book of Changes*, trans. Cary F. Baynes (Princeton, NJ: Princeton University Press, 1971), 218.

**35.** Kyger, *On Time*, 90.

**36.** Grace and Johnson, *Breaking the Rule of Cool*, 152.

## EPILOGUE

**1.** George Wilkins Kendall, *Narrative of the Texan Santa Fe Expedition* (London: 1847), 326, quoted in Cecil Robinson, "The Extended Presence: Mexico and Its Culture in North American Writing," *MELUS* 5, no. 3 (Autumn 1978): 3–4.

**2.** J. G. Brotherston, "Revolution and the Ancient Literature of Mexico, for D.H. Lawrence and Antonin Artaud," *Twentieth Century Literature* 18, no. 3 (July 1972): 182, 188.

**3.** Joanne Kyger, "Lecture," in *When Poetry Began It Practically Included Everything: Selections from Poetry Readings and Talks at the Boise Gallery of Art 1984–1985*, ed. Gail Kirgis and Norman Weinstein (Idaho Humanities Council, 1986), 41; Aldous Huxley, *Beyond the Mexique Bay* (London: Triad and Paladin, 1984), 149, 153. Stuart Chase, *Mexico: A Study of Two Americas* (New York: Macmillan, 1931).

**4.** William A. Richards, *Sacred Knowledge: Psychedelics and Religious Experiences* (New York: Columbia University Press, 2016); Michael Pollan, *How to Change Your Mind: What the New Science of Psychedelics Teaches Us about Consciousness, Dying, Addiction, and Transcendence* (New York: Penguin, 2018).

**5.** Maria Sabina, quoted in Joan Halifax, *Shamanic Voices: A Survey of Visionary Narratives* (New York: Arkana, 1991), 130.

# INDEX

Page numbers in *italics* indicate photographs.

# ABOUT THE AUTHOR

DAVID STEPHEN CALONNE is the author of *William Saroyan: My Real Work Is Being*, *The Spiritual Imagination of the Beats*, *Diane di Prima: Visionary Poetics and the Hidden Religions*, and *R. Crumb: Literature, Autobiography and the Quest for Self* and the editor of *Conversations with Allen Ginsberg* and *Conversations with Gary Snyder*. He has also written critical biographies of Charles Bukowski and Henry Miller. He has taught at the University of Texas at Austin, the University of Michigan, and the University of Chicago. He presently teaches at Eastern Michigan University.